CARIBBEAN WORLD

A COMPLETE GEOGRAPHY

NEIL SEALEY

CAMBRIDGE
UNIVERSITY PRESS

Author's acknowledgements

A book such as this is in many ways a compilation of primary and secondary sources, and the Bibliography on pp. 252-3 is in part an acknowledgement of the considerable help I have received.

Much of the factual information and statistics were gained by visiting the various governmental and quasi-governmental institutions in the region, and I would particularly like to thank the personnel in the following offices for their kindness and help:

- Departments of Fisheries and Tourism in Belize
- Statistics Office and Department of Education in Montserrat
- Department of Statistics in Antigua
- Ministry of Education, and the Statistics Division of the Ministry of Agriculture, in St Kitts and Nevis
- Urban Development Corporation, Kingston, Jamaica
- Hellshire Bay Development Corporation, Jamaica
- Ministry of Finance, Dominica
- Department of Tourism, Cayman Islands
- Ministry of Information and Culture, the Guyana Manufacturers' Association, the Department of Forestry, the Bank of Guyana, the Guyana Bauxite Company Limited, the Ministry of Economic Planning and Finance, the Guyana Geology and Mines Commission, and the University of Guyana, all in Georgetown, Guyana.
- Office of Economic Research, the Economic Development Administration, and Puerto Rico Development Company (FOMENTO) in San Juan, Puerto Rico
- Bureau of Mines and the US Geological Survey, US Department of the Interior
- Ministry of Tourism, Industrial Development Corporation, Arawak Cement Company, Ministry of Finance and Planning, and The Barbados Development Bank, in Barbados
- National Energy Corporation, The Central Statistical Office, Ministry of Finance, Point Lisas Industrial Port Development Corporation, in Trinidad and Tobago.
- Department of Lands and Surveys, the Department of Fisheries, the Department of Agriculture, The Bahamas Agricultural and Industrial Corporation, the Meteorological Department, the Department of Statistics, and the College of The Bahamas, Nassau, The Bahamas

Private companies, and local and regional associations have been equally helpful, and I would particularly like to thank the following:

- The Barbados Sugar Producers' Association, Fibrepol Limited, Intel Barbados Ltd, Four Square Sugar Factory, and R.L. Seale and Co. Ltd, of Barbados
- Reynolds Jamaica Mines Ltd, Lydford, Jamaica
- Amoco Trinidad Oil Company, Trinidad and Tobago
- Morton Salt Company, Marcona Industries Ltd, The Bahamas
- The Caribbean Tourism Research and Development Centre, Barbados
- The Caribbean Examinations Council, Barbados
- The University of the West Indies, all campuses
- The Caribbean Community Secretariat, Georgetown, Guyana

Many individuals – colleagues, friends, relatives and acquaintances – have been contributors in some way to this book. Regrettably it is not possible to name all of them. The following have made contributions well above the average:

- Mr Irvin Greenidge and family, of Warner's Terrace, Barbados
- Ms Florence Bryden of St Andrew's School, The Bahamas
- Mr Alim Hussein and family, of Georgetown, Guyana
- Mr Mike Morrissey and colleagues at the University of the West Indies, Jamaica
- Mrs Pamela Moss of the College of The Bahamas
- Dr John Mylroie and colleagues at Mississippi State University
- Mr Michael Tibbits of Bridgetown, Barbados
- Mr Kenrick Seepersad and Ms Betty Ann Rohlehr of Port of Spain, Trinidad

Contents

Introduction

This is a book about the West Indies. It is aimed at a readership in the secondary school system, and is intended to satisfy the requirements of the CXC Geography O-level and more recent GCSE syllabuses. It is not, however, simply a digest of geographical information at this level. These syllabuses recognize that geographical phenomena are the cause and effect of other phenomena, both within and outside the realm of geography, and the text acknowledges this through its systems approach. In this way the geographical features of the region can be studied as parts of a system, and their linkages and connections within and outside each system can be identified.

These secondary syllabuses provides for a comprehensive survey of Caribbean geography. In meeting their demands it has been necessary to produce a text that provides an introduction to the physical, social and economic systems of the region, and this book should also serve beyond the school syllabus for all those needing an introduction to the geography of the West Indies at college or university levels.

The West Indies are a collection of many large and small countries, islands and continental territories, and together these cover a large part of the western hemisphere. They are populated by people of many origins and cultures, and their natural wealth varies from the abundant to the meagre. In total we have an extraordinarily complex geographical region. This complexity cannot be ignored, but it is possible to bring order and organization to its study, and that is the ultimate aim of this book. If a phenomenon or an activity is properly described and explained, it can be understood more easily. Such an understanding cannot be gained from a cursory glance. The text must be studied carefully, and used in conjunction with other sources of information, for example an atlas, local maps, field trips, and the various magazines and newspapers that keep us up to date in a changing world.

The student – and the teacher – who takes this approach will be rewarded, not by knowledge alone, but also by a better understanding of the physical and human environment. Such a person will be able to contribute more to the management and use of the environment, ultimately for the benefit of all West Indians.

Questions in the text

It is not possible for geography alone to tell us everything about our environment. What we learn in geography must be related to what we learn in other areas – science and history, for instance. Many of the questions set in this book are designed to draw attention to other subjects and their importance in understanding geographical features. Nor is one textbook alone sufficient to study everything geographical. Every student should have a good atlas, and easy access to a large encyclopaedia and to books about other countries.

In some cases it is not books at all that provide the answers, but our own observations. Geography is all around us, and for many of the answers we should not look in any book, but at our environment and our activities in it.

PART ONE
The Physical Basis

1

The geology of the Caribbean: Plate tectonics

The world map has not always looked the way it does today, and the area we now know as the Caribbean did not always exist. Today this fact is fairly well known, but for a long time there was little evidence to support the *Theory of Continental Drift* as it was then known.

Most of the early ideas of continental drift were based on the fact that the two sides of the Atlantic looked as if they could be fitted together. This was noticed hundreds of years ago, and the early geologists found many clues in the rocks and fossils of the east and west coasts of the Atlantic to suggest that the continents had once been joined. The problem was that no one knew how they could have been separated.

The answer came eventually from the ocean floor, and not the land. In 1963, two English geophysicists, Vine and Matthews, proved conclusively that the ocean floor was

All Saints Church, Antigua, after an earthquake. Severe earthquake damage is not common in the Caribbean, but can leave a lasting impression.

spreading from a central crack. Such cracks are found in all the oceans (Fig. 1.1). In the Atlantic the crack is marked by the mid-Atlantic ridge.

Further investigation of the ocean floors showed that the Earth's crust actually consists of a large number of plates, and the edges of these plates are responsible for many features and phenomena that were not previously understood. Once the significance of *sea-floor spreading* was recognized, a major theory known as *plate tectonics* was developed to explain the behaviour of the Earth's crust. Geologists use the word *tectonics* to describe major movements in the Earth's crust.

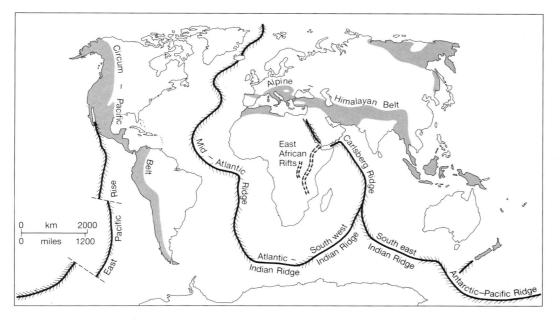

Fig. 1.1 The Oceanic Ridges. The Pacific is the only ocean that is not bisected by a mid-oceanic ridge. It was the original ocean and has a much more complex structure than those oceans that were created later.

Crustal *plates* are the separate fragments of the crust that make up the whole. Plate tectonics describes the movements of these plates. The term *continental drift* suggests that only the continents move. However, we now know that this is not true, so it is no longer used. In many cases the continents are merely parts of larger plates on which they ride. The continents themselves may be split; for example, Africa is splitting into two parts, along a line from the Red Sea through to the East African Rift Valley. The Rift Valley is a *potential ocean*, while the Red Sea is a *proto-ocean* (*proto* = primitive).

Our study of the Caribbean must therefore begin with the birth of the Atlantic and the formation of a proto-Caribbean Sea.

Birth of the Caribbean

The Atlantic started to form about 200 million years ago. Just what has happened in the Caribbean since then has only been seriously studied for the last 25 years. The explanation which follows is one *possible* likely reconstruction which seems to fit the known facts. Other reconstructions are possible, and new information will probably mean that existing theories will have to be revised.

Central to the story of the Caribbean is the formation and subsequent behaviour of a part of the crust known as the *Caribbean Plate*. When North and South America were joined to Europe and Africa, the only areas of the wider Caribbean region that existed were the mainland areas of the Guianas and Mexico. Southern Mexico (the Yucatan Peninsula) was at that time located in the Gulf of Mexico in the form of a minor crustal block or plate. All the other areas - the islands, large and small - were created later.

In geological terms the Atlantic opened at the end of the Triassic period (200 million years ago) as the North American Plate rotated away from South America and Africa (Table 1.1). As this occurred the Yucatan block moved southwards into

the Caribbean area and left behind a small ocean basin which became the Gulf of Mexico. Closer to the Atlantic a long tapering wedge of shallow-water sediments was laid down

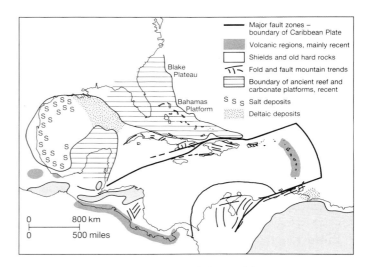

Fig. 1.2 Main structural features of the Caribbean region.

Geological time				Events
Era	Period	Epoch	Age*	
Cenozoic	Quaternary	Holocene Pleistocene	Last 10,000 Years 2	Barbados and limestone bank islands take present form. The Bahamas islands form. Ice ages. Appearance of modern human race.
Cenozoic	Tertiary	Pliocene	5	Caribbean Plate margins underthrust and uplifted. Caribbean separates from Pacific. Mountain building in Jamaica. Volcanism and formation of western Leeward Islands (St Kitts/ Nevis, Montserrat, etc.).
Cenozoic	Tertiary	Miocene	23	Trinidad and Jaimaica above sea level. Trinidad's oil deposits form.
Cenozoic	Tertiary	Oligocene	37	Much of the Greater Antilles, Bahamas and Belize are shallow-water banks fringed by coral reefs.
Cenozoic	Tertiary	Eocene	45 55	Subduction and volcanism ends in the Greater Antilles and begins in Lesser Antilles western belt and Windward Islands. Jamaica eroded and submerged.
Cenozoic	Tertiary	Paleocene	65	Caribbean Plate begins to move east causing mountain building in Greater Antilles and Trinidad/Venezuela.
Mesozoic	Cretaceous		110 140	Separation of Caribbean from Pacific Plate, with subduction beneath Central America. Greater Antilles forms as a series of volcanoes over a subduction zone.
Mesozoic	Jurassic		195	Atlantic rift opens - oldest known rocks in West Indies (Cuba, Trinidad).
Mesozoic	Triassic		225	Age of dinosaurs.
Paleozoic	Various		250 350 570	Oldest rocks in Belize. Main coal deposits laid down (Carboniferous). First life on Earth recorded.
Pre-Cambrian			3,800 4,600	Oldest rocks in the Caribbean region - Guyana shield. Beginning of geological record. Age of Earth.
* millions of years				

Table 1.1 Geological events in the Caribbean

in shallow seas. These sediments were later to form the Blake-Florida-Bahama-Cuba platform (Fig. 1.2). This particular set of movements continued for about 100 million years into the Cretaceous period. By then Central America, as far south as Guatemala, looked much as it does now. But before this was complete, about 135 million years ago South America had also started to move and form the South Atlantic. Both North and South America were travelling westwards, but also diverging, so that the gap between them was increasing. At this point the Caribbean Plate came into existence and the Caribbean region was formed (Fig. 1.3).

In order for the Americas to move westwards, they had to override the crust in the Pacific - the *Pacific Plate*. This they did, creating the resultant trenches, earthquakes, volcanoes and

mountain ranges associated with such activity (See p.18). Between the two continents, however, there was a gap into which an intact section of the Pacific Plate was forced. Eventually this was to become the Caribbean Plate, but for a long time it was not a separate piece of crust. The Caribbean Plate did not come into separate existence until about 100 million years ago. At first it was travelling north-eastwards, pushing up towards Cuba and the Bahamas platform. About 65 million years ago and until the present it has had a relative movement eastwards compared with the North American and South American Plates. At this time the Greater Antilles ceased being a subduction zone and volcanism ended there. By about 45 million years ago subduction had started in the Eastern Caribbean, and volcanism in this region started then.

The Caribbean Plate is now moving south-westwards and is being consumed rapidly under the Cocos and Nazca Plates,

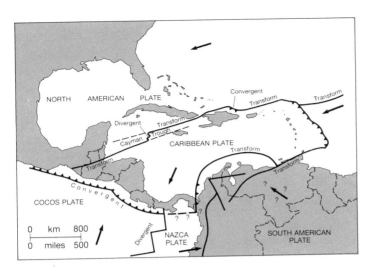

Fig. 1.3 The Caribbean Plate and its neighbours. Source: Peter H. Mattson (1984) *Caribbean Structural Breaks and Plate Movements*, Geological Society of America, Memoir 162.)

1. *The north-westward movement of the South American Plate may now have ended.*

2. *The boundary between the Caribbean and Nazca Plates has not been identified.., and they may actually be the same plate.*

3. *It should be noted that the Caribbean Plate is not actually moving eastwards (as is often suggested), but moves very slowly to the south-west. It is, however, being <u>overtaken</u> by both the North and South American Plates, so <u>relative</u> to them it has an eastward component, see Fig. 1.4.*

which have high rates of north-easterly movement. This accounts for the frequency of earthquake activity in Central America (Managua 1975, Mexico City 1985). In the Eastern Caribbean the Caribbean Plate is being overtaken by both the

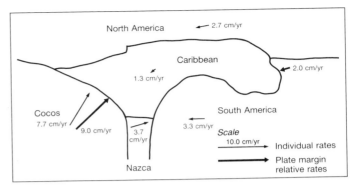

Fig. 1.4 Movement of the Caribbean and adjacent plates in the last 5 million years. Source: As Fig 1.3.

North American and the South American Plates at a rate of about 2 cm each year (Fig. 1.4).

At the eastern edge of the proto-Caribbean Plate a variety of forces were at work. These were caused by the collision and destruction of the Atlantic Plate at its contact with the young Caribbean Plate. In order to understand this process we need to consider the forces at work around a crustal plate, and the features they create.

---

1   How many major plates make up the Earth's crust?

2   Using an atlas, name the Central and South American countries on the edges of the Caribbean Plate.

3   What countries does the East African Rift Valley run through?

4   Find America on a map. In which parts would you expect to feel an earthquake?

The margins of the crustal plates

In its simplest form a plate has four sides : a leading edge in collision with other plates, a trailing edge where the plate is actually constructed, and two sides. Each of these is a response to the Earth's internal forces that move the plate, and each in turn creates major crustal features that are quite distinct from each other (Fig. 1.5). We consider each edge in turn (Fig. 1.6).

The trailing edge - a zone of divergence

Several names used for the edges of plates, or the zones of activity that separate them from other plates. The most important feature of the trailing edge is that it is where new crust is being created. This is the *constructive* zone where the crust

splits. Here there is volcanic activity, and new crust is created from the continual outpouring of molten material along the split or *rift* (Fig. 1.7). All the mid-oceanic ridges, such as the mid-Atlantic Ridge, are *divergent zones*.

There are no divergent zones in the Caribbean region, nor do there ever appear to have been. Figure 1.1 shows that the divergent zones which affect the region are in fact outside it, in the Atlantic and Pacific Oceans. The plates are pushed from these zones, and then collisions take place in the Caribbean.

The combined mid-Atlantic Ridge is over 60,000km (36,000 miles) long and occupies as much as one-third of the ocean floor. The central part of the ridge is usually a rift valley of up to 50km (30 miles) wide and over 1km (½ mile) deep.

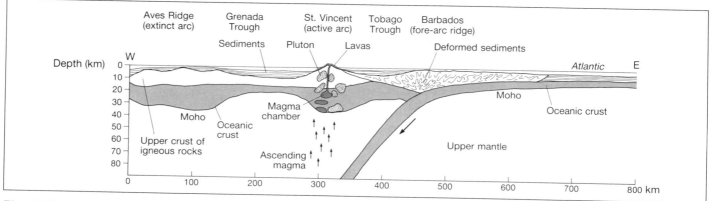

Fig. 1.5 Cross-section of the Lesser Antilles in the latitude of St Vincent. In the region of Barbados, where the Atlantic Plate sinks below the Caribbean Plate, the trench that would normally exist has been filled with sediments, forming a eugeosyncline. The uplift of Barbados is thus accounted for. Source: M.H.P. Bott (1982) The Interior of the Earth, Elsevier, p223.)

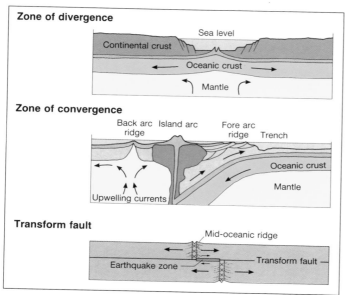

Fig. 1.6 The margins of crustal plates. Formed wherever two plates are moving past each other. It is most common in small sections between parts of the mid-oceanic ridges, which tend to get out of line wherever they are curved. The Cayman Trench is a major plate boundary.

1 Fore arc ridge   A jumbled mass of crustal rock and sediments severely folded, faulted and metamorphosed. This is the eugeosynclinal area.
2 Island arc   The descending crust is heated and melted, and the magma so formed rises up periodically to form a curved chain of volcanic material.
3 Back arc ridge   This is a minor zone of divergence caused by eddying currents behind the island arc. Compare this with the Aves Ridge (Fig. 1.12).

Volcanic activity takes place along the ridge, and in certain places, called *hot spots*, it reaches sea level. Iceland is a good example. Accompanying the vulcanicity are shallow earthquakes - that is, fracturing of the Earth's crust within 60km (36 miles) of the surface. As the upwelling lava forces its way through and between the overlying plates, they are cracked and forced apart, causing earthquakes. The rate of movement, or *sea-floor spreading*, varies between 1 and 10 cm (0.4 and 4.0 in.) each year. It is about 6 cm (2.5 in.) in the Pacific, but only about 1.5-2 cm (0.6-0.8 in.) in the Atlantic.

The leading edge - a zone of convergence

For every constructive zone we must assume there is a destructive or *subduction* zone. After all, if the Earth's size is fixed, as it appears to be, we cannot add crust in one place without removing it from somewhere else. Ideally this happens on the other side of the plate as it is pushed out from the mid-oceanic ridge (Fig. 1.7). A striking set of geological

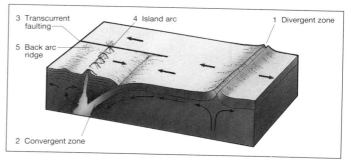

Fig. 1.7 Volcanoes and earthquakes at plate margins.
Earthquakes Shallow earthquakes occur where upwelling currents split the crust (1). Intermediate and deep earthquakes occur where friction is greatest, at (2) where the descending crust is forced beneath another plate, and at (3), where two plates grind past each other in opposite directions.
Volcanoes Frequent volcanic activity takes place along the mid-oceanic ridges as magma wells up through the rifted crust (1). Intermittent activity is associated with fractures in the convergent zone (2) and results in the formation of a volcanic island arc (4).

features marks these edges, which are particularly important to us because land areas are usually formed here.

The Caribbean Plate is perhaps unique in having had each of its edges at some time in the destructive category. The northern edge was the first, then the southern edge for a limited time, and the eastern and western edges are very active at present.

The destructive edges are extremely complex zones. They are not all the same, and many of their features are not yet understood. Within the last ten years one group of researchers commented, 'The Eastern Caribbean region is so complex that a simple subduction theory cannot fit the observed seismic facts'. (*Seismic* is the term used to describe measurements made by bouncing sound waves off the geologic strata on the sea floor, so as to get a picture of the various layers present.) We can only consider a few of the main features in detail here, although a fuller picture is given in the diagrams (Figs 1.5 - 1.7).

Parts of the mantle

Geologists tend to use the following terms in plate tectonics:

Lithosphere   The set of brittle crustal plates that move about.

Asthenosphere   The upper part of the mantle; a 'plastic' or resilient layer on which the lithosphere rides.

Mesosphere   A stronger resistant zone in the mantle, 250km (150 miles) below the surface.

Deep-sea trenches

These mark the line along which the lithosphere is forced under an opposing plate. Trenches are up to 100km (60 miles) wide, and extremely long. In the Caribbean we have the following:

- The Puerto Rico Trench: 1,030km (640 miles) long, up to 8,648 m (28,382 ft) deep.
- The Cayman Trench: 1,500km (930 miles) long, up to 7,535 m (24,730 ft) deep.
- Bonaire Trench: 290km (180 miles) long.
- Cariaco Trench: 160km (100 miles) long.
- Los Roques Trench: 570km (230 miles) long.

Earthquakes

As the lithosphere is forced down into the asthenosphere, it is heated and eventually becomes so hot and fluid that it loses its identity and merges with the mantle. This probably occurs in the mesosphere, at no deeper than 700km (400 miles). The path of the descending crust is known to us because by its movement it creates earthquakes. If the centres or *foci* of these earthquakes are plotted, they map out the path of the descending plate. The depths of earthquakes, unlike those of the mid-oceanic ridges, can vary from shallow, through intermediate, to deep. In the Eastern Caribbean the number of faults created is considerable, and there are many complications in the subduction process. Along the eastern edge of the Caribbean Plate, shallow earthquakes occur in a zone up to 80km (50 miles) east of the Windward Island chain, while earthquakes at intermediate depth (65 -130km / 40-80 miles deep) are within 40km (25 miles) of these islands. The deep earthquakes, over 130km (80 miles) down, are much fewer, but occur under the chain itself, or even west of it. The centre of the chain is most affected, roughly from Guadeloupe to St Vincent, and this is also the zone of presently active volcanoes. This distribution fits in nicely with the theory of a *steeply* slanting and plunging crust.

Earthquakes are not of course confined to the Eastern Caribbean. They also affect Jamaica and the rest of the Greater Antilles. Central America is also a major earthquake zone (for example, Managua 1975), and like the Eastern Caribbean this area is affected by earthquakes with deep foci, indicating subduction. Central America has in fact suffered from severe earthquakes much more than the Eastern Caribbean. In the last 80 years there have been seven major, catastrophic earthquakes in Central America which seem directly related to underthrusting at the plate margin. There have been no earthquakes at all on this scale in the Eastern Caribbean, probably because of the slower rate of subduction.

Earthquakes in the Greater Antilles are, however, shallow and are not related to subduction zones. North of the Greater

The ruins of St Pierre, Martinique, still remain after the 1902 eruption of Mt Pelée. The French moved their capital to Fort de France and abandoned this site.

Antilles, earthquakes are virtually unknown, and the Bahamas-South Florida platform is one of the most stable geological regions on the Earth.

---

1 What are the nearest countries to each of the trenches listed on this page?

2 Explain why some Caribbean countries have earthquakes and others do not.

Volcanoes and island arcs

As the lithosphere descends, the various sediments on its surface, and those collected in the trench, are dragged down

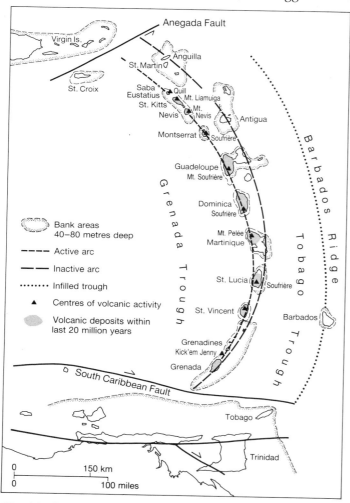

Fig. 1.8 The Eastern Caribbean Plate margin. This map should be compared with Fig. 1.5, which is an E–W section through St Vincent and Barbados. The areas of shallow water, which are the main fishing grounds for this area, should be noted. (Source: R.H.A. Martin-Kaye (1969) A summary of the Geology of the Lesser Antilles, Overseas Geology and Mineral Resources, vol. 10, No. 2.)

with it. They become folded, faulted, crushed and eventually melted, producing a magma that can find its way back to the surface along the many fractures caused by the collision of the plates (See Fig. 1.6). The initial result is the appearance of a chain of small volcanic islands - an *island arc* (Fig. 1.8). The islands of the Eastern Caribbean are a typical example, but there are several others around the world:

Pacific Ocean: Aleutian Islands
                Mariana Islands
Atlantic Ocean: South Georgia
                South Sandwich Islands
Indian Ocean: Andaman Islands
                Indonesian Islands

If the activity continues, the islands combine to form larger islands, but still with a generally curved shape. Java and Sumatra in Indonesia are examples, as is (perhaps) part of the Greater Antilles. With further volcanic activity a major landmass could develop, and this is believed to be the origin of Central America from Nicaragua south to Colombia. However, this is a considerable simplification of what amounts to *mountain building*, which is discussed separately below.

As well as the length of *time* during which the subduction of a plate occurs, we must also consider the *rate of movement*. The East Pacific or Cocos Plate is moving three to four times faster than the North American Plate (Fig 1.4) and this may be

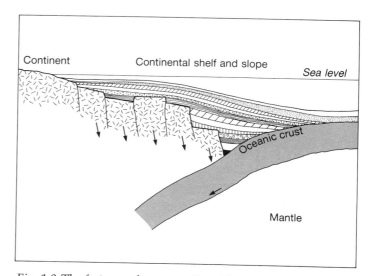

Fig. 1.9 The features of a geosyncline. There are several types of geosyncline, but all have the essential feature of great thicknesses of sediment accumulating on a subsiding crust. Here, a wedge of sediments 6,000 metres (20,000 ft) or more thick has accumulated at the continental margin, which is fractured. The increasing weight of sediment pushes the blocks of continental crust down into the flexible oceanic crust. This particular situation is similar to that found at the Atlantic edge of North America.

Plate Margin	Number of Volcanoes	Volcanoes Active in the Last 300 years	Magma Erupted (km^3)	Magma Production Rate per 1,000 yrs
Central America	42	20	19	65
Eastern Caribbean	12	3	1	4

Table 1.2 Comparison of volcanic activity at the Caribbean Plate margins in the last 300 years

why there is much more volcanic activity at the western edge of the Caribbean Plate. It has been shown that volcanicity at plate margins depends on the rate of subduction. In the case of the Caribbean Plate there are two destructive margins, with subduction at the Central American margin four or five times as great as at the Atlantic margin. Table 1.2 shows how volcanic activity in Central America is much greater than in the Eastern Caribbean because of this.

Mountain building

What happens when subduction *stops*? The cause of subduction - that is, 'sinking' - is the irresistible movement of the lithosphere. Once this pressure is removed, the crust 'relaxes' and the great accumulation of fractured crust, sediment, volcanic and metamorphosed rocks (geologists call it a *melange*) rises up. This is a most important process in land building, and explains why *active* subduction zones only have small islands. The mountain-building process is essentially one of *uplift*, whereas volcanoes are the result of *accretion* - layers of lava and ash piling up on top of each other. Accretion can only occur at the point of eruption, but uplift is regional and can cover thousands of square kilometres. The Greater Antilles are largely the product of uplift over some 208,000km^2 (80,000 sq. miles), while the Eastern Caribbean, which is mainly volcanic, covers only about 6,000km^2 (2,300 sq. miles).

Mountain building is definitely related to plate tectonics. Prior to the theory of plate tectonics, it was considered that mountain ranges originated in great troughs known as *geosynclines* (Fig 1.9). As a trough filled with sediment, the crust below sagged with the weight until at a certain point the geosyncline became active - strata were folded and turned over - and great masses of magma were injected into it. How all this took place was a matter of considerable argument, but it was responsible for three great mountain-building phases in the Earth's history:

Caledonian: 400 million years ago
Hercynian (Appalachian): 250 million years ago
Laramide (Alpine): 35 million years ago.

All of these took place over a very long period, perhaps 30 million years, and the last phase is considered to be still going on in some parts of the world. These great episodes were known as *orogenies*, and the mountain ranges as *orogenic belts*.

With the theory of plate tectonics, the solution to the puzzle of mountain building was revealed: the geosynclines were the boundaries of the plates. When active they 'filled up', but when movement ceased, an orogeny took place. As rather different types of mountain were formed at the constructive and destructive edges, the word 'geosyncline' was not considered sufficient to explain what happened, and two new terms came into being:

eugeosyncline   at the collision edge
miogeosyncline   at the trailing edge

Caribbean geologists now refer to a *eugeosyncline* along the northern edge of the Caribbean Plate from Cuba to Puerto Rico, and uplift probably took place at the time of the Laramide orogeny when the northward thrust of South America against North America ended. The considerable amount of limestone found at thousands of metres above sea level in the Greater Antilles shows the great extent of uplift in these islands (Fig. 1.10). Limestone can only form below sea level. This limestone is known to be 25-50 million years old, which fits in with the theory.

When a plate's leading edge is also the edge of a continent, the amount of sediment available is greatly increased and the mountain ranges are much larger. Mountain ranges like the Andes, the Alps, and the Western Cordillera of North America are examples. There has been no orogenic activity on this scale in the Caribbean, where mountains rarely exceed 3,000 metres (9,750 ft).

The sides

As a plate moves, it must slide past other plates, and this usually creates major weaknesses in the crust. As in the other two zones, earthquakes and volcanicity are present, but on a much reduced scale. There are, for instance, no active volcanoes known in such parts of the Caribbean, and no significant landforms result from this activity. Beneath the sea the situation is different.

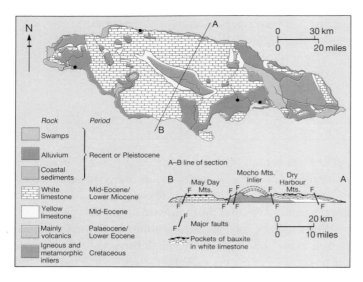

Fig 1.10 Simplified geological map of Jamaica. Jamaica is mainly a limestone island with a core of older igneous rocks which have been exposed from beneath the limestone and form the mountainous areas. Source: Based on Fig 8.2 in Minerals and Rocks of Jamaica, *Anthony R.D. Poter et al, Jamaican publishing House 1982.*

Transform fault zones

The Cayman Trench is today a remarkably visible expression of transform faulting, although it may well have started life as a subduction trench. It separates the North American Plate from the Caribbean Plate. As one author noted: 'Here the two plates grind and creep past each other; here earthquakes are born.' (Robert D. Ballard, *National Geographic Magazine*, August 1976, p. 232) The rate of movement is about 1cm (0.4 in.) a year. Investigation of the trench by research submarine has identified 3-million-year-old sediments in the nearly vertical sides and, more surprisingly, fresh lava at 3,600 metres (12,000 ft). The presence of this lava in a small 'dog's-leg' in the transform fault (See Fig. 1.6) just south of Grand Cayman, may in fact indicate that the sea floor is spreading. This could be the Caribbean's first and only zone of crustal separation - a construction zone.

As long as the plates move there will be earthquakes, and this particular fault has been considered to be very similar to the famous San Andreas Fault, which is also a transform fault. In February 1976 a series of shocks in Guatemala caused the deaths of over 20,000 people. At the same time, earthquakes measuring up to 6 on the Richter Scale were recorded in Jamaica and Cuba. The Guatemalan earthquake registered 7.5, which was much more serious, as Table 1.3 shows.

Earthquakes, volcanoes and human activity

Mankind does not try to avoid zones of natural disaster to any great extent. Farmers cultivate the slopes of active volcanoes, and cities are built on fault lines that are noted for their earthquake activity. People settle in hurricane belts, flood zones and areas that are subject to drought. There are several reasons for this.

Unlike the constantly difficult conditions of the polar regions or the hot deserts, for example, earthquakes and volcanoes are only occasionally dangerous. More important, most people *think* they occur less frequently than they do, and with less severity. As a result, when major earthquakes or

Table 1.3 The Richter Scale of earthquake magnitude

Richter Scale	Effect	Comments
8.0+	Total devastation	About 2 a year, but only 1 in every 10 years affects people. The largest ever recorded was in Ecuador 1906 = 8.9. San Francisco 1906 = 8.3. 700 deaths.
7.4-7.9	Extensive serious damage	Guatemala 1976 = 7.5. 27,000 deaths. Mexico 1985 = 7.9. 9,500 deaths. Iran 1962 = 7.3. 14,000 deaths.
6.2-6.9	Considerable damage	San Francisco 1989 = 6.6.
5.5-6.1	Slight damage	Typical of Cayman Trench earthquakes affecting Jamaica and Cuba.
4.9-5.4	Felt by all	
4.3-4.8	Felt by many	
3.5-4.2	Felt by some	
2.0-3.5	None	Only recorded by instruments.

Earthquake zones and major events		Volcanic zones and major eruptions	
Cayman Trench		**Eastern Caribbean**	
Port Royal	2,000 killed in 1692 earthquake, 4,000 by disease and starvation. City destroyed and about half of it submerged.	Guadeloupe	Soufrière, 1694, 1798, 1838, 1956, 1977.
Kingston	1907, much destroyed by fire and by tidal wave.	Martinique	Mt Pelée, 1851 lateral outbreak. In 1902, 30,000 killed (28,000 St Pierre inhabitants, and 2,000 refugees). Active 1929-32.
Cuba	Santiago/Guantanamo Basins – serious earthquakes causing much damage and casualties, e.g. 1852	St Vincent	Soufrière erupted in 1718, 1812, 1902 (2,000 killed), and 1974.
Puerto Rico Trench		St Kitts	Mt Misery (Mt. Liamuiga) erupted, 1692.
Haiti	1842, Cap Haitien destroyed.	St Lucia	Eruption of Qualibon Soufrière, 1766.
Dominican Republic	Santiago destroyed on several occasions, e.g. 1946	Kick' Em-Jenny (Near Grenada)	Submarine volcano discovered in 1939. Has erupted 2 – 3 times every 10 years.
Puerto Rico (western end)	Frequent earthquakes. Mayaquez and Aquadilla both destroyed in 1918.		
Eastern Caribbean			
Guadeloupe	Severe damage, in Pointe-à-Pitre		
Antigua/Barbuda	1975, minor damage. (See photo. p.6)		
Antigua/Montserrat/Nevis	Severe earthquake and damage, 1843.		

Minor volcanic activity and phenomena	
Dominica	A gas emission in 1765, and a violent steam explosion in 1880 are the only recorded activities. The Valley of Desolation has soufrières (See p.21), which are not uncommon on the island.
Nevis	Here there are two fumaroles which only show minor activity. The main one was activated by an earthquake in 1950 which damaged several buildings.
St Eustatius	A volcano, the Quill, has not erupted in historic times, but has probably done so in the last thousand years. It cannot be considered extinct.
St Kitts	Mt Misery shows minor fumarole activity in its crater, but there is no evidence of an eruption in recent times.
Grenada	Inactive on land, but there was a submarine eruption in the 1960s off the northern coast.
Montserrat	Three years of earthquakes and gas emissions started in 1894, and four years of further activity in 1934.

Table 1.4 Major earthquakes and volcanic activity in the Caribbean since the late seventeenth century. (Sources: Various, including Richard A. Howard, Volcanism and Vegetation in the Lesser Antilles, Journal of Arnold Arboretum, V.XLIII, No.3, July 1962.)

volcanic eruptions do occur, their effect can be catastrophic. The two most notable disasters of this kind in the West Indies were the earthquake of 1692 which hit Port Royal, Jamaica, and the Mt Pelée volcanic eruption of 1902. Table 1.4 lists some of the major earthquakes and volcanic activity in the Caribbean region during the last 300 years.

Mt Pelée on Martinique is a quite recent example of the threat that we face from volcanoes. In 1902, in the period before the eruption, the volcano gave considerable signs of activity, and farmers on its broad slopes were sent to the town of St Pierre, at that time the island's capital. Many warnings were issued to evacuate the town, but the French government did not consider the threat a serious one and the Governor informed the population that they would be safe. Unfortunately the eruption was in the form of an explosive *nuée ardente*, which can best be described as a mass of incandescent gas fired like a fireball over the town from a split in the side of Mt Pelée. Only two people - one on a ship and another in the town gaol-survived out of a population of 30,000. The French government subsequently abandoned St Pierre, which is not much more than a large village today, and made Fort de France - well away from Mt Pelée - the capital. The full circumstances surrounding this tragedy have still not been

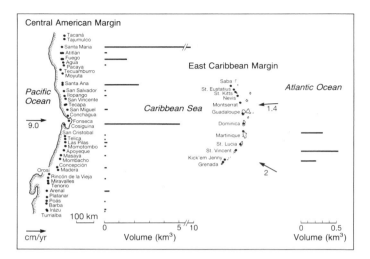

Fig. 1.11 Magma produced at Caribbean plate margins, 1680-1980. The horizontal bars show the quantity of magma erupted from active volcanoes in the last 300 years. The dots indicate active volcanoes, and the arrows the relative rate of convergence at the Caribbean plate margins. (Source: G. Wadge (1984) Geology *Vol. 12.)*

entirely revealed, as the French government originally closed the area off to researchers. Even today evidence of the destruction is still visible.

It is likely that there is a common source for the three volcanoes that are active in the East Caribbean today. When Mt Pelée erupted, it was accompanied by a major eruption of Soufrière on St Vincent which killed 2,000 people, and in the 1970s both Soufrière and Mt Pelée were active and ejected much ash. Guadeloupe's Soufrière was also active in the 1970s. Although ash is not usually dangerous to human life, it is devastating to plant life, and the banana crop of St Vincent was largely destroyed. The expense and inconvenience of cleaning up the ash is also considerable, as it is easily carried by the wind and is fine enough to penetrate cars and buildings. Barbados received a covering of ash from St. Vincent in 1980.

When volcanic activity begins along a subduction zone, no islands have yet formed and the volcanoes erupt under the sea. The Lesser Antilles arc is now fairly mature, many volcanoes are extinct, and nearly all the activity is above sea level (known as *subaerial*). Some submarine activity still exists, however, and the most striking example is the submarine volcano Kick'em Jenny, in the Grenadines just north of Grenada (Fig. 1.11). Kick'em Jenny has frequent eruptions and its cone, which is about 200 metres (660 ft) across, is rising at a rate of about 4 metres (13 ft) a year. As it was estimated to be 165 metres (541 ft) below sea level in 1974, it is unlikely to reach the surface until well into the next century.

When there is an earthquake, most deaths are caused by the consequences of the tremor, and not directly as a result of the earthquake itself, or the cracking or faulting of the earth. In Port Royal, the greatest devastation was caused by the *tsunami* or tidal wave that followed the earthquake, as this knocked down the already weakened buildings and drowned hundreds of people. The earthquake also caused some subsidence, and part of the town never recovered from the flooding, but stayed beneath the sea. The city was not finally abandoned for another 17 years, when it was destroyed by fire, and Kingston across the harbour began to replace it. Fire is a great hazard during earthquakes. It was fire that destroyed San Francisco in 1906, in the world's most famous earthquake. Fire started by the earthquake could not be put out because all the water pipes had been broken as well, and the city burned for three days and nights.

The Caribbean Plate

The 'typical' plate and its margins described so far are not as common as we might like to believe. Perhaps the South American Plate is as near to a perfect example as we can get (Fig. 1.3). There are several factors affecting plate movements.

- The Earth is a sphere and the plates help form its shell; they are themselves curved. The total sum of the movements must interact over the whole spherical surface, and as a result most plates do not move in straight lines, but curve or rotate as they move.

- The forces that create new crust and move the plates vary over time, in location, number and strength.

- The plates may break up and form smaller plates, which set up their own minor movements, or they may collide and become welded together.

The Caribbean Plate has some typical features, notably its 'island arc' system in the Eastern Caribbean, but it is not a 'typical' plate: it has two destructive edges, but no constructive zone. On the other hand it has two sides of transform

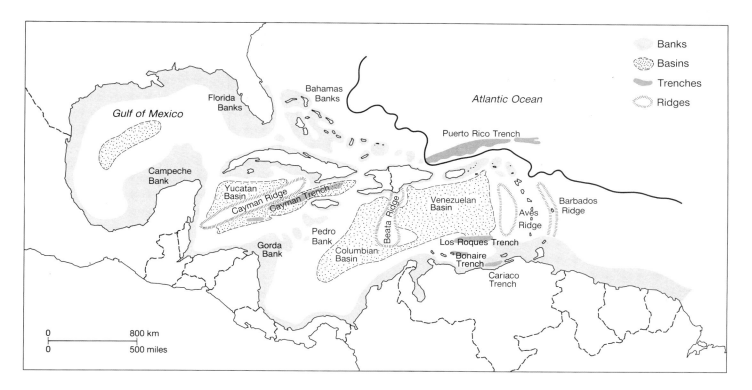

Fig. 1.12 Main oceanographic features of the Caribbean region.

faults. In the past these were also destructive zones, which have changed their nature owing to a change in the direction of crustal movements.

The history of the Caribbean Plate

Once the East Pacific Plate had penetrated the Caribbean area (about 70 million years ago, at the end of the Cretaceous period), it developed a characteristic destructive edge in the Greater Antilles region, stretching from Cuba to Puerto Rico. Along this edge there was a complicated trench system, with the proto-Caribbean plate *under*thrusting the Atlantic Plate, in the vicinity of Cuba and Hispaniola, but *overriding* it further east where Puerto Rico now is.

The result of this activity was the formation of the Greater Antilles. Two things help us confirm this:

1   Most of the igneous rocks originated in the Cretaceous period, and none is younger than 35 million years. They were formed long before the islands of the Eastern Caribbean.

2   The enormous disruption of the Earth's crust that was needed to form these large islands could not have come from the edge of the Caribbean Plate as it is today. Transform zones cannot create this scale of mountain building. The Greater Antilles must have been formed in a subduction zone which has since ceased to exist.

Between these two zones of activity was a split in the plate which had the character of a transform fault. The volcanic activity of this split created the *Beata Ridge*, which is clearly seen on oceanographic maps (Fig. 1.12). At this time the plate's destructive edge was to the north, but south of the Puerto Rico Trench there was further activity at the eastern edge of the plate which is today represented by another underwater feature, the *Aves Ridge*. The Aves Ridge was probably active until the early Tertiary period, about 60 million years ago.

At the same time as the Proto-Caribbean Plate was thrusting northwards and eastwards against the North American Plate (See Fig. 1.3), it was itself being thrust from the south by the South American Plate, which at this time seems to have changed direction more towards North America. This created much volcanic and mountain-building activity which is seen today in the coastal mountain ranges stretching from Lake Maracaibo to Trinidad and Tobago, and under the sea as far as Barbados. This is why the mountains of Trinidad run east-west and Trinidad has its characteristic shape.

In the early Tertiary period the Caribbean Plate was detached from its parent in the Pacific. This occurred because of the 'pinching' movement caused by South America moving north-westwards, at 90° to the north-east movement of the East Pacific Plate. Once separated, the Caribbean Plate settled down to a totally eastward movement, and no more major activity took place along its northern edge. This is basically the situation today (Fig. 1.3).

2
Two geological landscapes

A new eruption filled the crater lake of Mt Soufrière on St Vincent in 1973.

Our survey so far has dealt with the crust of the Earth at a scale that cannot be seen on the ground. Only a map or satellite photograph can show the crustal arrangements of plates, islands, continents and trenches. It is now time to consider in greater detail the landscape we live in. The features that make up a landscape are the *landforms*; that is, individual geographical features, such as a volcano, a sand dune or a sea cliff. A region that is characterized by related landforms, such as rivers, valleys and hills, is collectively known as a *landscape*.

In order to simplify the fairly complex physical geology of the various Caribbean landscapes, it is useful to view them from a more *geographical* point of view. This means identifying the landscapes as we see them, even though the geology overlaps from one landscape to another. There are four main landscapes of the Caribbean:

- Volcanic landscapes
- Limestone landscapes
- Upland landscapes
- Coastal landscapes

In this chapter we deal with volcanic and limestone landscapes. Upland landscapes are examined in chapter 3, and coastal processes and landforms are described in chapter 5.

Volcanism is the most spectacular part of igneous activity, and refers to all that activity that breaks through the crust, as *extrusions*. Igneous *intrusions*, on the other hand, stay underground, and are usually referred to as *plutonic* activity. (Pluto was the Greek god of the underworld.)

The Eastern Caribbean exhibits a great variety of volcanism. The area from Saba in the north to Grenada in the south can be said to have a *volcanic landscape* - but note the exceptions on Fig. 1.8. This same map shows that there are in fact two distinct chains of volcanism. The younger chain is in the east, the older one in the west. In the east, therefore, landforms are fresher and less eroded, but features are considerably eroded and less recognizable in the west.

Volcanic types

There are many different types of volcano. This is because the lava that is extruded from a volcano can vary in character from very fluid to thick (viscous) or even solid.

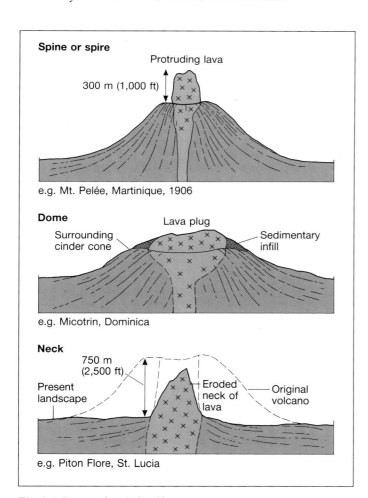

Fig. 2.1 Some volcanic landforms.

A sulphurous vent in Dominica

It is not only lava that comes out of a volcano. Other material includes:

Cinders gravel-sized fragments
Ash fine particles
Pumice lava that has been made frothy by large quantities of erupting gas and steam
Bombs blocks, usually part of the existing volcano or other strata, up to 100 tonnes in size!

Together, these are known as *pyroclastic material*. The presence of gases under pressure is a serious complicating factor in volcanoes that are made up of lava of the less fluid types.

The most fluid type is known as a *shield volcano*, or *Hawaiian type*. The Hawaiian volcanoes such as Mauna Loa are typical examples. Thin layers of basaltic lava build up a very gently sloping cone, and ash and other light material is generally absent. These volcanoes are most common on the mid-oceanic ridges. None of this type is found in the Caribbean.

Another volcanic type has a cone made up of alternate layers of lava and pyroclastic debris, and these volcanoes are therefore called *composite* or *strato-volcanoes* (*strato* means 'layered'). Such famous volcanoes as Vesuvius in Italy and Mt Fuji in Japan are typical examples, and most people are familiar with this shape of volcano. Some of the features of a classical volcano are a conical shape, a circular crater with a lake, and little erosion. There are many examples of such volcanoes in the Caribbean, both old and young. The best known are the young, active ones (See Table 1.3), but there are others that are still young enough to show all the classic features (See Table 2.1).

Volcanism in the Caribbean has been mainly explosive and the deposits from eruptions are therefore of the pyroclastic

Volcano	Height (metres)	Island	Activity
Quill	590	St Eustatius	Dormant
Mt Liamuiga (Mt Misery)	1,155	St Kitts	Sulphur gases escaping
Nevis Peak	985	Nevis	Dormant
Mt Pelée	1,398	Martinique	Active
Soufrière	1,219	St Vincent	Active

Table 2.1 Some Caribbean volcanoes

type. Much of this material falls directly into the sea, and most of what falls on land is easily washed into the sea shortly after an eruption. In the 1979 eruption of St Vincent's Soufrière, mudflows and flash-floods transported most of the volcanic material into the sea within a few months of the eruption. Only in the southern part of the Caribbean are lava flows likely, such as on St Vincent, and especially around the crater of Kick'em Jenny.

Much of the remaining volcanic scenery is of strato-volcanic origin. For example, Dominica has been described as 'comprising several young volcanic centres on an older complex of eroded volcanoes'. *(Source: R.H.A. Martin-Kaye, Summary of the Geology of the Lesser Antilles, Overseas Geology and Mineral Resources, V.10, No.2, 1969, p.193.)*

---

1 Make a list of all the things that might be produced during a volcanic eruption.

2 Explain the effect of each of these volcanic products on the natural world and on our own activities.

Volcanic features

The strato-volcanoes of the Caribbean tend to be composed of increasingly viscous lavas. Many of the volcanic features we see in the Caribbean today are actually the remains of this lava (Fig. 2.1), and include:

Plug　The solid or near-solid lava stuck in the pipe of the volcano.

Spine　Here the lava was too solid to flow and simply stuck up in the air.

Piton　This may be a spine or, more commonly, an exposed plug after the erosion of the surrounding layers of ash and volcanic debris.

Dome　This is the rounded summit of a volcano whose crater has been filled with a plug.

The formation of a dome was recorded relatively recently following the 1902 eruption of Mt Pelée on Martinique.

'When the violently explosive phase ended, a viscous, stiff lava was extruded into the summit crater, ending with the construction of a dome-like protrusion of blocky lava, encrusted with lesser spires and pinnacles. By September 1903 the spire had attained the height of perhaps 305 m (1,000 feet) and a diameter about twice as great... Such *volcanic domes* are more common than many people think.'

(Source: Peter W. Birkeland and Edwin E. Larson (1978) Putnam's Geology, 3rd edition, Oxford University Press, p. 148.)

Dominica has several notable domes, for example Morne Diablotin, Morne Trois Pitons, and Morne Macaque (Microtrin). The very high pitons of St Lucia mark the sites of old volcanic activity, the surrounding composite cone having eroded away.

The Caribbean has only three active volcanoes, with possibly two others dormant. There is therefore much less construction than erosion, and much volcanic material, such as the ash and cinder deposits, is rapidly eroded. The resulting landscapes are therefore very complex and often, as in Dominica, St Lucia and Grenada, the islands seem to consist of rugged masses of confused and unrelated hills, numerous steep-sided valleys, and many small, near-vertical outcrops. This very confusion is in fact a characteristic of the eroded volcanic landscape. The clean-cut lines of an active volcano are rare, and although the crater of St Vincent's Soufrière is indeed remarkably well formed, the region's three active volcanoes are not particularly spectacular.

Galway's soufrière on Montserrat has destroyed the vegetation and weakened the rocks, allowing excessive erosion.

Fumaroles

The most common volcanic features in the Windward Islands are the small but usually smelly features that are called sulphur springs, soufrières or solfataras by the local people. The correct name for a single vent is a *fumarole*, but multiple fumaroles are usually called *soufrières*. They can be found high up in the mountains, as in the Valley of Desolation in Dominica, along valley sides, as at Galways in Montserrat, or at or below sea level as in the case of several extinct examples in Nevis.

St Lucia's soufrières are among the best known and show the most common features: the emission of steam; the venting of hot sulphurous gases; yellow deposits of sulphur; blackened rock and black pools of boiling water; and a smell of hydrogen sulphide.

The gases, heat and steam kill the surrounding vegetation and rot the surrounding rocks, so fumaroles are characterized by highly visible erosion. Steam from St Lucia's Qualibou soufrière reaches 185°C (365°F) and is a possible source of geothermal energy (See p. 121).

---

1 Locate Fort de France on an atlas map. Explain why it was believed to be a better location for the capital of Martinique than St Pierre.

2 What is a 'solfatara'?

3 Why are there no plants near fumaroles?

4 Give two reasons why fumaroles may be of economic value.

5 Why would people want to bathe in volcanic water?

Plutonic features

The remaining igneous features are those that have intruded into the earlier rocks, known as the *country rock*. Although they were buried when they were formed, erosion often exposes these features, and so they are now sometimes visible, at least in part.

The general name for an intrusive feature is a *pluton*, and this name is widely used in the Caribbean where many of the intrusions are not clearly identified. Underlying all volcanic activity is an intrusive body. On the continents this may be of truly massive dimensions, hundreds or thousands of kilometres across. The typical rock of such intrusions, which are known as *batholiths*, is *granite*, or its relative *granodiorite*. Both are coarse-grained (the minerals in them are large and easily visible) owing to the slow cooling of the magma underground. This provided time for the crystals to form, in contrast to the faster-cooling volcanic rocks, such as basalt, which are fine-grained.

The only batholith in the Caribbean region is that of the Guiana Shield, and granite and granodiorite rocks are widely exposed (and rotted) in the interior of Guyana, particularly in the Rupununi and Kanuku mountain areas. There are smaller plutons in the Greater Antilles, for example the Above Rocks area - 50km² (20sq. miles) - north of Kingston, Jamaica. Investigation of this body suggests that it was intruded some 65 million years ago under at least 2,000 metres (6,500 ft) of sedimentary rocks. These rocks were later eroded and replaced in part by limestone, but the granodiorite core is readily accessible at various places in the parish of St Andrew. (*Source: Anthony R.D. Porter et al, Mineral and Rocks of Jamaica, Jamaica Publishing House, 1982*). Finer-grained plutons are known in Dominica, where the mountains of Morne Watt, Morne Anglais and Couronne were formed by intrusion, but under a much thinner cover than in Jamaica. All of these plutons form relatively high ground, over 500 metres (1,600 ft) in the Above Rocks area and in parts of the Blue Mountains, and as much as 1,224 metres (4,017 ft) at Morne Watt.

Around any igneous body, whether it is volcanic or plutonic, magma will be injected into any weaknesses in the country rock. The main weaknesses are faults and bedding planes, and as the magma fills them they give rise to vertical (or nearly so) and horizontal sheets of igneous rock. The former are called *dykes*, and the latter *sills*.

Dykes are much more common as they are often exposed at the surface. There are dykes in all West Indian countries with igneous rocks. Examples are numerous in Guyana, but more restricted, for example, in St Vincent (in the Mesopotamia Valley and on Bequia). Dykes may run for a long distance, but are quite narrow, usually less than 30 cm (12 in.) across in the West Indies.

Sills are less common here as they depend for their formation on well-bedded layers of sedimentary rocks. Guyana has several well-known examples, some of which, in the Roraima area, are thick intrusions between beds of sandstones, conglomerates and shales.

---

1 Why do some volcanic islands not have a volcanic crater?

2 Where does lava come from?

3 Why do people settle on the slopes of volcanoes?

4 What kind of weathering is associated with fumaroles? (See also p.31.)

5 What is the main type of erosion in a volcanic landscape? (See also ch.4.)

The most widespread rock in the Caribbean, and indeed in the world, is limestone. In some ways this is strange, as it is only formed in water and must later be exposed (by earth movements or sea-level changes) to form land. Despite this, almost every country in the Caribbean has some limestone, including the volcanic Windward Islands.

In the Caribbean there are several types of limestone, each of which is formed in a different way.

Types of limestone

Coral limestone

Coral reefs are formed by minute organisms which extract calcium carbonate ($CaCO_3$, the chief and often the only mineral found in limestone) from the sea and build a skeleton with it. Unlike other limestones, coral limestone starts life as a *massive* (solid) rock, and not as a sediment.

The coral limestone that covers most of Barbados originated as coral reefs, which are still abundant throughout the region. Both the Atlantic Ocean and the Caribbean Sea support a wide range of coral species.

Ideally, coral requires sea temperatures in the range 25-29°C (77-84°F) (c.f. ch. 8 etc), and can live in depths of up to 100 metres (330 ft), although the water must be clear and free of sediments and pollution. The necessary climatic conditions exist throughout the region, but clear, unpolluted water is generally only found around the smaller islands such as the Virgin Islands, the Grenadines and The Bahamas. Islands like Puerto Rico and Hispaniola have many rivers, and serious soil erosion has led to excessive sedimentation offshore. Fine sediment stays in suspension in the water and reduces the penetration of sunlight. It also chokes the tiny coral polyps on the surface of the coral structures. As a result, reef development is not widespread near muddy estuaries, and with increased sedimentation in more recent times, many reefs have been damaged or destroyed.

Coral polyps live in colonies, on the outer surface of what we know as 'coral'. This contains the outer skeleton, or 'cups', that the coral polyps live in. The coral polyps secrete calcium carbonate which they extract from the sea to build a skeleton, layer by layer. The accumulation of corals makes the coral reef, which supports many other animal and plant life forms, which also secrete or deposit calcium carbonate. Reefs can

A fringing reef protects the shore of Cannouan in The Grenadines.

22

therefore grow into quite large structures, and in the Caribbean, as over the rest of the world, these can take several forms:

Barrier reef   This is a linear reef that is separated from the land by a substantial body of water. Quite long systems exist in the West Indies, for example off the coast of Belize, and Andros in The Bahamas. In Belize the barrier reef is 20-40km (12-25 miles) offshore, sufficiently far to be unaffected by the sediment brought down by rivers from the interior.

Fringing reef   This is also a linear reef but lies much closer to the shore, with a shallow lagoon between them. Many islands have such reefs, especially on their Atlantic or windward shores, including the north coast of Jamaica and the eastern coast of Antigua. Barrier and fringing reefs may merge into each other, and be broken or continuous. In some cases, such as Andros, a reef might be considered to be either a barrier or a fringing reef, as the difference is not in their origin, but rather in the depth and width of the shelf on which the reef is built.

Patch reef   While linear reefs are largely a response to wave action offshore, the patch reef inhabits the more sheltered areas in the lagoon behind the linear reef, and the wider expanses of quiet water on the banks of areas like The Bahamas. Quite often they occur in clusters of several hundred, rising up to 10 metres (30 ft) from the sandy sea floor in water 10 to 15 metres (30 to 50 ft) deep.

Atoll   This is not so much a separate type of reef as the circular arrangement of a linear reef. The classic types are those of the Pacific which have developed around the summits of submerged volcanoes. With time and subsidence, great thicknesses of coral have formed and create a wall which surrounds equally great thicknesses of lagoon sediments. To explain this process a theory known as *The Bucket Theory of Atoll Formation* has been devised (Fig. 2.2). It is useful to study this as it shows the relationship of the coral wall (side of the bucket) to the inner sediments which it prevents from escaping, and the volcano itself.

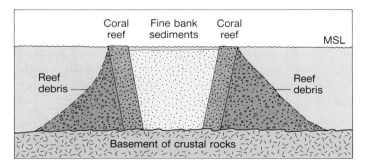

Fig. 2.2 The bucket theory of atoll formation. The theory explains the way in which a coral reef wall grows vertically, and retains the fine biological sediments produced within the rim.

Atolls are not abundant in the West Indies, but some 15 have been identified in the Caribbean Sea, and a few more on the major banks outside the area. The very large banks of The Bahamas, although quite irregularly shaped, are otherwise identical to atolls in structure, and could be described as 'mega-atolls'. They are not, however, built on volcanoes.

The coral reef can therefore be a very large geological feature. It can grow horizontally (with minor sea-level changes) and vertically (with subsidence) and so form a substantial body of limestone rock, such as that which covers 90% of Barbados.

1   What conditions are essential for the growth of coral?

2   Why do we find coral limestone above sea level today? (See photograph on p.46.)

3   What is the nearest coral reef to you? What type of reef is it?

4   Are coral reefs good or bad for fishing? Does your answer apply to all types of fish? (See also ch.14)

5   Are the Grenadine Islands of coral or volcanic origins? How can you tell? (Look at the photograph on p.22.)

Coralgal limestone

In and around coral reefs are many other plants and animals, and most important of these are the *green calcareous algae*. These also extract calcium carbonate from the sea and grow prolifically on the sandy sea floor. When they die their bodies disintegrate to form more sand. Together with the debris from all the other life in and around a coral reef, they provide a mass of coral and algal - *coralgal* - sediment, which when cemented to form a rock creates coralgal limestone. The outer parts of all the major banks - The Bahamas, Turks and Caicos, Caymans, Barbuda - contain this material.

Oolitic limestone

This only forms in shallow water but is nevertheless abundant along the edges of the banks referred to above. It originates as very fine sand in sand banks within 5km (3 miles) of the bank edges (Fig. 2.3). The origin of the tiny spherical grains is not known for certain, but it is believed to be the result of the heating up of sea water in shallow areas. This causes the calcium carbonate to be precipitated out (similar to the formation of salt) and it 'rains down' on the sea floor. The Bahamas and the Turks and Caicos Islands are almost entirely made up from oolitic limestone.

1 What are algae? Do all algae form sediments, or just one type?

2 With the aid of your biology or science department, find some marine algae that make sediment. Examine the roots and foliage, and draw the sample. (One example is *Halimeda*, the most common type.)

3 Why are The Bahamas so flat and low, but Barbados higher, and hilly in the centre?

Limestone landforms

Together these three limestones account for most of the islands found on shallow banks in the Caribbean. The islands themselves have basically two sets of landforms: a flat, low-lying limestone plain, which is often swampy; and lines of curving ridges up to 60 metres (200 ft) high. The former represent the exposed sea bed which was originally laid down when sea level was higher (between ice ages); the latter are fossilized sand dunes made up of the fine-grained oolitic limestone. These islands are invariably found on the edges of the banks they belong to, where the production of sediment was greatest.

With the exception of coral-capped Barbados, these landscapes are unspectacular and unproductive. They have little relief, and shallow soils. In some cases, notably Barbados, the marine limestones have been lifted above sea level and may exceed 300 metres (1,000 ft) in height. In addition, much uplifted limestone is to be found in the Greater Antilles, where the visual aspect of the landscape is quite different, and often spectacular. Jamaica, Cuba and Puerto Rico all show extensive areas of what is known as *tropical karst*. In order to understand the development of such scenery we must learn a little about the peculiar nature of limestones.

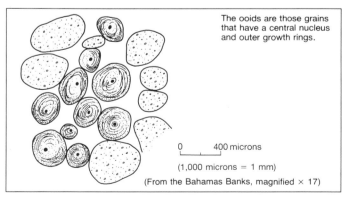

The ooids are those grains that have a central nucleus and outer growth rings.

0   400 microns

(1,000 microns = 1 mm)

(From the Bahamas Banks, magnified × 17)

Fig. 2.3 Diagram of fine to medium oolitic sand, with other sediments. The ooids are those grains showing a central nucleus and outer growth rings.

The long snaking ridge of Salt Cay in The Bahamas is typical of the long thin islands that develop from sand dunes on shallow-water banks in the Caribbean.

In the tropics, limestones develop rather differently from those in other parts of the world. The reasons for this are mainly due to the *climate* - a wet season with heavy downpours and high temperatures - and to the nature of the *limestone* itself.

Limestone is calcium carbonate ($CaCO_3$), which dissolves in rain water and percolating ground water. (This chemical process is described under 'Weathering', page 31.) The dissolving of the limestone takes place both on the surface and beneath it. The surface is etched and eroded, while below the ground it is tunnelled and hollowed out until the entire limestone stratum has been honeycombed into a state of collapse. At this point many collapses do occur, creating a variety of hollows and holes, and providing new material for the ground water to work on.

Eventually the limestone surface is worn down to the water table, below which erosion is much slower. It can therefore be said that the erosion of a limestone landscape follows a *cycle*, from a new surface down to a level plain. Most of the Caribbean limestone outcrops are fairly young, so the final stages are rarely seen here.

We can now go through this cycle and pinpoint specific landforms as they appear (Fig. 2.4). As limestone is usually a fairly pure rock (over 70% $CaCO_3$), it generates little soil and is often exposed to rain and sun. This has two results, which are quite different in character:

1 Surface corrosion results in a fluting or grooving of the limestone surface. These small-scale rills or runnels are also known as *karren*.

2 High temperatures cause rapid evaporation of soil moisture, leaving behind deposits of calcium carbonate that

was dissolved in the water. These deposits form a *limestone crust* beneath the shallow soils. Limestone crust is widespread throughout the Caribbean. It forms a dense, impervious cover over the rock below it, which can be a major problem in agriculture.

As the water penetrates underground through any natural weaknesses, such as joints (shrinkage cracks) or faults in the rock, it widens them to give a pot-holed surface. The 'pot holes' are correctly termed *solution holes* and they generally vary from 2 - 30 cm (1 to 12 in.) across. Large holes are usually the result of several smaller ones joining when the surface layer collapses.

These features represent the early stages in the cycle of destruction of the limestone landscape. The next stage represents a more *mature* stage and is characterized by much larger features, mainly holes and depressions, caused by the collapse of the honeycombed upper layers into a cavern below. In the tropics these features are known as *cockpits* after the famous Cockpit Country of Jamaica.

This stage has not yet been reached in the younger limestones (usualy less than 1 million years old) of the banks islands, but in the Greater Antilles the limestone is often 30-50 million years old. In addition it has often been elevated to several hundred metres, which allows the development of a more massive relief (that is, there is a greater vertical height in the various landforms).

A related feature is the *blue hole* (or ocean hole). These are found extensively in the shallow seas of The Bahamas, and also in Belize. The vertical holes are usually circular, 15-150 metres (50-500 ft) across, and may be over 90 metres (300 ft) deep. Today they are generally flooded to within a metre of the top of the hole, and many are completely submerged by the sea (Fig. 2.5). Blue holes are a relict landform of the Ice Ages, and were formed when sea level was at times over 90 metres (300 ft) lower than it is today. The land was therefore much higher above sea level. The holes are mostly a combination of vertical weathering and collapse, and can be compared with the cave climbers' 'pot holes' of Europe. They are a major tourist attraction for divers, and provide a 'window' into the islands' recent history.

Several different underground features may be found in a limestone landscape:

Tunnels (or *conduits*) These passages are followed by the underground drainage system. Surface drainage is not common on limestone, although it will be seen when the water table rises after heavy rains, or if the tunnel system is unable to carry the water away quickly enough. The absence of surface water under normal conditions provides a false sense of security, and flooding in limestone areas can be very dangerous. On 12th June 1979, for example, in the Newmar-

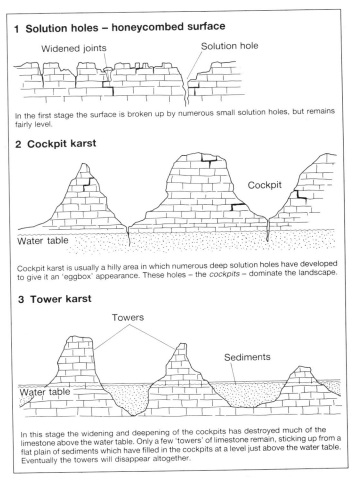

Fig. 2.4 *The cycle of limestone denudation in the tropics.*

ket area of western Jamaica, it was reported that some 90 lakes were created after exceptionally heavy rain. Up to 50 people drowned, mainly where torrential underground streams flooded above the limestone surface in quite unexpected places.

Caves and *caverns* Caves have a direct opening to the surface, while caverns are totally underground and must be reached by a tunnel. They are popular attractions and some can be developed to allow access by visitors, as at Harrison's Cave in Barbados, for example. In practice most caverns are either inaccessible or are dangerous to reach. Caverns usually form where major weaknesses in the rock encourage a greater degree of erosion. They are often the meeting place of several tunnels. Caverns are very prone to collapse, as they have a large unsupported roof area and are generally in areas that are already structurally weak. Such collapses form some kinds of blue hole. If they do not collapse they may exhibit a variety of *speleothems*.

Speleothem This is the generic name for any underground depositional feature such as a *stalactite* or a *stalagmite, columns*

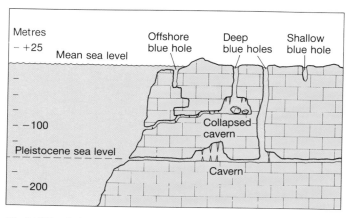

Fig 2.5 Blue holes may be on land or in the shallow seas offshore. They are flooded vertical solution holes formed when sea level was much lower, during the Ice Ages. Their maximum depth is often related to the water table at the time of formation.

Solution holes filled with bauxite, exposed in a road cutting at Lydford, Jamaica.

(a combined stalactite/stalagmite) and *curtains* (on the walls). All are made of re-deposited calcium carbonate, which in these forms is known as *travertine*. (This is the same mineral material that forms the limestone crust described on p. 25.)

Tower karst

This name is a general term to describe the remnants of a karst landscape when more has been destroyed than remains. Such a landscape is particularly striking because of the contrasts it provides. The lowland is absolutely flat and usually cultivated, as the water table is close to the surface. It is similar to a flood plain, and represents the base level to which the limestone relief has been weathered down. Standing up from it are towers of limestone with steep or even vertical sides which are often well forested. These towers are the remains of the original limestone strata, being the more massive sections which for some reason were more resistant to erosion. They are nevertheless honeycombed with tunnels and caverns, and some of these have an exit or exits at the foot of the tower. The largest area of tower karst in the West Indies is in Cuba, near Holguin, but other parts of Cuba, and Puerto Rico and Jamaica, also show these final stages.

Cockpit Country, near Ulster Spring, Jamaica.

---

1 Where does limestone go after it is dissolved by solution weathering? (See p.31.)

2 What is likely to fill solution holes?

3 Name and sketch features of deposition in a cavern. Provide a scale for each sketch.

4 What kinds of deposit might you find on the floor of a cave? Are these of any use to us?

3
Geological forces and geographical processes

A normal fault in limestone cliffs at Clifton, Nassau, The Bahamas.

We have examined how two distinct groups of rocks - volcanic rocks and limestone - can result in a particular kind of landscape. Wherever the *geology* - in this case the rock *type* - is the main reason for the features we see, we consider *geological controls* to be dominant. We have looked at the *creative* forces of volcanism that formed the landscape, and at the *destructive* forces of weathering and erosion on one particular type of rock. We now examine the main geological and geographical *forces* that affect the landscape:

- Folding
- Faulting
- Weathering
- Erosion, by mass wasting, rivers and marine forces - see chapters 4 and 5.

Sometimes these *processes* are so important that they create a particular kind of landscape, whatever the rock type.

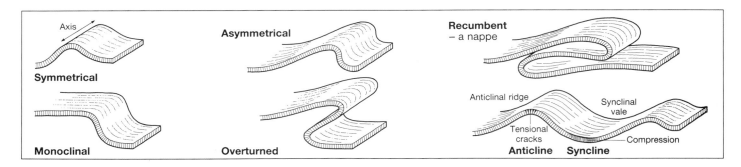

Fig. 3.1 Types of folds.

We already know that the Earth's surface is mobile. Folding is one of the results of this movement, and there are few places on Earth where rocks are completely horizontal and undisturbed (Fig. 3.1).

Folding is most noticeable in mountainous areas, where *uplift* has taken place. In fact, the more recent mountain ranges of the world are often called *fold mountains*, as their strata show extreme degrees of folding on a very large scale. However, any movement of the Earth's crust will disrupt the strata which will either bend (fold) or crack (fault). Geologists have classified folds into two main types:

1 *Minor folds*   These are relatively small, such as those seen in a quarry or cliff face. Examples are common in the Greater Antilles and Scotland District, Barbados.

2 *Major folds*   These can affect hundreds of square kilometres and may include minor folds and faults within them. Perhaps only in Trinidad do we see any evidence of this. The Greater Antilles are too rigid to fold, and break into large blocks instead.

In many cases the larger folds have been severely eroded and the original form has to be reconstructed from the remnants. It is important to note that the *shape* of the fold does not necessarily create landforms of that shape - anticlines are not usually hills and ridges, nor are synclines valleys. The landscape is usually much more complex and the synclines may be higher than the anticlines. An anticline is weakened by tension cracks when the upper part of the fold is stretched, and in mountain areas these are at the highest points and therefore exposed to more severe physical weathering. Consequently, *eroded anticlines* are a common feature in their own right (Fig. 3.2).

These sloping strata near Maracas are the result of folding in Trinidad's Northern Range

The *nappe* is only well known in the more recent mountain ranges, such as the Alps or the Rockies. They represent the effect of massive thrusting that has caused the fold to overlap itself. Such movements are usually accompanied by metamorphism, faulting, crushing and perhaps volcanism.

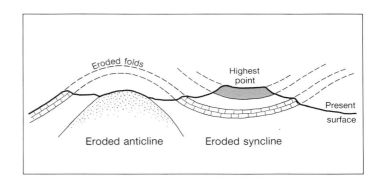

Fig. 3.2 Erosion of anticlines and synclines. Although the anticline is originally a higher feature of relief than a syncline, after erosion it may well form lower ground than the syncline. In this sketch the bottom of the syncline now forms the highest ground.

Faulting

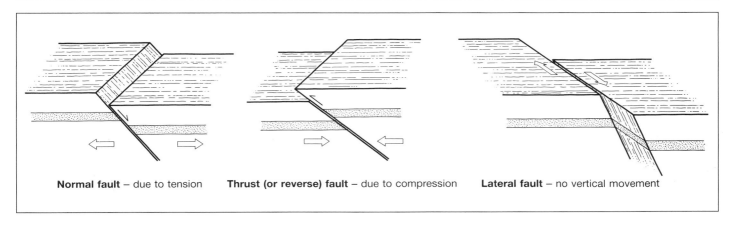

Fig. 3.3 Types of faults.

Like folds, faults can be classified into several distinct types (Fig. 3.3).

Minor faults These faults are common and are visible at the smallest scales of only a few centimetres. Minor faults can be seen throughout the West Indies in cliff faces.

Major faults Major faults may appear to be nothing more than long minor faults. The famous San Andreas Fault is a lateral fault running for 1,000km (600 miles) in California. However, in detail these faults become quite complex. The San Andreas Fault, for instance, splits and subdivides into as many as four parallel faults in southern California. Major faults criss-cross all the islands of the Greater Antilles, and often form a *fault scarp*, such as at Spur Tree Hill in Jamaica. When they extend over large areas they are termed *regional faults*.

Multiple faulting is common in major fault zones and can give rise to impressive landforms (Fig. 3.4).

1 What causes rocks to fold. What parts of the Caribbean might have folded rocks?

2 In Fig. 3.4 the names *graben* and *horst* are used. What language is that? From a map, find an example of each feature in the country that uses that language.

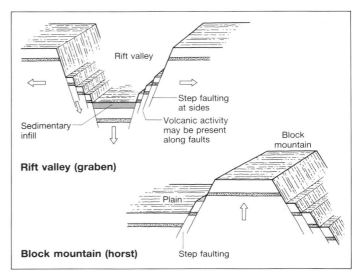

Fig. 3.4 Rifting.

29

The terms 'erosion' and 'weathering' are often used loosely, but they do have specific meanings.

Weathering involves the destruction of solid rock *in situ* (without it being moved), by physical and chemical means.

Erosion is the wearing away of the landscape by physical action, and transportation is involved. Although erosion affects solid rocks, it is most effective on rock that has been weathered, and much erosion is of the weathered layer. The combined destruction and removal of the rock surface is best known as *denudation*, and should not simply be referred to as 'erosion'.

As in much of physical geography, the alteration of the landscape is the result of certain *processes*, and the way these processes work is affected by certain *factors*. Weathering can be explained by examining each of these processes and factors in turn.

The *processes* are essentially of two kinds:

- physical
- chemical

A third process, *biological*, is sometimes included, but in fact it is more correctly considered as an *agent* that encourages physical or chemical processes, as every biological process is a chemical process.

We need also to consider two more factors:

- The environment   - climate
  - hydrology (availability of underground or surface water)
- The rocks and their minerals

Physical weathering

As we shall see, the Caribbean is not very prone to this kind of weathering.

Load release

This is rather difficult to identify without extensive sampling and fieldwork. It is most common in old landscapes where deeply buried rocks are eventually exposed at the surface by denudation. Any rock buried underground is compressed, but once the pressure is removed from above, it can expand. This is why granite at the surface, as in tors, has so many cracks (called *joints*). It is best known as a phenomenon in mines, where floors may rise and walls 'explode'.

Freeze-thaw

As water expands by about 9% when it is frozen, and it cannot be compressed, it is quite capable of shattering the strongest rocks. Rocky areas in cold countries, such as cliff faces, mountainsides or quarries, are always littered with angular rock fragments after the winter, a sure sign that there has been frost-shattering. In the tropics, freeze-thaw is only possible on the highest mountains. A rather similar process does take place in tropical dry regions, however. This is the expansion of *salt crystals* as they grow. Anywhere exposed to a salty atmosphere can be subject to this type of weathering, but it is most noticeable in buildings and other structures where there is salt in the building sand or water.

Insolation

This includes a type of weathering known as *exfoliation*. It is the result of the surface or structure of a rock being weakened by repeated heating - causing expansion - and cooling - causing contraction. It is most common where there are great differences in temperature between day and night. Such conditions are rare in the Caribbean region, but important in hot, dry, desert areas. Exfoliation can also occur when rocks are cooled by rain after they have been exposed to the sun, and loose surface layers of rock are quite common in many parts of the Caribbean. It may be that the loose flaky surface of limestone in some dry areas is at least partly due to this action.

Onion-skin weathering is the most common type of exfoliation, as it is obviously the surface layers that are most vulnerable. A variation is known as *blocky disintegration*, when the surface layer becomes crazed into very small fragments. In both cases, when something dislodges the loosened fragments, the lower layers are exposed and the process is repeated. Some igneous rocks, such as granite, are made up of different minerals with different colours. These heat up at different rates and gradually separate from each other, weakening the rock. This is called *granular disintegration*.

Wetting and drying

This is probably very common in the Caribbean, but is difficult to detect. Whenever a rock is wetted, some physical and chemical changes occur, and when it is dried there is a further change. Probably a variety of processes act together, such as insolation, chemical weathering and drying. Studies suggest that it is most effective in the softer fine-grained sedimentary rocks, such as clays and shales.

Chemical weathering

Under many conditions an actual chemical change takes place in the rock to produce a new, water-soluble material. In

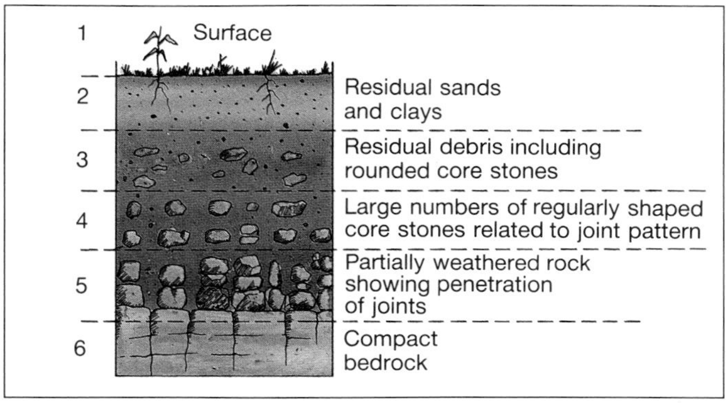
1
Surface
2
Residual sands and clays
3
Residual debris including rounded core stones
4
Large numbers of regularly shaped core stones related to joint pattern
5
Partially weathered rock showing penetration of joints
6
Compact bedrock

Fig. 3.5 Chemical weathering. This diagram shows the typical deep rotting that can occur in the igneous rocks of the Greater Antilles or the Guianas.

effect the surface of the rock is dissolved and washed away, or is at least rotted and can easily be eroded away.

The likelihood of chemical weathering depends on the presence of water - the more water, the more likely it is that a chemical reaction will take place. Also, with higher temperatures the chemical reactions will be faster. Acids derived from rotting vegetation can also be important. Clearly, then, a hot wet climate is ideal for chemical weathering, and indeed this is undoubtedly the most important element in the destruction of rock surfaces, exposed or beneath a soil, in the Caribbean and in the tropics in general (Fig. 3.5). There are several different types of chemical weathering.

Solution

There are few examples of weathering by solution alone. The dissolving of rock salt in water is one of the few cases. Most rocks are too resistant simply to be dissolved. However, solution is an important part of chemical weathering.

- It often *starts off* a process by dissolving one of the minerals or chemicals in a rock. This solution then reacts with another chemical, and so a whole series of reactions is created.
- It is also the *end* of many processes which produce a soluble material. This is then dissolved and washed away.

Sea water contains many chemicals, but the main one is salt (sodium chloride). Virtually all of the chemicals come from rivers which collect the dissolved chemicals from weathered rocks. A more recent example of solution in action is caused by human pollution of the atmosphere. Sulphur compounds emitted by cars and factories are dissolved in rainwater and form an acid which attacks natural rock surfaces, especially the limestone that is often used for buildings. This produces a soluble compound and the rock facings simply dissolve bit by bit each time it rains. This is what is meant by *'acid rain'*.

Carbonation

This is one of the best-known natural reactions, as it is the one that attacks limestone and creates a karst scenery. The basic process is as follows:

1. Rain (H_2O) dissolves carbon dioxide (CO_2) from the atmosphere and forms dilute carbonic acid (H_2CO_3).
2. The carbonic acid converts the limestone ($CaCO_3$) into calcium bicarbonate ($Ca(HCO_3)_2$).
3. Water dissolves the calcium bicarbonate (solution) and the rock is thus dissolved.

Any rock containing a carbonate or bicarbonate in its mineral structure is susceptible to this process.

Oxidation

Any mineral that reacts with oxygen in the atmosphere (which is 16% oxygen) will produce an oxide, which is usually soluble. Iron, manganese and sulphur are the elements most affected, and as iron is the second most abundant mineral on earth, oxidation is an important process. Iron oxide is what we know as rust, and the red colour of many soils is due to the presence of iron in them. (See also ch.9).

Reduction

This occurs in the absence of oxygen, such as in waterlogged areas like swamps and tidal flats. Hydrogen sulphide is generated under these conditions and may be smelled if a sample of swamp peat is removed. The sulphur combines with the metallic minerals and produces a sulphide such as iron sulphide, or nickel sulphide, and this is a much softer material. The typical colour is black, as can be seen in the steel parts of shipwrecks rotting under water, or in peat.

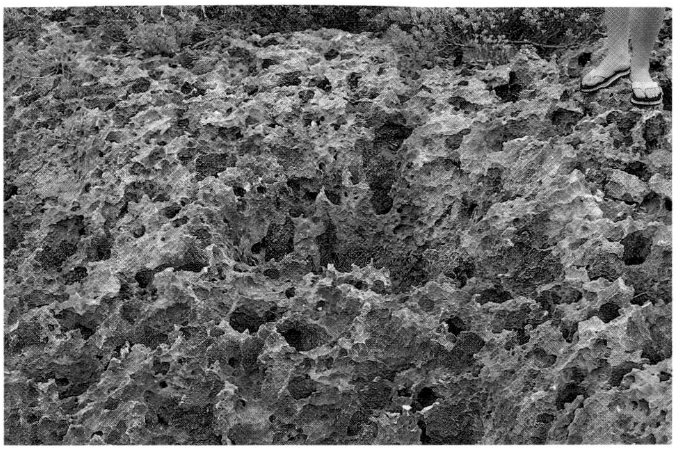

Solution holes developing in oolitic limestone on Andros, The Bahamas.

Hydration

In the same way that combining oxygen or sulphur with a mineral can produce a soluble or weaker mineral, so can the *addition* of water, which is known as hydration. It is not usually identifiable as a single process, but is part of other processes, often being the first step in 'softening up' a mineral for oxidation or reduction. The end product is usually a clay, which is nature's most indestructible material. Clays are the product of weathering, and almost nothing can destroy them. Bauxite is a clay in whose formation hydration plays a part.

Hydrolysis

Hydration is the adding of water to a mineral. Hydrolysis involves a *chemical reaction* between the two. Many igneous minerals are vulnerable to this, and it is important because nothing else is needed except water. This is also a major process in the production of bauxite from basalt, in which calcium, magnesium, sodium and potassium are removed by water alone.

Biological agents of weathering

Physical
(a)   Breaking up of particles by tree roots, algae, fungi, or by organisms eating or burrowing the rock, e.g. algae, worms, termites.

(b)   Transfer and mixing of materials by animals. In this way material can be brought up to the zone of oxidation.

Chemical
(a)   Increased solution due to carbon dioxide released by plant transpiration.
(b)   Increased moisture due to plant cover. This increases the potential for chemical activity.
(c)   Fermentation produced by rotting vegetation.
(d)   Increase in acidity due to plant activity.
(e)   Bacteria encourage *oxidation*, and probably cause most of the *reduction* (rotting in the absence of oxygen).

The extent of biologically induced weathering is enormous in the tropics and should not be underestimated. Beneath the tropical forests of Guyana are some 30-60 metres (100-200 ft) of rotted material (mainly sands and clays) before solid rock in encountered.

---

1 What kind of *weathering* do you see where you live?

2 What kind of *erosion* do you see where you live?

3 What is 'acid rain'?

4 Why are some soils a rusty-red colour?

5 Make a list of all the biological agents that affect the soil or rock near your home. For each physical effect, state *exactly* what is happening.

Summary: Rock type and structure

Every rock type reacts differently to weathering, and each climate produces a different result in the same rock. For example, temperate limestone weathering is different from tropical limestone weathering. The structure of the rocks largely governs the movement of water in the rock - *permeability* - and the amount of water a rock can hold - *porosity*. The varying combinations of these, and the fact that many weathering processes are in action at the same time, and interacting with each other, make this a very complex process. Despite this, the basic processes are still clearly identifiable in the field. They can also be studied in school by trying out different experiments on rock samples in the laboratory.

Experiments on rock samples

1   To estimate porosity, obtain a variety of limestone rock, about the size of your fist. The rock should be clean and freshly broken from a natural exposure. Samples may be taken from a cave, cliffs, road-cuttings and along the coast at sea level.

The samples must be labelled and thoroughly dried out in the sun for several days at least. Each one is weighed, then immersed in the bottom of a bucket of water and left for several days. Once the rock has been thoroughly soaked it should be taken out of the bucket, dried on the surface with a towel and weighed immediately. The porosity in percentage is then:

$$\frac{2.7 \; (\text{weight wet - weight dry})}{\text{weight wet}} \times 100 = P\%$$

This is an approximation only as porosity is a measurement of volume, not of weight. The constant 2.7 is the average density of limestone, and as it is water (density 1.0) that is filling the pore spaces, it must be multiplied by 2.7 to make it the equivalent of limestone.

2 To estimate weathering rates, proceed as before, but obtain four sets of samples. All should be weighed accurately. Place one set in the sea, one in a large source of fresh water such as a barrel of rainwater, one out in the open exposed to the weather, and one in the intertidal zone. A fifth sample can be kept in a sheltered area as a control. After as long a period as possible - at least 1-2 months (a year is better) - retrieve the rocks and dry them thoroughly in the sun for several days. They must be as dry as when they were first weighed. Then weigh them precisely and note the differences (in percentages):

(a)   for each type of limestone,

(b)   for each type of environment.

This will indicate the rate of solution (chemical) weathering taking place, and you will be able to tell which kind of limestone is most vulnerable, and which environment is most aggressive.

A large blue hole at Cargill Creek, North Andros, in the Bahamas. This deep solution hole has several underwater caverns leading away from it. It is used as a local swimming pool.

4
Upland fluvial landscapes

A mountain stream on Grande Terre, Guadeloupe. During a flood the road bridge (remains in foreground) was destroyed and the large boulders washed downstream.

In the Caribbean, and especially in the Greater Antilles, many people live inland, away from the coast, in regions where the weathering and erosion of the surface is dominated by the weather rather than by the rock type. This type of landscape is distinguished by its surface drainage and the formation of valleys and other water-eroded features.

Volcanic landscapes and limestone landscapes (See chapter 2) both form upland, but the former is distinguished by its exceptionally steep slopes while the latter has no surface drainage. Surface drainage is also the main feature of the heavily populated coastal lowlands, so our division into four types of landscape (See p.18) is more useful as a description

of the environment than as a description of the physical geography.

Once the land rises above about 200 metres (600 feet), there is enough height for a hilly relief to develop. Much of the Greater Antilles consist of blocks of sedimentary rocks that have been lifted up as much as 1,000 metres (3,300 ft), and except where this rock is limestone, as in the Dry Harbour Mountains and White Mountains of Jamaica, the landscape is typically a succession of valleys with ridges between them. In many cases the ridges are broad enough to be called plateaus and so there is a large area available for settlement and cultivation up to about 700 metres (2,000 ft). Above that, increased rainfall and erosion, and difficulty of access, limit occupation, but for some special crops like coffee this is the most favoured area. The main areas for Blue Mountain coffee, for example, are between 900 and 1,500 metres (2,700 and 4,500 ft).

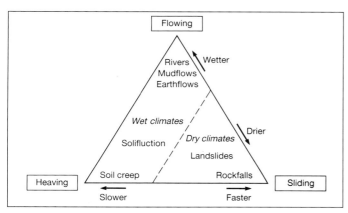

Fig 4.1 Types of mass wasting. The various types of mass movement depend mainly on the wetness of the climate. Wetter climates invariably produce more debris and there is more frequent movement. (Source: M. Clark and J. Small (1982) Slopes and Weathering, Cambridge University Press.)

This term simply means *the movement of solid material down slopes*. Basically, the drier the climate, the bigger but less frequent are the movements (Fig. 4.1).

Water is a lubricant, and wetter climates move smaller particles frequently, as in soil creep. There are four main types of movement:

- Rockfalls
- Landslides
- Soil creep
- Mudflows

Table 4.1 gives some idea of the relative quantities of material displaced by these movements. It is important to note that the movement is due to the force of *gravity*, and not transport by river, wind, sea or ice, as is the case in other types of erosion.

There are various *types* of movement:

Heave   a limited movement over a long time.

Flow   a continuous movement of small particles in association with water - it is a generally *fluid* movement.

Slide   a fast continuous movement of usually dry particles, sometime quite large.

Rockfalls

These are most common on cliff faces, in quarries, or on bare mountain slopes. Suitable conditions are most likely to exist in arid areas with a limited growth of vegetation. The lack of rain prevents the development of clay particles and so *cohesion* - the ability of particles to stick together - is low. In addition, the binding action of plant roots is absent.

Movement	Index of amount of material moved
Soil creep	1 x
Rock falls	7 x
Landslides	28 x
Chemical weathering (for comparison)	50 x

Note A figure for mudflows was not calculated for this study, which was made in a cold mountainous environment. The values have been shown to be relatively true elsewhere.

Table 4.1 Material displaced by mass movement

In most parts of the world freeze-thaw is the agent that disturbs rock particles from their resting position. This is rare in the Caribbean, and falls are more likely to be triggered by earthquakes, storms or hurricanes, by unseasonal showers or by human interference.

Landslides

The point at which a 'fall' becomes a 'slide' is not an obvious one. The main difference is that in a slide the individual particles move as a *mass*, so that a large piece of *land* is displaced (Fig. 4.2). The geological structure is important

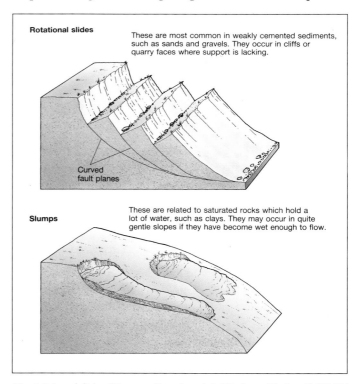

Fig 4.2 Landslides (Source: Based on M. Clark and J. Small (1982) Slopes and Weathering, Cambridge University Press.)

because the weaknesses that lead to the slippage usually develop along joints or faults. Where massive rock formations break up, the mass movement is known as a *rockslide*. Softer rocks such as sands and clays are more likely to slump and may even begin to flow at the lower end. The boundary between a slide and a flow in this case is not clearly defined. Rain, wetting and waterlogging increase the weight of the rocks and the water also acts as a lubricant. A landslide will take place when the weight of the cohesive rocks increases so much that friction is overcome, and the coherent mass slides downhill, often in a rotational and stepped fashion.

Soil creep

This is usually confined to the surface layers of a slope. It may include the soil and any loose weathered material at the surface or below the soil. Such a non-soil layer is called a *regolith*. Creep is caused by a variety of factors which have one thing in common: they disturb the surface material, and combine with gravity to create a net downward movement. The movements are small but frequent and it is the result rather than the movement itself that is seen (Fig. 4.3).

Several factors can cause soil creep:
• Heating and cooling ⎞ expansion and contraction
• Wetting and drying ⎠
• Trampling and burrowing by animals
• Raindrop impact
• Earth tremors

Solifluction is the name given to a similar movement, over greater depth and area, which is found in areas close to permanent ice (*periglacial* regions).

Mudflows

Mudflows can best be imagined as rivers of mud, or like lava flows. They can vary from thick, slow-moving but fluid masses, to fast-moving streams of mud only one step re-

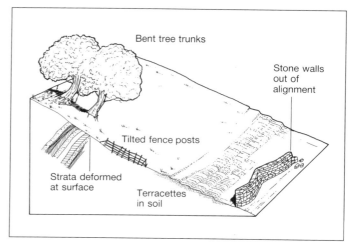

Fig. 4.3 Some indicators of soil creep.

moved from a muddy river. The presence of water, usually to the saturation point of the material in question, is crucial. Unlike most of the other types, mudflows present a very real danger to life. Rockfalls, for example, take place in an environment where they can be seen and predicted, but mudflows usually develop at a distance. Once started they can travel many kilometres along gentle slopes, but are extremely powerful and suffocating. The depth of the flow may vary from 30-60 cm to 10 metres (1-2 ft to 30 ft) or more, and speeds may reach 50-65km p h (30-40 m p h).

---

1 Under what climatic conditions is each type of mass wasting likely to occur?

2 What else besides climate causes mass movement of rock and sediment?

3 How can raindrops cause erosion?

4 How can the wind erode the soil? (See p.91.)

Rivers and river systems

In most countries, rivers are the main agents of erosion and deposition, and of all the geological agents have the greatest relevance to us. Water supply, irrigation and navigation are often dependent on rivers, and they may cause problems of flooding, or be obstacles to communications.

The importance of a river must be judged by its *discharge rate*; that is, the amount of water passing one point in a given time. This is usually measured in cubic metres or feet per second (See Table 4.2).

The true size of a river is not its length, but its discharge rate. Except for those in the Guianas, Caribbean rivers are small, with very few exceeding 30m³/s (1,000 cu. ft/s). The discharge rate can also show marked variation between the dry and wet seasons.

Rivers are dependent on rainfall, and their flow varies according to the amount of rainfall. In limestone areas, and fairly dry areas, few rivers develop, as water sinks underground or is evaporated quickly. As rainfall increases the

River	Discharge (m³/s)	Length (km)
Amazon	127,000	6,290
Congo	40,000	4,680
Mississippi	17,000	6,290
Nile	3,000	6,710
Rio Grande, Jamaica	24,000	32

Table 4.2 *Discharge rates for selected rivers*

ground becomes increasingly saturated and more and more water runs over the surface. This is known as *runoff* by geographers, and as *surface flow* by hydrologists.

It is important to distinguish between a river *channel*, in which the river flows, and a *valley*, which contains the channel. The river channel is cut directly (eroded) by the river. Although we are often told that rivers erode valleys, this is not correct. The river erodes the channel, and acts as a transporting agent for all the debris eroded by other agents on the valley sides.

This can be illustrated with reference to an area where erosion of any kind is very limited - an arid or desert area. Rivers often cross such areas on their way from a wet mountainous zone to the sea. They invariably cut a *gorge*, a valley which is about the same width as the river channel. This is what a river will do on its own. If a V-shaped valley is cut, then something else was responsible, and far more was eroded by

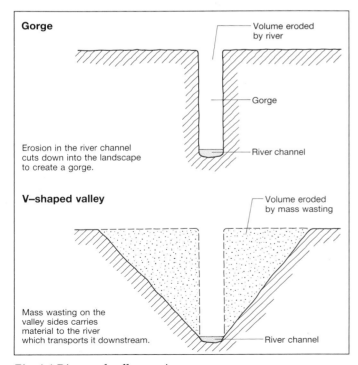

Fig. 4.4 *River and valley erosion.*

this other agent than by the river (Fig. 4.4). The agent is *mass wasting* (See p. 35). The river is nevertheless a vital factor in allowing this erosion to continue, for the products of mass wasting always end up on the floor of the valley. If it was not removed the valley would fill up and erosion would become insignificant.

The work of rivers

Bearing this in mind, we can now examine the work of rivers under three headings:

- Erosion of the channel
- Transportation of the stream load
- Deposition of the stream load

Erosion

A river erodes its channel in several different ways.

Abrasion
This is the mechanical wearing away of the rock. *Corrasion* refers to abrasion of the channel bottom or sides, and *attrition* to the grinding or crushing of particles against each other. Most of the debris lies on the channel floor, so this is worn down the most. Careful examination of the floor often reveals *fluting*; that is, grooves scoured by debris on the floor. *Pot holes* are also common; these are holes about the size of saucepans, which contain stones that are continually swilled around by eddies in the water.

It is important to note that the debris in the channel has not been created by the river itself. It is the product of mass wasting and is merely used by the river as an erosive agent during transportation.

Corrosion
Much of what has been said about weathering and limestone landscapes (See p. 24 and 32) is relevant here. Very little of the dissolved material in the river is from the channel. Most has drained into the river via the valley slopes.

Hydraulic action
This is simply the river's ability to carry loose material away in suspension, such as sand grains or clay particles.

Waterfalls and floods
The ability of a river to erode in any of the ways described above depends on its speed. Any increase in the amount of water increases the discharge rate, and any increase in slope causes an increase in speed. In either case there is more *power*, which is much greater during flooding and when water is falling. This is because the erosive force of water increases at a rate that is equal to the square of the speed. So if a

river travels twice as fast, it will do four times as much damage ($2^2 = 4$ x).

An example: Rocks in a river are hitting a bridge. Normally one rock hits the bridge every hour. If the river doubles its speed, two rocks will hit the bridge every hour, as twice as many are now going past the bridge. But in addition, they will hit the bridge twice as hard, because they are going twice as fast. Therefore four times as much damage can be done. During major floods, rivers can increase their rate of discharge 100 times, and be 10,000 times as destructive!

Waterfall sites mark major areas of river erosion. Downstream from every waterfall there is usually a gorge, and this is a product of river erosion alone (See above). Waterfalls are common in mountainous areas, but are usually small and therefore do not attract much attention. The best-known waterfalls are where large rivers cross a major geographical boundary (Fig. 4.5).

Examples are found where rivers leave the Canadian Shield and descend to the St Lawrence River, the Great Lakes and the Atlantic Ocean (numerous falls can be found on an atlas map of this area, for example Cameron Falls, Shawinigan Falls, Churchill Falls; and off the African Plateau, for example Victoria Falls on the Zambezi River, Kabelega Falls on the

Niagara Falls, with viewing points for tourists. At night the falls are 'switched off', and the water is used to generate hydro-electric power.

Nile and Stanley Falls on the Congo. In the Caribbean there is a similar situation where rivers leave the Guiana Highlands. The Canadian Shield, the African Plateau and the Guianian Highlands are all Precambrian shield areas. This is significant: these ancient surfaces have a large water catchment, and there has been enough time for major rivers to form here. The hard igneous and metamorphosed rocks are more resistant to erosion than the younger sedimentary rocks around them. Venezuela and the Guianas all have major waterfalls, for example the Angel Falls in Venezuela, and the Kaieteur Falls and Tiboku Falls in Guyana.

Once the water falls from one level to another it acquires an enormous amount of energy from the force of gravity. In this case the *hydraulic* power of the water is important - the water by itself is the main agent of erosion. The tremendous force of the water is enough to shake, fracture, dislodge and transport rocks of all sizes from the ground. The lip of the waterfall is undercut and continually collapses, so that a gorge is formed. Any debris in the water is just further 'ammunition' for this continuous process.

Waterfalls are fairly easy to understand as they are relatively permanent features, but floods only affect us occasionally. A river that floods is a very powerful and dangerous phenomenon, and for a while it may acquire the force of a waterfall along its entire length. During a flood the amount of water is greatly increased and this in turn causes several other changes which make it a much more powerful erosive force.

- There is more water - greater hydraulic force.
- There is more energy - greater transporting power,
    - greater amount of debris to cause abrasion.
- The protective layer of debris on the channel floor is stripped away.
- The river is likely to flood its banks and erode the valley sides.

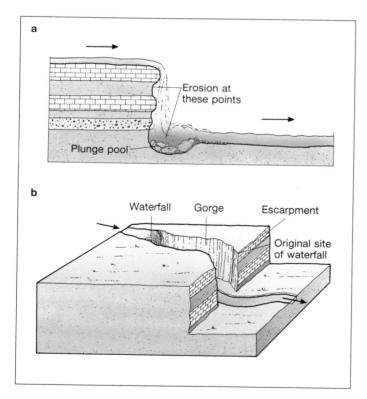

Fig. 4.5 Erosion at waterfalls. Waterfalls occur at sharp changes in relief, such as escarpments. Because of the rapid way in which they erode (a), they soon wear a gorge back into the landscape, often for several miles (b).

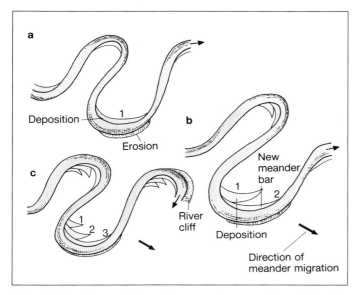

Fig. 4.6 Erosion and deposition on river meanders. Meanders continually migrate downstream, eroding on the outside of their bends and depositing on the inside. Over a period a succession of meander bars is created and eroded.

- The river may change course and erode areas that have never been exposed to the river before.

Most of the time, a river in its lower course has very little erosive power. Here it is a more constructive force, and deposits material that has been eroded elsewhere. Perhaps once a year, or once in every ten years, the river floods. The erosion at this time is often greater than during the much longer period of normal flow. The river can now carry a much greater load and, armed with this, can cause much more damage (See p. 37). The channel floor is usually eroded, and all the material carried down the valley sides and accumulated here over many years can now be removed.

The effects of a flood can be striking, and are often visible until the next one. In particular, large boulders will stay where the flood left them, and new channels may be used and old ones abandoned. It may well be that the erosion we see in river channels and valleys is not a continuous process, but is the result of just a few hours' flooding every few years.

Lateral erosion

So far we have discussed rivers cutting *down*. Rivers can also widen their valleys by eroding their banks on the outsides of bends. A river is more likely to do this in its lower courses, and material eroded from the outside of one bend is often deposited a little further downstream on the inside of another bend (Fig. 4.6). This is particularly true of *meanders*, which are the extreme curves of a river that has almost no gradient, and is usually flowing across a flood plain.

Higher up the river lateral erosion is more important in

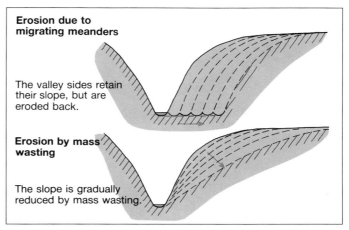

Fig 4.7 Lateral erosion and valley widening.

undermining the interfluves, and removing the interlocking spurs of younger valleys. In such cases the river combines with mass wasting to widen the valley (Fig. 4.7). Generally speaking, the steeper the valley side, the more likely it is that river erosion created the valley. Mass wasting tends to produce gentler slopes, while rivers cause parallel slope retreat; that is, the slopes maintain the same steepness.

---

1 Explain how valleys become V-shaped.

2 Why is there a gorge in front (downstream) of a waterfall?

3 How do rivers erode sideways?

4 Why are there dry valleys in some types of rock (for example in Barbados and Jamaica)?

Transportation

A river can transport material in three different ways;
- In solution   - the *dissolved* load
- In suspension   - the *suspended* load
- Along the ground   - the *bed* load

The minerals transported in *solution* require no energy from the river and can be carried by any stream in any state. Most of the dissolved content will be restricted to five salts (Table 4.3). These salts will end up in the sea, or in a lake, which is why the ocean is salty and lakes without an outlet are *salt lakes*.

The *suspended* load is dependent on the velocity of the river. In perfectly still water there will be no suspended load, but as the velocity increases the smallest grains of *sand* will be picked up. Surprisingly, the finer *silts* and *clays* are not so easily picked up because they tend to stick together. Only when there is some turbulence in the water are they lifted, but after that they can stay suspended almost indefinitely until the water has been still for some time (See Fig. 4.8).

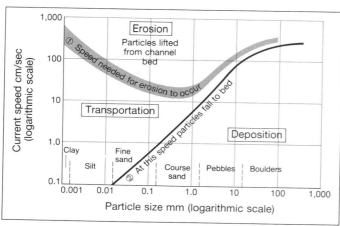

Fig. 4.8 Relationship between speed and load size for erosion and deposition in a river. When the critical speed (1) is reached, particles are lifted from the banks or channel floor. Thereafter they are transported until the speed reaches the lower critical value (2), when deposition occurs.

Particles of *coarse sand*, or larger matter, require considerable speeds to lift them off the floor, although once lifted they can be carried long distances. This is due to the distribution of speed in the channel - it is faster above the floor than on it (Fig. 4.9).

The *bed load* consists of material that is too heavy ever to be lifted up, but which is pushed or rolled along the bottom, usually in stops and starts. Some of the smaller material, such as *sand and gravel*, is intermediate between the suspended and the bed load, and undergoes what is known as *saltation*. This is a form of temporary suspension in which particles are lifted up, but soon fall back to the bottom again. The largest particles, pebbles and boulders do not move very often, and boulders in particular are normally only moved during floods.

Fig. 4.9 River current speeds in differently shaped channels. In all cases, the central and surface sections have the fastest current, while the slowest speeds are found on the channel bed.

Salts	Dissolved load (%)
Bicarbonates	41
Sulphates	26
Calcium	12
Sodium	8
Chlorides	3
Others	10

Note Pollution may constitute up to 50% of the dissolved load. This table is based on average figures for the Missouri, Colorado and Columbia Rivers.

Table 4.3 Typical dissolved load of an unpolluted stream

Deposition

Anything that reduces the transporting ability of a stream encourages deposition. As has been noted, the lower course of a river is often subject to deposition. In fact deposition can - and does - take place anywhere along a river's course if certain conditions are met (Fig. 4.10).

Decrease in gradient Most commonly this happens when a river leaves the mountains and starts to cross a plain. A river can start in mountains, descend to a plateau, fall again to a plain, and then run into the sea. Both the plateau and the plain will be areas of deposition, normally in the form of a *fan* at the foot of the slope.

Decreased volume This is not so common, but is perhaps more frequent than is realized. Rivers crossing dry zones lose water by evaporation and infiltration into the ground. In areas of heavy vegetation, much of the water is removed by plant transpiration.

Increase in amount or size of load This can be caused by a tributary entering the main river with an excessive amount of material, or a change in geology that takes the river over more easily eroded rocks.

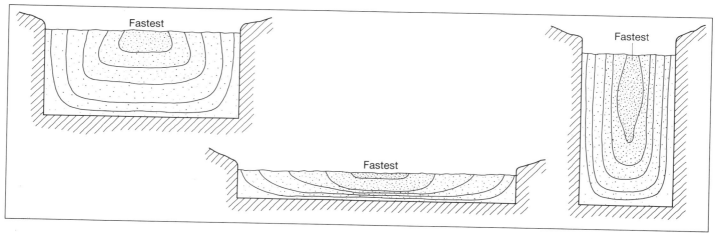

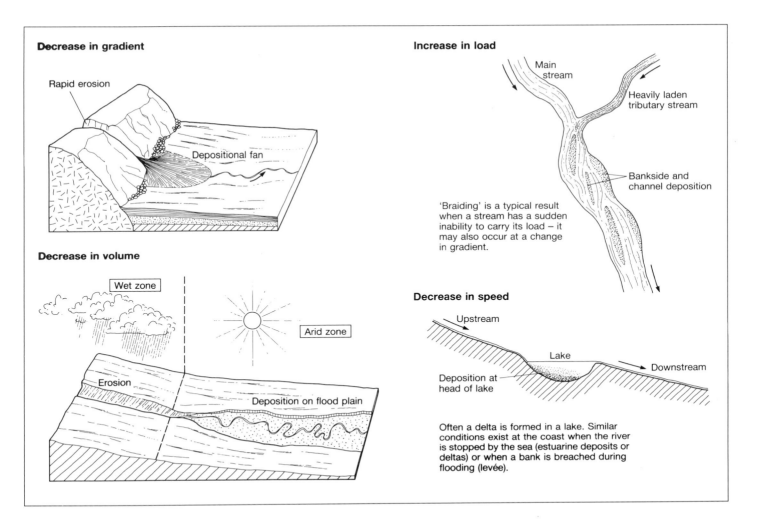

Fig. 4.10 River deposition.

The largest deposits of a river are usually found in its *flood plain* and *delta*. These are deposits which build up vertically. There is, however, another type of deposit which builds up laterally, and this is the *meander deposit*.

Flood plain deposits
As the name suggests, these deposits only occur during flooding. When the river breaks its banks it spreads out and rapidly loses its energy and therefore its ability to carry its suspended load. As this loss of energy occurs immediately on leaving the channel, most of the load is deposited close to it, on the banks. This forms a feature known as a *levée*, and in fact the driest part of a flood plain is that part which is closest to the river. The outer parts of the plain are often swampy - they are commonly called the *backswamp* and may even contain a secondary river.

Many Caribbean rivers have flood plains. Rivers of any size may have them on any level part of their course. Trinidad's River Ortoire has a flood plain which extends for some 25km (15 miles) and is up to 1km (½ mile) wide. In Jamaica there is the Cabarita River in the west, and Haiti's famous Artibonite Valley has extensive flood plain sections. In Cuba the Rio Cauto in the south provides one of the finest examples of a river with mature meanders crossing a broad flood plain and building out a delta. Settlements in this area (Holguin) are highly concentrated on the levées, especially in the delta, and avoid the swampy areas. Much of the land has been cut with ditches to prevent excessive flooding, and planted with sugar cane. Unreclaimed areas are used as pasture, and the delta is a swamp.

Deltas are of limited use to us, and often their historic neglect has caused them to become wildlife sanctuaries today. Trinidad's Caroni Swamp is a good example of this, although the classic delta shape is absent. Traditional deltas are not too common, as it takes a really large river to build out into the sea. The small quantity of debris deposited from island rivers is rarely sufficient to prevent tidal and coastal currents from sweeping it away. A delta can only develop if the sediments are allowed to build up. Consequently, around the Caribbean we only see classic deltas at the mouths of the

41

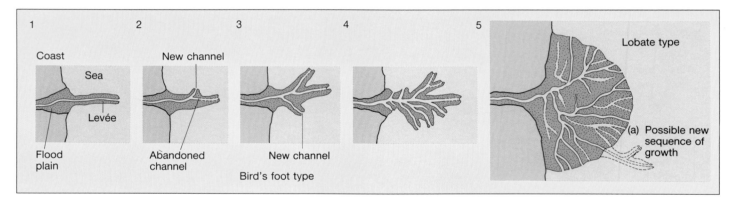

Fig. 4.11 Formation of a simple delta. The river continues building its flood plain and levée out to sea (1), but after a time it will look for a shorter route to the sea and form a new channel (2). This will be repeated whenever a route gets too long. Some of these old channels silt up and are abandoned. Eventually this produces a bird's-foot delta (3). As the process goes on, silting closes off all the easy accesses to the sea and the delta advances on a broad front (5), producing a lobate shape. At any point one of these channels may build out independently from the lobe and start a new sequence of delta building (5a).

Mississippi (Gulf of Mexico) and the Orinoco, and in Cuba, which has several small but nevertheless well-developed examples: Sagua la Grande and Sagua la Chica in Villa Clara Province, the Cauto in Holguin, and a nicely developed bird's-foot delta on the Rio Manati in the south-central province of Sancti Spiriti.

A bird's-foot delta is so described because instead of marshland between the interfluves, there is the sea. A delta continues below sea level, but in the bird's-foot delta the sea level is perhaps just a metre higher, and the deposits between the levées (which are the 'toes' of the 'bird's foot') are submerged (See Fig. 4.11).

---

1 Look back at Table 4.2. Use an atlas to locate the Missouri, Colorado and Columbia Rivers. Will the dissolved load of any of these rivers be of any importance to the Caribbean. If so, of which rivers?

2 With the aid of sketches, explain the difference between a *fan* and a *delta*.

3 What are the advantages and disadvantages of a flood plain?

River systems

River systems often show a distinct pattern. Under 'normal' conditions - that is, where there is a uniform geology - rivers eventually develop a *dendritic* pattern, which is the most efficient way of draining a uniform plain. The pattern is similar to that of a tree with a well-developed branch system.

Other patterns form when the geology is varied within the drainage basin. As certain geological structures are quite common, the river patterns that form on them are well known. Some of the simpler ones are described here (Fig. 4.12 and 4.13).

Radial The most perfect example is the pattern that often forms around a new volcano - numerous streams flowing like spokes from the volcanic hub. In fact most of the smaller

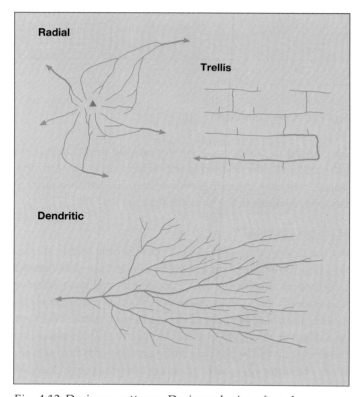

Fig. 4.12 Drainage patterns. Drainage basins often show a geometric pattern of streams, but it is more likely that a major river system will show several patterns in different areas, according to the geology of its basin.

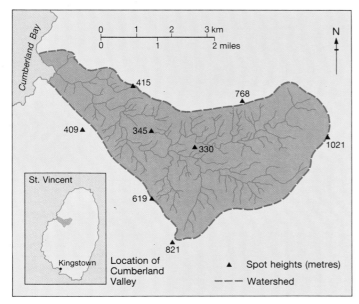

Fig. 4.13 St Vincent's Cumberland River basin. The Cumberland basin is fairly small (about 20km² or 7.5 sq. miles), but it has a very dense network of streams. Rainfall is high at about 2,500 mm (100 in.) overall, but reaches 5,000 mm (200 in.) near the centre of the island. The spot heights show that the average height of the basin is over 300 metres and reaches more than 1,000 metres in the east. The small area is therefore compensated for by the high rainfall, steep gradients, and high runoff. The potential for HEP here is good.

volcanic islands in the Eastern Caribbean still have dendritic patterns, although the regularity is not now so perfect. St Lucia, especially the southern half, has a very well-preserved radial pattern, and Nevis is almost perfect.

Trellis This is a system full of right-angle bends. Whenever the geology forms scarplands - long parallel ridges - the rivers tend to flow in the vales between them. Occasionally the ridges are breached and the rivers link up, especially if the ridges are parallel to the coast. Such patterns are most likely on moderately tilted geological strata, which is not commonly found in the Caribbean.

Dendritic patterns These are widespread (See above). The Caroni River in northern Trinidad is a fairly large example, and is matched by the Oropouche on the south side. Both are fed by water from hills in the north and south, and cross unresistant sands and clays on their way to the sea.

Rivers and human activity

People are much attracted to rivers. They have various uses:

- Harbours
- Drinking water
- Navigable waterways
- Routes through hills, forests, marshlands, etc.
- Irrigation
- Farmland
- Settlement sites
- Hydro-electric power
- Scenic or tourist routes and water sports

Unfortunately rivers are liable to flood and destroy all that is built on or near them! It is important therefore that we know how to protect ourselves from these problems, and indeed how to control rivers to such an extent that they are even more valuable to us.

Methods of controlling rivers

The causes and destructiveness of floods have already been discussed, but a much more practical knowledge of indi-

Control of gully erosion by lining the channel of a stream, in the northern Punjab of India. The colour of the water in the river indicates the amount of material that is being transported.

A small dam on St Croix controls the river and provides a reservoir for drinking water.

vidual rivers is needed if the proper precautions are to be taken. In any water basin there is a drainage system, surface or underground, the channels of which can cope with a certain amount of water. It is the *rate of flow* that is important, not the quantity of water alone. A high level of annual rainfall will not cause flooding if it is evenly distributed, but one day's particularly heavy rain could be disastrous. It is not possible to predict rainfall accurately, but the likelihood of flooding can still be calculated. To do this it is most important that proper recording instruments are set up and regular records maintained. A rain gauge and water-level gauge are relatively cheap, even the self-recording type. Stream-flow meters should also be used. If this information is collected and analysed, the frequency of flooding can be established. Local knowledge about past floods should also be gathered; this is not usually difficult, as disasters are well-remembered. For each river a frequency can be ascertained of, say, 1 flood in 10 years (1:10), or 1:20, or 1:100, or perhaps one every year.

If it is decided that the frequency of flooding is unacceptable - land use and settlement in the valley are too valuable to be at risk - then flood prevention can be practised, or it may

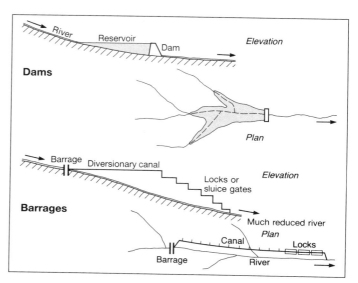

Fig. 4.15 Dams and barrages. *While a dam simply ponds the water back up the valley and floods the surrounding area, a barrage diverts the water into a canal, which can then be used for navigation or for irrigation. Sluices (gates) on the barrage and canal control the water level above the barrage, in the river and in the canal.*

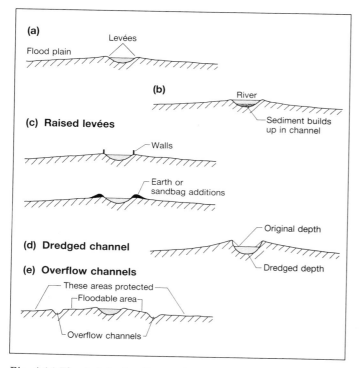

Fig. 4.14 Flood plain flooding and protection. *The river in a flood plain is controlled by its levées, but over a period it will build up its channel floor with sediment, which raises its level. Any increase in volume in the river, such as seasonal rains or storms, will cause it to flood. This is of course a normal, natural, sequence of events. If the river is to remain in one place, we must take one of the precautions shown in (c)-(e).*

be recognized that the expense of flood control would be too great. In such cases measures of a more negative kind can be taken. For example, settlement and land use can be restricted, the flood plain can be limited to use as permanent pasture, or cultivated using the flood waters for irrigation. Protection can be of several forms (Figs. 4.14 and 4.15).

Improved banks   These might be artificial raised levées, walls, reinforced banks or dykes. The aim here is to keep the water in its channel by preventing it from breaking through, or overflowing, its banks.

Deepened channel   This requires dredging the channel. It also provides more room for floodwater, especially as a river tends to raise its channel above its flood plain if it is left alone.

Overflow channels and improved drainage   Usually these are combined with the above. The assumption is that flooding will occur, but it is kept under control by channelling the flood water around and away from settled areas. The 'monsoon ditch' is the common name for artificial channels which remain dry except in the rainy season. Most of Kingston's natural gullies have been converted to such features.

Dams and barrages   The above features do not prevent the river from rising - they are just an attempt to control the increased flow. A dam is intended to keep the water back entirely. During flood conditions the dam sluices are closed sufficiently to prevent flooding downstream and the water is contained in a reservoir. Later on the water can be released safely. A barrage does not normally create a reservoir, but acts

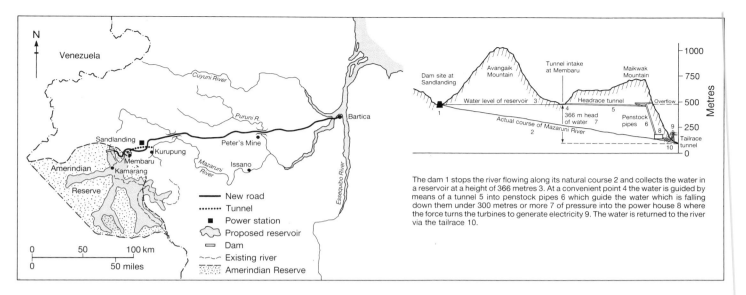

as a control on the river level above and below it. In particular it 'irons out' flood surges by holding back flood water in one section of the river to protect another.

Diversion   Quite simply, the river is given another course to flow in where it will do no harm, either permanently or in conjunction with a barrage to divert flood waters to another area.

Rivers under control

The production of domestic, industrial and irrigation water, and hydro-electric power (HEP), are the ultimate aims of major water catchment schemes. Water and power shortages are a permanent problem for most Caribbean countries, yet there is enough water in our river systems to solve the first and help overcome the second. Nevertheless there are few schemes in operation of any note, and we should consider why this is so.

Within the region, major works have only been carried out in a few countries - Cuba, Dominican Republic, and Suriname. Plans for Jamaica and Guyana are in hand (Fig. 4.16). We should immediately note two things that these countries have in common:

1   They are large enough to have big river systems that justify dams and an HEP scheme. Only large systems can provide power at a rate that is cheaper than imported oil.

Fig. 4.16 Guyana's Upper Mazaruni HEP project. The water impounded by the dam will create a reservoir bigger than Barbados! Water will flow through a massive tunnel (the headrace tunnel) and then descend to the power station before entering the river at Kurupung.

2   They have a large enough population to make use of the power and water, and the power can be produced in sufficiently large quantities to pay for the overall project.

Quite simply, HEP and water projects must be large, and only the bigger industrial countries are likely to be able to use them to the full. (See also chapters 6 and 11.)

---

1   What are the disadvantages of building dams and reservoirs? (For example, think of what happens behind a dam.)

2   Why is it necessary to control some rivers?

3   What are the conditions necessary for a river to be suitable for HEP?

4   Where is HEP produced in the Caribbean? Can you name the rivers that are used?

5
The coastal landscape and its processes

The sea, through its agent, the waves, is responsible for erosion, transportation and deposition along the coast in much the same way that rivers are on land. With waves we also need to distinguish exactly what they are responsible for along a coast, because the various land-based agents continue acting right up to the waterline, and so there is some overlap. It should also be noted that storms - the sea's equivalent of

Extreme underutting of coral limestone cliffs near Sam Lord's, Barbados

floods - are responsible for many features seen on a coast, and this is particularly so in a region that has many storms and hurricanes passing through it in the course of a year.

Some terms and definitions

The *coast* is the general area that is subject to the influence of the sea. The *coastline* is the line (on a map rather than on the ground) where land and sea meet; it is usually based on the highest high tides. The *shore* is the term most widely used in

geography, and has a more precise meaning - it is the area affected by wave action. Figure 5.1 explains the subdivisions, *offshore, foreshore, backshore* and *onshore*. The *beach* is any loose material on the shore. The *shoreline* is the actual boundary

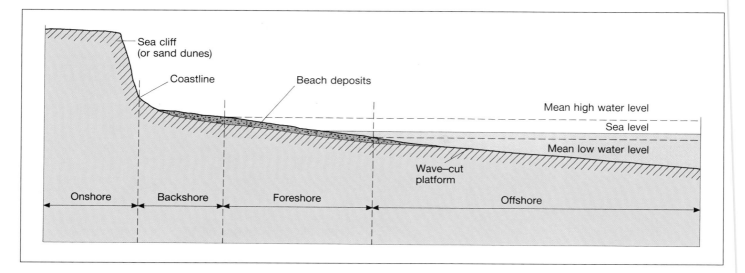

Labels in figure: Sea cliff (or sand dunes); Coastline; Beach deposits; Mean high water level; Sea level; Mean low water level; Wave–cut platform; Onshore; Backshore; Foreshore; Offshore

Fig. 5.1 Coastal features defined. These terms are not always used precisely, and others can also be used. Inshore is often used to mean 'close to the shore', as opposed to 'in the ocean' or 'in distant waters'. Backshore means the area above the high water mark that is still affected by the sea.

between land and sea. It varies with the tides, and *high water level* or *low water level* are more precise terms for the same thing.

Marine erosion

The erosive force is the waves, assisted by the wind which generates them, and the tides which raise and lower them. In the Caribbean the *tidal range* (the difference between high and low tide) is only about a metre (3-4 ft). In some parts of the world it is as much as 6 metres (20 feet), for example in north-west Europe or north-east USA. If we regard marine erosion as a saw cutting horizontally into the land, then the width of the saw-blade is equivalent to the tidal range. On land the erosional processes have an effect more like sandpaper being rubbed down over the entire surface. Although marine erosion is often spectacular, it is a much more limited force.

The pressure on the 'saw-blade' is related to the wind speed. Higher wind speeds produce bigger waves, and like rivers their destructive power increases as the square of the wind speed. For this reason hurricanes are particularly damaging to the coast, but there is another factor: during a hurricane, the sea level can rise as much as 4-5 metres (12-15 feet), and so the 'saw-edge' is 'lifted', and in effect is taken to a fresh surface, often further inland.

A headland formed where a ridge of high ground projects into the sea. Bequia, The Grenadines.

Apart from the *waves*, we must also consider the *coast* that is being eroded. Its relief, geological structure and composition all affect the rate of erosion and the kind of landforms that result from it.

---

1 Find out the high tide and low tide levels near you, and calculate the *tidal range*. Does this vary during a month? What are the maximum and minimum ranges? What are these called?

2 What is the importance of tides in marine erosion?

Wave action

Waves erode in different ways:
- By the impact of water against the coast. This is called *hydraulic action*.
- By the impact of suspended or bottom particles against the coast. This is called *abrasion*.
- By *attrition* of already eroded material on the shore.

Hydraulic action is of several types:

(a) *Pressure oscillations* are set up by the rhythmic beating of waves against a cliff. This is equivalent to a gentle but perpetual shaking of the rock face, resulting in the loosening of already weakened rock blocks. Coasts on the windward side of islands are exposed to this throughout the region, as the Trade Winds bring in well-formed waves of 1-1.5 metres (4-6 feet) almost throughout the year. Well-jointed rocks like limestone are particularly affected.

(b) *Pressure impacts* are due to the slap of larger breaking waves. These are the equivalent of sledge-hammer blows and during storms they are extremely destructive, with a large wave carrying many tonnes of water at speed high on to the cliff face or coastal sand dunes.

(c) Finally, *compression impacts* are also present with breaking waves wherever there is undercutting, cave development, or even open joints or faulting. In all these openings the air inside is greatly compressed when hit by a wave, and so the wave impact is transmitted far into the cliff structure where water cannot reach. *Blowholes* are created where the compressed air in a cave forces itself out at the point where the resistance is weakest - in the *roof* of the cave.

Abrasion on the coast is not very different from abrasion in a river. There is a suspended and a bed load. *Attrition* is continuous, and the end product is *sand*, which is still abrasive, but is too light to damage itself on other grains of sand. Most of the load is on or near the sea bed, and therefore most erosion takes place at the foot of the cliff, giving rise to *undercutting*, and creating a *notch* (Fig. 5.2).

These and related features are well illustrated along rocky and cliffed coasts throughout the Caribbean. Wave action undercuts a cliff mainly through abrasion. The notch deepens until the overhang gives way, probably as a result of the

Fig. 5.2 Erosion along the coast. The features shown here are all related and are the products of wave erosion. As the cliff is undercut it is weakened until the upper portion collapses, which provides boulders at the foot of the cliff. These are themselves eroded but are also used by the waves as ammunition to further erode the cliff base. As the cliff is worn back, a wave-cut platform is left in front of it.

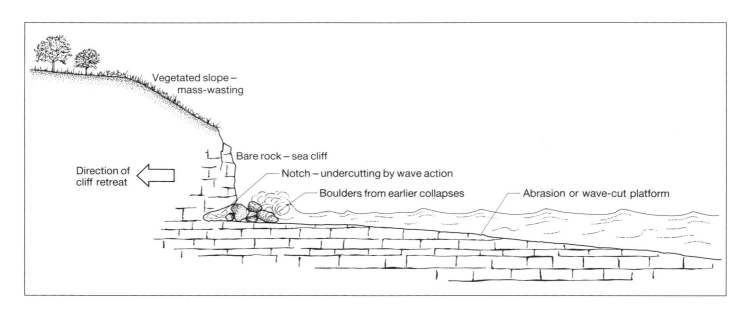

percussive hydraulic action common during rough seas. The debris is subject to attrition, and also provides ammunition for further erosion. Undercutting continues, but *cliff recession* also takes place, the cliff itself gradually being replaced by an *abrasion* or *wave-cut platform*. Scour over this platform will deepen it to some extent, but eventually it becomes wide enough to reduce the energy of the waves that cross it, and cliff erosion and recession slow down. Any significant erosion will then be limited to storm conditions, and this is indicated by a less steep cliff face, which is often vegetated. In effect this indicates that other forms of erosion are dominant on the cliff face.

Although these are the typical features of marine erosion, under certain circumstances other landforms are produced, notably wherever headlands have developed. Again a systematic progression can be identified. Undercutting is in effect taking place on both sides of the headland, and at some point will meet to produce a tunnel, and perhaps an *arch*. Later on the seaward end of the headland becomes detached to form a *stack*. Many of the rocks or cays adjacent to headlands in the West Indies were originally stacks (See Fig. 5.3).

1 What is *attrition*? Can it take place in rivers as well as the sea?

2 What features of marine erosion can still be seen long after the erosion has stopped and sea level has fallen (or the land has risen)?

3 Examine the photographs in this book. How many show (a) a cliff (b) a notch (c) a wave-cut platform?

4 Why do some parts of a coast have headlands and other parts have beaches?

5 Describe a stretch of the coast nearest to you, for about 5 kilometres (3 miles) of its length.

Fig. 5.3 Headlands and bays. The waves are refracted when they reach the headland, and so curve around it. Wave energy is therefore concentrated on the headland, which undergoes severe erosion. Within the bay the waves have lost much of their power, and sediment from both offshore and the headlands forms a beach against the shore.

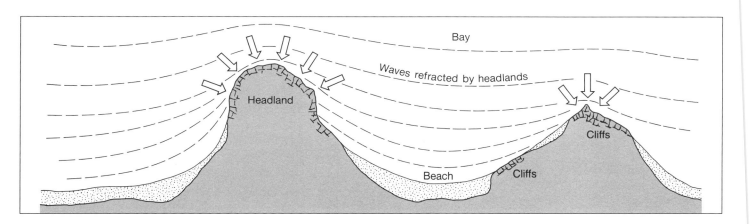

Marine transportation

Wave action readily moves beach material through the individual actions of *swash* and *backwash*, and through their combined action which is known as *longshore drift*.

(a) *Swash* is the action of a breaking wave moving up a beach. Most small waves push material up a beach, and as a result beaches get bigger.

(b) *Backwash* is the dragging action (*undertow*) as a wave recedes down the beach. Larger waves usually have a stronger backwash and erode beaches. However, very large waves can lift extremely heavy objects up a beach, and these may be too heavy to be washed down again. So

although large waves transport material off a beach, under storm conditions they can deposit a *storm beach*, or *berm*, high up on the shore.

(c) *Longshore drift* is a combination of swash, which is due to the force of the waves caused by wind and can be at any angle up a beach, and backwash, which is due to gravity, with the sea draining directly down the beach.

As Fig. 5.4 shows, the net effect is a sort of crab-like movement *along* the beach, and this is indeed the path taken by individual pebbles or grains of sand. The persistence of wave action converts these very small individual movements

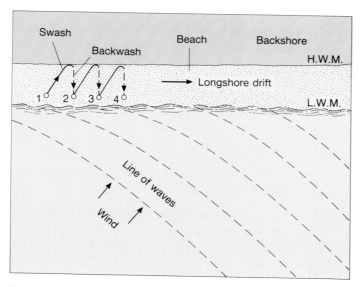

Fig. 5.4 Longshore drift. Waves usually hit a beach at an angle, and carry any particles of sand up the beach with the swash. However, after the energy of the wave is spent, the water runs back down the beach owing to gravity. This is the backwash, and it takes the shortest route to the sea. The result is that the sand is moved from 1 to 2 and then on to 3, 4, etc. (See also Fig. 5.5.)

snaking its way along a coast. The end of the line for this movement is deep water at the far end of the windward coast.

Longshore drift is very marked in Barbados, and has been the subject of much controversy and eventually legislation. Along the south coast in particular, the 1960s saw the construction of several breakwaters or groynes perpendicular to the beach, as at the Hilton Hotel at Needham's Point. Sand accumulated very quickly on the eastern side and created broad beaches where previously there had only been a rocky foreshore. Not all local residents were happy about this, as in effect a private backyard had become a tourist beach! The most inconsiderate construction was that of the Coast Guard dock at Oistins. A large beach immediately formed east of the jetty, and then spilled around to silt up the dock. Within a few years the dock was a beach, and a little later the site was abandoned and turned into a public bathing area!

After that, much closer attention was paid to the construction of groynes in this area, and several that had been built by new hotels along the Maxwell coast were removed. The message as far as beaches are concerned is very clear: longshore drift and beach construction or erosion is a complex process. Despite this it should be common knowledge that it is always present and any human interference will almost certainly

into a major transporting activity. Along any coast, massive and continuous movement of sediments is taking place, and most beaches that appear permanent are no more than temporary resting places for a river of sand that is continually

This beach near the Crane, Barbados, was once much higher. The original level is shown by the change in colour on the rock above the palm tree. Beach erosion has caused the coconut palms to collapse. Note the oil (tar) pollution on the sand.

Pinneys Beach and Railroad Vine.

alter the existing situation and create widespread disturbance for a long way on either side of the site. Any coastal construction that projects into the sea must be the subject of expert investigation for its effect on the shoreline.

Longshore drift is by far the most important mover of beach material, but there are other currents in the sea that transport sediment. *Tidal currents* are most active in shallow or constricted channels, such as over reefs or between islands. They *scour* the channels in very much the same way as a river does, and erode the floor and sides.

Fig 5.5 Coastal deposition - beaches.

(a) *Beach sand and longshore drift. If longshore drift is removing too much sand it can be partly stopped by building <u>groynes</u> (fences). These trap some of the sand which tends to collect mostly on the downdrift side. The beach then protects the shore during storms.*

(b) *Beach cusps. On exposed beaches with no significant drift, the waves turn on themselves and create cusps, which can be as high as 2 metres (6 feet).*

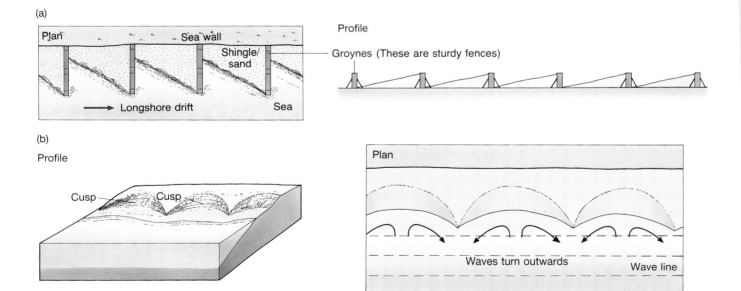

Ocean currents, which are more correctly called *wind-driven currents* because they are created by the friction of the major wind systems on the ocean surface, are less important. They are too weak to carry suspended sediment except in a few cases. The Gulf Stream is one of the faster currents, reaching 5 knots (about 10km/hour) in the Straits of Florida, and there it does have an impact because it carries away sediment swept off the Florida and Bahamas Banks by tidal currents, and keeps the platform slopes clear of debris.

Turbidity currents are submarine currents of great energy, being something like an underwater avalanche. Sediment from shallow water will gradually accumulate in certain localities, but eventually will be triggered into movement. Once started, the turbidity current, which is basically a fluid mass of sediment rolling downslope, gathers momentum and flows downhill and out onto the oceanic plains. Like an avalanche the turbidity current can be most destructive, and has been responsible for breaking telephone cables on the sea floor, and scouring great V-shaped canyons, as along the floor of the old Bahamas Channel, between Cuba and The Bahamas.

1 Describe the various currents that affect the coast near where you live.

2 Describe two beaches that you have visited, mentioning (a) width (b) shape (c) wave size (d) beach material (e.g. sand, fine sand, etc. - examine the grains carefully and describe them).

3 With the aid of a diagram, explain how longshore drift takes place.

Marine deposition

This results in a great variety of forms of which the most common are beaches, sand bars, spits, sand dunes, and salt marshes. In many cases these features are very important to

Fig. 5.6 Coastal sand dunes. The vegetated sand dune is a natural progression from the beach in exposed areas. At low tide the foreshore dries at the surface and the wind carries fine sand to the backshore. Once far enough from waves and heavy spray, the upper part of the backshore is colonized by tough, salt-tolerant plants. They in turn prevent the sand from travelling much further inland, and so the sand now builds up vertically, and the main or fixed dune is formed. More plants provide more shelter, and the dune can reach a considerable height.

us and so the processes should be thoroughly understood before any major construction is allowed on the coast. Deposition is very active in Caribbean coastal areas and much damage has already been done by such activities as building groynes, breakwaters, piers, marinas and docks, and dredging sand, taking beach sand, cutting through sand dunes, destroying beach vegetation, and altering drainage channels (Fig. 5.5).

Beaches and sand dunes

These two are related and so can be considered together. We should consider a beach as being built by constructive wave

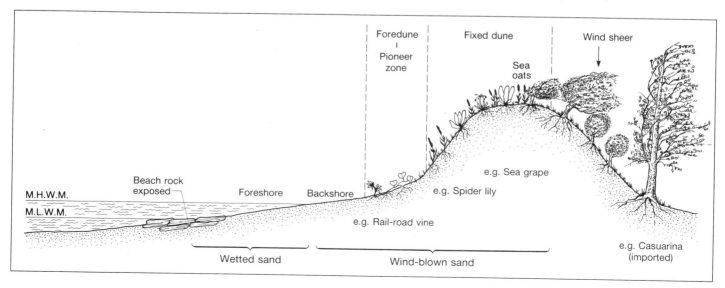

action (dominant swash). When it is exposed at low tide, the sand is blown further up the beach by the wind. Once the sand has been blown far enough from the sea, salt-resistant vegetation starts to grow in it, and the horizontal movement of the sand is restricted. Instead, the sand starts to build up, more vegetation grows, and a sand dune develops (Fig. 5.6). With steady winds like the Trade Winds and a good supply of sand from coral reefs, extensive sand dunes can be created. All the hills and ridges of The Bahamas were formed in this way, and indeed most of those islands owe their existence to this process, which was extensive during the Ice Ages. (See photo p.23.) These fossil sand dunes are now ridges of limestone, but there are modern sand dunes on many windward shores, such as Walker's Savannah in Barbados and along the windward shores of many of the low-lying Bahamian islands.

Bars and spits

These are the most complicated of all the depositional landforms as they are continually changing. Often part of a feature is eroded in a storm and deposition starts in a new

Fig. 5.7 Coastal deposition - spits and tombolos.

(a) *Spits usually develop on the more sheltered sides of West Indian islands, but they can be found wherever there is sufficient sediment to build them.*

(b) *The twin tombolos shown here join the islet of Scotch Bonnet to the mainland of St Kitts. This kind of spit development is not uncommon, and single and double tombolos joining islands or cays together can be found throughout the Caribbean. The Palisadoes of Jamaica is a composite tombolo.*

place, or the whole or part of the feature actually migrates across the sea floor.

Bars in their simplest form are what are more commonly called sandbanks. They are normally covered by the sea at high tide, and develop parallel to the shore at a point where a supply of sediment is dumped owing to a decline in wave energy. The mouths of rivers are noted for this, such as Jamaica's Rio Grande. Here the bar has been built up above sea level and has migrated towards the shore that it is attached to. This is a common feature of bars, and it is not always possible to say whether such a landform began life as a bar or a spit. A *spit* is a tongue of sand attached to the land but built out from it. The tip, called the *distal* end, is often hooked, this being where sediment is carried around the end by winds from another direction. The main arm of the spit will be a response to the *dominant* winds (the winds that determine the longshore drift). The material is built up by wave action, and continues until the water becomes so deep that the waves become destructive. At this point the spit will possibly continue in a new direction which is facing the waves caused by winds from another direction (See fig. 5.7).

Spits often show many bulges which mark previous positions of the tip as they grew. They are usually the result of longshore drift continuing out from the coast at a point where the coast turns inland. The famous Port Royal/Palisadoes spit represents the continuing deposition of sand carried westwards by longshore drift, until the coast here turns north-westwards to form Kingston Harbour.

An interesting version of the spit is the *tombolo*, a spit which links an island to the mainland, or to another island. This might seem to be a rather special situation, but there are many examples in the Caribbean. On the island of New Providence

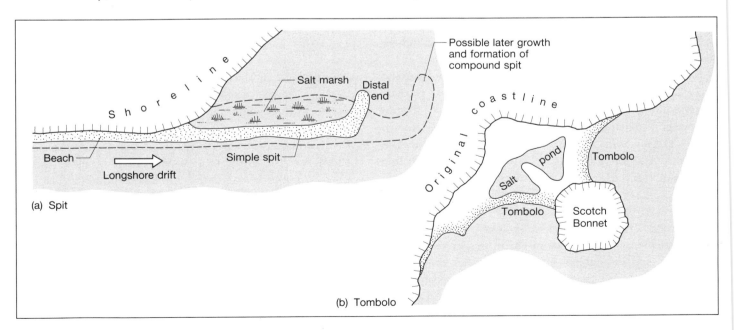

Dense mangrove swamp between the beach and solid ground on Grand Bahama Island.

the settlement of Lyford Cay is partly built on the arms of a double tombolo, and the golf course occupies the triangular swampy area between them. Charts of the early nineteenth century show that boats could pass between the cay and New Providence. The Virgin Islands and Antigua also provide good examples at several locations.

Mangrove swamps and salt marshes

In the Caribbean most coastal marshland is colonized by the mangrove, but *salt marsh* is a more general term that is also more correct, as there are marshy areas that do not have mangroves. Most mangrove swamps include areas where sedges and other species are common.

Salt marshes are of two broad types, the exposed and the enclosed. The *exposed* salt marsh is directly open to the sea, perhaps along the shore of a tidal creek or lagoon, or simply at the edge of a sheltered stretch of shoreline. A *tidal flat* is often between the swamp and the sea but, particularly in the case of mangrove swamps, the sea may end abruptly against a line of vegetation standing in 0.5-1.5 metres (2-5 feet) of water.

There are several types of mangrove: the true or red mangrove, the black mangrove, the white mangrove, and the buttonwood. They survive where the water is not too deep and where there is a good rooting medium. The water must be salty or brackish, and calm. They establish themselves easily on any ground that is exposed at high tide, and their extensive root systems help trap more sediment and so encourage further vegetation. In this way they can rapidly build out the coast, which will eventually trap so much sediment, and accumulate so much peat (dead swamp vegetation), that the area will become relatively dry land, colonized by casuarinas or palmettos, for instance. Any gently shelving offshore area is likely to be reclaimed in this way, for example the sheltered eastern coast of Belize, and the coastal areas of Guyana.

Enclosed marshes are equally common. We can usually see a progression in landforms along outbuilding coasts:

- Tidal flats
- Lagoons - sections partly enclosed by spits or bars
- Ponds - totally enclosed lagoons
- Marshes - colonized ponds

Alternatively, a tidal creek may be sealed off by bar or beach deposits. Numerous swamps of all sizes are created in this way, such as Graeme Hall Swamp in Barbados, behind the St Lawrence beaches, and the Great Morass behind Negril Beach in Jamaica. The north-western coast of Antigua also has a variety of ponds and swamps, all formed by the linking of a series of small islands to the mainland by tombolos, and the tombolos themselves are the sites of several hotels, e.g. Jolly Beach, Runaway Beach, Galley Bay Beach.

---

1 What plants inhabit a tidal flat?

2 Why are swamps eventually filled in?

Fig 5.8 Types of coasts. (Source: Valentin's <u>Coastal Classification</u>.)

Advancing coasts

Emergent	*Exposed sea floor forming land, e.g. rockland in the Bahamas, Barbados' coral cap, volcanic islands*
Outbuilding	*Organic deposition: mangroves, e.g. Belize coral, e.g. Barbados*
	Marine deposition: spits and bars, e.g. locally in south-west Cuba, Jamaica, etc.
	Deltas and terrestrial depositon, e.g. Guyana coast

Retreating coasts

Submergent	*Drowned landscapes, e.g. The Bahamas, Cayman Banks. Exposed in the Ice Ages. Drowned swamps, karst features*
Erosion	*All cliff shorelines, e.g. Atlantic coast of Dominica, north coast of Trinidad, east coast of Jamaica*

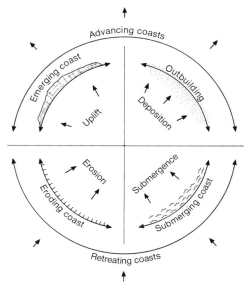

The diagram (Fig. 5.8) is a simple way of fitting the processes described above, and coastal landforms, into a single system. All coastlines can be considered as either retreating or advancing. In most cases this means they are either eroding or depositing respectively. But it may be that sea level is changing or the land is moving. In some parts of the Caribbean we need to take account of the latter possibility, as not all features can be explained simply by erosion or deposition. Barbados is particularly noted for having risen well above sea level in recent times - raised sea cliffs in coral limestone can be traced almost up to the 300-metre (1,000-feet) contour. A newly exposed coastline tends to promote deposition because it exposes marine sediment to the waves and has a gently sloping profile that reduces the power of the waves. Much of the West Indies north of Cuba, and including northern Cuba, is of this type, and these conditions continue far up the eastern seaboard of North America as a result of sea level falling some 5-6 metres (16-20 feet) from a high point about 125,000 years ago.

Coastal pollution

Pollution of the coastal areas can be

- direct
- seaborne
- landborne

Direct pollution

This mainly involves *litter* and *sewage*. Litter is the most visible for a variety of reasons. The beaches are heavily used and many items taken to, or used on, a beach are less degradable than they used to be. Polythene bags, polystyrene cups and plastic packaging are much less easily decomposed than paper and cardboard, for example. Our society is more prone to litter than it used to be - a social problem that affects all parts of the environment, including the coast (See p.249).

In many countries it is illegal to remove sand from a beach. This beach was accidentally made by human activities near Oistins, Barbados.

The increased use of the beach has made coastal settlement much more popular, and as a result much sewage escapes onto the shore. This is partly due to bad planning - or evasion of it - as sewage treatment costs money. Both litter and sewage are likely to cause some or all of the following:

- Death or damage to coastal plants and animals
- Increase in unpleasant activity, such as seaweed, flies, ants
- Unsanitary conditions on beaches and in the sea
- Possible disease in shellfish, especially oysters, whelks and crabs
- Unsightly surroundings

Seaborne pollution

This is similar to direct pollution, but to it must be added *oil* and *tar*. Litter is dumped from commercial vessels, cruise ships, yachts and boats in much greater amounts than ever before. Much more of it can float, and it lasts much longer. These vessels also invariably dump their sewage while out at sea, so it is very difficult to control or police it. By far the most dangerous form of pollution is from the fuels that these vessels either transport or use. Numerous minor spillages and losses from wrecks provide a continuous, if small, supply of pollutants which is totally uncontrolled.

Discharges from oil tankers are even more serious, with virtually all of the tar that we see on windward beaches especially, being deliberately dumped into the sea. After delivering a cargo of crude oil to a refinery, oil tankers must wash out their cargo tanks. They do this by means of high-pressure water jets, and the water must be drained from the tanks before loading can start again. The more reputable companies have holding tanks on their ships, and the refineries off-load the 'washings' when the ship arrives. However, it costs money to do this: the ship has to 'waste' space for storage; the process requires additional equipment on the ship; and the refinery has to unload unwanted water and separate the oil from it. Many ships simply pour the washings over their stern, and this is still legal over most of the world's open seas. Finally, collisions and other disasters can cause colossal amounts of crude oil to be released into the sea. The effects are well known - dirty beaches, and death to all marine life.

Landborne pollution

This is certainly the least serious form of pollution in the Caribbean, and is mainly associated with *industrial pollution*, although *agricultural pollution* and *river dredging* and *diversions* are also important. The classic case of industrial pollution took place in Japan, where a factory on the shores of Minimata Bay poured chemical wastes containing mercury into the sea for many years. Fish is the major source of protein in Japan and the bay was extensively fished. Unfortunately the fish stored the mercury in their bodies and this was passed on to the population who were stricken by incurable diseases many years later, and the effects of these were passed on to their children. This is not the type of pollution that should be stopped only after it has started - it must be prevented from ever happening.

Any addition to sea water in the tropics is likely to be damaging to the coastal area. The ecology of the Caribbean is largely based on the penetration of sunlight to the sea floor and coral reefs. Nearly all the food chains start here and are based on filter feeders such as coral. Any pollution that reduces the clarity of the water or chokes the filter feeders can damage the environment. Bathers and divers will also be discouraged. This kind of pollution can be caused by any kind of building activity which stirs up the soil and drains silt or mud into the sea; the dredging of a river; drainage from a swamp, such as was proposed at Negril in Jamaica in pursuit of a peat-powered electricity plant project; drainage of fertilizers, pesticides and fungicides from farmland; and the drainage of effluent from industrial plants, such as chemical or mineral wastes from refineries and bauxite plants.

---

1 What type of coastline does Guyana have?

2 Why is there more pollution of the sea today than in the past?

3 What parts of the Caribbean are most vulnerable to oil pollution? (Consider the location of oilfields and refineries, and major shipping routes.)

4 How can coral reefs be damaged?

5 How do you think the features in the photograph on this page were formed?

6 What evidence is there for loss of beach sand in the photograph on p.50

Part Two
Natural Systems

6

Water resources

Fresh water is a much neglected resource in many parts of the Caribbean. In many places the local water supply is less certain than in the days of the Arawaks, and the water is often less pure. Much water is wasted or unused, while a few supplies are overused. This is partly due to insufficient

A domestic water tank typical of the homemade systems that are constructed on small islands, Nevis.

development by local authorities, but it is also due to a general lack of education in the nature of resources.

Collection, storage and distribution

Most fresh water in the Caribbean comes from rainfall. A small amount is desalinated. Most parts of the Caribbean have enough rainfall to supply their needs, but in some parts it is too dry and the rainfall has to be supplemented with purified sea water or other salty (brackish) water.

Rain water is not used directly except for agriculture. It has

to be *collected* first, and then *distributed*. Collection can be *natural* in

- rivers

- lakes

- aquifers (underground storage in freshwater lenses),

or it can be artificial, in

- reservoirs fed by rivers, often with specially made diversions
- rain tanks (cisterns) fed by sealed catchment slopes, or from the roofs of houses and other buildings.

Distribution is usually by means of a pumping station and pipeline, but may also be by tanker lorry to places that are not served by pipeline. *Purification* is carried out by *settling* and *filtering out* sediment, and adding *chlorine* at the pumping station to kill *bacteria*.

Surface drainage and supply

All the larger islands, like Jamaica, and the smaller mountainous islands, like St Lucia, have rivers. Here the water resources are ample, but supply is often limited because the resources have not been developed. Kingston, Jamaica, is a good example of this problem. It has a large population, but Jamaica's rivers are far away, and so there is a problem getting the water to the city. People do not expect to pay much for water, but major river and water works are very expensive. Jamaica plans to solve this problem by combining water supply with HEP production in its Blue Mountain Scheme. It is hoped that the profits from the sale of electricity will help to pay for the cost of the water works.

In St Lucia it is planned to build a reservoir on the Roseau River south of Castries. In many of the smaller islands, surface catchment is supplemented by rain tanks which are fed by guttering on roofs. This is common in the British Virgin Islands, the Cayman Islands, the Turks and Caicos Islands, Nevis, and Bermuda, which has an especially well-organized system. It is also the common method of collection in Belize City despite its abundant rainfall and many rivers.

Part of complex rainwater catchment which collects fresh water for Cockburn Town, Grand Turk. In the background there are disused salt pans.

Underground storage

As this is not visible it is less easily understood. All rocks are *porous* to some extent; that is, they can hold a certain percentage of their volume in water. A rock such as sandstone or limestone that contains a good supply of water is known as an *aquifer*, and the surface of the water in the aquifer is known as the *water table* (Fig. 6.1). It is this level that can be seen in a well or borehole. Limestone is the most common aquifer in the Caribbean, and a few islands depend on water lenses to supply virtually all their water, the notable examples being Barbados, The Bahamas and Anguilla. All the larger islands like Trinidad and Jamaica, and some smaller ones, for example Grand Cayman, use underground water as well as surface water for about half of their needs.

In some cases the water in these aquifers comes to the surface naturally:

As a spring Springs occur wherever the water table reaches the surface, usually on a hillside.

As an artesian spring This is a special case where hydrostatic pressure forces water to the surface in an *artesian basin* (Fig. 6.2). In this case the strata must form a syncline so that some part of the aquifer is above the ground level of the basin.

As a lake This is simply due to the land surface dipping below the water table of the surrounding area, as in a vale between two ridges (See Fig. 6.1).

Organized water supply systems guard the *catchment* areas of aquifers, usually by leaving them forested and in a natural state. This ensures a minimum of wastage by evaporation and prevents pollution or 'stealing'. The amount extracted is carefully monitored, and regulated to match the amount

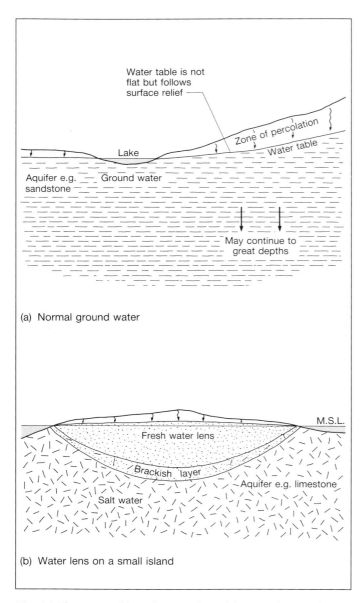

Fig. 6.1 *The water table and a water lens. (a) Normal ground water (b) Water lens on a small island.*

supplied by the rainfall. Usually about 20-30% of the rainfall is captured; the rest evaporates, is lost by plant transpiration, or runs off the surface to the sea. Private wells are common in some areas - the island of New Providence in The Bahamas is reputed to have some 7,000 private wells - and under these conditions it is impossible to control the storage and supply of water. A particular problem in the Caribbean is that the freshwater lenses are underlain by salty water, and if wells are overpumped this salty water is drawn towards the surface and pollutes the aquifer. It can take more than 30 years for a medium-sized lens to rebuild itself if it is overpumped.

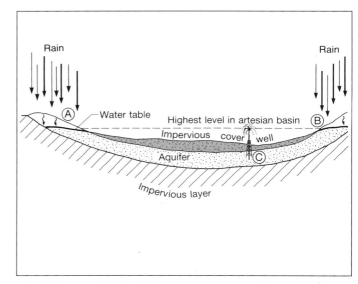

Fig. 6.2 *An artesian basin. In any water system, the water level will try to rise to the highest level in the system. The water is therefore under pressure in proportion to the 'head' of water above it. In an artesian basin, the basin itself is below the highest level of water, as shown at A and B. Water in the basin at C is under pressure and will try to rise to the higher level. If a well is dug, the water comes out as a gusher. (A water gusher is not the same as a gusher in an oil well, which is usually the result of high gas pressure.)*

Desalination

This is the purifying of water so as to remove the salt. Usually sea water is treated by a plant that can produce between 0.5 million and 5 million gallons a day for a large town. There are many smaller plants for communities on small islands or cays. There are two common ways of purifying salt water: by *distilling* it, or by *reverse osmosis*. The first method requires the water to be boiled and then the steam is condensed to provide water that is 99% free of contaminants. Unfortunately boiling

the water is expensive as it needs fuel, usually oil, for heating. Reverse osmosis only requires the water to be pumped through a special membrane which acts as a filter, and if the water is sediment-free this is quite efficient.

Islands that depend heavily on desalination include Antigua, Grand Cayman (about 90% of its water is desalinated), Aruba, Curacao, St Maarten, and the US Virgin Islands of St Thomas and St Croix.

Pollution

There are many ways in which water can be polluted, but the following are the most important:

- Overpumping, as described above.
- Industrial effluent, e.g. red mud and caustic soda from alumina plants in Jamaica.
- Agricultural herbicides, pesticides, fungicides, and fertilizers.
- Domestic effluent. There are few treated sewage systems in the Caribbean, and these only exist in some of the towns. Domestic waste is drained into cesspits and soakaways - that is, the ground and the aquifers. Usually there is a law controlling the location of these, but it may only require that a pit is 15 metres (50 feet) away from a well. The rapidly increasing population has caused a great increase in this form of pollution. The Barbados Government recently reported: 'Of major concern also is the danger of pollution of our water system by the improper disposal of human waste', and a $40million project aided by a $25million loan will be used to build a new sewage system for Bridgetown.
- Oil, and other fuel spills and leaks. Today there are numerous pipelines in and around our towns, and every service station with its underground storage tanks can be a source of pollution. Gasoline in urban water supplies is not an uncommon problem faced by water engineers.

Conservation

There are several major areas of *conservation*. The prevention of pollution, of course, is one. Others are as follows:

Maintenance of the natural vegetation cover   Although plants do transpire water back to the atmosphere, they reduce the amount of evaporation and run-off by a far greater amount. The following report from Haiti, which has the worst soil erosion in the Caribbean, emphasizes this: 'The Government has forbidden the cutting of trees in the region of the Saint Mathurine hydro-electric plant (Les Cayes). . . the scheme is endangered by severe erosion caused by almost total destruction of the forest cover protecting the watershed of the river supplying the hydro-electric reservoir.' The generation of HEP is of course another, but less common, use of our water resources.

Enhanced catchment   For example, the use of domestic gutters and tanks, and specially constructed underground storage systems. Well-maintained distribution systems are also necessary. Many old water systems in the Caribbean lose up to half of their supply through leaks; for example, 35% of Jamaica's water production is unaccounted for.

Recycling water   Modern factories can conserve water by condensing it, or purifying it, and re-using it. This applies particularly to very large installations such as oil refineries which can use enormous amounts of water for cooling purposes, but then discharge it untreated into the sea. Recycling also eliminates much pollution.

Recycling sewage   Domestic sewage can be collected and treated and then used for irrigation - a technique known as *waste-water treatment*. For example, St Croix treats its sewage water and then pumps it back into an aquifer to be re-used later.

---

1   Where does fresh water come from in your country, and in your home?

2   How can the water supply be polluted?

3   How can sea water be made drinkable?

4   How can water be recycled?

7
Weather: Its nature and causes

Convectional storms in the wet season can be exceptionally heavy. Local flooding is common. These floods were in Nassau, The Bahamas, in 1988.

What are weather and climate?

The *weather* is what we *experience* on a day-to-day basis, while the *climate* is the weather pattern that we *expect* to receive over a period (a year, say). If we put this more scientifically, we can say that the weather is a single event in the series of conditions that make up the climate. We can also say that the climate is the average condition of the atmosphere.

There are some other terms that should be understood. *Meteorology* is the physics of the atmosphere. A meteorologist is well qualified in physics and mathematics. *Climatology* is a much broader-based science, which describes and explains the climates of the world in relation to the various factors that influence them.

Some aspects of weather and climate are well known and help to explain the difference, and the connection, between the two. For example, the Caribbean region has a climate that includes hurricanes - hurricanes are a part of our climate. When we have a hurricane we experience a certain type of weather, such as very high winds.

The elements of weather, and how they are measured

Some of these elements are very familiar, but others are not because we do not react to them with our bodies. Table 7.1 lists the main elements of the weather. These are what weather recorders and forecasters concentrate on, and are the elements that are measured at weather stations.

Table 7.1 lists the elements in the order in which they affect us. Usually, people are very sensitive to temperature changes, even a few degrees, but it is quite impossible, for example, to detect normal pressure changes without an instrument.

All these elements of the weather are present at any one time, and it is merely the relative values of each that change and provide a certain type of weather. We now need to look at what makes each element change, daily, seasonally, or occasionally.

Table 7.1 The elements of the weather

	Element	Instrument	What is measured
1	Temperature	Thermometer	Actual temperature Maximum temperature Minimum temperature
		Thermograph: a recording device	As above, continuously
2	Rainfall	Rain gauge Recording rain gauge	Amount of rain Also measures duration and intensity of rainfall
3	Wind	Anemometer Weather vane Wind sock	Wind speed Wind direction Wind direction
4	Humidity	Wet and dry bulb thermometer Hygrometer: an instrument that reacts directly to humidity	Relative humidity As above
5	Sunshine	Sunshine recorder	Duration of sunshine
6	Cloudiness	Visual	Observer estimates cloud percentage and type of cloud cover
7	Visibility	Visual	Observer makes estimate, using landmarks at known distances.
8	Evaporation	Evaporimeter	Rate of water-loss from a pan
9	Pressure	Barometer Barograph	Atmospheric pressure Atmospheric pressure, continuously

Temperature

The Earth revolves around the sun in such a way that the equatorial areas are most exposed to it, and the poles least exposed (Fig. 7.1) This is due to the *angle* at which the sun's rays strike the Earth, and has nothing to do with *distance* from the sun. (The sun is 150 million km/93 million miles from both the Equator and the Poles.) In addition, because of the tilt of the Earth's axis, the northern hemisphere is more exposed to the sun from May to September (northern summer), and from October to April (the northern winter) the southern hemisphere is more exposed to the sun. The result of this is that the overall temperature of a place declines depending on how far it is from the Equator, or as its latitude increases. Other factors may hide this at times, but generally we can say that Trinidad is hotter than The Bahamas, or that Barbados is hotter than Jamaica (See Fig. 7.1 and Table 7.2).

63

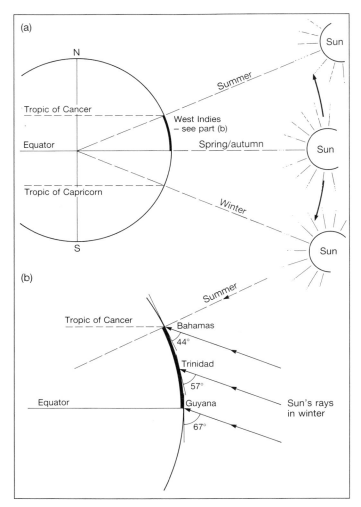

	Trinidad	Barbados	Jamaica (north coast)	The Bahamas (Nassau)
January	26	28	24	21
February	25	28	24	21
March	27	29	24	22
April	29	30	25	24
May	28	31	27	25
June	27	31	27	27
July	29	30	27	28
August	27	31	28	28
September	27	29	27	28
October	28	30	27	26
November	27	29	26	24
December	28	28	25	22
Average temperature	27.3	29.5	26.3	24.7
Range	4°	3°	4°	7°
Latitude	11°N	13°N	18°N	25°N

Table 7.2 Monthly temperatures for selected West Indian islands, °C

Fig. 7.1 Position of the West Indies in relation to the overhead sun. The sun migrates relative to the Earth so that it is overhead in the northern West Indies in summer, and over the Equator in March and September. In winter it is never overhead - inset (b) shows that its angle above the horizon varies from just below 70° in southern Guyana, to only 44° in The Bahamas.

1 Explain the relationship between pressure and temperature.

2 Why is it important to record the weather and keep the records?

3 What is the angle of the overhead sun in your home (a) in midwinter and (b) in midsummer? Use these formulae:

(a) Midwinter: 90° − (your latitude + 23 1/2°)
(b) Midsummer: 90° − (your latitude − 23 1/2°)
(remember, two minuses make a plus!).

(c) Explain your answer to (b).

Air masses

An *air mass* is a body of air that has a distinctive set of meteorological characteristics, the most important of which are its temperature and humidity.

Air masses can be created over any part of the earth that is large enough to influence a large mass of air. The continents and oceans are the most likely regions, but smaller areas, such as northern Canada, and Amazonia, are sufficiently big and uniform to create distinctive masses of air.

In the Caribbean the only regions close enough to affect the climate are the continent of North America, the North Atlantic Ocean and, to a lesser extent, South America.

The air masses that form over the continents are quite different from those that form over the oceans (See 'Continentality' p.65). Continental air masses are likely to start off cold or hot, and dry. Oceanic air masses are cool or warm, and moist. Both can be changed as they travel, the most likely result being a change from dry to wet as continental air masses cross water, for example when an air mass crosses the Great Lakes of North America in winter - which is why so

	Hot/Wet	Hot/Dry	Cold/Wet	Cold/Dry
North America	Never	Possible in summer	Possible in winter in northern Caribbean*	Frequent in winter in the northern Caribbean
South America	Possible in summer (rare)	Occasionally in winter	Never	Never
Atlantic	Common all year round	Possible in spring**	Never	Never

* Cold air masses from North America are dry to start with but may absorb moisture as they cross the sea. Once the front has passed they usually bring dry weather.

** Africa may send us a hot, dry air mass via the Atlantic in the spring.

Table 7.3 Air masses that affect the Caribbean region.

much snow falls south of the lakes - or when a cold front (See below) crosses the Gulf of Mexico or the Straits of Florida.

At the geographical level we can describe air masses in the Caribbean as being hot/warm or cool/cold and wet or dry. This gives us four possibilities from the three areas affecting our region, and we can relate these as in Table 7.3.

Finally, we should note that to most of us an air mass is experienced as a *wind* - the North Atlantic air mass is the north-east trade wind (See p. 76).

Virtually all of the inhabitants of the Caribbean region live in a *maritime* rather than a *continental* environment. The most common and important air masses are the trade winds, and we can consider the weather of the trade winds to be the normal conditions except when air masses from the continents replace them. As we can see from Fig. 7.2 and Table 7.3, this does happen at certain times and in certain places in the Caribbean, and so continentality is an important factor in the region.

Continentality - the influence of North America

Continentality is the seasonal reaction to solar heating experienced by the continents. It is sometimes described as *thermal modification*. Unlike the oceans, land surfaces react very quickly to changes in temperature, as is shown by the development of land and sea breezes on a daily basis.

On a seasonal basis the effect is much more dramatic. In winter the northern continents cool down and then stay cold until the sun 'returns' to heat up the land in spring. The reaction in summer is also dramatic, with intense heat spots developing in the drier interiors. Both the coldest and hottest spots on Earth are found in the continental interiors, and not at the North Pole or the Equator. (See chapter 8.)

In winter the North American continent gets very cold. The cold air is heavy (open a refrigerator door and feel the cold air falling around your feet) and sinks to the ground, spreading out over the land, travelling southwards and south-eastwards in particular. As the continent is surrounded by seas and oceans to the east, west and south, and these stay relatively warm, the cold air is surrounded by warm air - a cold air mass surrounded by warm air masses. Sometimes a warm air mass pushes into parts of North America and creates high temperatures in winter (in January 1983, for example, temperatures in West Virginia were in the 20-30°C range (70-80°F), but well below 0°C (32°F) in Chicago). More often the cold air pushes under the warm air and spreads south to Florida, The Bahamas and the Greater Antilles. In Jamaica these surges of cold air are called 'northers' and in The Bahamas 'cold fronts'. Both terms are accurate - the wind comes from the north, and the edge of the cold air mass is correctly termed a *cold front* (Fig. 7.3). The front itself has its own weather system, because the cold and warm air do not mix easily. Because the heavier cold air pushes the warmer air upwards, cloudiness and rain are common at the cold front. The colder the cold air mass, the more violent the interaction, and thunderstorms can easily develop. As the front is quite independent of the land, the disturbance it creates is present over the sea as well, creating *squalls* and often a *squall line*, which is a whole series of squalls along the front. (This is rather different from the convectional thunderstorms found over hot land in summer - (See p. 71.) A front takes several hours to pass, and the cold air will remain for one to three days.

The front and the cold air mass are not unaffected as they leave North America. First they have to cross the warm Gulf Stream, and then they come into contact with other warm areas such as the Bahamas Banks, the Cuban land mass, and other islands. The air cannot stay cold, and it never arrives as cold as when it leaves the United States. For instance, air that is freezing in Florida will be over 10°C (50°F) when it reaches The Bahamas, and over 15°C (60°F) in Jamaica. The air will also become more humid, although rain is unlikely once the front has passed.

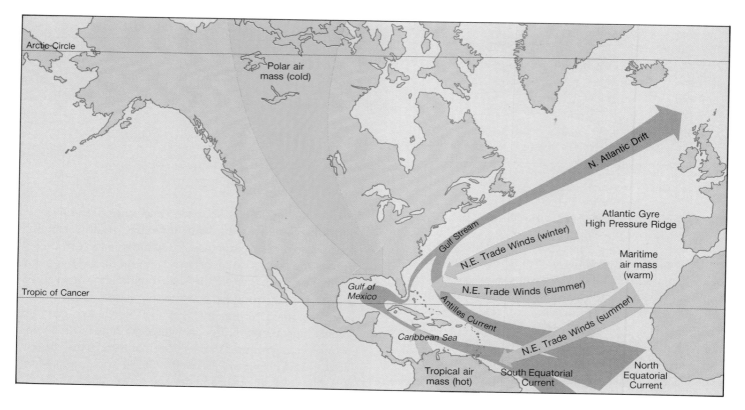

Fig. 7.2 Air masses and ocean currents affecting the West Indies.

---

1 Look again at Table 7.2. Why do you think The Bahamas has the coldest winter?

2 Observe today's approximate wind direction, the temperature and humidity. What air mass is present?

3 If the entire Caribbean region was land, would Jamaica be hotter or cooler, and wetter or drier, in (a) winter, (b) summer?

The maritime influence

Most of the Caribbean territories are islands, and most of the people live near the sea. The previous section explained how a land mass affects climate, but although this is significant, for most of the year, and for most of the region, it is far less important than the influence of the sea. The sea is the great modifier. It cools the hot summers and it warms the cold winds. It produces what is known as an *equable* climate - that is, a climate without great extremes of temperature. For most coastal locations the range of temperature is only 3° or 4°C. Only The Bahamas is significantly different (7°C).

The following points are a summary of the ways in which a water mass modifies temperature and transfers its effect to the land.

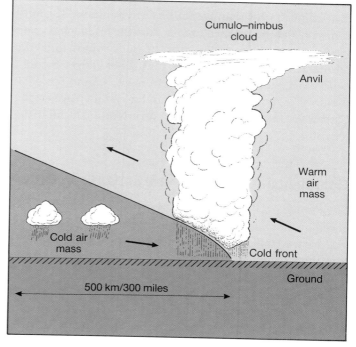

Fig. 7.3 Structure of a cold front. This diagram shows a typical cold front with a large temperature difference between the warm and cold air masses. Often the cold air has been warmed by the time it reaches the West Indies, and instead of cumulo-nimbus storm clouds, thinner stratus clouds giving only light rain are present. However, they may be quite extensive and give overcast conditions for a day or more.

66

(a) Water reacts much more slowly than land to temperature changes - it heats up slowly and cools down slowly. It never gets as hot as the land. In summer the sea heats up slowly and does not reach its maximum temperature (about 28°C) until September, several months after the land maximum. Therefore during the hottest summer months the sea is still relatively cool. In the slightly cooler winter season the sea again lags behind - it is coldest in March or April, making it relatively warm (26°C) in the coldest months, usually January and February.

(b) For the sea to affect us on land, its characteristics must be transferred to the land. This is done through the air - all air is heated or cooled according to the surface that it is in contact with. It cannot be heated directly by the sun. As almost all the air masses reaching the Caribbean have to cross the sea to get here, they are all affected by it. In general, an air mass crossing the sea adjusts to the sea's temperature. As the most prevalent winds here are the north-east trade winds, which cross the Atlantic, island and coastal temperatures in the Caribbean are very closely related to the sea temperatures (compare the sea temperatures in Fig. 7.4 with the land temperatures in Table 7.4). Even North America's cold fronts are rapidly warmed up as they cross the sea.

(c) The sea gets its heat from the overhead sun. Hot water rises, and the warm water stays on the surface of the sea where it is blown over the ocean in the form of wind-driven currents like the Gulf Stream, the Antilles Current, and the North and South Equatorial Currents. All Caribbean currents originate in the hot equatorial regions. If *cold* currents entered the Caribbean, the climate would be different. So not only is the sea subject to tropical heating from the sun, it is also the bringer of heat from the Equator. These currents act like a heat-shield that prevents cold air entering the Caribbean.

(d) Large shallow seas, as in The Bahamas and on other

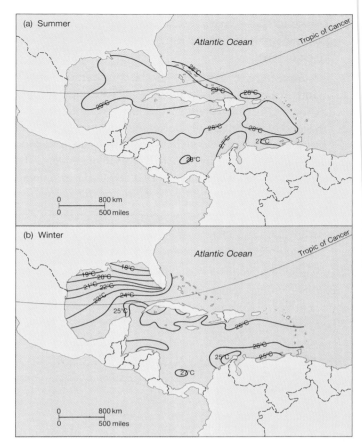

Fig. 7.4 Sea temperatures in the West Indies.

(a) Summer Note that the hottest area is in the Gulf of Mexico and along the Tropic of Cancer. The position of the overhead sun is significant. Also important is the passage of the north and South Equatorial Currents through the Caribbean Sea.

(b) Winter In winter the sun is too far south to be the controlling factor. Instead the warmest zone is the Caribbean Sea, only 2° cooler than in summer, due to the presence of the incoming Equatorial Currents. In the Gulf of Mexico the coldness of North America causes rapid cooling to the north.

	Winter, lowest monthly mean	Summer, highest monthly mean	Seasonal range	
Northern Bahamas	17.5°C (63.5°F)	27.8°C (82.0°F)	10.3°C (18.5°F)	Closest to USA
Central Bahamas	21.1°C (70.0°F)	28.9°C (84.0°F)	7.8°C (14.0°F)	
Southern Bahamas	23.6°C (74.5)	28.6°C (83.5°F)	5.0°C (9.0°F)	Furthest from USA
Geographical range	6.1°C (11°F)	1.1°C (2°F)		

Table 7.4 Winter and summer temperatures in The Bahamas

This simple analysis of seasonal temperatures can be applied to any country. The figures clearly show that The Bahamas have relatively similar conditions everywhere in the summer, when the north-east trade winds are dominant. In winter there is a marked difference in temperatures between the north and south, owing to the spread of cold air out of North America. The figures show how this influence declines with distance from the continent.

67

banks and large lakes, react more quickly to heating and cooling and have greater ranges of temperature than the deep ocean.

(e) Distance from the sea must also be considered. Once the wind, or air mass, crosses the coast it is no longer affected by the sea. Instead it starts to develop the characteristics of the land, which is usually hotter. As they progress inland the relatively cool trade winds become hotter, and probably weaker if there are hills in the way. Consequently the inland areas of large islands, and sheltered or leeward coasts, are least affected by the maritime influence.

---

1 What is an *equable* climate? Which of the following has an equable climate: Iceland; Hawaii, Disneyworld in Orlando, Florida, New York?

2 When are sea temperatures at their coolest in the Caribbean? Does this make spring cooler or warmer than autumn, or is there no difference? (Look back at Fig. 7.4.)

3 Why are there no cold currents in the Caribbean?

Other influences

Several other things affect the temperature of places in the Caribbean.

Shelter As winds are usually a cooling influence, any barrier to them will raise the temperature. Valleys, the leeward coast, and the leeward sides of mountains are all hotter than more exposed areas.

Height above sea level On the larger islands there is a noticeable drop in temperature with height, usually about 6°C per 1,000 metres (3.5°F per 1,000 feet). As average sea-level temperatures are about 27°C, we would reach freezing point if we went up $\frac{27}{6} \times 1,000 = 4,500$ metres.

The highest mountain is only just over 3,000 metres, so this is not possible. However, in the islands of Jamaica, Hispaniola, Puerto Rico, and the far south-east of Cuba, there are towns and villages between 1,000 and 2,000 metres.

Vegetation Areas covered with forest, grassland or farmland are significantly cooler than areas of bare rock and built-up areas. Vegetation contains a lot of water and therefore absorbs a lot of heat before it reaches the ground. Trees shade the ground. On the other hand, dark road surfaces and concrete buildings heat up quickly and store heat. Also, large buildings obstruct the cooling breezes. On sunny days the larger towns and cities of the Caribbean are hotter during the day than the surrounding areas.

Rainfall

Rainfall is always produced by a change of temperature in the air. As we have already examined most of the factors affecting temperature, we are now in a good position to understand why and where it rains in the Caribbean (See Fig. 7.5).

To create rain there must be a mass of air that is humid enough to give up its moisture. It will do this if it is cooled, because the amount of moisture (*water vapour*) that the air can hold depends on its temperature. If the temperature is reduced, the air is less able to hold its moisture. At a certain temperature (*the dew point*) the water vapour *condenses* into *water droplets*. We see this phenomenon as *cloud*, or if at ground level, as *fog*.

There are therefore three very important conditions for rain:

1 The air mass must be moist. If there is not sufficient water vapour there will be no rain, regardless of whether there are mountains or convectional currents.

2 There must be cooling. All air is moist to some degree, and the night-time relative humidity in the West Indies is rarely less than 70%, which means that the air contains 70% of the amount of water vapour it could hold without condensing some (See Table 7.5).

3 Technically, there is a third requirement. There must be something for the water vapour to condense on, and this is known as the *condensation nucleus*. In practice there is usually no shortage of these nuclei, which include dust, salt, and particles from chemical pollution. However, in the much purer upper atmosphere, the temperature is often below the dew point, but there is no condensation. If nuclei are introduced, such as by a jet airliner, then condensation occurs immediately on the exhaust gases from the engines, creating the well-known *condensation trail*. The term *vapour trail* is not correct, as it is the condensation, not the vapour, that we see.

The importance of these figures lies in the dew point and

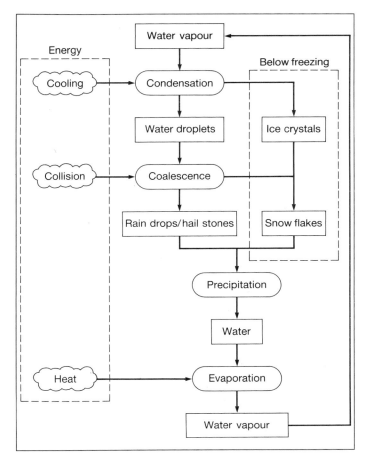

Fig. 7.5 Condensation and precipitation. The water cycle is the product of energy input or output processes which change water into its various atmospheric forms. The diagram identifies the processes and products at each stage.

relative humidity - in the dry season the air is drier, the dew point is lower, and even though it is colder, it does not rain. In summer the air is full of moisture - it is very *unstable* - and only a small drop in temperature is enough to release large amounts of water.

Table 7.5 Dew point, relative humidity and rainfall

Season	Max. temp	Min. temp	Dew point	Relative humidity (%)	Condensation (rain possible)
Dry	23°C (73°F)	18.5°C (65°F)	15.5°C (60°F)	65-85	No
Wet	32°C (90°F)	26.5°C (80°F)	29°C (84°F)	85-100	Yes

1 Why are towns hotter than vegetated areas?

2 Is hail possible in the tropics? Why/why not?

3 Why are mountain tops often covered in cloud?

Dew and rain

Both of these are the product of condensation when the dew point is reached. *Rain* is produced when water droplets combine in the air to form raindrops which are too heavy to stay up, and so fall to earth. *Dew* is formed on the ground or on other cool surfaces, usually at night. When the sun goes down, the ground cools and the air in contact with it can be cooled to its dew point. The condensation only takes place on cold surfaces, such as car bodies or grass.

The air near the ground may also be cooled to its dew point creating a morning mist, more correctly known as *radiation fog*. Such fog is usually experienced only in the more sheltered mountain areas (See photo p. 70).

Types of rain

Rain can be either *local*, or *regional*:

Local	Regional
Convectional	Frontal
	Tropical (easterly) waves
Orographic (relief)	Tropical revolving storms (hurricanes)

Local rain is produced by the geographical conditions at a particular place, and the area over which the rain falls is limited. Regional rain is produced by atmospheric conditions, and is independent of ground conditions. Such rain affects land and sea alike.

Convectional rain

One of the most common forms of summer rain in the Caribbean is caused initially by heating. When the sun heats

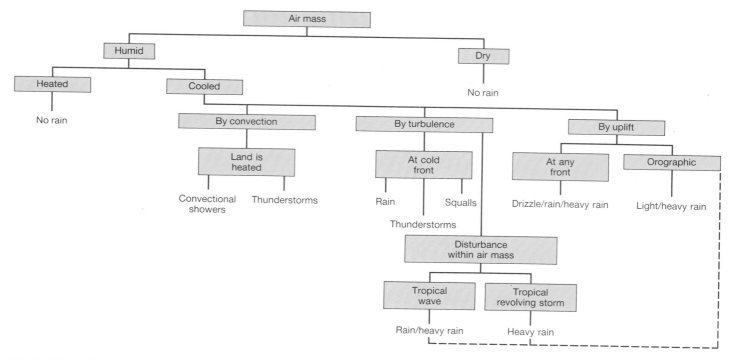

Fig. 7.6 Rainfall types.

the land, the air in contact with it is heated, and it rises. Although it starts off hot, because it is rising it begins to cool down at the rate of about 6°C per 1,000 metres (3.5°F per 1,000 feet) (Fig. 7.7). As heating continues during the day, a vast amount of air is lifted up, forming vertical streams rising thousands of metres into the atmosphere. In many cases the air is concentrated and speeded up, and may reach over 160km p h (100 m p h). In these cases it ascends to great heights, perhaps over 6,000 metres (20,000 feet), and even up to 15,000 metres, or 15km (50,000 feet or 9 miles). Condensa-

Radiation fog (caused by cooling at night) in the Central Mountains of Puerto Rico in the early morning. This fog disappears soon after sunrise.

Fig 7.7 Convectional rainfall under different conditions.
(a) Normal   (b) On small islands and cays.

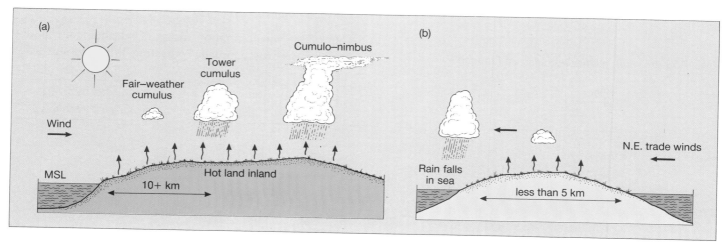

The anvil tops of nimbo-stratus clouds over Cuba in summer.

tion may then occur at as low as 600-900 metres (2,000 - 3,000 feet), and continues as the air rises.

Enormous quantities of water are produced and intense downpours are the result. Because the action is so violent, several other meteorological features may be present;

Lightning Any intense movement in a conducting medium creates static electricity. In a convectional cell (cloud), water rushes up and down, creating enormous amounts of electricity. This can be discharged to the ground or the sea, or simply to another part of the cell. If we see it clearly it is *forked lightning*, but often it is masked by cloud and we see a diffused flash or *sheet lightning*.

Thunder This sound is created by the lightning as it instantly vapourises the water that it passes through.

Hail The rising currents are so strong that quite large rain-drops are carried high up into the convectional cell, past the freezing level, which may be at about 4,500-6,000 metres (15,000-20,000 feet). As a result, they are frozen and become hail. Often this melts before it reaches the ground, but this is why the rain seems cold - it *is* cold! In severe storms the hailstones may be caught up in another current and carried back up to the freezing zone. If this happens they become larger, and this may be repeated several times until eventually they become too heavy and fall to earth.

Gusty winds This is the incoming wind which feeds the rising currents. These can be noticeably cool and dangerous at sea.

Convectional rain is common in summer over most inhabited islands. The larger islands generate the most heat, so they have the most rain per square kilometre. Small islands do not usually develop convectional cells, or if they do, the rain usually falls into the sea on the leeward side. On hilly or mountainous islands, relief rainfall may be added to convectional rain, and it is difficult to tell which is dominant.

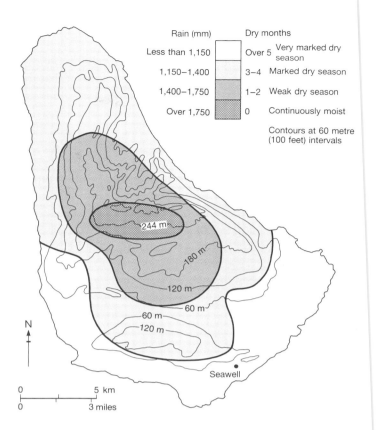

Fig. 7.8 Altitude and rainfall, Barbados. This map shows the <u>humidity</u> of the land based on the amount of rain and the length of the dry season. The location of Seawell airport should be noted and compared with the data in Fig. 8.2. (Source: K.C. Vernon and D.M. Carvol (1965) <u>Soil and Land Use Survey of Barbados</u>, V.W.I. Trinidad.)

The reason we do not have convectional rain in winter is not because it is cooler, although this is the reason usually given! We have already seen that the temperature range for most of the Caribbean is about 4°C (40°F), and convection does not simply switch off because the temperature drops a few degrees (See Table 7.2)

On most 'winter' days the temperatures are quite sufficient to generate a considerable amount of convection, but it does not rain. The reason is in the air itself, and not the convectional current. In the winter season the Caribbean is exposed to the northern part of the north-east trade winds (Fig. 7.8). These are much drier than the southern margins, as the air in the Hadley Cell is descending. Only the lower 1,500 metres (5,000 feet) or so, in contact with the ocean, are quite moist, and this is not enough to allow a convectional cell to develop. As soon as the rising air reaches the drier air above at about 1,500 metres (5,000 feet), its ability to continue rising and condensing moisture is limited and the cell dies out, although small 'cotton-wool' cumulus clouds are a common sign of what is happening.

Orographic or relief rain

The mountainous islands of the Caribbean are well known for their heavy rainfall (Fig. 7.8). It is also well known that the highest areas are the wettest, and the windward sides are wetter than the leeward sides. In these areas annual rainfall totals may be over 2,500 mm (100 in.) and often exceed 5,000 mm (200 in.). What is not always appreciated is that quite low hills also generate rain, and that orographic rainfall rarely acts on its own, but combines with convectional or other types. Whenever there is a moist, unstable air mass, the uplift caused by the air rising up the mountain or hillsides combines with any other factor, for example a convectional current, that might be present. Relief rain is essentially additional to what would take place if the mountains were not there.

The air mass conditions must also be right. In 1986, in June and July (the wet season) there was a drought on the hilly island of Puerto Rico, and to a lesser extent in Hispaniola and Jamaica. This was due to unusually stable north-east trade winds, which did not contain enough moisture to allow condensation to take place.

Frontal rain

Frontal conditions are only significant in the northern Caribbean, but as they are most common in the dry season they are valued for the rain they produce.

Both cold and warm fronts produce rain, although not always, and all parts of the Caribbean can be affected. However, the northern Bahamas can receive as many as 50 cold fronts in the season from October to March. Here is part of the January 1985 weather report for The Bahamas:

'On the 15th a cold front associated with scattered showers and isolated thunderstorms quickly advanced across the north-east and central Bahamas. The following two days were fair and sunny.

On the 18th and 19th a slow-moving cold front drifting over the north-west and central Bahamas gave occasional rain or showers. The system became stationary in the south-east Bahamas.

On the 21st an active cold front followed by a strong surge of Arctic air behind it crossed The Bahamas, causing temperatures to dip into the upper forties (°F) in the northern Bahamas. For the rest of the month, despite the movements of three weak cold fronts over The Bahamas on the 25th, 26th and 29th, there was a predominance of fair to fine weather everywhere.'

It is a peculiarity of air that masses of a different temperature do not mix easily. In the case of a cold front, the cold air advances as a shallow curved wedge, sliding along at ground level under the warmer trade winds (See Fig. 7.3). Rain can be caused in two ways:

1   At the front itself there is some mixing of the air masses, causing turbulence. Pockets of warm air are trapped in the cold air and ascend rapidly through it, just like a convection cell, and the result is very similar, with a line of cumulo-nimbus storm clouds marking the front and causing heavy rain at scattered locations. The greater the difference in temperature between the two air masses, and the faster the speed of advance, then the more likely it is that heavy rain will result. (See Fig. 7.3.)

2   Above and behind the front, the warm north-east trade winds are lifted to thousands of metres, creating extensive layers of stratus and strato-cumulus cloud as condensation occurs. In many cases the trade winds are too dry and stable for rain to form, but if uplift is significant there can be extensive continuous rain, perhaps lasting as long as a whole day.

Other types of front are less common, but the activity taking place is very similar - warm air is forced to rise over cooler air, causing condensation and possibly rain.

Easterly waves

We need to think of the trade winds as having a lower moist layer, owing to contact with the ocean, and an upper drier layer. If the lower air is lifted up in any way, it cools, causing condensation and eventually rain. An *easterly wave* is something like a tidal wave at sea, except that it is a steep wave of moist air, the top of which is usually more than twice as high as usual (Fig. 7.9). It is called 'easterly', because it travels from the east within the trade winds. The result is that in the area of the wave, especially in summer, large areas of cloud give showers, and in places there may be thunderstorms and continuous heavy rain. These waves can occur all year round, but they are more common in summer. As they cross land they become much more vulnerable to orographic or convectional influences, and then produce much more rain than when over the ocean. This is why it does not rain on every hot day in summer - rain comes in cycles that usually coincide with the passage of easterly waves. In between it is dry and sunny.

An easterly wave can also be described as a *trough of low pressure*. This is because the area of the wave is warmer than its surrounding air, and warm air, being lighter, creates a low-pressure zone. Pressure is the common feature recorded on weather maps, and the easterly wave will appear on it as a trough-shaped zone of low pressure, hence its other name. In the Caribbean, troughs of low pressure usually mean easterly waves in the trade winds.

Other factors affecting rainfall

Vegetation cover   It has been proved that when an area is

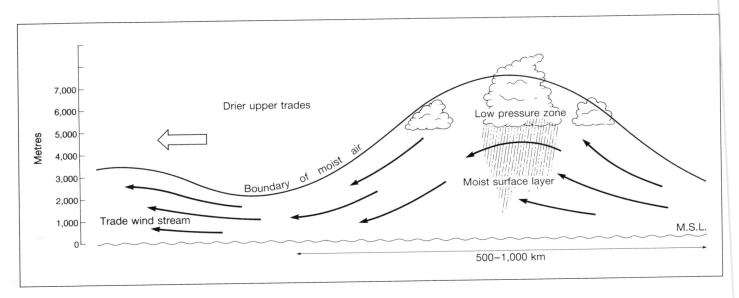

Fig 7.9 An easterly wave. Because of the wave, air rises and cools to its dew point, creating a cloudy belt within the trade wind stream. If the wave is high enough, rain will develop, and the West Indies may experience heavy rain as the wave crosses land, and convectional and/or relief conditions are added to the unstable rising air already present. This is particularly common in the Greater Antilles in early summer.

deforested the rainfall of that place decreases. Vegetation holds large amounts of moisture, which it returns to the atmosphere through the process of *transpiration*. If the vegetation is removed, this source of water vapour is lost. As a result the humidity of the air over the land drops and there is less chance of rain.

Size of an island   Small islands, such as cays, and very narrow islands, such as many of the Grenadines, receive very little rain. They are too small or narrow to create convectional

currents, they have little vegetation, and even if they have some relief the rain may fall offshore on the leeward side of the island.

1 Describe the weather you would experience as a cold front passed over you.

2 Describe the conditions that are most likely for the development of a thunderstorm.

3 Why are high mountains wetter than lowlands?

4 Why is winter in the Caribbean generally drier than the summer? Can you explain why California and the Mediterranean have dry summers and wet winters?

5 Look at Fig. 7.9. The wave travels at about 15km (9 miles) per hour. How long might the rain last as the easterly wave crosses the land?

Tropical revolving storms - hurricanes

A *hurricane* is the Atlantic and Caribbean name given to the largest type of tropical revolving storm. Any tropical disturbance or storm that has the following features is a tropical revolving storm and can become a hurricane, typhoon (in the Pacific) or cyclone (in the Indian Ocean), when the winds exceed 120km p h (75 m p h). See Table 7.6 and Fig. 7.10.

- An anti-clockwise rotation, known as *cyclonic*.
- A central 'eye' without cloud surrounded by a large circular pattern of heavy cloud.

In addition we should note several other features:

- The tropical revolving storm forms over warm water, not less than 27°C (80°F). In this it is quite different from convectional thunderstorms which form over land.

- The disturbed area is extremely large. Cloud may extend 300-550km (200-350 miles) from the eye, and areas within this radius can experience a marked change in weather conditions, often receiving rain for several days.

- Wind speeds can be extremely high, severe hurricanes having been recorded with winds between 160 and 320km p h (100 and 200 m p h) close to the eye.

Class of Hurricane	Wind speed (km/h)	Sea surge (metres)	Extent of damage	
1	119–153	1.2–1.5	Minimal	
2	154–177	1.6–2.4	Moderate	
3	178–209	2.5–3.7	Extensive	e.g. Hurricane Betsy, 1965
4	210–243	3.8-5.5	Extreme	e.g. Hurricane David, 1979
5	Over 243	Over 5.5	Catastrophic	e.g. Hurricane Gilbert, 1988
				Hurricane Camille, 1969

Table 7.6 Saffir-Simpson hurricane scale

Rain from tropical revolving storms

Rain is the most widespread effect of a tropical storm or a hurricane. Although we do not know exactly how hurricanes form, we do know a lot about their workings once they are formed. Sometimes they are called 'heat engines', as they generate heat which gives them their tremendous energy.

Basically, if we start at the sea surface, we can imagine vast amounts of water being evaporated from the warm sea. As this rises it cools and condenses, but the act of condensation releases more heat (this is 'latent' heat, the same heat that was originally used to convert the water into water vapour). The heat released provides more uplift, and so on in a sort of perpetual motion. Eventually this operation becomes so ex-

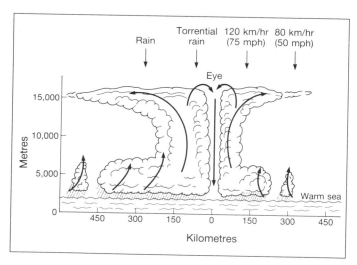

Fig 7.10 Typical hurricane structure. Hurricanes usually have one sector wetter than the other. Wind speeds shown here are for a minimum hurricane (class 1 on the hurricane scale - see Table 7.6). The scale here should be noted, as the hurricane is about 900km across and 15km high. If this diagram was drawn without vertical exaggeration, its height would be about the same as the width of the 'eye'.

tensive that an upward rotating pattern develops which will continue as long as the system is fed with water vapour from the sea. If the hurricane crosses land its supply is cut off and it weakens rapidly.

From this account it should be clear that a hurricane is a huge rain-making machine. The spiralling air carries the moisture far up and away from the centre. As a rough guide we can expect any place that comes within 80km (50 miles) of the centre of a hurricane to receive 100-250mm (4-10 in.) of rain over a period of one to four days. Places farther away, up to 320km (200 miles), will still be affected, and on average 10-25% of the rain received in the northern Caribbean in any year is due to tropical revolving storm activity.

The tracks of hurricanes

Nowadays the tracks of all hurricanes can be plotted precisely using satellite photographs. Unfortunately it is not possible to forecast where a hurricane will go. What can be done is to look at past hurricanes and see what they did. The following is a list of likely routes (See also Fig. 7.11).

Origin in the Atlantic between 10° and 20°N

1 Travels westwards, either north or south of the Greater Antilles, until it reaches Texas, Mexico or Belize, e.g. Hurricanes Allen 1980, Hattie 1961, Gilbert 1988.

2 Travels westwards and turns north or north-east into The Bahamas, the Atlantic, or the USA, e.g. Hurricanes David 1979, Camille 1969, Hugo 1989.

3 Travels north, or north-west and then north. These do not affect the Caribbean at all but may pass close to Bermuda. Sometimes they continue as far as New York or New England where they can cause considerable damage, e.g. Hurricane Diane 1955.

Origin in the Caribbean Sea

4 These form to the south of Cuba and nearly always head northwards, crossing western Cuba and Florida. (These are less common, but in some years several may form. There were three in 1968.)

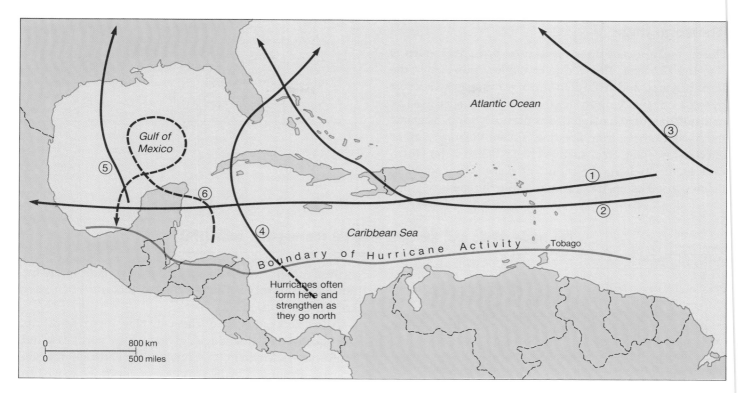

Fig. 7.11 Typical hurricane tracks. The numbers refer to the classification of hurricanes in Table 7.6. Each track represents an actual hurricane that has hit the Caribbean in the last 30 years. No hurricanes have hit land south of the boundary shown, although Tobago was hit in 1963 and Belize in 1961 (twice) and 1969. Both of these are on the boundary.

Origin in the Gulf of Mexico

5   These can take any direction from west to north. They usually form late in the season - September onwards - and as they soon reach land are not as severe as Atlantic hurricanes. However, as they are almost guaranteed to hit the well-populated Mexican or US Gulf coast, they are extremely damaging. There were five in 1957, all of which hit the US coast, and one in 1985 which hit the Mississippi Delta after staying offshore for several days.

Unpredictable hurricanes

6   Wherever they originate, hurricanes can sometimes take the most unpredictable and surprising courses. For example:

(a) A hurricane may turn north, but then turn right around and come south again, hitting places they have just left, a second time, e.g. Hurricane Betsy 1965.

(b) A hurricane may make a complete loop over several days, and then continue in its original direction.

(c) A hurricane may head south, usually in the western Caribbean or the Gulf of Mexico.

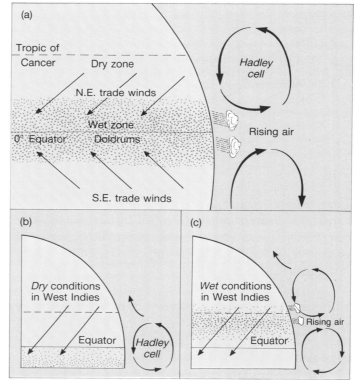

Fig. 7.12 The north-east trade winds. The wet part of the Trade Wind system is related to the rising air at the heat Equator, which is at the southern edge of the N.E. Trade Wind cell. The northern part of the cell has descending air (a) which is stable and dry. in winter (b) the cell shifts southwards so that the West Indies are in the dry sector, but in summer it shifts northwards and produces the wet season (c).

The storm surge

During the hurricane the sea level rises, perhaps as much as 7 metres (22 feet). This is due to the low pressure in the hurricane area, and to the piling up of water against the coast by the strong winds. In an area that is confined, such as a bay or a gulf, the surge is magnified as the sea is trapped against the coast. Damage from flooding is often the most serious effect in low-lying areas such as coastal Belize. After Hurricane Hattie in 1961, the capital of Belize was moved to Belmopan, 50 kilometres (30 miles) from the coast.

1 Why is the storm surge such a danger in a hurricane?

2 Why is it that hurricanes can reach New York, yet Guyana never has any?

3 Where are the strongest winds in a hurricane?

The trade winds and the inter-tropical convergence zone (ITCZ)

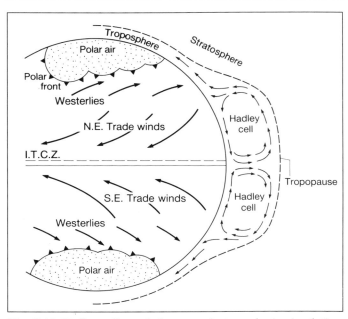

Fig. 7.13 Hadley cells and the general atmospheric circulation. There are two Hadley cells generated by the hot air rising from the intertropical convergence zone (ITCZ). They carry hot moist air away from the Equator, but it descends through the troposphere at about 30°N and S of the Equator, mostly returning as a surface flow - the trade winds - back to the ITCZ.

The trade winds are the most extensive part of the *planetary system* of winds. This is the wind system that would exist if there were no land masses. The trade winds (Fig. 7.12) are generated by two forces:

1 The heating of the equatorial regions by the sun.
2 The Earth's rotation.

The diagrams (Figs 7.12 - 7.14) show how heating in the equatorial regions causes massive amounts of air to rise up. This creates a cellular circulation in which air rises, travels north or south at high altitude, sinks to ground level, and then returns to the equatorial region. The area of rising air is known

as the *doldrums* as there are no prevailing winds, but to the north and south of it the huge air masses that are drawn in are known as the *trade winds*.

As we know, they do not actually blow directly towards the Equator, but at an angle, giving us the north-east and south-east trade winds. If we imagine the Earth spinning on its axis surrounded by its envelope of atmosphere, we can understand that air at its surface will be dragged over its surface rather slower than the Earth is rotating. As the Earth spins towards the east, an observer will feel the wind in his face if he looks east. In other words, the spin of the Earth creates an easterly wind.

We therefore have two forces at work - air sucked to the Equator (flowing north and south), and air coming from the east. These combine to give us the north-east and south-east winds.

The intertropical convergence zone (ITCZ) is the area in which the air is rising. It coincides with the doldrums and is sometimes known as the *heat equator*, as it marks the area of greatest heating by the sun (Fig. 7.12). As the overhead sun migrates north and south during the year, so does the ITCZ. If the Earth had no land masses it would appear on a map as a zone parallel to the Equator but north (northern summer) or south (northern winter) of it, depending on the season. In practice the increased heating by the land masses in summer distorts it and it bulges polewards wherever there is land, as this is where the heat is greatest. (See Fig. 7.15)

In the Caribbean it lies along the line of the Greater Antilles in summer, and runs through Brazil in winter. This has the following effects:

• In winter only the north-east trade winds are present in the Caribbean.

• In midsummer the north-east trade winds only affect the northern half of the Caribbean. The southern and eastern Caribbean are just in the northern section of the south-east trades. Between them are the doldrums.

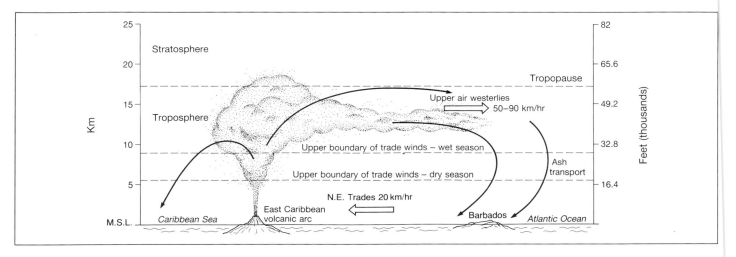

Fig. 7.14 The trade winds and the transport of volcanic ash in the eastern Caribbean. The trade winds are surface winds, and above them lie the upper air westerlies, the 'top half' of the Hadley cell (See Fig. 7.13). Volcanic eruptions easily reach these winds in the upper troposphere, and the ash is carried westwards towards islands like Barbados, where as a result the soils contain much volcanic ash. (Source: H. Sigurdsson et al (1980) <u>Volcanic Sedimentation in the Lesser Antilles,</u> Journal of Geology Vol. 88, Fig. 5.)

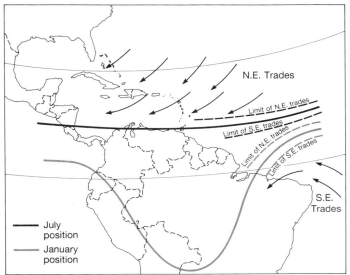

Fig. 7.15 The intertropical convergence zone in the Caribbean.

- The moist parts of the trade winds are the areas nearest the ITCZ, as this is where the air is rising. This is why the rainy season comes in summer, as this is when the moist unstable air is present over virtually the whole region.
- When the ITCZ shifts south, the rainy zone goes with it. Only Trinidad and Guyana are close enough to receive rain at this time, and this is why they are able to have two sugar and rice harvests, instead of one as in the rest of the region.

The monsoon effect

When a continental land mass is *cooled*, its air *sinks* to the ground and flows outwards. On the other hand if the land mass is *heated* the air *rises* and sucks in more air. This happens naturally over a continent like Asia which has a great difference in temperature between winter and summer. The result is the formation of a major system of winds that blow out in winter, but blow inland in summer. This has been referred to as 'Asia breathing in and Asia breathing out'. This striking reversal of the major wind system is known as the *monsoon effect*; the *monsoons* are the winds themselves. The main countries affected are China and the south-east Asian countries, including India, Pakistan, Bangladesh and Sri Lanka. In winter the north-east monsoon brings severe cold and snow to most of China, and the north-west monsoon brings cool weather to India.

The summer monsoon blows across the Indian Ocean from the south-west - it is so strong that it actually reverses the north-east trade winds which would normally blow in these latitudes - and eventually crosses the whole of southern Asia as far as the Himalayas. In South-east Asia and China, the monsoon wind is from the south-east and the north-east trade winds are turned through 90°.

Although North America is not as big as Asia, it does create a monsoon effect, but not true monsoon winds. The winter cold fronts are part of this effect, and in summer the north-east trade winds are deflected to come from a southerly, south-

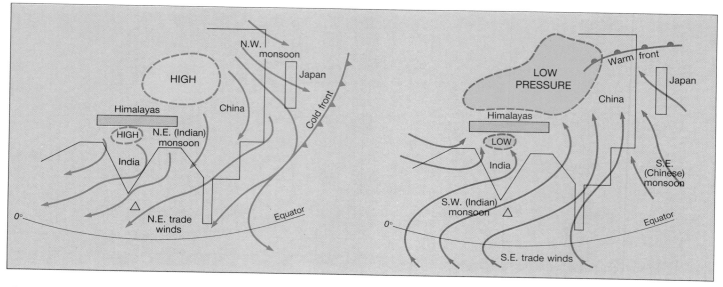

Fig. 7.16 The monsoons of Asia.

(a) Winter. Low temperatures over Asia cause cold air to drain outwards over the coastal countries. This is a 'dry' monsoon except where it crosses the sea after leaving the mainland. Then it brings rain and snow to Japan, and rain to Malaysia and Sri Lanka.

(b) Summer. High temperatures over Asia cause humid air masses to be sucked in, creating heavy rain in all coastal areas and on high ground. Note that the Himalayas are a barrier between India and the rest of Asia, but that northern India creates its own high and low pressure cells.

easterly, or easterly direction. It is a common mistake for people in the northern countries of the Caribbean to believe they are affected by the south-east trade winds in summer. They actually get the north-east trade winds, which are deflected through 90° by the monsoon effect of North America.

1 What is the intertropical convergence zone? How does it affect the trade winds?

2 Which trade winds blow in your country?

3 Is there a monsoon effect in the Caribbean? Compare it with the Asian monsoon.

Anticyclones

Cyclonic circulation is the name given to any low-pressure system that rotates anticlockwise. The opposite is an anticyclonic system, rotating clockwise.

Any cold spot will generate high pressure, and if it persists this is termed an *anticyclone*. For example, North America has a seasonal anticyclone stationary over it in winter. In summer the North Atlantic is cooler than the land and an anticyclone forms there, known as the 'Azores High'.

Some anticyclones are much more active than these large seasonal ones. They are either cold or warm types, and the latter occasionally enter the Caribbean.

Cold anticyclones are cells of cold air that travel across continents in very cold latitudes, such as Canada and the USA in winter. They are quite big features, often over 1,500km (1,000 miles) across. They create very cold, dry conditions.

The warm anticyclone is equally large and slow-moving, and once established it can persist for some time. These are only present in the northern Caribbean, usually entering from North America, and are essentially limited to the subtropical zone. The weather is clear and warm without rain, and the system is a stable one which often blocks other systems - even the trade winds may be deflected around it.

8

Major climatic types

West Indian mountains are often high enough to be at the condensation level, and so are much wetter than the lowlands. This is the cloud base at 1,200 metres (4,000 ft) on an October morning at Newcastle in Jamaica's Blue Mountains.

Most climatic types are distinguished by the range and seasonality of their temperature and rainfall. At the simplest level we can divide the Earth into broad temperature belts.

Most of the Caribbean region is in the tropical zone. This zone can also be divided up according to rainfall, so that there are subtypes for the Caribbean region.

Many attempts have been made to divide the world up into climatic regions. The system that was originally created by A.A. Miller is used in this book because it is relatively simple, and is based more on geographical than meteorological factors (Table 8.1).

Major division	Subdivision	Examples
Hot No month below 18°C (64°F)	* Equatorial * Tropical marine * Tropical continental	Amazon basin Caribbean Texas and northern Mexico
Cool temperate 1-5 months below 6°C (43°F)	Marine * Continental	Western Europe Eastern Europe and west USSR
Cold 6-9 months below 6°C (43°F)	Marine * Continental	Alaska and Scandinavia Siberia
Arctic Less than 3 months over 6°C (43°F)	Tundra Ice or polar	Arctic Canada Antarctica
Desert No significant rainfall	Hot (no month below 6°C (43°F)) Cold or mid-latitude desert (one or more months below 6°C(43°F))	Sahara Nevada/Colorado
Mountains Altitude causes a marked deviation from expected climate	Andes, Himalayas	

*All of these also have a monsoon version (See p.77 and below).

Table 8.1 Major world climatic regions

Some climate types

Equatorial

This is always hot and wet. The sun is never far from the overhead position and daily heating (known as *insolation*) is considerable. Convection currents are so strong that by early afternoon thunderstorms have usually developed. It rains almost every day, and everywhere seems permanently damp.

The resultant landscape is one of dense rain forest which both encourages the humidity and thrives on it. To drain away the water, massive river systems develop, such as the Amazon and Congo rivers.

Tropical marine

This is only slightly different in temperature to the equatorial climate. It is hot all the year round, but slightly cooler in 'winter'. The main difference is that there is a seasonal variation in rainfall, more rain falling in summer than in winter. The Caribbean and Central American lands, as well much of the Brazilian and East African coast, have this climate. All lie at the eastern end of the trade wind belt.

Tropical continental

This is like the tropical marine type, but has less rain as both temperature and humidity are too low in winter to provide any rain. In summer the moist trade winds penetrate far enough inland for the high temperatures to create convectional rain. Much of Venezuela, Brazil south of Amazonia, Central Africa, and Texas and Mexico have this climate.

Tropical monsoon

The Asiatic monsoon includes both marine and continental versions:

(a) South-east Asia, the Philippines, the East Indies and northern Australia all receive the south-east monsoon in summer, and the north-west monsoon in winter. As a result it is a wetter region than, say, the Caribbean.

(b) Further north lie South Asia and those countries which most people think of as the heart of the monsoon lands - India and its neighbours. The winds reverse completely with the seasons, the summer monsoon bringing rain to almost every part (except the deserts of Rajasthan and Pakistan), much of it triggered by the hills and mountains along the coasts of these countries. In winter the monsoon wind is cooler and drier, but as it crosses water it can still bring rain, for example to southern India and Ethiopia.

Warm temperate west coast (Mediterranean)

The temperate climates are those that have a clearly identifiable winter season. In this case temperatures may reach freezing, but do not average less than 6°C (43°F) for any month. This temperature is significant as it is the point at which most vegetation stops growing. The climate can be summed up in the simple phrase, 'cool wet winters, warm dry summers'.

The most typical area is the Mediterranean region, which in effect 'borrows' the climate of Western Europe in winter, and of North Africa in summer. Other Mediterranean - type climates exist in similar latitudes. They are equally well populated, and have one other factor in common: the grapevine grows well there - California, Chile, Cape Province in South Africa, and south-west and south-east Australia all lie between 30° and 40° north and south and are noted for the wine that they produce.

Cool temperate interior (continental)

The cool temperate climate has severe winters, and in the continental interiors they can be long, with much snow and freezing temperatures. It is these conditions that drive many tourists south to the Caribbean in winter.

Much of the central parts of North America and Europe have this type of climate. With the end of winter, temperatures rise quickly in the spring, and the summers can be very hot - hotter than the Caribbean - with heat waves of over 40°C (104°F) not uncommon. This heat generates much rain, which makes summer a time of great agricultural activity. The traditional four seasons are more well defined here than in any other climatic region.

Cold temperate interior (continental)

This is an extremely cold version of the cool temperate continental climate. Not only are winter temperatures below 6°C (43°F) for up to nine months (as opposed to five months in the cool temperate region), but actual temperatures may be much lower. In fact this region includes the coldest places on Earth, in Siberia, where Verkhoyansk averages -51°C (-59°F) in January! Summers are very short, with temperatures not usually averaging more than 15°C (60°F). Because this area is far from the sea and lacks any convectional heating of the atmosphere, the climate is mainly dry - too cold and too dry for much human activity. Most of Siberia, northern USSR and northern Canada are in this zone, but none of the southern continents extends far enough south to be included.

---

1 What are the differences between a tropical marine climate and a tropical continental climate in (a) winter (b) summer?

2 What is the climate of (a) Ontario in Canada (b) Calcutta in India, (c) Beirut?

The Caribbean climates

The Caribbean is almost entirely tropical marine in character. Only the northern Bahamas area has sufficiently mild winters to be close to being classified as warm temperate (east margin), with one month only averaging 18°C (64°F) or less, approximately every other year.

Generally, temperatures are fairly uniform throughout the region, but rainfall does vary to quite a large degree (Fig. 8.1). We can recognize three rainfall zones:

(a) Tropical marine dry - less than 1,000mm (40 in.) per year.

(b) Tropical marine wet and dry season - 1,000-2,000mm (40-80 in.) per year.

(c) Tropical marine wet - over 2,000mm (80 in.) per year.

A common and important feature of the tropical marine climate is that convectional rainfall (See p. 69) can combine with relief rainfall (p. 72), which is encouraged by the trade winds. The distinction between these three climatic subtypes is largely due to the extent to which the relevant land mass and relief of an area can generate convectional and relief rain, respectively. (See Fig. 8.2).

Tropical marine dry

This includes:

Southern Bahamas	Southern Hispaniola
Turks and Caicos Islands	Southern Puerto Rico
Southern Dutch Antilles	British Virgin Islands
South-central Jamaica	Anguilla and Barbuda

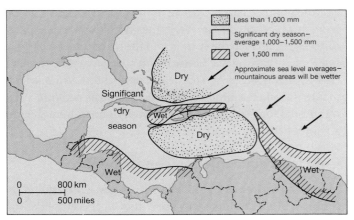

Fig. 8.1 Rainfall regions in the West Indies. *This map shows the main rainfall zones with respect to water supply. Wet zones should have no water supply problems, but dry zones will have continuing difficulty in meeting demand. The remaining areas will need to have storage systems to hold water over from wet season surpluses for dry season shortages.*

These represent two situations: small islands that are too small and flat to generate rain on their own account, and areas of larger islands that fall in the rainshadow of their mountain ranges.

We should consider this subtype as a dry variation of the normal type - the wet and dry season with up to 2,000mm (80 in.) rain.

Tropical marine wet and dry season

This includes:

Southern Jamaica
Northern Bahamas
Cuba, Haiti, northern and upland Puerto Rico
Leeward Islands
Northern Belize
Barbados
Western Trinidad and Tobago

These countries have a climate that is made up from the weather systems already described. Rain is possible all the year round, but two-thirds of it falls in the rainy summer season. A drought in the months from March to May is possible.

Tropical marine wet

This includes:

Northern and upland Jamaica
Eastern Trinidad and Tobago
Windward Islands
Guyana
Southern Belize

Dry zone		
North		
Inagua, Bahamas	685 mm (27")	
Grand Turk	750 mm (29")	
South		
Kingston, Jamaica	800 mm (32")	
Azua, Dominican Rep.	735 mm (29")	
Ponce, P. Rico	910 mm (36")	
Bonaire	510 mm (20")	
Margarita	700 mm (28")	
Wet/dry zone		
North		
Nassau, Bahamas	1270 mm (50")	
Havana, Cuba	1220 mm (48")	
Camaguey, Cuba	1420 mm (56")	
Port au Prince, Haiti	1370 mm (54")	
Santo Domingo, D. Rep.	1395 mm (55")	
Montego Bay, Jamaica	1320 mm (52")	
Grand Cayman	1295 mm (51")	
East		
Montserrat	1525 mm (60")	
St. Johns, Antigua	1250 mm (49")	
Port of Spain, Trinidad	1525 mm (60")	
Seawell, Barbados	1270 mm (50")	
Wet zone		
North		
Port Antonio, Jamaica	3430 mm (135")	
Limbe, Haiti	2060 mm (81")	
Humacao, P. Rico	2120 mm (83")	
West		
Belize airport	1855 mm (73")	
South		
Roseau, Dominica	1930 mm (76")	
St. Vincent	2185 mm (86")	
Fort de France, Martinique	2030 mm (80")	
St. Georges, Grenada	1840 mm (72")	
Tobago	2030 mm (80")	
Piarco, Trinidad	1800 mm (71")	
East Coast, Trinidad	2800 mm (110")	
Georgetown, Guyana	2300 mm (90")	
Cayenne, French Guiana	3310 mm (130")	

Fig 8.2 Selected annual totals of rainfall in the West Indies.

A high altitude, creating orographic rainfall, is the main reason for these territories being wetter than might be expected. Trinidad and Guyana are also far enough south to be on the fringe of the equatorial climatic region, and therefore are hardly ever out of the wetter area of the trade winds (See p. 77).

1 What is the total rainfall in your country for (a) November to April, (b) May to October? What climate type does this put you in?

2 Draw a *histogram* for your nearest rainfall station.

9
Soils and soil processes

Bare rock and severe gullying cut into areas of intensive farming on a hillside at Kenscoff, Haiti.

Nature and formation of soils

A mature soil can be defined as the structured layer of animal, vegetable and mineral matter at the surface of the earth. It is subject to certain internal processes.

The 'structured layer' refers to zones, known as *horizons*, within the soil. The various components are derived from the underlying parent rock, the vegetation, and animal, insect

and bacterial life. The processes are mainly those that are due to the movement of water upwards and downwards through the soil.

Most soil starts off as the weathered mantle, known as the *regolith*, lying above the bedrock. In unconsolidated sediments, such as sand or clay, it is the sediment itself that provides the

83

mineral content. However, such material does not constitute a soil. It only becomes a soil when vegetation starts to grow, and die, in it. The addition of vegetable matter, and of course water, is the first step towards an *immature soil*, or in technical terms, an *azonal* soil. It has no profile and is often very stony and shallow. Most of the Caribbean islands have such a recent geological history that many of their soils fall into this category. In The Bahamas, for example, virtually all the soils are immature; in Barbados about half the soils are immature, especially in the Scotland District and in the south and south-eastern parishes. In the more ancient and varied landscape of Trinidad, about one-fifth of the soils are immature, but this is still a high proportion of the total.

Certain factors govern the formation of a soil:

- Parent rock
- Climate - rainfall and temperature
- Biological activity - vegetation, bacteria, insects, ants, termites, worms, etc.
- Relief - mainly slope, which controls the water supply
- Time - which leads us towards maturity

Figure 9.1 sums up the way in which these factors determine the main soil groups.

Fig. 9.1 The major world soil groups.

Parent rock

In the Caribbean this is often more important than climate. Generally it is assumed that fully mature soils will develop according to the *climate*, regardless of the rock they initially formed on; that is, they are *zonal soils*. However, some soils do depend on non-climatic factors and these are the *intrazonal* soils; within this group are soils formed on limestones. Finally, immature soils are called *azonal* and are always strongly related to the underlying geology. As limestone and immaturity are so characteristic of the Caribbean, parent rock is obviously important as a soil-forming factor in the region.

Climate

As Figure 9.1 shows, climate accounts for more soils worldwide than any other factor. The group known as the *pedalfers* depend on temperature differences, while the *pedocals* vary according to rainfall. Examples of both are found in the Caribbean.

The study of soils has shown that whatever the parent rock, in the end a type of soil will develop that depends entirely on the climate, providing that good drainage is present. (Swamp, desert or limestone environments all prevent the normal movement of soil water.)

Temperature as it increases allows chemical reactions to

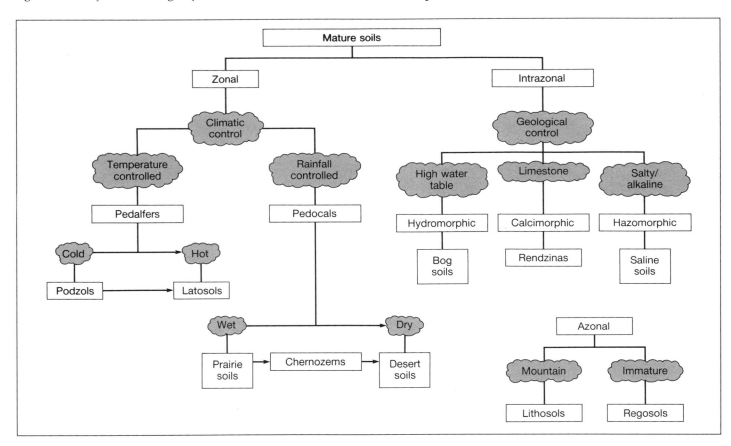

take place more rapidly. Soils in hotter climates are therefore much more uniform, as they have undergone major chemical changes. In cooler climates much more of the original materials are present. In the case of wet and dry climates, the result depends more on where the chemicals end up. With heavy rain the minerals are washed down into the lower layers, a process known as *leaching* (or *eluviation*). In drier climates evaporation causes the water to rise up through the soil by capillary action, and deposit the minerals at the surface, a process known as *illuviation*. (Capillarity is the ability of water to rise upwards through a granular material. It is the same process by which a sponge soaks up water.)

Biological activity

This in itself does not determine soil types. Vegetation is largely a product of the climate, and the degree of activity depends on the temperature and water content more than anything else. However, certain soil characteristics and processes are very dependent on biological activity:

- Vegetable content (humus)
- Mineral content
- Acidity
- Water retention (soil moisture)
- Aeration (oxygen and nitrogen content)

Relief

The slope of the land can affect the thickness of a soil because *soil creep* and other forms of erosion are at work (See p. 36). These activities greatly increase as slopes get steeper. Level areas normally have the deepest soils, whether they are in a valley floor, on a plain or on a plateau. In contrast, slopes often have a thin soil which fails to mature because the surface layers keep migrating downhill.

The movement of water within the soil is also dependent on the relief. Level areas tend to hold water longer, and may even become waterlogged. Slopes are naturally well drained, although it is this characteristic that causes the soil loss.

Relief on its own does nothing to influence the soil type. It merely allows gravity to act on it in varying ways, mainly through the agency of water which makes the soil more fluid.

Time

All of these factors depend on time in order to exert their influence. With increasing age the parent rock is decomposed, biolgical activity becomes stable, and climatic controls dominate as far as the local relief will allow.

The detailed impact of these factors is best understood by examining the characteristics of soils in general, and a selection of the best-known types.

---

1 Answer these questions about the soil near you:

   (a) What is the parent rock?

   (b) What is the average temperature and rainfall?

   (c) What is the relief?

   (d) How far down is the water table?

   (e) How young is the rock?

2 From the answers to question (1), what quantity (depth) and texture of soil would you expect? Go and dig up some soil and check your answer.

3 Is leaching good or bad? Is it evident in your soil?

Soil characteristics

Profile, hard pan, and crusts

The horizons (See p. 89) are normally visible layers of different colour, texture and content. The horizons of the topsoil are referred to as A and B, and these are often subdivided. Horizons C and D refer to the weathered and solid rock respectively. The horizons of a soil are a summary of its identity. The degree to which the horizons are developed indicate its maturity, and absent or incomplete horizons indicate deficiencies. Horizon A is basically the zone from which minerals are removed, and horizon B is the zone in which they are deposited. A mature soil will eventually be as

deep as the water table, at which point the vertical movement of water almost ceases. This means that minerals may collect in a layer just above the water table. This layer, which can become impermeable, is known as a *pan*. If clay minerals are common it is a *clay pan*; if iron is common it is known as an *iron pan*.

In drier climates nodules or layers can also collect in the soil. Water rises by capillary action, bringing with it whatever minerals are present in the parent rock, and then the water is evaporated leaving the minerals behind.

In the Caribbean this can happen in limestone sands to form *concretions* or a pan known as *caliche*. Hard pan of any type is a serious problem in many areas, for example in the European uplands where it prevents drainage and causes waterlogging and the formation of *peat bog*. The bogs of Dartmoor in England developed in this way, but in many areas, such as in the eastern Netherlands, the pan has been ploughed up and the land reclaimed.

Not all leaching of minerals is bad, however. Small amounts of valuable metals such as copper and nickel can become concetrated at the bottom of the B horizon. This has happened in the Greater Antilles on a fairly large scale, and both copper and nickel mines have been developed to exploit it.

If the climate is so dry that there is an upward movement of water carrying minerals, then the equivalent of a pan, known as *duricrust*, may form at the surface.

Texture

A soil's most obvious physical characteristics are its texture and its colour (See p. 87). The texture is initially related to the parent rock, but as the soil matures the texture depends more on the end product of physical and chemical weathering

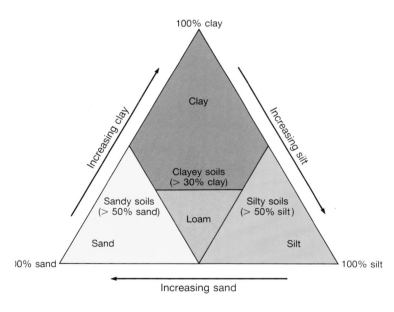

Fig. 9.2 Basic types of soil texture. Texture depends on the proportions of sand, silt and clay in the soil, which can be found by using sieves. Particle sizes: Sand 0.05-1.0 mm
Silt 0.002-0.05 mm
Clay Below 0.002 mm
(Source: Modified version of US Department of Agriculture classification of textures, which has 12 classes.)

(Fig. 9.2). In cold climates, with little chemical action, a sandy material may be the final product. For example, the common mineral quartz forms a coarse sand when it is weathered out of granite rocks in temperate climates, but in the humid tropics, for example in Guyana, it breaks down completely and dissolves away. The only residue from granite in the tropics is likely to be an insoluble clay.

In general, *sandy soils* do not hold water easily. They need a lot of humus to fill the pore spaces and reduce rapid drainage. As long as they are not too well drained they provide a good medium for plants, because they provide easy access to water and air, are quickly warmed by the sun, and are easily tilled. *Clay soils* are the opposite. They hold water, but do not release it to plant roots easily. They stay cold and do not drain well. They are sticky when wet and brick-hard when dry. Neither pure sand nor pure clay makes a good soil texture. A mixture is ideal, and is known as a *loam*. Farmers have a habit of calling any relatively good soil a loam, but technically it should contain roughly equal amounts of sand, silt and clay.

Mineral content

Much of the mineral content of a soil comes from the parent material:

Calcium (Ca) This is also referred to as *lime*, and is usually in the form of calcium carbonate. Most soils developed on limestone in the Caribbean have a high calcium content and are alkaline (See below). Calcium is useful in improving the structure of a sticky soil as it allows it to break up more easily. Chemically it helps plants absorb other minerals, but it is not itself used by the plant.

Potassium (K) This is an essential mineral for leaf development and photosynthesis in plants.

Phosphorus (P) This is equally important for root and seed formation.

Iron (Fe) This is such a common metal that it is nearly always present. It is largely responsible for the colour of the soil (See below). It is essential for many plants but may be present in a non-soluble form known as *sesquioxides*. An iron fertilizer may therefore be necessary, even on red soils, for some crops, for example mangoes.

The other minerals that may be present in the soil are sulphur, magnesium, chlorine, manganese, copper and zinc. Other elements are obtained from different sources:

Nitrogen (N) Along with oxygen and carbon, nitrogen is obtained from the air, and released into the soil through plants and humus. Many plants remove nitrogen, such as grain crops and cotton, but others, like peas and beans, can add it if their roots are ploughed back into the soil. *Soil exhaustion* is the term used to indicate a nitrogen deficiency.

N-P-K Nitrogen (N), phosphates (P), and potassium (K) are the most important chemicals in a soil. Tropical soils are nearly always deficient in these, and compound fertilizers, known as NPK fertilizers, are used to replace them. These fertilizers are invariably coded with the percentage of each nutrient. For example, 8-18-8 means:

8% nitrogen (usually an ammonia (NH_4) compound)
18% phosphates (usually phosphoric acid, P_2O_5)
8% potassium (usually potash, K_2O)

This is a concentrated general-purpose fertilizer for vegetables and fruit trees. Tomatoes might require 18-18-21.

Humus

Vegetation provides *humus*, which is the decaying vegetable matter that gives a dark colour to soil. Humus has several functions, the most important being that it returns many of the minerals the plant has used to the soil. This is why stubble and sugar cane should not be burnt, for every time this happens large amounts of nitrogen, sulphur and carbon are lost. Humus is also important in loosening up clay soils, and increasing the ability of sandy soils to hold moisture. However, the rotting process requires oxygen, as it is carried out by oxygen-using (*aerobic*) bacteria. If the soil is waterlogged, rotting takes place by non-oxygen-using (*anaerobic*) bacteria

and *peat* is formed. Peat can subsequently be used as a fertilizer if it is dried and mixed with another soil.

The distinction between fresh-water and salt-water peat should be noted. Peat formed in the lakes and bogs of Europe is well known for its use in horticulture, especially moss peat. Most peat in the Caribbean is the product of salty mangrove swamps. This peat is not nearly as valuable as its northern relative because its salt content must be washed out before it can be used, and because it is not very nutritious. Northern *Sphagnum* peat moss, which is often imported for gardening and nursery use, contains largely unrotted moss remains which rapidly break down into a rich humus when exposed to water and oxygen. Peat from lake beds is often very rich in nutrients and is valued agriculturally for vegetable, salad and fruit crops. Such areas are reclaimed by draining, and by adding lime to counteract the peat's natural acidity. In the West Indies, mangrove-swamp peat can be dredged and mixed with any limestone soil to improve it. After a season of rain it would be suitable for Irish potatoes, for example.

Colour

This is merely an indication of the mineral content, but it is much used by small farmers as a guide to fertility. In the Caribbean the following colours usually have these meanings:

Black This indicates a high humic content. For example, peat is black. A typical mixed hardwood forest (poison wood,

Black soils in St George's Valley, Barbados.

gum elemi, pigeon plum, etc.) on a limestone rock produces an organic soil consisting of dark brown/black humus mixed with limestone fragments.

In coastal sand dunes the white sand goes from white to grey to dark grey. On inspection it will be seen to consist of a mixture of white sand grains and black particles of humus. This is sometimes called *salt and pepper soil*.

White This usually indicates that a white parent material is dominant. Very thin soils often show up white on aerial photographs. Alternatively it may indicate salt and the formation of an alkaline crust.

Red This is very common and is associated with laterite and bauxite lands in Jamaica, Haiti and the Dominican Republic. It indicates a high percentage of insoluble iron, and a probably sterile clay soil. In some countries this is mistakenly believed to be a nutritious soil because of its ability to grow pineapples which will not grow on soils containing calcium. Pineapples simply like acidic soils, and red lateritic soils are so leached that all the calcium has been washed out, along with all the other minerals.

Yellow This also indicates iron, but in a different form due to poor drainage. The red formed by oxidation (rusting) is restricted, and the iron sesquioxide combines with water to give a yellow colour.

Acidity and alkalinity (pH)

This is measured on a scale from 1 to 14, of which 7 is neutral. Soil is usually in the range 5-9, of which 5-7 is acid and 7-9 alkaline. Any tendency to extreme acid or alkali conditions is generally not good for plants. Poorly drained soils tend to be acidic; limestone soils are always alkaline. Crushed limestone can be added to acidic soils, and peat to alkaline soils.

---

1 What causes hardpan in a soil, and what problems does it create?

2 Why is texture important in soils?

3 Where does humus come from? How can you add it to the soil? What is *mulching*? What is *compost*? How do these help?

4 What is the significance of colour in a soil?

Soil types

In detail there are numerous soil types for even the simplest geographical regions. For instance, there are nine *associations* for the coral cap of Barbados:

> '... an association is a group of soils developed from the parent material within one climatic area and representing the range of profile types produced as a result of differences in drainage.'

(Source: *Soil and Land Use Survey of Barbados*, K.C. Vernon and D.M Carroll, U.W.I. Trinidad, 1966, p.13.)

Each association is subdivided into several types, giving a total of 86 soils altogether. The much smaller Scotland District has been assigned another 80 types, giving a total of 166 types, one for every square mile of the island! Trinidad has been assigned over 200 soil types.

It is clearly not possible to identify all of these. For most countries there are fewer than 10 easily distinguishable soil groups which with a little practice can be easily recognized. All soils should be analysed by a soil laboratory before any form of agriculture takes place, and it is at this stage that the minor characteristics of the soil can be identified.

The following major soil types are described here because they are fairly widespread and illustrate the most important soil processes. They include those soils found in the Caribbean (See Figs 9.3, 9.4).

Podzols

These are the classic soils of cool humid areas. They are not found in the tropics, and are most common in places with a cold winter and rain all the year round. Most of northern Europe, northern Asia and Canada have podzolic soils.

The dominant process in the formation of podzols is leaching by acidic soil water. This is *podzolization*. As the climate is cold, organic matter is slow to decompose and many organic acids are absorbed by the percolating rainwater. The top is often a thickly matted layer of only partly rotted organic matter. As the water moves down through the soil it does two things:

1 Dissolves and carries away any salts or alkalis in the upper layers.

2 Washes out the clay particles.

Both are carried down into the B horizon where the concentrations are high enough to cause the salts to precipitate out. The results are also twofold:

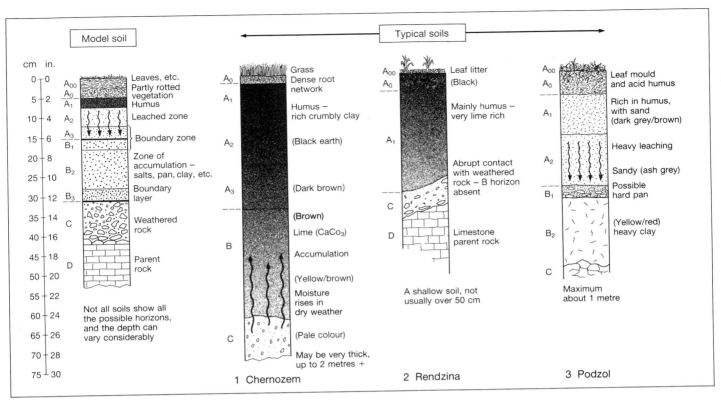

Fig. 9.3 Soil profiles.

1 The A horizon is clay-free and develops a *whitish* or *ash-grey colour* because of the removal of the iron oxide and humus. Because there is no clay left it is coarse and sandy.

2 The B horizon is increasingly clayey and if enough oxides are deposited a *hard pan* may form. If iron oxide is included a rusty red colour will be present at this level (See Fig. 9.4).

Podzols are not very good soils and are mostly associated with the coniferous forest belt. Conifers do not need minerals such as potassium, phosphorus and calcium, so absence of these through leaching is not a problem.

Chernozems

These are another major group of soils, but they are confined to the continental interiors and are not as widespread as the podzols. The two great areas of chernozem soils are the Great Plains of North America and the Russian Steppes. They support natural temperate grassland and are much farmed for cereal-growing. They also occur in parts of Argentina and Australia, but never in the Caribbean. They are very closely related to a climate that is relatively arid with hot summers and cold winters.

The soil itself is noted for its black colour and is often referred to as a *black earth*, which lies below a protective layer of matted and compacted grass.

The black A horizon is that colour because of the high percentage of humus. Rainfall is low, so the humus is not leached out. Lower down in the B horizon the colour is lightish-brown with concentrations of calcium carbonate. The drier it is the higher up this *lime horizon* is found: about 60cm (2 ft) down in dry areas, but as much as 150cm (5 ft) down with higher rainfall.

These soils are dry and crumbly with large amounts of humus, so they are very vulnerable to wind erosion if the natural grass cover is removed. For this reason, and the unreliability of the rainfall, they are difficult to farm, but their considerable natural fertility has led to their extensive use for wheat-growing, especially using dry-farming techniques (See p.146).

Latosols

These are the soils of the tropical wet areas and they are widespread in the Caribbean, except in the drier areas. For instance, about 20% of Trinidad's soils are latosols, most being found in the Northern Range, and the red soils of upland Barbados are also of a latosol type - red/brown and yellow/brown clay soils. On a worldwide scale they are most abundant in the hottest and wettest areas - the equatorial regions - but they also extend into the tropical wet/dry season areas. As Fig. 9.3 shows, this includes most of West, Central

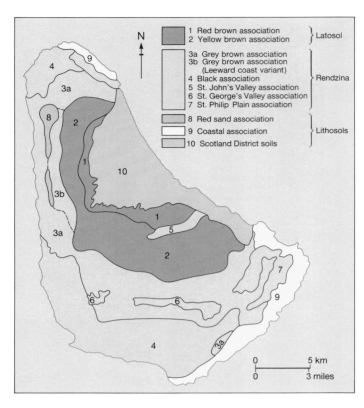

Fig. 9.4 The soil types of Barbados.

Map legend:

1 Red brown association
2 Yellow brown association } Latosol

3a Grey brown association
3b Grey brown association (Leeward coast variant)
4 Black association
5 St. John's Valley association
6 St. George's Valley association
7 St. Philip Plain association } Rendzina

8 Red sand association

9 Coastal association } Lithosols

10 Scotland District soils

and East Africa, Central and South America, and South and South-east Asia.

The upper layers of these soils consist of a deep red clay which gradually changes to a dark grey or bluish colour with depth. This change in colour occurs as the water table is reached and oxidation can no longer take place. The usual horizons are not visible, and the changes are gradual. The process is basically one of extreme leaching so that only the most chemically inert minerals are left behind. This process is known as *laterization*, and the clay is *laterite* (See p. 86). Great depths of this soil are known.

Laterites have virtually no humus or minerals other than the insoluble oxides of iron and aluminium that are left behind. As a result they are infertile. Their texture is clayey, wet and sticky in the wet season, brick-hard in the dry season. In fact the name 'laterite' means 'brick' (Latin *later* = brick), and in India it is common to see large pits dug in the ground, sometimes with simple ovens nearby to bake the clay into bricks, although they can simply be left to dry in the open air.

The laterization process is a process of concentration of the insoluble minerals, and *bauxite* in particular is formed in this way. Bauxite is simply laterite with a higher than average

Black volcanic rocks (basaltic) produce a black sand, such as here at Ste Marie on Martinique.

aluminium hydroxide content. Iron and manganese can also be formed in this way, and all are present in Guyana, Suriname and French Guiana (See p. 109).

Rendzinas

These are all intrazonal soils which forms on limestones. In an immature form they are widespread in the Caribbean, and the lowland black and grey-brown soils of Barbados have been called rendzinas.

However, true rendzinas are less common, only accounting for 2% of Trinidad's surface for example. On a worldwide scale their distribution depends on the occurrence of limestone, and they are mainly limited to the subtropical areas. The most famous example is the Black Belt of Alabama, a very fertile area that was once famous for cotton, but most Mediterranean climates, like those in California and Italy, have rendzinas. A mature rendzina is one that is very dark brown or black and contains calcium carbonate throughout its pro-

file. The C and D horizons are entirely limestone, and the softer it is the more rapidly the soil develops. If there is too much rain the free drainage of limestone areas allows the humus to be carried away, so the truly tropical wet areas do not develop a mature rendzina soil.

Many of the 'black land' leafmould soils of the limestone lands of the northern Caribbean can be described as immature rendzinas. They are simply shallow layers of humus and rotting vegetation, covering a rugged, potholed limestone bedrock, which is crumbling away within 30cm (12 in.) of the surface.

---

1   According to Fig. 9.3, what type of climate is associated with podzols?

2   What is the importance of vegetation in a chernozem?

3   Describe the soils found on limestones.

Soil erosion

Soil erosion is a natural process that can never be stopped completely. The aim must be to keep it under control and replace the losses. Extreme climatic events like floods or drought, or bad land management, can cause increased erosion and serious soil losses. Haiti is the most often quoted example in the Caribbean, but soil erosion is widespread. The main types of erosion are described below.

Gullying   This is caused by excessive runoff of water on sloping land. It is most likely to happen where there is a sudden release of water, as in tropical storms. The Haitian hillsides and the Scotland District of Barbados are well-studied examples, but all areas with marked wet and dry seasons suffer from it, for example the Southern Appalachians and the Tennessee Valley. Snow meltwaters also cause this kind of flooding, typified by the numerous ravines of the Badlands of South Dakota.

Sheet erosion   This is more likely on gently sloping or even flat land where the water is less likely to be channelled along a particular course. It is particularly damaging where it removes the topsoil from a very large area. West African countries and the monsoon areas of Asia are particularly vulnerable. The Caribbean is also affected locally, for example in the deforested areas of Haiti and the Dominican Republic, and in other places where shifting cultivation is practised.

Wind erosion   All light soils (chernozems, rendzinas, sandy soils, etc.) are at risk when the natural vegetation is removed,

or after harvest. Much of the Caribbean sugar cane lands are protected by the practice of ratooning, but cane-burning, or the more recent diversification to other crops, has made them much more vulnerable.

The Dust Bowl of the dry high plains of the United States was created by the removal of the grassland and the planting of wheat and other grains which only covered the ground for three or four months of the year. The level land allowed high winds to sweep away millions of tonnes of soil, and much of the land had to be abandoned.

Land reclaimed from bauxite mining at Lydford, Jamaica, makes a good pasture for a herd of cows.

Conservation measures

The causes of soil erosion; and the ways of preventing erosion or improving land that has already been eroded, are listed in Table 9.1.

Table 9.1 The causes of erosion and measures for conservation

Causes of erosion	Conservation measures
Natural • Steep slopes • Occasional torrential rain • High winds • Lack of vegetation *Human* • Removal of grass cover from flat land • Removal of forests from slopes • Land left fallow between crops • Overgrazing, especially by goats, which graze right down to the roots of plants • Farming of dry land • Shifting cultivation practices (slash and burn) which destroy the vegetation and the soil structure • Bad farming practices: ploughing and planting in rows that encourage gullying; and inadequate manmade drainage	• Reafforestation of hills and slopes • Brushwood dams across gulleys; infilling of gulleys; establishing lined drainage channels • Terracing of hillsides, e.g. ricefields of South-east Asia • Contour ploughing - similar to terracing, but less effective • Strip-cropping: avoiding large areas of bare soil by growing different crops side by side, e.g. bananas with eddoes, citrus with papaya • Smaller fields (similar to strip-cropping) • Conversion of crop land to pasture • Crop rotations to avoid exposed fallow land • Controlled animal grazing (especially of goats) • Planting of shelter-belts of trees to reduce the impact of wind

The Scotland District of Barbados – a case study in conservation

Gullying and landslides have been a problem in the Scotland District of Barbados since the first days of settlement. Systematic erosion control began in the 1940s, and a Soil Conservation Service was set up in 1957. In the 1960s major successes were achieved, and the area is now a model for future reclamation and conservation.

Some of the problems of the region were due to the geology, to road locations and village situations. The two causes most relevant to the Caribbean as a whole are *excessive rainfall* and *poor agricultural techniques*.

Reclamation of land eroded by excessive rainfall

Over 400 ha (1,000 acres) of rough ground were reshaped by bulldozers and returned to cultivation. This was done by reducing the slope and filling in the gullies. The most effective method was to create terraces 4-9 m (15-30 ft) wide, sloping at only 2° or less. This was too gentle a slope to encourage further gullying. In order to allow the rainfall to drain away, drainage channels were built with weirs to reduce the gradient. By 1967 50km (30 miles) of terraces had been constructed.

Reclamation of land eroded as a result of poor agricultural techniques

By the eighteenth century Barbadians had discovered the dangers of planting sugar cane in straight lines or furrows, and switched to the well-known 'can hole system', which was also used in other islands, especially St Kitts. These were so successful that furrows died out until quite recent times, when tractors began to be used for ploughing.

Farmers in the Scotland District prefer to plough their furrows up and down the slope because:

- tractor drivers find it harder to plough across the slope;

- ploughing across the slope takes longer and tractors need more maintenance;

- harvesting is more difficult.

However, contour ploughing can hold water in the soil and encourage landslips, which have also occurred.

The terracing technique described above has been a satisfactory solution to this problem, although the Conservation Service has to maintain the terraces.

Overgrazing has been the other main problem, mainly by sheep and goats. Reclamation starts with the exclusion of livestock, although this is a problem because it creates hardship for the farmers who lose their pasture. However, much land has had to be abandoned owing to overgrazing, so reclamation is obviously a wise thing to do. In future all animals will have to be controlled and grazing lands used only under supervision. The next stage in many cases is afforestation, usually with species yielding construction timber or fence posts, or in some cases fruit trees.

Further study of the Scotland District can be made by reading Bulletins 49 (1967) and 53 (1970) by E.R. St J. Cumberbatch, published by the Barbados Ministry of Agriculture.

---

1 What are the main types of soil erosion? Give a local example for each type.

2 Why are slopes particularly liable to suffer from soil erosion?

3 How does climate affect soil erosion?

4 What can be done to prevent gully erosion?

5 If there are gullies, what can be done to remove them?

6 For the crops grown in your country, say what is good and/or bad about each one as far as soil erosion is concerned.

Previously eroded hillsides can be reshaped by bulldozing. Proper drainage (centre) prevents future erosion. Cherry Tree Hill, Barbados.

10

Vegetation and forestry resources

Commercial Caribbean pine trees in Grand Bahama, with an understorey of Sabal palmetto. The wide avenue between the trees is a fire-break.

When the vegetation of a region has fully adapted to the local conditions, and is not changing in density or species, it is known as a *climax vegetation*. This is the *natural* or *primary vegetation*, and it is mainly a response to the climate of a place (Fig. 10.1).

If this vegetation is removed, it will be a long time before it re-establishes itself, perhaps several hundred years in the tropics. The vegetation that develops in the meantime is known as the *secondary vegetation*. In much of the Caribbean it is the secondary vegetation that we are seeing today. The natural or primary vegetation that is present has survived only because it was too inaccessible - as in central and southern Guyana, Suriname and French Guiana where it was too far away from the coastal settlements - or where it was too mountainous, as in a few areas of the Dominican Republic, Cuba and Jamaica.

In many countries much of the forest has gone for ever - nearly 100% in Barbados and 50% in Trinidad - although in Guyana as much as 80% still remains.

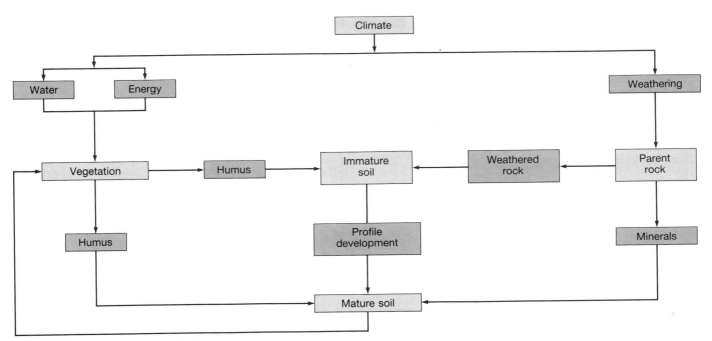

Fig. 10.1 Climate, vegetation and soil.

The major formations of natural vegetation

In general the three major formations of natural vegetation - *forests*, *grasslands* and *deserts* - are distributed according to variations in rainfall (Table 10.1). As rainfall decreases the species get smaller, the density decreases, and trees in particular become stunted or appear in bush form. Many botanists believe that grasslands are not a climax vegetation, but occupy areas that were once forested. The trees were removed, sometimes by deliberate burning, and were replaced by grazing animals.

Forests

Equatorial rain forest - selvas

Tropical monsoon forest - jungle

Tropical thorn forest

Evergreen forest - Mediterranean type

Temperature forest - deciduous

Coniferous forest - taiga

Grassland

Tropical grassland - savanna, llanos, campos

Temperate grassland - prairies, plains, steppes, pampas, veldt

Arctic grassland - tundra

Deserts

Hot deserts - Sahara, Kalahari, Australian, Atacama

Cold deserts - Gobi, Colorado, Patagonian

Ice deserts - Greenland and Antarctica

Table 10.1 *Major formations of natural vegetation, with examples and common names.*

Rain forest on the flanks of Mt Pelée, Martinique.

Factors affecting vegetation type

Rainfall This is the most important factor affecting vegetation type. However the value of the rainfall also depends on the accompanying temperature: the hotter the climate, the greater the evaporation and transpiration (See p. 68). For instance, in cold latitudes a rainfall of 25 mm (10 in.) is enough to sustain a coniferous forest but in the tropics this would create a semi-desert.

Just as important is the *seasonal distribution* of the rainfall, an even distribution being more favourable to plant growth. Long dry seasons are the main reasons for grasslands, and in the Caribbean region they account for much of the scrub vegetation.

Temperature This is important for its effect on the *type* of vegetation, the *size* of plants, and their *rates of growth*. For example, the cold latitudes are noted for coniferous forests, the temperate latitudes for deciduous forests, and the hotter regions for evergreen forests.

Trees need a growing season of at least three months, and few plants can grow in average daily temperatures of under 6°C (43°F). This is equivalent to the 10°C (50°F) July isotherm on world rainfall maps, and marks the boundary between the taiga and the tundra. It is also for this reason that the world's climates are subdivided according to the 6°C (43°F) monthly temperature boundary (See p. 80).

Altitude Temperatures decrease with altitude, and rainfall increases. As a result, mountains have their own vegetational zones.

Soils These are much less important than might be thought, because they are formed by the climate and the vegetation itself. However, they may be a factor locally, especially when the soils are immature (See p.84), because they may lack certain qualities that the local vegetation normally requires. Examples are best seen in countries like Germany or Great Britain which would naturally have a mature deciduous forest throughout. In these countries sandy soils instead support conifers or moorland, and thin limestone soils are limited to grassland - the 'downs' of England, for example.

---

1 What is evapotranspiration?

2 How does temperature affect the value of rainfall?

3 What are the critical temperatures for plant life? Why are they critical?

4 What are the effects of altitude on climate? How is vegetation affected?

Selected vegetation types

Equatorial (rain) forest

These forests are found where there are hot, wet climatic conditions. The rain forest is noted for the numerous different species present in it, many of them hardwoods, but all mixed up. Over 2,500 tree species have been recorded in Amazonia, with 40,000 other plants. Some of the better-known varieties which have an economic value include rubber, brazil nut tree, cacao, mahogany (Madeira), oil palm, ebony, silk cotton and rosewood.

The trees themselves are often very tall - over 30 metres (100 ft) - and form a canopy well above the jungle floor, which reduces the amount of daylight reaching the ground, and therefore limits the growth of other plants in the lower layers of vegetation. The ground is covered with rotting vegetation which encourages fungi, mosses, orchids, air plants and ferns. Characteristics of these plants include leathery leaves to withstand the heat, and a continual rather than seasonal leaf fall. Many trees have buttress roots, and lianas and other creepers hang from the upper limbs and encircle the trunks.

In the Caribbean the rain forest is fairly well represented between Hispaniola and the Guianas in those areas where rainfall is over 2,000 mm (80 in.): on the wetter lowlands of the Guianas in the south; in southern Belize in the west; in the Great Antilles in the north; and on the windward slopes of the smaller volcanic islands in the east. The higher parts of the mountains - certainly those over 600 metres (2,000 ft) - do not have rain forest owing to the effect of altitude on temperature. Above this level is a mountain vegetation with shorter trees, fewer species, and more ferns.

In Trinidad the *mora*, a useful commercial tree, is most unusual in being a homogeneous species (that is, it is not mixed up with others), and over 80,000 ha (200,000 acres) of mora forest exist.

Coniferous forest (taiga)

This is the natural forest of the cold temperate climate, with many well-known species like larch, fir, spruce, pine and birch in uniform stands for thousands of square kilometres across Canada, Scandinavia and the northern USSR.

These trees are straight and tall, and grow close together. Most of the foliage is near the top, and there is little undergrowth. The most characteristic adaptation is reduction of the leaves to needles, a response to the need to keep transpiration to a minimum. The streamlined shape of both the needles and the trees allows them to resist wind and shed snow in the severe winter. These trees are the source of most the world's softwood timbers used for construction, and for pulp used to produce paper.

Obviously the Caribbean does not have the right climate for coniferous forest, but one species, the Caribbean pine, an export of this region, has adapted itself to Caribbean conditions (Fig. 10.2). It is only found in the northern Caribbean, in the northern Bahamas where it has often been cut for export, in Cuba (hence the name Isle of Pines), northern Belize and parts of the Dominican Republic. It has however been used widely in reafforestation projects as far south as Guyana (See p. 103).

It should be noted that the casuarina, also known as the Australian pine, is not a pine tree or a conifer, although it looks rather like one. The species was introduced to the Caribbean from Australia.

Fig 10.2 The Caribbean pine in The Bahamas.

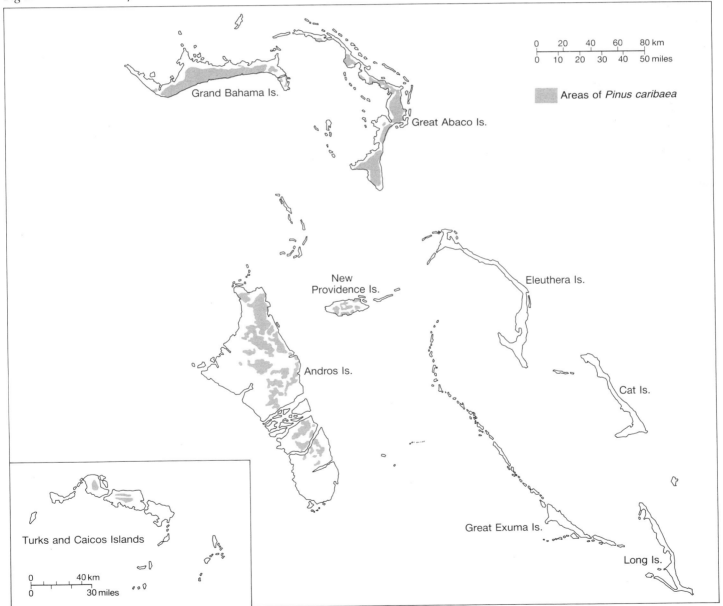

97

Coniferous forest (taiga) in the Begna Valley of Norway.

Tropical grassland (savanna)

On a worldwide scale the savanna lands lie either side of the equatorial forests, in the climatic zone of the tropical continental region. Here it is too dry for trees to survive under present conditions, although they are to be found in scattered locations throughout the grassland.

The long dry season - anything from five to eight months - is the important factor in preventing tree growth. Annual rainfall might be quite high, 1,000-1,500 mm (40-60in.) in the savannas of parts of West and East Africa, but the long dry season inhibits tree growth. The grass itself is long and tough, such as elephant grass which reaches a height of 5 metres (15 ft) in the wetter parts. Nearer the drier margins, such as in Ethiopia, the grass is shorter and grows in tufts. Guinea grass, which has been introduced widely into the Caribbean as a fodder, is a typical savanna grass, as is Seymour grass which is a native type. The Rupununi Savanna in Guyana is well known, but there are other savanna lands in the Caribbean region, notably in the Greater Antilles.

West Indian savanna lands

The Rupununi savannas

These cover about 12,000km² (4,500 sq. miles) and are divided into northern and southern parts by the Kanuku Mountains. The southern savannas are hillier, but both areas receive 1,750-2,000 mm (70-80 in.) of rain a year, and consist of rolling hills covered with grassland and studded with clumps of trees.

Cuba

The plains of Las Villas and Camagüey cover most of central Cuba. The Arawak word *sabana*, meaning 'treeless land', is widely used in these areas - there are 10 places named La Sabana, and 36 other towns with similar names, such as Sabanalamar and Sabanilla. The Cubans recognize several different types of savanna:

- humid sandy savanna with clumps of Sabal Palmetto
- Royal Palm and Ceiba savannas
- Serpentine savannas, often waterlogged.

Mostly these are areas where soil conditions prevent tree development, and rainfall is about 1,250-1,500 mm (50-60 in.).

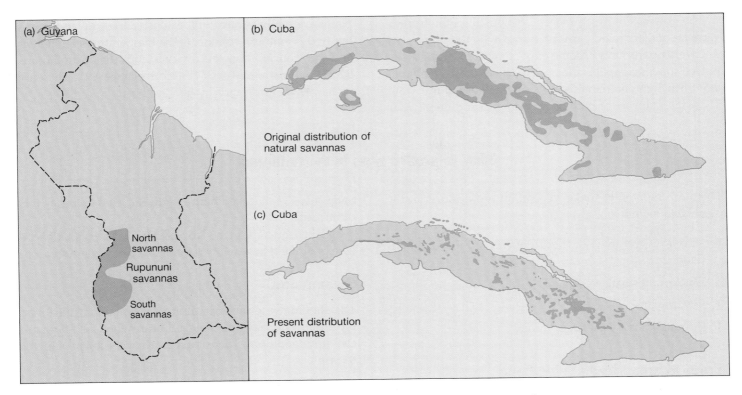

Fig. 10.3 Caribbean savannas.

(a) Guyana.

(b) Cuba - original distribution of natural savannas.

(c) Cuba - present distribution of savannas.

The original natural savannas of Cuba have been much reduced through cultivation of sugar, planting of pines, and by erosion. This applies especially to western and central Cuba (compare the map, above and below). In the east much remains, although it is more fragmented than originally. In some areas forest clearance has created new savannas.

Although rather scattered, in total they add up to a greater area than the savanna lands in Guyana.

Haiti, the Dominican Republic and Puerto Rico
There are a number of dry and moist savannas in the coastal and upland areas, especially on the southern side of the Dominican Republic, for example around the capital of Santo Domingo, and in the upland river basins such as the Ville de San Juan.

Trinidad
South of the Northern Range lie the flooded or water savannas of the upper Caroni and Orapuche Rivers, and the Aripo savanna which closely resembles the nearby *llanos* of Venezuela. The Llanos is one of the world's great savannas covering over 400,000km² (150,000 sq. miles) in the Orinoco basin.

Temperate grassland

The temperate grasslands, known as plains, prairies, pampas, steppes or veldt, are located, like the savannas, in the interiors of the continents where the rainfall is insufficient to sustain forest growth. As with the tropical grasslands, it is the dry season that is the problem in restricting a fuller development of vegetation. Usually these grasslands receive less than 500 mm (20 in.) of rain a year. In the USA, where the plains are extensive, the wetter eastern portion is known as the long grass prairie and the drier western part is called the short grass prairie.

Rain clouds and rain falling over the rain forest of Morne Watt, Dominica.

The grasses are much more nutritious than the tropical varieties and are widely used for grazing in the drier areas. The wetter parts have become major grain-producing areas. In fact, so widespread is the human use of these grasslands that virtually none remains in its original, or natural, state. The winter climate of both North America and the Russian plains is usually severe, with extensive freezing and snow, but in the southern continents the temperatures are higher and snow uncommon. It is on such lands that the infamous 'Dust Bowl' of the mid-west USA formed (See p.91). There are no temperate grasslands in the Caribbean.

Other vegetation types in the Caribbean

There are four other major vegetation types found in the Caribbean region:

1   Tropical (evergreen and deciduous) broad-leaved woodland

2   Thorn and shrub woodland

3   Swampland

4   Mountain (montane) vegetation

Tropical broad-leaved woodland

The striking difference between this type and the rain forest is the loss of leaves in the cool dry season. The trees do not lose all their leaves, but they have far fewer, and there is no significant new growth. In the wet season this forest looks much more impressive. Virtually all the wooded areas receiving between 750 and 2,000 mm (30 and 80 in.) a year fall into this category. The trees are often the same as those found in the rain forest, such as mahogany, and as those found in the savannas, such as the palmetto, but heights do not go much over 10 metres (30 ft). Much of the secondary vegetation is of this type as well, even in the very wet areas. Undergrowth is well developed and in the drier areas especially is very thorny. Some of the most characteristic species are mastic, gum elemi, pigeon plum, palmetto, poison wood and sea grape.

This is the natural vegetation of the central Bahamas and it is widespread in the areas of the Greater Antilles and the eastern Caribbean that have marked wet and dry seasons.

Thorn and shrub forest

Once the rainfall is as low as 750 mm (30 in.), plants have to be adapted in some way to withstand the shortage of water. Many of the plants of the broad-leaved woodland grow here in stunted or bush forms, such as the sea grape, but the palmetto is absent and in the driest areas cactus is common. Trees include rams horn, cinnecord and brasiletto. Without the presence of a canopy the ground cover is dense and thorny, although in the driest areas, such as parts of the Turks and Caicos Islands, southern Puerto Rico and Curaçao, it is quite sparse.

All these areas lie in the Tropical Marine Dry climatic type (See p. 81), and have a low rainfall and a dry winter season.

Swampland

This should be seen as a variation of the equatorial rain forest type, and is present in the Caribbean wherever there are swampy conditions. There is a typical succession of plants in these areas:

wettest - red mangrove
         - black mangrove
         - white mangrove
         - buttonwood
driest   - sabal palmetto

All of these have special adaptations such as aerial roots (red mangrove), breathing tubes or *pneumatophores* (black mangrove), and various filters on the leaves to extract salt from the water they need.

Other plants are present, such as sedges - like saw-grass - and bullrushes, but the swampland vegetation has the least number of species. Wherever there is a flooded coastal zone, or brackish or salty lakes, these plants will be found. It is doubtful if there is any country in the Caribbean that does not have a mangrove swamp. There are some very large swamps in Belize, Guyana and Cuba.

All mangrove swamps are temporary, because they are great reclaimers of flooded lands. In coastal areas the mangroves trap material in their dense network of stilt-like roots, and every change of the tide brings in more debris. The mangroves and other plants, and the various swamp fauna that live here also provide material to build up and reclaim the peaty floor (See p. 87). For instance, mangrove leaves provide vegetable matter for peat, and radiolaria (a pinhead-size shelly organism) live off the dead leaves. When they die they help to form a sandy sediment. Algae, like batophora (a green club-shaped alga about 1 cm long), can form an algal mat which traps tidal mud, brought from nearby tidal creeks or rivers or from offshore. Coastal reclamation under these conditions is continuous and can be rapid. Brackish lakes are similarly affected. They soon develop a fringe of mangroves, then a few islands appear, and in time the lake becomes a swamp. The swamp builds up until in the dry season it starts to dry out, and this allows a greater variety of plants to develop, such as palmetto, sedges and bullrushes, which also signify the changeover to freshwater conditions. In some parts of the Caribbean the final stage of reclamation has been speeded up by human activity, such as on New Providence Island where an extensive area of swamp behind the Cable Beach Hotel has been taken over for domestic housing, a golf course, and more recently by a canalized village.

Mountain woodlands and moorland

Mountain vegetation is much more variable than any other type. This is because it is usually the most inaccessible, and therefore contains a high degree of *indigenous* species (species native to that land, not imported). Almost every mountain has one or more zones above the rain forest that fall into this category. Jamaica's Blue Mountains and John Crow Mountains probably still have the original forest cover, which includes blue mahoe, ironwood, yucca, juniper, cedar and bloodwood trees. In areas affected by people, bamboo is now

very common on the upper slopes and can be seen in Jamaica, Martinique and Trinidad.

The highest areas of all begin to lose their trees, and those that survive are stunted and twisted owing to high winds and exposure. For this reason such vegetation is given the name *elfin woodland*. As it is still very wet, tree ferns - also stunted - and mosses are abundant, along with lichens which in places cover everything. These conditions are only found on the highest ranges - Jamaica's Blue Mountains, Guadeloupe's Soufrière, and Belize's Maya Mountains, for instance. Two trees that are found in the highest regions are charianthus and didymopamax.

---

1 Describe the kind of vegetation changes you would notice going from sea level to 3,000 metres (10,000 ft) in the Greater Antilles.

2 What is the importance of the taiga commercially, and how does the Caribbean benefit from it?

3 Locate the plains, prairies, pampas, selvas and veldt on a world map. What do they have in common?

Deforestation and its consequences

Throughout the Caribbean, deforestation has been practised since the first days of settlement, and is probably going on at a faster rate today than ever before. However, we must not assume that this is necessarily a bad thing, as there are many ways in which the land can be put to a more economic use. Barbados would hardly be the prosperous country it is today if it still had its forest, and Dominica, which is still heavily forested, gets very little benefit from its many trees (See p. 104).

There are, though, many areas which have been deforested in such a way that the environment has been damaged, and is now *less* valuable than it would have been. Unfortunately there are some extreme cases in the Caribbean, for example in Haiti, northern Belize, parts of coastal Guyana, and in much of the upland areas of the Dominican Republic. Deforestation can be due to several factors:

Organized cultivation Large areas of lowland have been cleared for sugar cane, as in Trinidad, Barbados, Guyana and Jamaica. Hillier areas have been stripped and planted with tree or bush crops, such as coffee in the Greater Antilles, citrus in Trinidad and Jamaica, cocoa in Trinidad and Grenada, and so on.

Slash-and-burn cultivation Many areas have been ruined in this way. Jamaica actually uses the term 'ruinate' to describe abandoned agricultural land, although not all of these were of the slash-and-burn type. Slash-and-burn cultivation is still widely practised in Haiti and the Dominican Republic, Belize and Guyana. Much of the erosion of hillsides in these countries is due to the exposure of the soil to tropical rain.

Firewood Collecting is widespread in countries with large rural populations, notably Guyana, Haiti and the Dominican Republic. Often immature trees or those that would be valuable for other uses are destroyed. The situation is so serious in the Dominican Republic that firewood cutting is banned without a licence, but in fact the ban is largely ignored.

Timber cutting This need not result in the loss of the forest if seed trees are left behind, and only mature trees cut. This has been the practice in The Bahamas and much of Guyana, Trinidad and Belize in modern times. However, in the past, a 'robber economy' of felling all the valuable trees, especially logwood, mahogany and greenheart, has been practised with no thought for the future.

Built-up areas Large cities like Kingston and Havana take up

Farming on steep slopes encourages soil erosion, like this area of the Maraval valley, Trinidad.

a considerable amount of land, as do tourist resorts and golf courses. These uses of land are typical of the modern West Indies.

There is no simple answer to management of the Caribbean's forests. The mixed broad-leaf and rain forests in total have little value, although they contain valuable trees. Only Guyana is capable of sustaining a major export industry, and this is particularly dependent on greenheart, which is used for outdoor construction and especially for use in and near sea water. This species alone accounts for half of Guyana's production, the rest being made up of wallaba (for posts and telephone poles), mora and crabwood.

The problems faced by *Guyana* are typical of those found in the region:

- Most of the world's demand is for softwoods for pulp, and for processed wood such as plywood and chipboard.
- Hardwoods are produced more economically from large resources that are still untapped in places like the Congo, Papua New Guinea and Indonesia.
- Transport from the interior of Guyana to the coast is very difficult. Roads and railways are enormously expensive and few extend more than 150km (100 miles) from the coast. Rivers are prone to flooding and have rapids and waterfalls.
- Export is restricted to relatively small ships owing to the presence of offshore bars at the mouths of the rivers.
- The best trees have been taken in many areas, and both the quality and quantity of these left is often poor.
- Power for sawmills is limited, and the capital cost for these is high. Also, the local market is not big enough to support a large modern sawmill.

Although forestry is not a hopeless case in the Caribbean, it does have a very limited role. Its most profitable use now is to provide local timber, instead of expensive imported timber, for fuel, building and handicrafts. Up until the 1950s about 75% of Belize's export income came from timber. It is much less today, but much better managed. About 400,000 ha (1 million acres) are reserved for forestry use and about 25,000 m³ (883,000 cu. ft) were produced in 1983, and 45% of it, worth US$1.3 m, was exported. For 1987 Guyana earned about US$4 m. These are the two main exporters in the West Indies at present. Suriname did have a plywood factory some years ago, and was a significant exporter, but the factory has now closed.

Conservation and reafforestation

Conservation is necessary to prevent loss of soil, loss of timber, and to maintain water supplies. In many countries, notably The Bahamas, Jamaica and Trinidad and Tobago, the government has taken over ownership of most of the forestry land. Trinidad and Jamaica in particular have been successful in implementing conservation policies. In some countries even more extreme measures are necessary, such as in Thailand, where the government banned logging throughout the country in 1989, after flooding and mudslides killed 350 people. Trinidad has divided its forests into *forest reserves*, which must remain as forest for ever unless an Act of Parliament releases them for some other purpose. Out of about 130,000 ha (325,000 acres) of reserves in Trinidad and Tobago, fewer than 4,000 ha (10,000 acres) have been lost, mainly to agriculture, in the last 30 years. The remaining State Forest covers some 90,000 ha

(225,000 acres) and this is not protected in the same way. As a result the loss is much greater, with over 20,000 ha (50,000 acres) being lost in the last 20 years, about half to agriculture. Private forests only account for 10,000 ha (25,000 acres). Clearly, government protection is necessary. One reason is that replanting forest is very expensive and no economic returns are likely for a number of years. Obviously only governments and large corporations have the capital to do this.

In addition to commercial forestry, the government in Trinidad and Tobago has set aside more than 16,000 ha (40,000 acres) of its forest reserves as nature reserves, wildlife sanctuaries and national parks, mainly for educational and recreational purposes. The Caroni Swamp Wildlife Sanctuary is a good example, with thousands of visitors every year (Fig. 10.4).

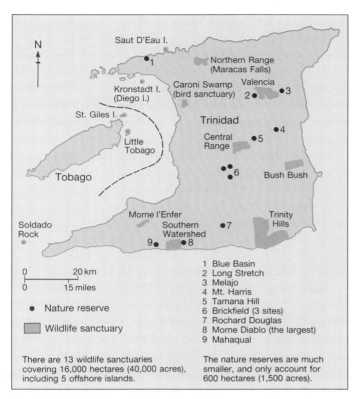

Fig. 10.4 Trinidad and Tobago: wildlife sanctuaries and nature reserves.

Map labels:

N

Saut D'Eau I.

Northern Range (Maracas Falls)

Caroni Swamp (bird sanctuary)

Valencia

Kronstadt I. (Diego I.)

St. Giles I.

Little Tobago

Trinidad

Central Range

Tobago

Bush Bush

Soldado Rock

Morne l'Enfer Southern Watershed

Trinity Hills

0   20 km
0   15 miles

● Nature reserve

▨ Wildlife sanctuary

1 Blue Basin
2 Long Stretch
3 Melajo
4 Mt. Harris
5 Tamana Hill
6 Brickfield (3 sites)
7 Rochard Douglas
8 Morne Diablo (the largest)
9 Mahaqual

There are 13 wildlife sanctuaries covering 16,000 hectares (40,000 acres), including 5 offshore islands.

The nature reserves are much smaller, and only account for 600 hectares (1,500 acres).

Reafforestation, or *sylviculture* as it is often called, involves the scientific management and planting of trees for a particular purpose. In the Caribbean, although some replanting takes place for soil conservation purposes, most of the reafforestation is restricted to the Caribbean pine, although teak is important in Trinidad and acacia is an alternative to the pine. In terms of area the amount is very small owing to the high cost, and it is unlikely that forestry will ever be a major activity in the region.

In Guyana, experimental plantings of *pines* were made some years ago to supply pulp and paper, but have not been pursued owing to lack of funds. About 4,000 hectares (10,000 acres) of Caribbean pines have also been planted in Trinidad, but this is less than 2% of the total forest cover. It is useful as a replacement for the much slower-growing mora.

Other projects involving pines have been undertaken in Cuba and the Dominican Republic. The advantages of the pine are that it grows quickly, it is suitable for firewood or charcoal within a few years, for pulp and paper within 25 years, and for construction timber within 35 years. It is much less susceptible to disease and pests than other species, notably acacia, which has also been tried as it grows even

Logs of Trinidad and Tobago's most popular native wood, Mora, awaiting the sawmill at Valencia.

103

faster than the pine. Once the pine is past the juvenile stage it is also fire-resistant owing to its thick protective bark. During the dry season, pine forest fires are common, but only the youngest trees suffer. The undergrowth of competing trees is destroyed, however, and the pine faces less competition as a result. Nevertheless, fire is not good for the forests as it weakens the trees and allows insects and disease to spread. Young trees are destroyed, and if there is a strong wind the fire may be fierce enough to destroy the foliage and even large mature trees. Modern practice is to cut firebreaks so that any fire will be confined to one block of forest only. The firebreaks are simply wide avenues that are kept clear of vegetation. They can also be used as access roads (See photo p. 94).

Teak was introduced into Trinidad early in the twentieth century and is the most successful example of sylviculture in the Caribbean. Five to six years after planting, the young teak trees are thinned to allow the stronger plants room to grow. The thinnings are used for fencing. The main use of teak, however, is for sawn timber, but this requires mature trees, which takes 50 years. It is only now that Trinidad is realizing the full potential of its earlier plantings, which cover about 3.5% of the forested area.

Jamaica has about 12,000 hectares (30,000 acres) of Caribbean pine in plantations, which is about 2% of its total forest cover. Pine is widely used in the construction industry, and over 80% of it has to be imported. By planting an additional 2,000 hectares (5,000 acres) every year, local production should increase about threefold by the year 2000, and supply perhaps half the demand.

The Jamaican government has also planted over 1,200 hectares (3,000 acres) each of blue mahoe and mahogany trees, which are mainly used in the furniture industry. Two of the problems faced are typical of the difficulties most forestry departments face in the Caribbean. It was intended to plant enough blue mahoe trees to supply a small sawmill. The first problem was that the land had to be bought from private owners, some of whom could not be found. Others did not want to sell, or if they did could not prove that they legally owned the land. In some cases there were squatters on the land, who did not want to leave. The second problem came when the trees had to be planted. As the forestry equipment had to be imported, import licences were required, and foreign exchange was hard to get. When machinery broke down there were no spare parts. For these reasons there was never enough equipment and the trees could not all be planted.

Despite this, inflation has made the trees particularly valuable, and the plantations are likely to be a profitable source of hardwood timber in the future.

Jamaica has long been almost self-sufficient in cedar, which is in great demand from the construction industry and furniture makers. Cedar grows naturally in the native forests of the John Crow Mountains and the Blue Mountains, and is by far the most important commercial tree in Jamaica.

Among the smaller countries, Dominica is notable for having two sawmills which together produce about 5,000 m³ metres (177,000 cu. ft) of lumber a year. This is used to build prefabricated houses at Woodford Hill, and to supply the construction industry. The forest industry was greatly stimulated by a project to recover the fallen and damaged trees that littered the island after it was hit by Hurricane David in 1979.

---

1 Why has so much of the Caribbean forest been cut down?

2 Name some of the introduced (exotic) plants that are common in your country (not crops).

3 What can your country's natural vegetation be used for today?

4 Which countries in the Caribbean have timber industries?

5 What is sylviculture, and how important is it in the Caribbean?

Lumbering on the Canadian Shield

Much of the lumber that is imported into the Caribbean comes from Canada, and Canadian forests are also the main source of paper.

Canada has two main lumbering regions, British Columbia in the west, and the southern edge of the Canadian Shield in the east.

A large part of the Shield is forested, about 20% of the total area of forest being classed as commercial, although not all of this is exploited. Because of the cold climate the forest is mainly coniferous, and trees gradually give way to tundra further north. Most of the exploitation has been along the accessible southern margin, where the Shield meets the St Lawrence River and the Great Lakes, and especially along the larger rivers which can be used to float the logs towards these waterways (Fig. 10.5).

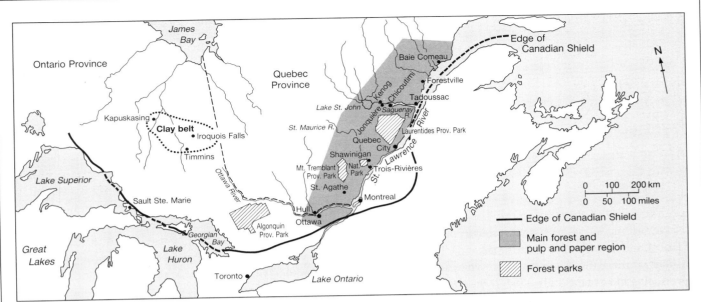

Fig. 10.5 Forestry on the Canadian Shield.

The trees that grow in this region are pines (white pine, jack pine), spruce (black and white), fir and larch. Where they are large enough they are used to provide lumber, mainly for constructional use and for veneers. However, trees grow slowly on the Shield and many are too small for these purposes. These are converted to pulp and then paper, much of it for export to the USA.

As Table 10.2 shows, three-quarters of Canadian forests

Table 10.2 Distribution of Canadian forests, 1986

| Province | Total reserves (million m³) | | Total cut (million m³) |
	Softwoods	Hardwoods	
British Columbia	8,180 (46%)	688 (13%)	77.5 (44%)
Canadian Shield			
Quebec	3,020 ⎫	1,204 ⎫	38.1 ⎫
Ontario	2,205 ⎭ (29%)	1,325 ⎭ (48%)	30.2 ⎭ (38%)
Rest of Canada	4,429 (25%)	2,103 (39%)	31.3 (18%)
Total	17,834	5,320	177.1

(Source: Canada Year Book 1990.)

Table 10.3 Canadian forestry production, 1986 (Canadian $billion)

	Lumber	Pulp and paper	Total
British Columbia	2.45 (44%)	1.80 (20%)	4.25 (29%)
Canadian Shield			
Quebec	1.28 ⎫	3.10 ⎫	4.38 ⎫
Ontario	1.09 ⎭ (43%)	2.79 ⎭ (66%)	3.88 ⎭ (57%)
Rest of Canada	0.70 (13%)	1.23 (14%)	1.93 (14%)
Total	5.52	8.92	14.44
Export value	6.32	11.37	17.69

(Source: Canada Year Book 1990.)

Spruce and Balsam fir	1,565
Douglas fir	286
Hemlock	589
Red and white cedar	587
Pine (white, red, jack and lodgepole)	324
All species	4,736

Table 10.4 Value of main commercial lumber species, 1984 (million Canadian $) (Source: Canada Year Book 1990.)

are found in the three main provinces, almost equally shared by British Columbia (the western mountain ranges), Quebec and Ontario (the Canadian Shield). The use of this timber is quite different, however, with British Columbia producing most of the lumber (64%) and the Shield most of the paper (71%). As Table 10.3 shows, the paper is by far the most valuable, worth about $9 billion in 1986, mainly newsprint going to the United States.

Altogether Canada's forestry industry employed about 277,000 persons and earned over $17 billion in 1986. Canada is the world's largest exporter of forest products.

A tree that has a trunk diameter of 23 cm (9 in.) at chest height can be used for pulping, and takes about 50 years to grow in this climate. Even longer - about 75-100 years - is needed for a tree 30 cm (12 in.) in diameter, which can be used for lumber. As a result of this long regeneration time, forestry has had to keep moving further north where the trees are smaller, and this has caused the industry to change from mainly lumbering early in the century to pulp and paper today.

The pulp and paper industry is highly concentrated along the edge of the Shield where hydro-electric power (HEP) can be generated. This power is used in the pulp mills in towns such as those around Lake St John on the Saguenay River, at Three Rivers and Kenog in Quebec, and at Ottawa, Port Arthur and Sault Ste Marie in Ontario.

There has been much concern about deforestation in Canada and the industry is now subject to many regulations. There are two particular problems:

Clear felling This is the practice of cutting everything in a concession area, regardless of its value or size. It provides no cover for seedlings to grow under, and does not leave any seed-trees behind. It also leaves the ground particu-

larly vulnerable to soil erosion, but it is the cheapest way to get the timber out.

Fire This is encouraged by the practice of leaving the unwanted branches of trees on the ground and just removing the logs. Modern equipment strips a tree in minutes and only the trunk is removed. The dried foliage is a major fire hazard.

Although much damage was done in the past, the slow regrowth of trees and the great expense of transport into the Shield has forced Canada to practise conservation measures. Replanting and nurseries are common in cut-over areas, and as a result of new techniques, previously unwanted species can now be used by the pulp and paper industry. The result is that reserves are now expanding more quickly than they are being depleted, and Canadian forests are becoming a true example of a renewable resource.

One of the most devastated areas was between Georgian Bay and the upper Ottawa River, which was left derelict for many years. It was first cut at the end of the nineteenth century. Today it is the main recreation area for the Toronto region and contains the Algonquin Provincial Park, with numerous chalets, motels, camps and second homes set among the many lakes and replanted trees. A similar area, around Ste Agathe and including the Mt Tremblant Provincial Park, lies north of Montreal.

The most active forestry zone is still within reach of the rivers and power stations of the lower St Lawrence Valley, and the stretch from Ottawa to Baie Comeau has been described as having the world's greatest concentration of pulp and paper mills.

Smaller centres of production exist elsewhere in the Shield wherever there is access and transport available. An example is in the Clay Belt farming and mining area around Timmins, where Kapuskasing and Iroquois Falls depend entirely on the pulp and paper industry.

1 What are the natural advantages of the Canadian Shield for lumbering?

2 What damage has been done by forestry (a) in the Caribbean, (b) in Canada?

11
Mineral resources and energy

The manufacture of alumina creates red mud, a waste product that cannot easily be disposed of. At Ewarton the red mud lakes cover four times the area of the rest of the operation!

It is usual to think of natural resources as anything produced by nature that is of *economic value* to people (Fig. 11.1). However, we should first of all distinguish between those

that every nation is likely to possess, which are *ubiquituous*, and those that only a few nations have, and are considered *sporadic*.

In the first group there are climate, soils, water, vegetation, rivers, fish, and so on. They are of course important, but usually of low value unless they are exceptionally rich or abundant. For instance, the combined warmth, sunshine and

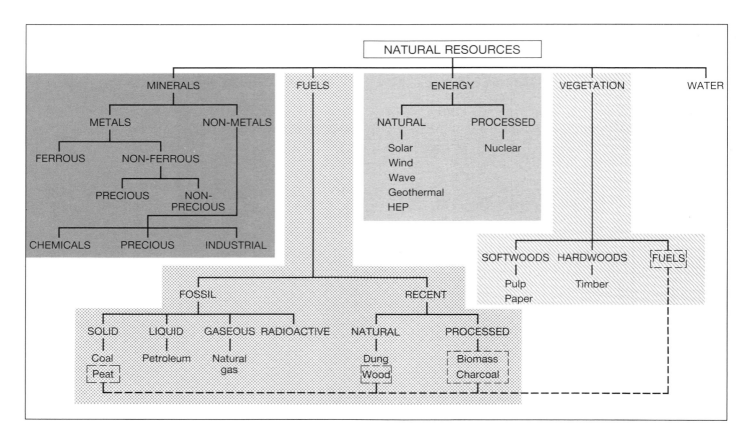

Fig. 11.1 Natural resources

relative dryness of the climate makes this an economic resource for the Caribbean. Water and soils are usually much less abundant and although used of necessity, have no export value in themselves.

The second group can be extremely valuable. They are not evenly distributed, many countries have need of them, and so there is an *economic* demand which enhances their value to a very great extent. The Caribbean is notable in being a signifi-cant producer of four such natural resources: bauxite, petroleum, nickel and salt.

In order to better understand our resources, we need to consider the full range of possibilities: what a country does *not* have is often more important than what it does have! Figure 11.1 covers most of the possibilities.

Value of a resource

Before considering some of our resources in detail, some general principles need to be established if we are to understand their true value.

Renewable and non-renewable resources

In the last few decades there has been considerable concern about the rate at which we are using up 'non-renewable' resources, such as certain metals and petroleum. There is the suggestion that we should concentrate on the renewable resources. The term 'renewable' surprisingly does not have a precise definition: it suggests that having used the resource once it will be freely available again. 'Non-renewable' means that there is a fixed quantity, possibly very large, that eventually must be exhausted. The problem lies in taking too simple a view of these two terms, and forgetting that a resource must have economic value. If it cannot produce a product at an economic price it is no longer a resource.

Truly renewable resources are things like solar energy, hydro-electric power, water, and salt from the sea. However much we take, they will always be replaced. Non-renewable resources are in fact those that can only be replaced by geological processes operating over a geological time-scale. Virtually all the fossil fuels, and the metallic and non-metallic minerals, are of this type.

There is nevertheless some confusion about this. Despite

their non-renewable status, resources like oil, coal, iron ore and bauxite are widely available throughout the world in large quantities. Techniques for locating and recovering them are probably improving at least as fast as demand is. All the shortages and price increases in recent years have been the result of political action, not geological limitations. On the other hand the abundance of renewable resources is offset by the difficulty of converting or storing their energy.

Finally we must always recognize that 'renewable' has to be qualified by time. A plantation of Caribbean pines that is replanted as it is used is a renewable resource within a time-frame of about 35 years. A forest of mahogany trees that takes 150-300 years to grow again is not a renewable resource - nowhere in the Caribbean are the original hardwood forests renewing themselves.

Capital cost

Harnessing a natural resource or refining a metal requires capital investment. This has the effect of putting an extraction cost on an apparently 'free' resource. At the present time producing electricity from water - hydro-electric power - (HEP), or refining aluminium from bauxite, requires a very large investment in dams and power-houses, or mining, processing and refining equipment. The water is both free and infinitely renewable, and the bauxite is readily available near the surface. Nevertheless, hundreds - possibly thousands - of millions of dollars are needed to finance these projects. The problems can be summarized as follows:

- The money has to be found, and in the Caribbean this means borrowed. Even a 'soft' loan of 5% on $1,000 million dollars means that the interest alone will come to $50 million a year, and the capital still has to be paid back.
- Even if the money can be found and the repayments afforded, probably only one such project could be managed every ten years. There are many other things that such money could be spent on - how do you choose?
- If a major project was not undertaken, a country would theoretically have $50 million a year to spend on importing substitutes and establishing smaller projects. It is often seen as cheaper to import 'expensive' oil than to develop 'free' water power!

Bauxite

Bauxite is the non-ferrous ore of the metal aluminium. In Jamaica, Haiti and the Dominican Republic it is a red, rusty-coloured clay. As well as containing aluminium, there is a high percentage of iron in it. This bauxite is found exclusively in pockets on top of limestone. In Guyana the bauxite has much less iron in it, it is pale in colour, and hard enough to have to be mined with the aid of explosives. It lies under a layer of sand or sandy clay which has to be removed.

Bauxite was first extracted in the Caribbean from Suriname (then Dutch Guiana) and Guyana (then British Guiana), at the beginning of the twentieth century. The industries still exist here and are very important as they are the main exports of these two countries. Suriname is the only country in the Caribbean actually producing aluminium. It is able to do this because it has developed a major HEP resource, which provides the enormous quantities of electricity that are needed to produce aluminium.

Bauxite, like all ores, only contains a limited amount of the required metal in it. The process of removing the aluminium is generally known as *refining*, and it is done in two stages (Fig. 11.2). The first stage is to remove all the unwanted material such as iron oxides, and to obtain *aluminium oxide*, which is known as *alumina*. The alumina is then further refined to produce the *aluminium*.

It can be seen from Table 11.1 that although the first stage of aluminium processing is well-represented in the Caribbean, very little aluminium metal is produced here. The

Country	Number of bauxite operations	Alumina refinery	Aluminium smelters
Jamaica	5	4	0
Haiti	1+	0	0
Dominican Republic	1+	0	0
Guyana	2	1	0
Suriname	2	2	1*
St Croix, US Virgin Is.	0	1**	0
Total	11	8	1

*   Production at the smelter has frequently been interrupted by civil war since 1987, and virtually stopped in 1991.

** Closed in 1985, this refinery processed African bauxite. Planned to re-open in 1991, but severely damaged by Hurricane Hugo in 1989.

+   Closed 1982/83.

Table 11.1 The aluminium industry in the Caribbean

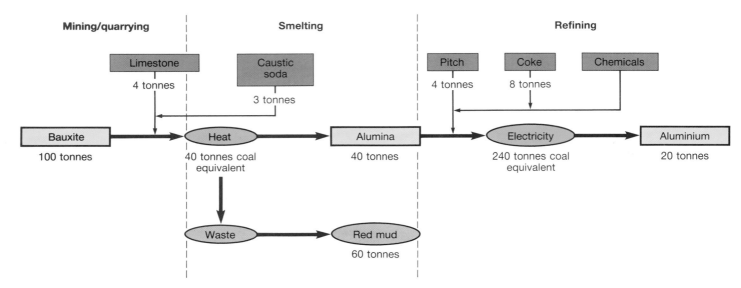

Fig. 11.2 *The bauxite-alumina-aluminium process.*

reason for this can be partly explained by the *process* (See Fig. 11.2) and partly by the *market* - that is, the location of users of the metal.

The bauxite/aluminium industry

In order to convert bauxite to alumina, certain other natural resources are needed. In the first stage fuel and caustic soda are required, both of which are usually imported. The expense of the factory and the imports explain why some bauxite, notably in Haiti and the Dominican Republic, was exported directly to North America. Nevertheless, as alumina is worth about ten times as much as bauxite, it is often considered worth the expense of producing it. This has been encouraged by the Jamaican government in particular, because it:

- creates more permanent jobs,
- creates temporary jobs during construction,
- increases investment in the country,
- earns more foreign exchange from exports, and
- makes it less likely that foreign investors will abandon their operations.

There would be the same advantages if aluminium were made here. The additional raw materials are not too expensive, but unfortunately six times as much energy is needed as in the first part of the process, and this has to be in the form of *direct current electricity*. Like alumina smelters, an aluminium refining smelter is in itself a major capital investment, and the additional cost of building and fuelling the very large electricity power station that is needed has made it economically impossible for most small countries to become aluminium producers. Suriname is fortunate in having a large HEP

source close to the bauxite mines. There are projects to build aluminium smelters in the Mazaruni District of Guyana, where the River Mazaruni is a major source of HEP (See p. 45), and at Point Lisas in Trinidad, where natural gas can be used to provide the electricity. Jamaica would supply Trinidad with alumina, and about 200,000 tonnes of aluminium would be produced each year. However, even with a good supply of electricity, there are still problems in producing aluminium in the West Indies:

1   The making of aluminium is an *electrolytic process*. It works something like a car battery on charge. A large amount of direct current (d.c.) electricity is passed through a solution (equivalent to the acid in a battery) which contains the molten alumina, and the aluminium is extracted and deposited at the bottom of the cell in a molten state (equivalent to the lead in a battery). Direct current

A bauxite transporter working the opencast pit at Lydford, Jamaica.

110

electricity cannot be transmitted far (unlike our normal alternating current), so the alumina or bauxite must be taken to the source of electricity. This is expensive, and also means that aluminium may be produced far from the consumers, such as aircraft companies or shipbuilders.

2 The large industrial European and American countries are the main users of aluminium. These countries can also afford to develop their own HEP resources more easily than the Caribbean countries. Countries like Norway, Canada and the USA have large HEP projects; Britain and the USA also have their own oil-powered plants (for example, Inverness in Scotland using North Sea oil; and Texas). Nuclear power can also be used.

3 The countries with existing aluminium plants do not want competition which might cause their own plants to close. Therefore they put customs duties (tariffs) on aluminium metal, but bauxite can be imported free. This encourages the mining companies to export the ore instead of making the metal.

4 A few very large companies - *multinational corporations* - control most of the world's bauxite and aluminium industry. They are Alcoa, Kaiser, Reynolds, Revère (USA), Alcan (Canada/USA), Alusuisse (Switzerland) and Pechiney (France). They prefer to have the final stages under the control of their own governments. This usually gives them security against takeovers like nationalization, and in the past allowed them to make larger profits than if they had all their operations in foreign countries. These companies are very powerful and without their co-operation it would be very difficult to be successful.

5 Political factors are often more important than any others. As aluminium is widely used in the defence industry, and the aluminium companies earn much from defence contracts, national security is a good reason for locating as much of the industry at home as possible. Alternatively, friendly powers are chosen in preference to those who are seen as unfriendly. For example, Jamaica was given favourable treatment when the USA began aluminium stockpiling in 1981, and this coincided with the change of government there.

6 The capital cost would be very high - as much as US$1billion for the Point Lisas project, which was being considered again in 1990 (See p. 163).

Bauxite in Guyana and Jamaica

Guyana has long been famous for its bauxite, and until the 1950s it was the largest producer in the British Commonwealth. Even today it is a significant producer and exported 1.3 million tonnes of bauxite in 1990. It is noted for the very high quality of its ores, which are used for a variety of purposes (Fig. 11.3).

While much of the bauxite is made into aluminium ingots, there is also a large demand for bauxite in other forms, of which calcined bauxite is the most important. 'Calcined' mean that the bauxite is heated to 1,132°C (2,800°F). At this temperature it is totally moisture free and

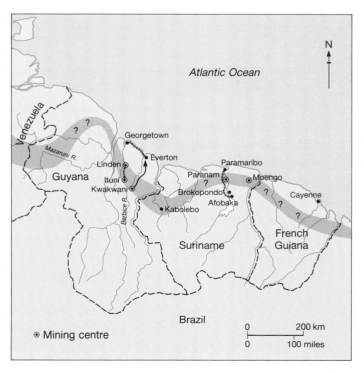

Fig. 11.3 Bauxite in the Guianas. All the Guianas have some bauxite deposits, although those in French Guiana are not worked. The deposits are part of a belt stretching through all the countries, which includes the proposed developments at Kabolebo (Suriname) and Mazaruni (Guyana), and continues west into Venezuela. The Kwakwani bauxite is sent to Everton by tug boat and barge down the Berbice River. Road or rail is used in all the other operations.

the crystal structure is altered in such a way that the bauxite becomes extremely *heat resistant*. Calcined, or heat-resistant, bauxite, is used for the following:

- Making *firebricks* to line furnaces.
- Making *heat resistant concrete* (ordinary concrete breaks down completely at very high temperatures).
- *Electrical porcelain*: when calcined bauxite is mixed with ordinary porcelain, the strength of electrical insulators is approximately doubled.
- *Coating welding electrodes*: The combined property of heat-resistance and the absence of iron, sulphur and phosphorus in bauxite make it ideal for electrode coatings.
- *Anti-skid surfaces*: calcined bauxite does not become smooth or polished with use, and it is therefore ideal for road surfaces, bridges, factory and warehouse floors, and airport runways.

Two out of every three tonnes of Guyanese bauxite is used for these purposes, and another 8% for chemical purposes. 'Metal' grade bauxite only accounts for about quarter of the total production and is of the lowest quality. Impurities of iron, titanium, silica, sulphur and phosphorus are much lower in Guyana than anywhere else in the world, and Guyana is the world's largest supplier of calcined and chemical-grade bauxite.

Guyana's two bauxite companies were owned by Alcan and Reynolds until the 1970s when they were nationalized. Guyana is the only Caribbean country other than Cuba to take over foreign investments. It had several reasons for doing this:

1   Guyana adopted a pro-Communist philosophy which demands state-ownership of all major resources and industries.

2   It was felt that the country was not profiting from the existing operations because the multinational corporations manipulated their profits so as to pay very low taxes.

3   The bauxite reserves, at least in the areas then worked, were not very large, and drastic action was believed necessary if any benefits were to be had before they ran out.

4   The bauxite companies would not agree to higher taxes or partial state control.

As a result the Guyanese government formed a bauxite mining company and production slumped or stagnated as it tried to manage its own operations and find new buyers

for its ores and alumina. It had some success in selling bauxite to its new political allies such as the USSR, China and Eastern Europe, and because its high-quality calcined bauxite could not be produced easily elsewhere.

It suffered by losing its old market, by the loss of skilled foreign workers, and especially by the loss of foreign money to buy and maintain all the equipment needed. Production fell severely owing to hold-ups especially in transport, and Guyana had to form its own shipping company (Guybulk, half Guyanese and half Norwegian) to handle exports. It also suffered from not having its own deepwater port. Bauxite is shipped to Chaguaramas in Trinidad, and then transferred to ocean-going vessels.

Guyana has long had detailed plans to develop the Mazaruni bauxite deposits, but as this area is disputed with Venezuela, it is unlikely that major development will be possible in the near future.

Jamaica has a different kind of bauxite, more of it, and more companies are involved in exploiting it (Fig. 11.4). It is a much newer industry, but has also been subjected to government controls and recent cutbacks and closures. Nevertheless it is still ranked third in the world, and fourth as an alumina producer. Much of its troubles in the 1980s were due to a decrease in world demand plus an increase in competitors - bauxite is really quite a common deposit, and countries like Brazil, Venezuela, India, Guinea in West Africa, and Australia, have all developed their own resources in the last 20 years. However, Jamaica is close to the USA and has considerable reserves yet to be developed. Some companies have closed down, but more as a result of their own problems than those of Jamaica. Some of the issues have been as follows:

1   In the 1970s Jamaica insisted on having a share in the ownership of the companies - 51% for bauxite companies, under 10% for alumina producers, in most cases.

2   The aluminium companies maintained inefficient practices which made them unprofitable when taxes were increased, when competition increased, and when prices fell.

3   Jamaica introduced a system of taxation based on the price of an ingot of aluminium on the open market. For every tonne of bauxite produced the companies had to pay a percentage of the price of the aluminium that would be produced from it.

By taxing the resource instead of the company, Jamaica greatly increased its income over the next ten years and effectively prevented the companies from evading taxa-

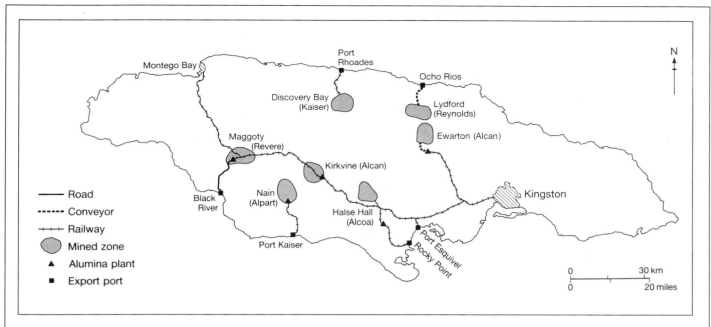

Fig. 11.4 Bauxite operations in Jamaica. Few parts of Jamaica are far from a bauxite mining area or its processing and export operations. At one time all seven operations were working, but by 1986 this had been reduced to four.

tion. The companies greatly resented this and when Reynolds closed down in 1984 it blamed the Jamaican government. In fact Reynolds had to close down its alumina and aluminium plants in Texas because the natural gas it used there was too expensive, so the bauxite was no longer needed.

Guyana has two bauxite mines, at Linden and Berbice (See Fig. 11.3). Linden is also fed with bauxite by rail from Ituni 58km (36 miles) further south. Linden, then known as Mackenzie, was the original location of Guyana's bauxite industry, which was established in 1916. Calcining kilns were added in 1938, and the alumina plant was built in 1961. The Ituni mines were opened in 1944.

The Berbice operations began at Kwakwani in 1937. The bauxite was mined there and sent in barges to Ewarton 233km (145 miles) further down the Berbice River. The bauxite is dried at Ewarton and then exported.

Jamaica has had as many as seven bauxite or bauxite/ alumina operations, similar to those in Guyana. Not all of these are now operating. The small Revère operation closed in 1975, and the bauxite-only plant of Reynolds closed in 1985. Two other plants (Alcoa and Alpart) closed in 1985, but were re-opened as a result of vigorous government intervention. The Alcoa plant, renamed Jamalco, is now leased by the Jamaican government. The Kaiser plant was closed from 1986 to 1989. Jamaica was hit by the world decline in demand for aluminium, but in the early 1980s did not accept that its plants should close down. The closures were partly the result of inefficiencies of the companies themselves, and were also due to the companies trying to force the Jamaican government to reduce its bauxite taxation. The bauxite levy was revised in an effort to encourage production and save jobs. This seems to have been justified, as by 1990 bauxite output was 10.9 million tonnes, and alumina 2.9 million tonnes a year. Since 1986 the Jamaican industry has slowly recovered, and is now expanding most of its plants.

---

1 Where is bauxite found in the Caribbean?

2 What makes Jamaican bauxite red, and what happens to the red minerals after processing?

3 Multinational corporations are not only found in the aluminium industry. Name five other activities in the Caribbean that are controlled by multinational corporations. Name one or more corporations for each activity.

4 What is bauxite used for?

5 What are the benefits of bauxite mining to the local population?

6 What are the differences between Guyanese and Jamaican bauxite?

113

Salt

Almost every island has had salt pans at some time in its history. The first visitors to The Bahamas and the Turks and Caicos Islands came for salt. As well as these two countries, Curacao, Puerto Rico, the Dominican Republic, Cuba, Jamaica, St Maarten and Anguilla have all had important salt industries in the past.

Most of the Caribbean salt industries collapsed with the advent of imported salt from the industrialized countries at the beginning of the twentieth century. Salt is a common mineral, and it became the basis of many chemical industries in Europe and North America. However, by the middle of the twentieth century there was a great demand for salt: from the food industry; for melting snow; as a water softener; and in the chemical industry. At the same time the mines in the temperate zone became expensive to work, and in many cases were exhausted.

Today one of the world's largest solar salt plants is on Inagua, the most southerly island in The Bahamas. This produces about 1 million tonnes of salt a year, while Bonaire has a smaller works producing 350,000 tonnes. The company in Inagua, Morton Salt, prospers as a result of several significant geographical factors:

- Inagua is closer to the USA than any other Caribbean country except Cuba.

Disused salt ponds cover much of Grand Turk. Cockburn Town, the capital, lies on a narrow strip of land between the pans and the sea.

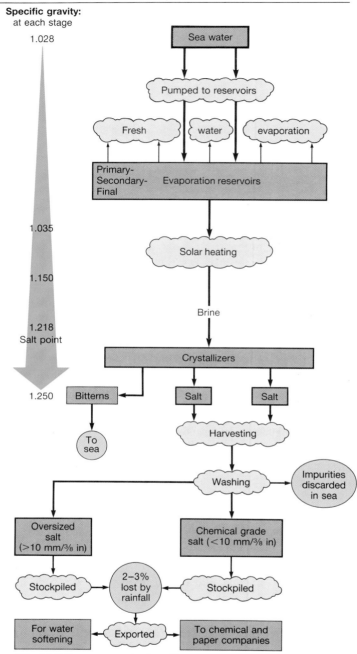

Fig. 11.5 From sea water to salt.

- It has a nearly perfect climate with 62.5 mm (25 in.) of rain and steady drying trade winds. Just 250km (160 miles) further north, on Long Island, the American Diamond Salt company had to stop operations in 1981 owing to excessive rain.
- A large natural lake and extensive flat land around it allow a very large scale of operation.
- Exceptionally pure sea water makes the salt commercially desirable.

Oil and natural gas, which in the West Indies are only found in Trinidad in any quantity, are both *hydrocarbons*. They are 'fossil fuels', and represent the concentrated remains of micro-organisms that lived 30 million or more years ago. Around the Caribbean good conditions existed for the creation, concentration and entrapment of oil and natural gas, especially in Texas, Mexico and Venezuela. The supplies found in and around the island of Trinidad, and also in Barbados, are related to the Venezuelan deposits (See p.120 and Fig. 11.6).

Natural deposits of tar are found in Barbados (where they are called *man-jak*) and Trinidad (the Pitch Lake, and local *Tarballs*), and gas bubbles up from Trinidad's mud volcanoes. As early as the nineteenth century these were recognized as indications of petroleum deposits in this part of the Caribbean. The most important developments in recent years have been the discoveries of large quantities of natural gas off Trinidad and Tobago, and the increasing production of oil in Barbados.

A close-up of a gas bubble on the surface of Trinidad's Pitch Lake. The pitch is much softer in these areas, which cannot be walked on.

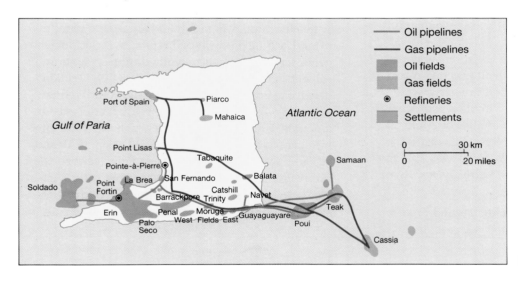

Fig. 11.6 The oil and gas fields of Trinidad.

Oil and natural gas in Trinidad and Tobago

Oil was produced in southern Trinidad early in the twentieth century, and by the 1950s it was also being sent ashore from the Gulf of Paria (Fig. 11.6). Since that time Trinidad has looked increasingly offshore for its oil, and this search was rewarded in the 1970s by major dicoveries off the east coast. By the end of the 1970s the Amoco fields were producing more oil than all the others put together.

However, despite these finds, known reserves are not large, and are unlikely to last more than 30 years. It may be that new finds will be made, and also that more oil can be got from old wells, as the present rate of recovery is only about 30% - that is, 70% of the oil is still in the ground! Trinidad is fortunate in also having discovered *natural gas* in the same offshore areas. There is much more of this than Trinidad can use, and eventually it should replace oil for many purposes, for example in the petrochemical industry, and for factory fuel and electricity generation. It can also be exported. At the present time much of this valuable gas is 'flared off' (burned off). In 1990 Trinidad produced 55 million barrels of oil.

Oil in the rest of the Caribbean

Despite encouraging prospects and some small finds in Belize, The Bahamas, Suriname and Guyana, and a great deal of exploration everywhere else, only Barbados and Cuba are significant producers elsewhere in the Caribbean. By world standards Barbados's production of oil (0.5 million barrels in 1986) and natural gas is negligible - less than 1% of Trinidad's small output. But for Barbados it is most valuable and supplies 45% of the oil and all the natural gas needed. Cuba produces about 5 million barrels a year, as well as natural gas, and supplies about 10% of her needs; and Suriname about 5% of her needs.

Oil refining in Trinidad

At a very early stage oil refineries were built to refine the oil at Pointe-à-Pierre and Point Fortin. Both expanded enormously over the years, but their profits have declined so much recently that their future is in considerable doubt. Originally, most crude oil - a dense black/brown/green viscous liquid, often polluted with sand and giving off dangerous gases - had to be treated before it could be shipped. Not all the crude oil could be used and as much as 50% might be wasted. Natural gas was rarely used and was considered a nuisance - it was burned off. The technology of supertankers had not yet been developed, and it made economic sense to refine the oil near the source and export the refined product.

As oil production increased in the 1940s, the refineries were enlarged to keep pace with it. After the Second World War, however, there was a revolution in energy as the Western world became heavily dependent on petroleum as its major source of fuel. Huge quantities of crude oil began to be shipped to Europe and North America in the 1950s and especially in the 1960s. Trinidad was able to benefit from this in two ways, as it already had two refineries:

1   It could expand the size of its refineries and process imported crude oil as well, thus earning money as a manufacturer. Eventually Trinidad and Tobago's refineries were handling three times as much imported crude oil, mainly from the Persian Gulf, as domestic oil.

2   A whole new range of chemicals - *petrochemicals* - were being produced from petroleum by a process known as 'cracking' (Fig. 11.7). This involves heating the oil to extremely high temperatures so that it breaks up into its component parts, ranging from gases (butane, propane, etc.) through liquids (naptha, gasoline, paraffin) to tar. The final products of this process include detergents, fertilizers, plastics, synthetic fibres, paints and solvents, and pharmaceuticals (Fig. 11.8). Trinidad decided to invest in this industry. The Texaco refinery at Pointe-à-Pierre, which is the largest, produces large amounts of ammonia products which are made into nitrogenous fertilizers for export. In the late 1970s and 1980s it was decided to considerably increase the production of ammonia products using natural gas. (See p. 164). Detergents, and products for the plastics, synthetic fibres and paint industries, are also made.

Unfortunately the demands of the industry changed again, to the detriment of the Caribbean refineries. In 1974 there was a world oil crisis, caused by the withholding of crude oil supplies by OPEC. This was followed by rapid increases in the price of crude oil. It took about ten years for the industrialized nations to recover from this crisis, but recovery was so successful that the demand for imported oil declined enormously. Some of the reasons for this were as follows:

- Use of energy-saving practices.
- Development of more efficient fuel-using engines - the American 'gas-guzzler' automobile was largely replaced by 'sub-compact' (very small) and 'compact' (small) models.
- Greatly increased oil exploration, with striking results in the North Sea, Alaska, northern Canada and Mexico.
- Stockpiling of crude oil so that temporary shortages could be handled.
- Economies in the oil industry itself. Many old and small refineries closed down. Offshore refineries became less popular. (Any refinery that is between the oil fields and the oil market is described as 'offshore'.) These included the Trinidad, Curaçao, Aruba and Bahamas oil refineries in the Caribbean. The most successful refineries are those that are closest to the users of the products: that is, the major industrial areas of Europe and North America. The extra cost of shipping refined products instead of crude oil became unacceptable by the mid-1980s.

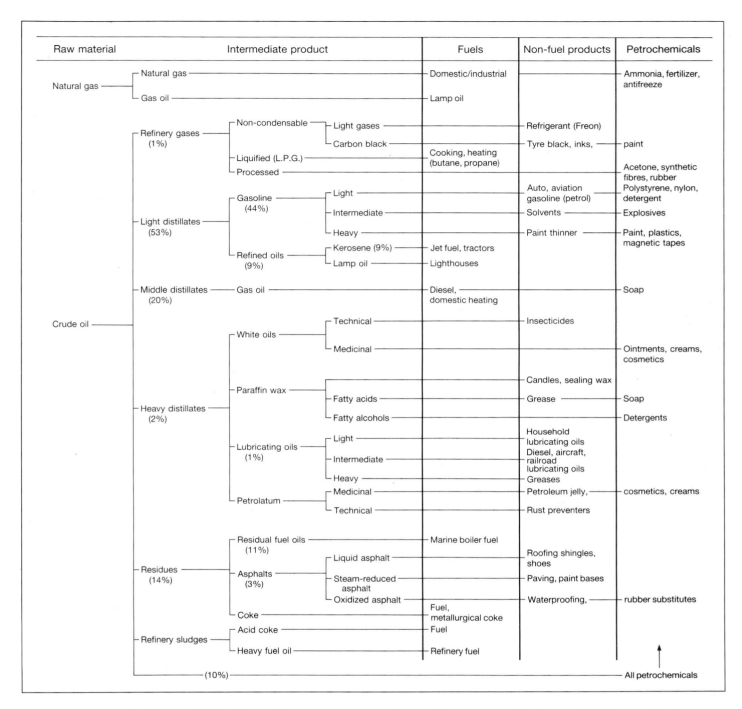

Fig. 11.7 Products of refining crude oil and natural gas.

Today imported oil is only about 40% of the total refined in Trinidad. Consequently Trinidad's refineries have become smaller. In 1970 the Texaco refinery produced over 350,000 barrels per day (bpd). In 1982 the capacity was reduced to 220,000 bpd, and in 1987 it sold the refinery to the government. It now only refines domestic oil.

The government refinery at Point Fortin is smaller, with a capacity of 100,000 bpd. It was a Shell refinery until 1974.

There is also a very small refinery at Brighton producing up to 5,000 bpd.

1 What is natural gas?

2 What are petrochemicals?

3 Is petroleum likely to be found anywhere else in the Caribbean besides Trinidad, Barbados and Cuba?

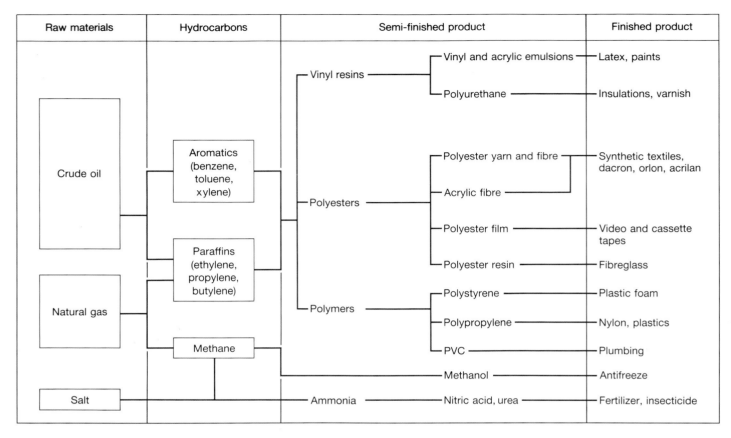

Raw materials	Hydrocarbons	Semi-finished product	Finished product

Raw materials: Crude oil, Natural gas, Salt

Hydrocarbons: Aromatics (benzene, toluene, xylene); Paraffins (ethylene, propylene, butylene); Methane

Semi-finished product / Finished product:
- Vinyl resins → Vinyl and acrylic emulsions → Latex, paints
- Vinyl resins → Polyurethane → Insulations, varnish
- Polyesters → Polyester yarn and fibre → Synthetic textiles, dacron, orlon, acrilan
- Polyesters → Acrylic fibre
- Polyesters → Polyester film → Video and cassette tapes
- Polyesters → Polyester resin → Fibreglass
- Polymers → Polystyrene → Plastic foam
- Polymers → Polypropylene → Nylon, plastics
- Polymers → PVC → Plumbing
- Methanol → Antifreeze
- Ammonia → Nitric acid, urea → Fertilizer, insecticide

Fig 11.8 Petrochemical products.

Oil refining and trans-shipment in the Caribbean

The oil industry is well represented throughout the Caribbean, which has about 20 refineries and 6 trans-shipment terminals. Some have closed, but may re-open; some are open but may close down. Often the future of a Caribbean refinery or terminal depends on the fortunes of a company far away from it, and ownership changes quite frequently. We can classify these operations into four main types.

Domestic refineries

The larger islands like Jamaica have found it more economic to have their own refinery to supply local needs, than to import refined products. This only works up to a point, as usually too many products are needed. A small refinery is unlikely to be able to supply all the following, for example:

Cooking gas	Aviation gas for propeller engines
Petrol (gasoline)	Paraffin
Diesel	Bunker 'C' for power stations
Lubricating oil	Fuel oil for ships
Road tar	Kerosene for jet engines

All countries in the Caribbean need these items. However, the bigger the country, the more likely it is to have a refinery (Table 11.2).

Offshore refineries

The location of the Caribbean territories between Venezuela and Europe/North America, and also at the end of the Persian Gulf-North American route via the Cape - the route which all the largest tankers have to take - has encouraged the development of large refineries here.

Three historical phases of development can be identified (Table 11.3):

1. In the first half of the twentieth century islands like Curaçao and Trinidad provided safe havens for the processing of Venezuelan and Persian Gulf oil.

2. From the 1960s, tankers of 250,000-500,000 tonnes became the most economical means of transport at a time when oil demand was increasing dramatically. Large refineries were built to process this oil, which was sent on to the USA in smaller tankers of 80,000 tonnes or less.

3. In the 1980s, the price of oil fell owing to a combination of fuel conservation measures and over-production. As a result, the savings from offshore production declined, and many refineries closed.

118

Location	Capacity	Operator and history
Antigua	18,000	Closed since 1976, briefly opened 1982
Barbados	3,000	Mobil
Cuba	5,000	Cabaiguan
	65,000	Santiago De Cuba, ex-Texaco, expanded
	85,000	Two in Havana, ex-Esso and Shell, recently expanded
	400,000	Cienfuegas, opened 1985, linked by pipeline to oilfields at Matanzas
Dominican	28,000	Nagua - Shell and government
Republic	16,000	Bonao, for ferro-nickel plant only
Jamaica	35,500	Government, ex-Esso: about 20,000 barrels per day in 1989
Martinique	10,000	
Puerto Rico	38,000	Catano
	161,000	Penuelas: Corco
	85,000	Yabucao
Trinidad	5,000	La Brea, Brighton
Total 15;	average size about 40,000 bpd (excluding Cienfuegas which is exceptionally large)	

Table 11.2 Oil refineries in the Caribbean

Table 11.3 Historical development of offshore refineries in the West Indies

Bahamas - Grand Bahamas	1972, Burmah Oil/Bahamas Government. $80m.
Bonaire	Reduced rate since 1981.
Curaçao	Adjacent to but distinct from the refinery. Reduced rate since 1981.
St Eustatius	Venezuelan (cancelled?)
St Lucia	Amerada Hess, $50m. Started 1980. South of Castries.
Planned:	
Cayman Islands - Little Cayman	$158m. Merril Lynch. Project suspended.
Bonaire	Amerada Hess (cancelled?)

Table 11.4 Trans-shipment terminals in the Caribbean

Trans-shipment terminals

These terminals mark a continuation of the offshore principle. There is no refining at a trans-shipment terminal. It merely allows an ultra-large crude carrier (ULCC) or a very large crude carrier (VLCC) to offload crude oil into storage tanks and return to the oil fields. (In some cases only part of the cargo is off-loaded, and the lightened tanker goes on to the USA.) The crude oil is then reloaded into smaller tankers of about 100,000 tonnes, known as 'supertankers', and shipped to refineries in the USA or Canada. These refineries have been built in places where the harbours are not deep enough to accommodate VLCCs or ULCCs, for example around the Gulf of Mexico (New Orleans) and along the eastern seaboard (Philadelphia). There are similar terminals in Wales, Ireland and Scotland (for the UK), and in France and the Netherlands (for Europe).

Location	Production (bpd)	Operator and history
Bahamas: Freeport	350,000	Chevron and Charter Oil, USA (50% each). Built 1967. Virtually closed down 1985. Bought by Venezuelan company in 1990, planned to re-open 1991.
Aruba	150,000	Government, ex-Esso. Built 1929. Closed 1984. Re-opening 1991 in co-operation with Coastal Oil, Texas. Originally 440,000 bpd.
Curaçao	320,000	Government, ex-Shell. Built 1919. Closed 1985.
Trinidad: Pointe-à-Pierre	160,000	Government. Originally 275,000 bpd.
Point Fortin	85,000	Government. Both now handle domestic oil only.
St Croix: US Virgin Is	728,000	Hess oil. Largest in western hemisphere. Operating well below capacity in 1988. Damaged by Hurricane Hugo in 1989.
	Total 6, Average 366,300	

It should be noted that these refineries are nine times the average size of domestic refineries.

Cayman Islands - Little Cayman	A precursor to the planned terminal. Started 1977, suspended 1980s.
Turks and Caicos Islands - West Caicos	US-owned. Started 1981, suspended by 1985.

Table 11.5 Caribbean ship-to-ship terminals

Ship-to-ship terminals

These are a cheaper version of the trans-shipment terminal, and are more recent (Table 11.5). They require no shore installations, only a deep, sheltered bay. The ULCC or VLCC receives the smaller tankers alongside and simply pumps oil into them.

In conclusion, although the production, refining and handling of petroleum in the Caribbean is less important than it was, the resource base is promising and the geographical advantages of location and deep harbours still exist. Should oil prices rise significantly, many of the islands of the Caribbean will again become refining or trans-shipment centres.

---

1 Where does your country's oil refinery get its oil from? If there is no oil refinery, which oil refinery do the imports come from?

2 Why did so many oil refineries close down in the 1980s?

3 What products in your classroom are made from petrochemicals?

Other sources of energy

Hydro-electric power

This depends on the power of water pressure to turn the turbine wheels of electrical generators. The amount of *pressure* depends on the *height* of the fall of the water. The more water that falls, the greater the number of turbines that can be turned, and so the *quantity* of water is also important. Small streams, even if they fall rapidly, do not have enough energy to produce much hydro-electric power. It therefore follows that only mountainous countries with large rivers have the potential for hydro-electric power. In the Caribbean, such conditions are found in the Greater Antilles, and in the Guianas in particular. The largest scheme is in Suriname, where the dam at Brokopondo generates more power than all other sources in the Guianas put together. Nearly all of it is used to refine aluminium.

There are much smaller schemes in Cuba, Jamaica, Dominica and the Dominican Republic. These are used mainly to supply electricity to the surrounding, mainly rural, areas.

Wind and solar power

These forms of power are the subject of much attention at present. They are both widely available in the Caribbean region. The north-east trade winds are a reliable and powerful source of energy on exposed coasts and hillsides, and six to eight hours of sunshine a day are common in most parts of the region. The old windmills of the sugar plantations, and the modern mills used in the twentieth century to raise water, are well known. Every time we dry grass for hay, or hang out washing to dry, we are using the sun's energy. Millions of dollars are spent in North America substituting for the sun's rays to dry clothes or crops with mechanical driers, which are usually powered by oil or oil-generated electricity. The Caribbean has long taken advantage of the wind and the sun, but in modern times these have had to be replaced by fuel-powered sources, because

(a) energy from the wind and sun cannot be stored easily or cheaply;

(b) the energy cannot be captured in large enough quantities to do large jobs.

Dunn's River HEP Station, Jamaica.

120

There are commercial windmills available for pumping water or for turning a 12-volt generator which can charge a 12-volt (car) battery, but most demands are for more powerful supplies. Much larger windmills are very expensive, and none has yet proved to be economical or reliable.

Similarly, solar water heaters are available and widely used in the more wealthy Caribbean countries, notably Barbados and The Bahamas. However, the capital cost is high - over US$1,000 for a solar heater for a small house - and widespread use is unlikely. Soap powders or detergents that wash properly in cold water are probably greater energy conservers than the present solar heaters.

The advantages of the sun and the wind as sources of energy, if their use could be made widely available, should not be ignored. They would save much in imported fuels (although this saving must be balanced against the cost of imported equipment), and provide a secure domestic supply that is non-polluting and totally 'renewable'.

Wood and charcoal

Wood, and to a much lesser extent, charcoal, are probably the most widely used fuels in the West Indies. This is because there are large numbers of rural dwellers in the hilly or remoter parts of the Guianas, Haiti and the Dominican Republic who have access to no other fuel. The same is true for smaller numbers in Cuba, Jamaica, Puerto Rico, Belize and the Windward Islands. Fuel for cooking is a basic human necessity, and in these countries there are large areas of forest and, for historical reasons, widely scattered communities. The economies of most of these countries have not allowed electricity or other fuel services to penetrate far inland because of the high costs of building power lines and roads in mountainous areas. Puerto Rico and Jamaica are the most advanced in this respect. As a result, vast areas of forest have been destroyed by woodcutters and charcoal burners and it is not likely that this can be changed for a long time, or indeed that wood will be replaced by say, paraffin or bottled gas. The remaining valuable sources of timber should be protected to prevent soil erosion caused by overcutting, and charcoal-burning should be organized so that the areas cut are controlled. In addition, replanting of fast-growing species should be undertaken to replace wood already cut.

Nuclear power

In Cuba, several Russian-designed nuclear power plants are under construction. In Puerto Rico a small nuclear reactor has been closed down for some years, but there were plans, now shelved, to build another one. The main advantage of nuclear power is that it can provide a very large continuous supply of electricity, which is essential for large-scale manufacturing or for very large urban areas. Obviously only Cuba and Puerto Rico are likely to provide a market for that kind of power at the present time. The disadvantages are well known. The dangers of serious explosions and radioactive contamination are great. In general the reactors are just as safe as any other generating plant, but the dangers from a breakdown are much greater. At the present time it is hard to justify any kind of nuclear activity in a region that is heavily dependent on tourism, and is regarded by the rest of the world as being unspoilt and unpolluted.

Geothermal energy

This unusual and apparently inexhaustible source of energy includes any source of heat from volcanic sources, and the various active volcanic features in the Caribbean (See p. 20) are all potential sources. So far only St Lucia appears to have a large enough supply for economic development. A large reservoir of steam has been found 1,200 metres (4,000 ft) underground at Soufrière with a temperature of 316°C (600°F), which is exceptionally hot. However, it is estimated that only 4.5 MW of power would be generated, which is less than half the 10 MW considered necessary for a successful project.

---

1 What can solar energy be used for at present?

2 In what ways has wind power been used in the Caribbean?

3 If St Lucia is successful in developing geothermal power, what other islands might do the same?

4 Compare the advantages and disadvantages of having

   (a) a coal mine
   (b) an oil refinery
   (c) a nuclear power station

   in your country.

Part Three
Human Systems

12
Agriculture in the Caribbean

Mechanical harvesting of cane in Barbados.

Agriculture can be looked at both from a cultural and an economic point of view. Culturally it may be either a *subsistence or commercial activity*, while economically it may involve either *intensive or extensive techniques*.

Subsistence agriculture is farming for one's own personal consumption. It usually involves a family and includes what is often called *peasant farming*. It is typical of isolated areas and the underdeveloped world, and is usually inefficient. Productivity per person is *low*.

Commercial agriculture is farming for profit. It is a business activity rather than a lifestyle. It is typical of developed societies and those with good communications. Productivity per person is *high*.

Intensive farming is any method that give high yields *per unit area*.

Extensive farming results in a low yield *per unit area*, but it can still be efficient.

If we combine these four possibilities we have a matrix that accounts for all the world's major farming types (Table 12.1).

Yield/person\yield/area	Subsistence (low yield/area)	Commercial (high yield/area)
Intensive (high yield/person)	• European 3-field system (medieval) • Asian rice cultivation • Polyculture, including West Indies peasant farming	• Market gardening/truck farming • European mixed farming • Dairying • Horticulture • Poultry, pigs • Cotton
Extensive (low yield/person)	• Hunting and gathering • Nomadism • Shifting cultivation	• Plantations • Ranching • Hill sheep • Grain • Orchards

Table 12.1 Different types of agriculture

The Caribbean

The Caribbean is both a consumer and a supplier of agricultural products. It produces a variety of meat, fruit and vegetables for local consumption, and fruit, sugar and other plantation crops for export. At the same time it imports a great variety of food, especially grain, meat and processed food. Agriculture is practised here in several forms, and is dependent on the success of agriculture in various other parts of the world (Table 12.2).

1 What are the main plantation crops besides sugar? Name at least two major producers of each one.

2 Today, most plantations are run like modern farms. What was a traditional plantation like?

3 Plantation crops often require some sort of processing before export. What is required for (a) sugar, (b) cocoa, (c) coffee, (d) tobacco? What further processing might be done overseas?

System	Product	Example
Commercial arable farming	Wheat and other grains	Prairies of Canada
	Sugar cane	Barbados
	Bananas and other estate crops	West Indies
	Rice	Guyana
Commercial pastoral farming	Beef cattle Dairying Livestock	Great Plains, USA Mid-West, USA Jamaica and Belize
Peasant farming	Subsistence farming Peasant farming	Nigeria Caribbean

Table 12.2 Systems of agriculture which are relevant to the Caribbean region

Sugar cane in the West Indies

Sugar is still the most important crop in the region and is produced by all the large islands and territories, plus Barbados and St Kitts. The smaller producers such as St Lucia and Antigua have long since abandoned production, and attempts to re-introduce the crop have failed, as in The Bahamas and St Vincent.

Country	ACP quotas 1975-90	US quotas 1988	Current Production	Peak (tonnes)
Barbados	49,300	8,205	69,000 (1990)	204,500 (1957)
Belize	39,400	11,045	100,000 (1990)	100,000 (1990)
Guyana	157,700	12,050	130,000 (1990)	370,000 (1969)
Jamaica	118,300	11,045	216,000 (1990)	413,000 (1966)
St Kitts- Nevis	14,800	8,000	15,000 (1990)	41,000 (1977)
Trinidad & Tobago	43,500*	8,205	118,000 (1990)	203,000 (1968)
Suriname	4,000	-	7,050 (1982)	-
Dominican Republic	-	123,200	1,250,000 (1982)	-
Haiti	-	5,770	71,000 (1983)	-
Total	207,000	187,520	1,976,050	

*Due to Trinidad's inability to meet its original quota of 69,000 tonnes, this was reduced to 43,500 tonnes in 1985. See also Table 12.5

Table12.3 Sugar quotas and production in the West Indies

Among the producers the output has declined greatly during the last 25-30 years. Table 12.3 shows some of the peak years for selected countries. There are several reasons for this decline, and these are described in detail below.

Independence and other political changes

Much of the sugar was grown by European or North American companies on land owned by them. This aspect of colonialism was unpopular and in some countries the change-over to local ownership has caused yields to decline or lands to be converted to other uses. In Guyana the Demerara Company was nationalized in 1975, and Cuba nationalized all holdings in 1959. About 40% of Cuba's 10 million tonnes industry was at that time owned directly by US interests. The previous owners had used large numbers of seasonal migrant labourers at very low wages. With the distribution of land to the peasants, there was a major problem of labour for harvesting which had to be met by brigades of 'volunteers' at first, and a conversion to mechanization later.

Another trend has been to convert land to food production and reduce imports.

Mechanization

Due to the growing organization of trades unions, competition from other industries paying higher wages - for example tourism, bauxite and manufacturing - and improved education, the availability of field labour declined rapidly in the 1960s. Mechanization led to a fall in acreages and yields for the following reasons:

(a) Some land was not suitable for tractors, for example gullied land, hilly land and stony land. These areas were eventually converted to other uses.

(b) Hand labour was relatively efficient *per area*. Machines are efficient *per man*. This led to declines in yield / area but an increase in yield / man. Put another way, sugar cane farming became more extensive. (See Table 12.6.)

(c) Suitable machines, especially harvesters, were not readily available and much time was lost with inadequate or insufficient equipment. Another problem was an increase in the amount of trash entering the factories. St Kitts introduced its first sugar cane harvesters in 1988 following a shortage of labour in 1987 which caused some 50,000 tonnes of cane to remain unharvested that year. (Fig. 12.1)

It should also be noted that as mechanization was introduced, it also *caused* unemployment in some jobs, such as ground preparation and weeding. Jamaica in particular had a reduced need for field labour all the year round, and this in turn led to increased out-imigration from the countryside, and consequently a shortage of casual labour at harvest time.

Cane fires

The practice of burning the cane is common in some countries, such as Trinidad and St Kitts. It is done to remove the cane trash and drive out snakes from the fields. However, because burnt cane is easier to cut, the practice became more widespread, both legally and illegally, as labour shortages increased. This led to lower yields because the sugar content declined when the cane was burned, and fell off rapidly if the canes were not harvested within 72 hours. Also, it limited the practice of *ratooning*, which is the cutting of several crops from the original plant. On good land, up to five ratoons could be harvested, but burnt land usually has to be replanted, which means an 18-month wait to the next crop, instead of 12 months. Finally, burning wastes valuable nutrients that should be returned to the soil, and increases soil erosion. Cane fires in Barbados increased from less than 10% of the crop in 1966 to 90% in 1974 and 1975, but was then checked. In 1990 about 5% of the land was burnt by malicious fires. It has been calculated that for every 1% of the land burnt in Barbados, 440 tonnes of sugar are lost.

The price of sugar

Over 80% of the world's sugar is sold in the country of origin, or exported under fixed agreements. For the West Indies, the following arrangements are the most important:

- The sugar protocol of the Lomé Convention, which governs the sale of sugar from the ACP countries to the EC. This accounts for most of the Commonwealth countries' sugar. (The ACP states are identified and explained on p. 226.)
- The International Sugar Agreement, under which exports are mainly to the USA and Canada but also to other countries. This includes Haiti, Dominican Republic and the Commonwealth Caribbean.
- Bilateral agreements between one country and another, such as Cuba and the USSR, or Guyana and China. Cuba gets about US 25 cents a pound for her sugar.

Fig. 12.1 Distribution of sugar cane land, St Kitts. The area shown represents about 4,000 hectares (10,000 acres) - about 23% of the total area. Unlike the other sugar-producing countries, this total has remained fairly constant since 1970.

Any other sales are made on a supply-and-demand basis at the existing world price, which is usually lower than any price under the agreements made above (Table 12.4).

The reason for the very low prices is that until recently the world produced 20-25% more sugar than it needed. The EC, for instance, does not need the Caribbean's sugar at all. It is self-sufficient, and most of what it buys it refines and re-exports. In 1989 the world produced 106 million tonnes compared with a demand for about 108 million tonnes.

The USA has also found that it must protect its own growers, and it puts a quota, an import duty, an import fee and a minimum selling price on all imports in order to inflate the final price. If imported sugar was allowed to enter unrestricted, US farmers would be unable to sell their own sugar and the US government would have to buy it from them. This kind of agreement is called the *domestic price support programme* in the USA, and is common in many countries in order to guarantee farmers an adequate income. In effect it usually produces surpluses. This kind of situation has recently kept the world price very low. If we examine Table 12.3 we will see that at best the six Commonwealth countries listed can normally only sell 60-80% of their crop at favourable

Table 12.4 Sugar prices in recent years

Sugar protocol	About 21-22 US cents a pound guaranteed for about 55% of the crop. The price is fixed annually.
USA	About 18-22 US cents a pound, guaranteed for about 15-20% of the crop.
World price	About 11-14 US cents a pound if a buyer can be found (1989 and 1990).

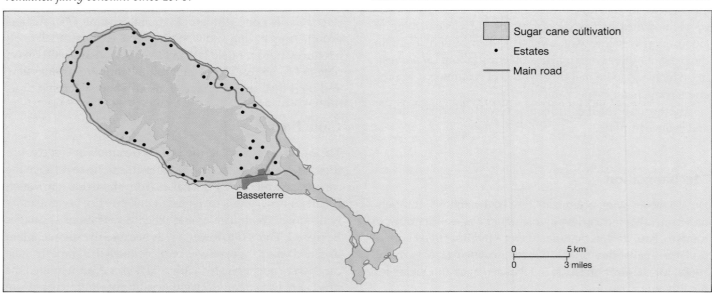

Sugar cane cultivation
• Estates
— Main road

Basseterre

0   5 km
0   3 miles

prices. Because of this they have reduced their sugar cane acreages. As long as the world price stays low, sugar production will continue to decline, because the cost of production in the Caribbean averages about 15 US cents a pound (Table 12.4).

Competition for land, and sugar substitutes

Competition for land, for housing, tourist development, and particularly for other forms of agriculture encouraged by policies of self-sufficiency and diversification, have also led to the decline in sugar production. Another problem is the use of non-sugar substances such as high-fructose corn syrup which is now used to sweeten many soft drinks. For instance, the Coca Cola company used to buy 1 million tonnes of sugar from Florida each year, but now buys none, and the USA as a whole has less need to import sugar. Similarly, in 1984 the US company Gulf & Western sold its sugar holdings in Florida (36,000 ha/90,000 acres) and in the Dominican Republic (96,000 ha/240,000 acres). As the press stated, this was due to 'a glut on the spot market for the past few years and because of competition from corn syrup and other sweeteners' (*Miami Herald*).

Nevertheless, sugar is still a major crop in the West Indies, employing many thousands of people and generating much foreign exchange (Table 12.5). Its development over the last

Country	Production (thousand tonnes)	
Cuba	7,600	(1990)
Puerto Rico	96	(1987)
Martinique	22	(1981)
Guadeloupe	59	(1981)
Total	7,777	

Table 12.5 Other sugar producers in the Caribbean

25 years in Barbados illustrates all the main problems and changes that have occurred.

1 How do world prices affect West Indian farming?

2 In what way is farming mechanized in your country? What further mechanization is possible? Why might mechanization be necessary?

3 What are the problems of growing food crops instead of export crops?

4 What are the advantages and disadvantages of cane fires?

5 What competition does Caribbean sugar face?

Sugar in Barbados

Barbados has long been a major sugar producer and even today produces about 2.5 tonnes for every hectare of land. However, sugar is not as important as it once was. For a long time it accounted for as much as 90% of all exports, but by the mid-1960s manufactured exports had become significant, and today sugar is down to 40% of the total. At the same time its contribution to the GDP fell from 33% to about 3%, being overtaken by manufacturing and tourism in the 1970s. In fact all agriculture, of which sugar is the major part, but which includes livestock, fruit and vegetables, is now less important than either manufacturing or tourism.

At one time most of the estates were owned by absentee foreigners. However, by the end of the 1970s there were only four estates owned by foreigners, accounting for a mere 3% of the area under cane. Altogether there are some 134 estates averaging about 115 ha (290 acres), which is rather small. There are far fewer owners - including the government which owns ten estates on about 6% of the

land - because many of the estates have the same owner.

The Barbados sugar industry is not simply a plantation system. There has always been a significant number (about 10,000) of peasant smallholdings accounting for about 15% of the cane land. On the smallholdings the owner does most of the work and rarely hires anyone. Usually he has a job somewhere else outside agriculture, but he may also be an estate worker. On the estates there is a management team which usually does not include the owner, a permanent workforce of about 3,500, and a seasonal labour force for harvesting of about 3,000. This is less than half of what it was ten years ago. The area of most concern has been the seasonal workforce, because since the time of independence there have never been enough seasonal workers to cut the cane.

For about ten years the government permitted the use of approximately 1,000 migrant cutters from St Vincent and St Lucia, but stopped this in 1976. The shortage of labour had two important results. First of all it led to an outbreak

System	Labour required	Cost (US$) per 100 tonnes		
		Labour	Machinery	Total
1 Manual cutting and loading	25 cutters 25 loaders 8 packers	725	0	725
2 Manual cutting and piling, mechanical loading	25 cutters 13 pilers 5 scrappers 1 machine operator	555	108	663
3 Mechanical cutting and loading, manual retrieving	25 retrievers 5 scrappers 2 machine operators	410	114 108	632
4 Mechanical cutting, mechanical cleaner-piler, mechanical loader	12 scrappers 3 machine operators	202	114 325 108	749
5 Chopper- harvester	1 field assistant 1 mechanic 1 machine operator	58	460	518

Machine costs include depreciation and running costs based on a workload of about 10,000 tonnes per year. Cost will be less if more is cut. It should be noted that system 4 is the most expensive as the mechanical cleaner-piler costs more to operate than the labour it replaces. All costs are approximate. (Source: Based on Andrew McGregor et al (1979), _The Barbados Sugar Industry_, Barbados Government.)

Table 12.6 Labour costs for harvesting sugar cane in Barbados, 1980

of illegal cane-burning by cutters, and then to controlled burning. Burnt canes are much easier to cut, so the labour force could earn more money per day and fewer were needed. Unfortunately this led to the serious effects already noted (p. 125) and burning was made illegal. The second result was the introduction of machinery. By the 1980s, 70% of the cane was loaded mechanically and about 15% cut by mechanical harvesters. Ultimately as much as 50% of the cane will probably be cut by machines. Not all

cane can be cut mechanically for the following reasons:

(a) The land must not slope more than 10-15° (this rules out 25% of the cane lands).

(b) Harvesters cannot work over gullies and sinkholes, and this takes out about another 3-5%.

(c) The land must be cleared of stones - this can be done over time, but has to be repeated regularly.

(d) The cane should be planted in long rows with proper spacing.

(e) The cane needs to be suitable for machine cutting - deep-rooted, upright, and with the trash hanging clear of the stalks.

In general it takes an estate about five years to convert

Table 12.7 Sugar production in Barbados, 1950-82

Year	Area harvested		Cane cut million tonnes	Sugar tonnes	Yield (tonnes)	
	hectares	(acres)			per hectare	(per acre)
1950	16,500	(41,240)	1.3	158,000	9.5	(3.8)
1960	19,630	(49,070)	1.4	153,500	7.8	(3.1)
1970	19,910	(49,780)	1.4	154,000	7.8	(3.1)
1982	15,580	(39,000)	1.0	85,500	5.5	(2.2)
1990	10,800	(27,000)	0.7	69,000	6.4	(2.6)

to mechanical harvesting. Under suitable conditions a harvester can cut 200 tonnes of cane a day, compared with a good worker who could cut 2.5 tonnes in a day. Put another way, a harvester is worth 80 cane cutters, and could cut 10,000 tonnes of cane in a season. It is worth noting that Cuba harvests well over half of its 8 million tonnes sugar crop with combine harvesters. These are manufactured in a Soviet-built factory that can produce 6,000 harvesters a year. 'We are going to make the machète obsolete', said the factory director!

Harvesters are by no means perfect, and in particular waste a lot of cane by crushing it, compacting the soil with their weight, and picking up a lot more trash which causes problems at the factory. They burn fuel, need repairs and maintenance, and put a new set of demands on the labour force, requiring new management techniques, and a new labour force of drivers and mechanics.

One remarkable aspect of mechanization has been the development by Barbados of its own mechanical harvesters, once it was found that imported machines were not really suitable for local conditions. Barbados thus developed the world's first harvester to cut and pile green sugar cane (not burnt). Most harvesters from abroad work best on burnt canes.

Processing and selling the sugar cane crop

Having harvested the cane it has to be converted into a saleable form, usually raw or brown sugar. There are several other things that it could be made into such as *ethanol*, which is the sugar alcohol used to make *gasohol*, a gasoline substitute. Other possibilities are to make *fibreboard* from the bagasse, use the bagasse as *fuel*, and use the pith to make *livestock feed*. Barbados has investigated all of these. It found that it could not produce ethanol cheaply enough to compete with gasoline. The production of fibreboard linked to that of livestock feed (See p. 162) would require a herd of 16,000 cattle to make it economical. It is possible that a combined fibreboard and sugar plant could profitably be built in the future. Livestock are already being fed with cane tops and chopped cane, and this aspect is likely to be developed further. Bagasse is the waste from normal sugar cane crushing processes, and the Barbadian factories are almost unique in the world in using it as their only source of fuel.

In 1985 St Kitts announced a project to produce electricity from surplus bagasse which, as in Barbados, powers the sugar cane factory. It is estimated that this will account for about 20% of St Kitts' electricity when it opens in 1987. Bagasse is a *by-product*. Another by-product is *molasses*. This is widely used in the *rum* industry (p. 160), which uses more than 70% of the molasses produced in Barbados.

The present situation is therefore that the sugar syrup produced in the factory is converted into sugar, with the exception of a small amount which is retained as fancy molasses. There are now only four sugar factories spread around Barbados, the one at Portvale being the only new one, finished in 1982. Although all the others have been continually modernized, this was the first new factory to be built for over 60 years! Today there are fewer factories than ever before, and they are all owned and operated by one organization. Two were closed in 1988 owing to the 'continued decline in production'. The Sugar Protocol guarantees the sale of 53,600 tonnes at a price, negotiated each year, that is much higher than the world price at present. This quota will stay the same unless Barbados fails to supply it in any year. The Protocol replaced the Commonwealth Sugar Agreement after Britain joined the EC. (See Table 12.3.)

The USA was not originally a major buyer, taking only 2,000 tonnes up to 1973 under the US Sugar Act. When this ended, US importers could buy as much as they wanted. Barbados sold all its remaining sugar to the USA until 1982, when the USA had to impose quotas to stop the flood of cheap sugar entering the country. The quota for Barbados was set at 17,800 tonnes, a big drop from the average sales of over 30,800 tonnes. After 1982 any production over the quota total had to be sold on the world market at world prices. In 1991 the quota was 14,239 tonnes, an increase from the low of 7,444 tonnes reached in 1989. This is due to shortfalls in US production (Table 12.8).

Table 12.8 Markets for Barbados sugar, 1973-77

Market	Tonnes	%
Used domestically	15,000	13%
Exported	112,000	87%
EC	53,600	48%
USA	30,000	27%
Canada	5,000	4%
Other countries	23,400	21%

Sugar in Trinidad

Trinidad provides the most striking example of the decline of sugar among the major exporters (See Table 12.9). Since 1984 it has had to import between 20,000 and 40,000 tonnes of raw sugar a year in order to meet export commitments and local demand. Production at 82,000 tonnes in 1988 was 44% of what it was in 1970, and the growing cost is now higher than the selling price. In 1988 the government was subsidizing the state-owned Caroni company to the extent of $2.00 for every $1.00 earned in foreign exchange. There seems little reason for Trinidad to continue growing sugar when it can buy it at a fraction of the production cost. Also the Caroni lands are quite suitable for other crops, and

Product	Value (US$ million)	%
Sugar*	23.2*	81
Cocoa	3.1	11
Coffee	2.0	7
Citrus	0.4	1
Total	28.7	100

* In 1986, 37,000 tonnes of sugar were imported to make up for the shortfall in production and meet export quotas. Imports have been necessary since 1984.

Table 12.9 Trinidad - value of exports of traditional crops, 1986

The moth borer is one of the many pests that can attack sugar cane.

Trinidad is too far south to be seriously affected by hurricanes, which are a threat to other crops. Despite this, sugar is a large employer of labour and is not being abandoned. Trinidad produced 118,000 tonnes in 1990, which was more than was expected, and was an increase on the 97,000 tonnes produced in 1989. With a greater demand from the USA in the 1990s, sugar may be having a revival.

1 Why does Barbados still grow sugar cane when most of its neighbours do not?

2 What can sugar cane be used for?

3 How do the EC and the USA help sugar producers?

Other export crops

Bananas, coffee, cocoa and citrus are the other main export crops after sugar. Coconuts are an important regional crop, but although coconut oil, meal and copra are used widely and exported among the islands, they are not significant foreign exchange earners.

There is a great variety of other crops that are important locally, but not widespread. These include the following:

Arrowroot (St Vincent)

Mace and nutmeg (Grenada)

Sea island cotton (Barbados)

Tobacco (Cuba and Jamaica)

Sisal (Haiti)

Pineapples (Puerto Rico and Martinique)

Cucumbers and melons (Dominica)

Live plants (Montserrat and Puerto Rico)

Coconut oil (Dominica)

Bananas

The export of bananas is much more recent than the trade in sugar, as it did not start on a large scale until early in the twentieth century, when fast refrigerated shipping services became available. (See Table 12.10.)

Most bananas grown in the Caribbean are used at home. Only Jamaica, Martinique and Guadeloupe have a long history of exports. This is because the trade was dominated by the major fruit companies who controlled the market, ran the

Preparing copra near Biabou Bay on St Vincent. Coconut oil is now in demand for the manufacture of soap.

Country	Export (tonnes)	% of UK market
Belize	27,000	6
Dominica	52,600	18
Grenada	8,600	3
Guadeloupe	87,800	-
Jamaica	43,000	10
Martinique	193,300	0.5
St Lucia	120,500	25
St Vincent	65,600	10
Suriname	35,000	10
Latin America	6,125,000	16

Table 12.10 Banana exports from the Caribbean, 1989

ships and established the estates. The largest estates, owned by the US United Fruit Company, are in Central and South America, but this company also established an estate in Jamaica in the name of its subsidiary, Fyffes. Until the 1950s Jamaica and West Cameroon (in West Africa) had the monopoly for supplying the UK, but with the independence of West Cameroon only Jamaica was left. In 1954 the Geest Company agreed to buy all the quality bananas produced in the four Windward Islands. Bananas grow best with 1,875 mm (75 in.) of rain and no dry season, and so are well suited to these islands. In many cases, notably St Lucia, the bananas were grown on old sugar cane land, and sugar production was abandoned, if it had not already stopped. The banana industry is structured somewhat differently from the sugar industry. Although originally set up by foreign companies,

Bananas now grow on old sugar cane land at Roseau in St Lucia. The railway was once used to take the cane to the sugar factory.

the land is owned locally mainly by many smallholders - there were 20,000 growers in the 1980s. Frequently other crops are grown in the shade of the bananas, such as dasheen, sweet potatoes, maize or pumpkins. For example, a small farmer at Port Casse in Dominica might own 3 hectares (8 acres), and also grow dasheen, sugar cane and grapefruit. Dasheen in particular is popular and fetches a good price.

Despite the variety, bananas are the crop around which a farmer's life revolves, and which guarantees a weekly income. Every week farmers pack bananas into boxes, about 20 boxes per hectare, each weighing 12-16 kg. The boxes are collected and sent to a packing station, such as at Barakua, where they are inspected and weighed. Farmers receive between 22 and 26 US cents per kilogram. In Dominica a banana boat from Geest or a charter company visits Roseau and Portsmouth once a week to load at least 1,000 tonnes of bananas for the UK. It also stops at St Vincent, St Lucia and Grenada.

Although production has been increasing, there have been problems, notably in Jamaica and Grenada. The former has had labour problems resulting in poor-quality produce, hurricane damage, and Panama disease, while Grenada reduced its acreages considerably after independence in 1974, and with the introduction of socialism in 1979. Jamaica's crop was severely damaged by Hurricane Frederick in 1979, and Hurricane Allen in 1980. As a result it only produced 10,000 tonnes in 1984, and 34,000 tonnes in 1987. In 1988 the crop was totally destroyed by Hurricane Gilbert, but 1990 was a good year: 60,000 tonnes were produced for export.

Hurricane damage is always a problem for any industry, but bananas and sugar cane are more resistant than most crops. Although the banana plant is very vulnerable to wind damage, its shoot usually survives to produce bananas the following year. Sugar cane, a tall grass, is equally sturdy, but tree crops that are destroyed have to be replaced at great expense and with a wait of five years or more for a full crop.

Severe hurricanes, such as Gilbert, have much longer-lasting effects, however. Infrastructure is destroyed, fallen plants or flattened cane lies rotting everywhere, and a whole year's crop is lost. The cost of recovery and the loss of income is so high that some farmers give up farming, and in the meantime markets are lost.

As Jamaica's industry declined, Suriname, and later Belize, became important suppliers. Since 1982 Suriname has averaged 35,000 tonnes a year for export to the UK, and Belize produced 28,000 tonnes in 1989. Both countries are expanding production by bringing new land into cultivation.

Despite its growth in the 1980s, the Commonwealth Caribbean's banana industry is threatened in much the same way that sugar was 20 years ago. This is particularly serious for the Windward Islands as there is no other crop that can be grown on their wet, hilly land to replace bananas as a source of income. The only market is the UK, which guarantees to take a quota of bananas from each West Indian producer. Unfortunately the West Indies is a 'high-cost' producer compared with Latin America, and if it had to compete with 'dollar' bananas (as Latin American bananas are called) it would go out of business immediately, even though 'dollar' bananas have to pay 20% customs duty. This may well happen, as the EC countries already import one million tonnes of bananas from Latin America, and the UK gave them a quota as well in 1988. As Britain is a member of the EC, its purchases are governed by the third Lomé Convention (See p. 226) which only lasts until 1990. It is unlikely that the EC will continue to allow much higher-priced bananas from the West Indies to be protected by the quota system when cheaper 'dollar' bananas are available. In 1990 455,000 tonnes of 'dollar' bananas were sold to the new east European market ('*Insight*' report).

---

1 Where were bananas first introduced into the Caribbean commercially?

2 What are the main differences in (a) cultivation, (b) processing, (c) labour requirements, between sugar cane and bananas?

3 What are the differences between the economic problems of sugar and bananas?

4 What are the differences in the climatic requirements for sugar cane and bananas?

5 What are the main hazards in growing bananas?

Coffee, cocoa and citrus - a valuable trio

Coffee

This is probably the next most important export after bananas in the West Indies, and it is the major export crop of Haiti. Unfortunately hurricane damage and salinity problems due to over-irrigation have led to a serious decline in Haiti.

Coffee has long been grown in the region, originally on large estates, but mainly by smallholders today. The significant producers are the Greater Antilles and Trinidad, with Jamaica's Blue Mountain coffee probably the best known. Coffee production has been declining, but because of its high world price there are many projects to enlarge and restock the main growing areas. The rainy mountain areas of these islands are well suited to coffee growing, but there has been much neglect and soil erosion. The small size of the holdings and overall production have prevented major long-term contracts from being given in Jamaica and Trinidad. Trinidad now produces a mere 40% of what it grew ten years ago and is no longer a significant producer. Production in Jamaica has been slowly increasing and the area under cultivation in the Blue Mountains has been expanded. Coffee is also grown in the other, mainly northern, mountain regions of Jamaica, and under the name of High Mountain Supreme it has been successfully marketed in the USA. (See Table 12.11.)

Production from the non-Commonwealth countries is consumed locally in large amounts, as coffee-drinking is a traditional activity in the Spanish-speaking areas; the surplus is sent to the USA. Puerto Rico earns ten times as much as Jamaica from coffee exports ($65m in 1987), and has a high local consumption.

Cocoa

Cocoa has had much the same performance as coffee. There are no acceptable substitutes and prices have traditionally been high compared with other possible land uses. Jamaica's crop, like its coffee, is regarded as a high-quality product and continues to fetch a good price. Despite this, orchards have been neglected and disease is a problem. Trinidad and Grenada are small but significant exporters.

Table 12.11 Coffee and cocoa exports from the Caribbean, 1989

Country	Coffee (tonnes)	Cocoa (tonnes)
Dominican Republic	32,400	40,600
Grenada	–	1,400
Haiti	13,400	2,800
Jamaica	900	1,100
Trinidad and Tobago	30	1,400

A typical response to the industry's various problems is a US$40 million project for both cocoa and coffee in the Dominican Republic, announced in 1981. The aim is to repair the damage of several earlier hurricanes. Some 16,000 ha (40,000 acres) will be replanted on nearly 10,000 small farms, and some 600 cocoa and coffee nurseries are being set up. In Belize the American Hershey Corporation has planted a large cocoa estate in Cayo, and local farmers are also growing the crop.

Citrus

The Caribbean has long been noted for its quality citrus products such as orange juice and marmalade, but Cuba produces by far the largest quantity - 880,000 tonnes in 1987, more than the rest of the region put together (Table 12.12). Of this, 500,000 to 600,000 tonnes was sent to the USSR and the Ex-Comecon countries (Comecon - the economic grouping of the East European communist countries and Cuba) each year, but there are plans to increase production considerably.

Traditionally, Trinidad and Tobago, Jamaica and Montserrat have been citrus growers in the Commonwealth Caribbean. Limes and lime juice produced in Montserrat in the late 1970s are no longer significant, and this was only a fraction of the production achieved 100 years ago. Trinidad's exports of orange and grapefruit juice have also declined dramatically, although production has been more or less constant in the 1980s. This is due to the increased domestic consumption, and distance from the USA, which was not its traditional market, and now limits its opportunity to compete with the northern suppliers.

Jamaica has been successful in continuing to export fresh fruit, fruit juice and marmalade, with fresh fruit being in greatest demand as a result of shortfalls in Florida.

In the winters of 1983/84 and 1984/85 there were severe freezes in Florida which destroyed or damaged thousands of hectares of citrus orchards. In a period of six years, 48,000 ha (120,000 acres) went out of cultivation in northern and central Florida. The response to this was to start new farms in the far south of Florida, but even these are not secure from severe frost, and land here is expensive. Several major growers, including Kendal Farms, the world's largest lime and lemon

Table 12.12 Citrus production in the Caribbean, 1987

Country	Production (tonnes)
Bahamas	10,500
Belize	84,000
Cuba	880,000
Jamaica	31,000
Trinidad and Tobago	4,000

juice producers, leased land in The Bahamas and Belize. In The Bahamas local producers have increased their holdings. Limes, lemons, grapefruit and the non-citrus papaya are the main crops, the papaya maturing much more quickly than the citrus and often being temporarily intercropped with it. The demand for fresh and processed citrus in North America is so great that the northern Caribbean has a major opportunity to diversify into this crop, which is relatively fast-growing and well suited to the climate. In 1985 Coca Cola purchased a large area of land in northern Belize, and the Harmon Fruit Company of Florida leased 8,000 ha (20,000 acres) on Abaco in The Bahamas.

Unfortunately the price of orange juice concentrate fell after several mild winters in Florida, and Coca Cola cancelled its project. Belize is still a major citrus grower, however, and has produced over 90,000 tonnes in recent years, mainly in the form of orange and grapefruit concentrates. By contrast, The Bahamas exports 10,000 tonnes, entirely in the form of fresh oranges, grapefruit, lemons and limes.

Further production will be encouraged in Jamaica, Dominica, and the Dominican Republic by a factory that is being built in Puerto Rico to process their citrus fruit. It will then be exported to the USA under a CBI agreement (See p. 227).

Caribbean export crops

The study of export crops in the Caribbean allows certain conclusions to be drawn:

1   For most products the Caribbean is a high-cost producer which cannot compete on the open market at world prices. Its competitors, notably Latin America, produce similar products more cheaply and in greater quantity.

2   Exports at specially negotiated prices are unlikely to continue because the markets want either to buy their own produce, e.g. sugar beet, which they subsidize, or to import the cheapest produce, e.g. 'dollar' bananas.

3   Even for crops in which the Caribbean is competitive at world prices, such as cocoa and coffee, it is too small a producer to influence these prices and is at the mercy of price changes. In particular, high prices lead to increased production in the major producing countries, causing a fall in price that is very damaging to the Caribbean grower.

4   Success in exports is possible under certain conditions:
    (a) A quick response to a new demand, e.g. tomatoes and cucumbers for the USA until the mid-1980s was a successful venture for Jamaica and The Bahamas. A high-investment orchard crop like citrus has been less successful.

Product	Value (US$million)	%
Sugar	62	54
Bananas	18	16
Coffee	9	8
Pimento	4	3.5
Citrus	3	2.5
Cocoa	2	2
Non-traditional*	16	14
Total	114	100

*mainly vegetables, tubers, fruits, ornamentals

Table 12.13 Jamaica - value of export of traditional crops, 1989

(b) Production of a minority product, such as nutmeg and mace in Grenada, and pimento in Jamaica. In 1987 pimento earned more for Jamaica than either citrus or cocoa, and sales are expected to increase (See Table 12.13).

Citrus-growing is having a revival in the West Indies, but it is by no means a new crop. Plants are first raised under controlled conditions in nurseries, such as this one at Graemes Hall, Barbados.

(c) Producing food crops for export to Caricom members. Dominica has done this well with dasheen and tannias, and Jamaica with yams, which also sell in the USA.

(d) Specializing in a high-quality product for a growing market, such as ornamentals (cut flowers, foliage and live plants). Puerto Rico and Jamaica have both entered this field successfully.

---

1 Why has citrus become a popular crop in some parts of the Caribbean in the 1980s?

2 Is citrus likely to lead to downstream industrial activities? If so, what might be possible? If not, what are the problems? (A *downstream* activity is one that uses the product of one industry to make a second product.)

3 What other crops might be successfully grown for export?

13
Farming at home and abroad

Growing rice in paddy fields near Debe, Trinidad.

Rice farming in Guyana

Rice is a major agricultural product in Guyana, grown on 100,000 ha (250,000 acres), which is about twice the area given to sugar cane. It is not a plantation crop, however, and in 1978 there were 29,000 farmers, many of these being small farmers with 6 ha (15 acres) plots. Despite a ban on wheat flour and the use of rice as a substitute, both area and yields have declined slowly over the last ten years. This is mainly due to low prices which discourage the many small farmers. The area for rice growing is the coastal strip (Fig. 13.1) which stretches 440km (270 miles) from the mouth of the Corentyne River to Essequibo. Not all of this is wet land, and some of it is ploughed and planted for other crops. On the wet or flooded land, seed beds (nurseries) are used to raise seedlings and then these are transplanted by hand. On the dry land the seeds are broadcast by hand, tractor, or even aeroplane directly onto the ploughed land. In the climatic conditions here it is possible to get two crops from the land in a year: the spring crop which grows from November to April, and the autumn crop from April to November. Rice needs about 1,000 mm (40 in.) of rain per crop. The autumn crop is the main one, giving better yields per hectare and occupying much more land, but the spring crop still produces about 60,000 tonnes or 30% of the total. More recently some farmers have been planting three crops using some of the new high-yielding varieties that respond well to fertilizers and irrigation. This is the same 'green revolution' rice that has transformed agriculture in India.

Areas that are entirely dependent on rainfall for water have poor yields, about half that of crops grown on irrigated land. Several projects are in hand to provide better drainage and irrigation for these areas, and also to increase the area at Tapakuma in Black Bush Polder, and the Mahaicony Abary district of eastern Demerara. Some sugar land in Demerara is also being converted to rice-growing. Although a lot of rice is exported, it is still the main part of the Guyanese diet. This means that much has to be retained for local use - once about one-third of the total, now about half. The remainder is exported mainly to the West Indies, but also to the UK and Canada, and to parts of eastern Europe. Total production in 1989 was only 142,000 tonnes.

Fig. 13.1 Agricultural land use in Guyana. Agriculture is confined to the coastal strip within about 100 kilometres of the coast. Most of the land not used for rice and sugar cane is pasture on the inland side of the cultivated strip. Coconuts are grown along the coast in all areas. Some coffee and maize are grown in the north-west. Green vegetables, root crops and fruits of many varieties are also grown privately and commercially throughout the coastal area. The reservoirs provide irrigation to the adjacent land.

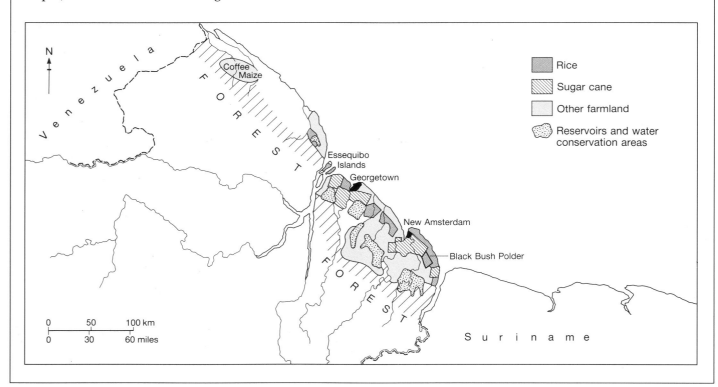

136

Guyana has made a great effort to increase the output of all its major foodstuffs (Table 13.1), and has long planned to increase the area of nearly all its major crops by a total of some 50,000 ha (126,000 acres). Most of this increase will be for sugar cane (16,000 ha/40,000 acres) and rice (24,000 ha/60,000 acres) which will increase foreign exchange earnings. Other increases are to save foreign exchange on food imports, which are virtually banned. The main import has been of wheat for flour, but in the 1980s this was also strictly limited, with severe penalties for smuggling. As far as possible rice flour is being used as a substitute. Unfortunately the attempted increase in land has not been matched by an increase in yields. Rice only yields about 0.6 tonne/ha, whereas 1-2.5 tonnes should be feasible. In most cases yield has declined, often considerably, suggesting the need for fertilizers, good seed, and better farming practices (maintenance of ditches, fences, roads and machinery). With the continued lack of foreign exchange in the 1980s, the situation has deteriorated. By 1989 it was clear that major coastal and river bank repairs were needed to prevent serious flooding, but the lack of machinery and spare parts prevented this, despite EC aid. In the summer of 1990, and again in early 1991, river and sea defences were breached and thousands of hectares were flooded in eastern Demerara, Corentyne and Mahaicony. One-third of the rice crop was lost, and the ban on wheat flour had to be relaxed. The estimate for repairs is US $1 billion. (Source: various 'Insight' reports, 1990-1991).

Sugar yields have declined from 1.3 tonnes/hectare (3.2 tonnes/acre) to 0.9 tonne/hectare (2.3 tonnes/acre). Yields also declined in Barbados with the introduction of mechanization in the 1970s, and the figures are very similar, so it should not be assumed that these declines are only a Guyanese problem.

Guyana is not the only rice grower in the region, as both Belize and Suriname have expanding industries. Most of Suriname's 200,000 tonnes annual production is exported to Europe, and the rest to the French West Indies. Trinidad produces about 4,500 tonnes a year for local use.

Table 13.1 Guyana - food production changes, 1960-78

Product	Area 1978 Hectares (Acres)		Production change %	Area change %	Yield change %
Sugar	56,000	(140,000)	0	+40	−25
Rice	120,000	(300,000)	+50	+25	+15
Corn	1,200	(3,000)	+800	Large increase	Large increase
Ground provisions (root crops)	2,000	(5,000)	−50	Same	Decline
Citrus	2,800	(7,000)	+20	+100	−40
Plantains	7,200	(18,000)	+25	+40	−70
Coconuts	19,200	(48,000)	−50	+20	−50
Coffee	1,320	(3,300)	+50	Increase	Increase
Cocoa	600	(1,500)	−70	Same	−75
Beef			0	Herd greatly increased	
Pork			+600	Herd +500	Weight +100
Mutton			+400	Herd +100	
Poultry			+2,000	Very large increase	Weight +40

Note: In most cases area or herd size was greatly increased, but yield declined so that there was not always an increase in production.

A ranch in Antigua.

The Caribbean is a major importer of food, and in particular of meat and dairy products. Beef and dairy products alone account for 34% of the food bill, worth about US $260 m in 1985. Caricom has designated certain areas as cattle-raising centres, notably Belize and Jamaica.

In Guyana livestock has also been an area of expansion, with enormous increases in pigs and poultry, and approxi-mately 100% increases in cattle and sheep numbers. Improved stock has led to significant increases in the weight of cattle, pigs and poultry, so the overall increase in meat production has been considerable, from 3.9 million kg (8.5 million lb) in 1960 to 14 million kg (30.8 million lb) in 1978.

Jamaica

Jamaica is particularly noted for its breeding performance in the past. It is most important for any form of livestock development to acquire or breed animals that are tolerant to the local climate, especially the heat, and are able to resist the local diseases, and parasites such as ticks. Heat and ticks are major problems to any European cattle in the tropics.

When attempts were made to produce meat in the tropics, the colonizers brought in British and European cattle, but these quickly deteriorated under tropical conditions. Nevertheless, as these cattle were highly efficient meat and milk producers, attempts were made to cross them with Indian and other tropical breeds so that they would eventually become resistant to tropical conditions, but still be good food producers. Indian cattle were introduced into the region in the nineteenth century, at the time when Indian indentured workers were migrating to Trinidad and Guyana. Rice and sugar cane are widely produced in India, and the Brahman breed has been the traditional draught animal until very recently, so it was natural that they should accompany the new agricultural labour force. Water buffalo were also introduced, but in smaller numbers, as draught animals, and to supply milk and butter.

Indian cattle belong to a group known as Zebu cattle. These are smaller than European cattle and take longer to mature, but they tolerate high temperatures and poor

138

A Jamaican bull and cows on a farm reclaimed from bauxite land in St Mary, Jamaica.

Item	1978	1987
Cattle slaughtered	57,700	67,400
Beef produced (tonnes)	12,800	13,900
Hogs slaughtered	126,300	109,600
Pork produced (tonnes)	8,400	6,500
Goats and sheep slaughtered	25,100	52,700
Goat meat and mutton produced (tonnes)	400	630
Poultry	33,900	37,800
Eggs (millions)	240	115
Milk (million litres)	47	21
Total meat produced (tonnes)	55,400	58,800
Total meat imported - fresh, chilled, frozen (tonnes)	76,900	33,800
% meat imported	58	37
Total consumption meat (tonnes)	132,300	92,600

Table 13.2 Jamaica - meat and milk production, 1978 and 1987

grazing remarkably well. Even more important is the Zebu's resistance to ticks. These animals are distinguished by their hump and a dewlap - loose skin hanging down under the neck. In India they are mainly kept to pull carts and ploughs, and in a few areas they also produce milk which can be used to make a native butter, but in India and many other Asian countries the meat is considered sacred and cannot be eaten. The Indian breeds used in the West Indies include the Myzore, Nellore, Red Cindy, Guzerat and Sahiwal, all generally known by the generic name Brahman.

The ideal in breeding is to provide an animal that produces the quantity and quality of the European animal but is as sturdy as the Zebu. In Jamaica the greatest success has been with the *Jamaica Hope*, which is about 80% Jersey with 5% Holstein and only 15% Sahiwal. This is a particularly productive *dairy* animal, and there are about 25,000 of them. The main *beef* animal, and the most common breed in Jamaica, is the *Jamaica Red*. It is a cross-bred cow from Red Poll, Zebu and Devon breeds, and the herd numbers about 100,000. Another breed used in the West Indies for beef is the *Santa Gertrudis*, 35% Brahman and 65% Shorthorn, bred in Texas and kept in smaller numbers in Jamaica, and to a lesser extent in The Bahamas.

While domestic meat production increased by about 25% up to 1978, actual consumption increased by about 100%. The balance was made up by a huge increase in imports - over 250%! This meant that Jamaica actually imported more meat than it produced, creating an enormous drain on its foreign currency. (See Table 13.2.)

At first sight it might appear that local farmers had been indifferent to the increasing demand, but the reasons were complex. A major problem was a shortage of foreign exchange to buy animals (for breeding), fodder, fertilizers, and the great number of other farm supplies needed to maintain and expand animal numbers and meat production. When the shortage reached the shops and the consumer, it was too late to go back to the farmer and start investing in new stock. Money had to be taken from other sources, and borrowed, to buy food to satisfy the existing shortages. Very quickly a vicious circle developed that has proved difficult to control.

Jamaica now has a total of about half a million cattle - almost half the Commonwealth Caribbean's entire stock. Of these 350,000 are pedigree and another 150,000 are recognized breeds. Most are beef cattle, with perhaps 10% dairy cattle. Dairy cattle have only been developed with the advent of large dairies, for example in Jamaica since 1941, and in Barbados when the Pine Hill dairy was built in 1966.

Guyana

The next largest herd is in Guyana on the savanna lands. Here there are about 280,000 head altogether, with some dairy herds in the wetter coastal savanna, and beef cattle on the inland Rupununi savannas. Georgetown and its Milk Plant dairy is the main market for the dairy herd. Some beef is also reared on the coast, but most comes from the interior where an abattoir has been built at Lethem.

Belize

Belize has been designated as particularly suitable for an increase in its cattle population. In 1983 it only had about 60,000 head, of which 10,000 were slaughtered each year. At present there are 43,200 ha (108,000 acres) of pasture, but this could be expanded considerably. In the meantime, Belize exports live cattle to Mexico and Martinique in particular, worth over US $2 m in 1984. There is a local modern abattoir and good local demand from the British garrison stationed here. However, expansion will be slow and costly, and overgrazing is already a problem. A further problem is that there are no deepwater ports in Belize; large vessels have to anchor offshore and livestock is ferried out to them.

In the Caribbean as a whole the biggest problem is that of pasture and nutrition. Few of the traditional farmers have been willing to plant grass or legumes as a crop, and cattle are usually left to forage for themselves. Alternatively, land too poor for other crops has been planted with local grasses, but these do not grow well on poor soils either, so the cattle are undernourished. Herd expansion in Jamaica and Guyana has repeatedly suffered from the shortage of imported feedstuffs and the inability to grow good-quality fodder at home. This problem has still not been solved.

1 Which countries grow rice in the Caribbean? What are the climatic requirements for growing rice?

2 Cattle are not widespread in the Caribbean compared with other countries. Why is this?

3 What are the breeds of cattle and sheep in your country?

4 What products do we get from pigs? Of those that you eat, which were produced locally?

Peasant farming in Haiti

Most of Haiti's agriculture is small scale - 90% of the farms are less than 3 ha (7 acres), and occupy about 60% of the farmland (Fig. 13.3). Nearly 90% of the population were subsistence farmers in 1971 and their average annual income was US$48 (Table 13.3). On average each family farmed two parcels of land, each less than one hectare. The term 'minifundia' is given to such small-scale farming. It prevents commercialization or improvement, as it is uneconomic to use machinery, irrigation or chemicals at this scale. Buying small quantities of fertilizer, for instance, would cost more per hectare than the crop was worth. Similarly, any improvements on a single parcel would be ruined by the lack of change in the fields surrounding it; for example, drainage improvements cannot be carried out in one field alone.

This situation is partly historic and partly geographic. Having been independent for nearly 200 years, the population farmed in the traditional subsistence fashion without the benefits of outside technology, which was introduced on the plantations of most of the rest of the Caribbean. This situation was compounded by the very hilly nature of the country, which led to extreme soil erosion

Table 13.3 Haiti - structure of agriculture in 1971

Size of holding (Ha)	No. of farms	Population
< 1 ha	362,000	1.5m
1-3 ha	296,000	1.0m
3-5 ha	36,000	0.2m
> 75 ha	23,000	0.14m

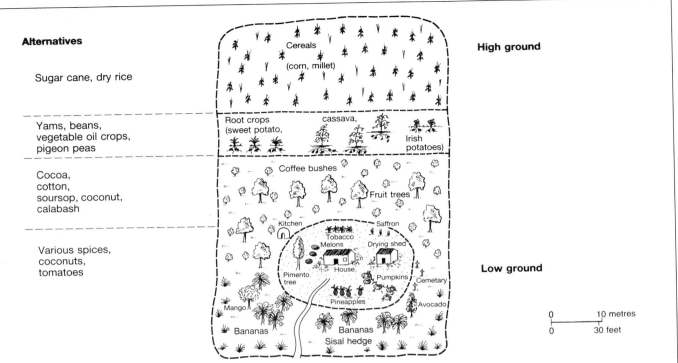

Alternatives

Sugar cane, dry rice

Yams, beans,
vegetable oil crops,
pigeon peas

Cocoa,
cotton,
soursop, coconut,
calabash

Various spices,
coconuts,
tomatoes

High ground

Cereals
(corn, millet)

Root crops
(sweet potato,   cassava,
                        Irish
                        potatoes)

Coffee bushes

Fruit trees

Kitchen   Saffron
      Tobacco
Melons   Drying shed
          House
Pimento
tree   Pumpkins
                  Cemetary
      Pineapples
            Avocado
Mango
Bananas   Bananas
      Sisal hedge

Low ground

0   10 metres
0   30 feet

Fig. 13.2 A Haitian subsistence farm (le jardin). The actual crops grown will vary considerably depending on where the farm is located, and how wet the climate is. There will also be chickens and a few cows on many farms. The appearance, especially in the dry season, will be more barren than the sketch suggests. (Source: Georges Anglade, L'Espaze Haitien, Editions Des Alizés, Montreal, 1981.)

under a climate of marked wet and dry seasons. Without external aid, agriculture remained trapped in a cycle of inefficiency and poverty. Only recently has the introduction of co-operatives and joint ownership brought any change.

Another part of the problem is *ownership of land*. The peasant can be the owner of his land, but because of the lack of proper surveys or deeds of ownership, probably less than a quarter of the peasant owners could actually prove their title to the land. Share-cropping, or *metayage*, is common, the farmer having to give a large part of his produce as rent to the owner of the land. This type of rental system is very discouraging to the peasant, who has no incentive to improve the land. *Tenant farmers* simply pay a rent in cash for the land.

The equipment used in most cases is the machète and a hoe. The farm is called a garden (*le jardin*). All farmers grow crops for subsistence, but also hope to produce a surplus - about a third of the crop - which they can sell at the local market for cash. This can be used to buy necessities. A great variety of crops are grown in order to meet as many needs as possible; this system is known as *polyculture*. Even so, some food must be bought, particularly butter, cooking oil, salt and seasoning.

There are well over a million gardens in Haiti. The most common crops are as follows:

Root crops: cassava, Irish potato, yams, sweet potato
Vines: water melon, tomato, pumpkin
Cereals: maize (corn), millet (sorghum)
Other crops: sugar cane, tobacco, cotton, coffee beans, spices, (pimento, saffron, peppers), cusceus-grass
Trees: mango, avocado, shade trees, soursop, coconut, bananas

These crops are arranged in most cases at a certain distance from the house so as to form three distinct rings or zones of cultivation (See Fig. 13.2). The crops nearest to the house are those that are most likely to be stolen, and therefore have to be watched, e.g. tobacco. Animals are also kept, being fed on scraps, and foraging wherever possible. Chickens, one or two pigs, a horse and occasionally a cow, are common.

Despite the great variety and apparent organization, yields are very low, and disease, pests and undernourishment are abundant. Everything is subject to the climate, to drought, floods and hurricanes. The only good thing that can be said is that over the centuries, experience has taught the peasant that whatever the disaster, with the right mix of crops at least something will survive to feed him and his family.

Subsistence farming in southern Nigeria

Nigeria is similar to Haiti in that where there was once a shifting cultivation, there is now a sedentary (permanently settled) population. The poor tropical soils are not fertilized and have to be left fallow for a period. As long as 15-25 years is really needed in most areas, but today 1-7 years is more common. This is because the population has increased and no new land is available. This leads to increased soil erosion and even lower yields.

Some crops are the same as in Haiti, others are different:

Roots and tubers:	cassava (increasingly popular)	
	yams	cocoyam
Ground level:	pineapples	melons
Above ground:	beans	peppers
	maize	rice
	groundnuts	
Trees:	mangoes	oil palm
	cocoa	kola nuts
	oranges	coconuts

A Haitian jardin, *in a typical hillside location.*

Animals are also kept, especially chickens, but disease and the tsetse fly are so prevalent here that no cattle can be kept in the south. Several goats and perhaps a sheep are common. Tools include a sort of cutlass, a digging stick and an axe. Farm size and income are generally the same as in Haiti, but probably more is taken to market and sold, often for export. This particularly applies to the vegetable oil that is extracted from the kernels of the *oil palm* tree. Some of this is also used locally, but for a long time the oil and palm kernels were Nigeria's most important agricultural export. Nowadays there is a trend towards diversification, and the increase in population has led to less oil being available for export, as it is the main oil used by Nigerians for cooking. Some of the crops now being grown for export are coffee, cocoa, rubber, tea and pineapples.

---

1 What are the differences between subsistence (peasant) farming in Haiti and Southern Nigeria?

2 Why do you think peasant farming is so widespread?

Local food has been traditionally supplied from the following sources:

- Smallholdings
- A portion (10-15%) of estates set aside for food crops
- Imports
- Commercial food-producing farms

Over the years it has become clear that the first two sources could not provide the quantity, quality and variety of food required. As a result of increasing incomes from tourism and manufacturing in particular, the deficiencies were met by imports. Only in a few cases have modern commercial farms attempted to go into fruit, vegetable or meat production, despite numerous plans and policies to diversify agriculture. There is also a wish to move away from dependence on export crops that are subject to falling prices, and to substitute for imports.

At first sight diversification into food crops or livestock seems an ideal solution for small countries with a history of agriculture, for the following reasons:

1   Food bills in the Caribbean are enormous and increasing. For example, Barbados spends US$100 m a year on imported food.

2   In many cases the dependency on foreign food supplies is very high - The Bahamas imports 80% of its food, Barbados 60%.

3   Imports of foreign food use up valuable foreign currency that could be used for other imports such as machinery, fuels, computers, for example.

4   A more diversified agriculture could supply the raw material for a variety of new food-processing and other

A typical small farm near Matura in Trinidad. Small amounts of many ground and tree crops are grown here, including dasheen, christophene, breadnuts, coffee, sugar cane and bananas.

Sweet potatoes intercropped with eddoes. St Philip, Barbados.

manufacturing industries, e.g. ham and bacon curing, processed meats, fertilizers, livestock feeds, soft and alcoholic drinks, etc.

5   There are a variety of related effects such as providing employment and reducing the pressure on urban areas that can also be seen as benefits.

Some countries have gone a long way towards *self-sufficiency*. Cuba has done so more or less by law, simply banning imports and rationing food. Most Cuban foodstuffs, especially rice, flour, fresh meat and vegetables, are rationed, with controlled prices and quantities. Very few other countries would accept this policy, but Guyana and Suriname have both gone a long way towards it.

In most of the West Indies the main use of farmland is still for growing an export crop, such as sugar cane. The advantages of keeping it in cane are that it grows well, it prevents soil erosion, it has guaranteed markets, and it is already established here. However, it is worth noting the case of St Vincent, which re-established its sugar cane industry in 1980. The operation was a small one intended to supply about 5,000 tonnes of sugar for local consumption and so save having to import it at a cost of US$0.40/kg. Unfortunately the operation had cost US$24 m by 1985, and had to be abandoned as it was only producing half the amount of sugar needed, at US$1/kg. The lesson to be learnt from this is that even with a crop that is thoroughly familiar to West Indians, producing locally can involve:

(a)   very high capital costs,

(b)   a product that is more expensive to produce locally than to import, and

(c)   unexpected problems resulting in much lower yields than forecast (in this case it was mainly a processing problem in the factory).

Diversification into new or traditional crops should therefore be cautious. Some of the main problems, which are common in other parts of the world, are as follows:

1   Land released from another use, or that has been unused, is often of poor quality or in an area of low rainfall. Marginal sugar cane land does not make good pasture land. If it has to be irrigated, this is a major expense. The new crop may cause soil erosion.

2   The land may have to be bought, although often it is leased. Further money has to be spent on seeds or stock, fertilizer, pesticides, fungicides, land preparation, drainage, fencing, irrigation, machinery, storage space, and so on. A new venture can be very expensive, and even profitable crops will probably bring in less money than the same investment in manufacturing or tourism.

3   Agricultural labouring is not popular. This has little to do with slavery in the past. In the developed countries the farm labour force fled from agriculture at the first opportunity and never went back. Virtually every country in the world loses agricultural labour as it develops. People will only work in fields if they are paid well or they are doing a skilled job. Consequently, cheap field labour must not be assumed. The citrus projects in Belize and The Bahamas described above (p. 133) have both been hampered by labour shortages, and the unpopular use of migrant workers as field labour. (See Table 13.4)

4   Modern agriculture will only be worth while if yields are high. This requires a sound education in agricultural science and proven business methods. Agriculture is a business, and few peasant farmers are capable of making the transition.

5   There must be suitable infrastructure to provide agricultural supplies, advice and education. Institutions such as co-operatives, banks and credit societies are necessary. Roads, transport, processing, storage and marketing all have to be considered. Government protection through import restrictions may be necessary.

6   Research is necessary into the best varieties to be grown, or livestock to rear. New breeds may have to be developed to suit local conditions. Diseases and pests may increase or be introduced as new crops appear. Sea island cotton, for example, has been unable to expand for decades, owing to pests.

7   Theft of fruit and vegetables will be a problem if security is not maintained.

8   The product may meet consumer resistance if it is not the same as the imported commodity. Shoppers are very quick to criticize something that looks ugly, dirty, marked, or over-ripe, that costs more than an imported product, or that tastes different.

9   Considerable effort must be made to find what the market wants, notably supermarkets, hotels, restaurants and foreign countries. Many projects grow a fruit or vegetable *and then* try to sell it. The correct way is to identify the market, grow precisely what it wants in the quantity it wants, and supply it regularly.

10 Scale is one of the greatest problems. If too little is grown, the individual price is high and the markets are not satisfied. If too much is grown, capital costs are high and the risk is greater. When there is likely to be some oversupply it should be processed or exported - this is the ideal situation.

11 Even if all these problems can be and are overcome, the product may still be dearer than the import or the competition.

It would not therefore be wise to persist in producing something that can always be imported more cheaply. No country can be truly and economically self-sufficient in all the major products, and despite the political credit that is often given to self-sufficiency, it is not a neighbourly ideal. It is wise to produce items that can be grown well and easily, notably Irish potatoes, onions, tomatoes, citrus and so on. Chicken and egg production is one example of a West Indian success story. Many countries in the Caribbean are now 90% or more self-sufficient in these commodities, whereas just 15-20 years ago they imported 50-70% of their needs. The production of pork is improving, but beef is more difficult. For most crops, the problem is one of seasonality: although many crops are grown, few are available all the year round. With careful selection some products, for example avocado pears, can always be in season. Irish potatoes are universally accepted and with proper storage keep well. Very few countries grow enough potatoes, and put up with poor quality imports. The case is similar for onions, although imports are usually of good quality. There is considerable scope for growing sorghum, cassava and legumes for animal feed, particularly for the new poultry industries. Much of this is imported at present.

Table 13.4 *Employment in agriculture* - estimates 1985-87*

Country	Employed	% of labour force
Guyana	308,000	31
Jamaica	280,000	33
Trinidad and Tobago	47,000	10
Suriname	30,000	30

*may include forestry and fishing

The crops and products that we have to import

Some basic foodstuffs, and many canned and processed ones, have to be imported. Conditions are such that the West Indies will never be able to produce things like wheat flour, breakfast cereals, canned soups, tea, instant coffee or cotton in the quantity or at the price that they can be supplied from abroad. This is mainly due to climatic limitations and to the scale of manufacturing.

Some examples of how such commodities are produced in North America, which is by far the world's largest producer and exporter of agricultural products, will illustrate this.

Food processing is the biggest and most valuable manufacturing industry in the USA.

1 If land is to be changed from producing export crops, what are the alternatives?

2 What is self-sufficiency? Is self-sufficiency (a) necessary, (b) practical, (c) desirable, (d) economic?

Wheat on the prairies of Canada and the plains of the USA

The prairies and plains are a vast area of temperate grassland, which is divided into two regions :

Spring wheat   the prairies of Canada, North and South Dakota, and Montana. The wheat is planted in spring after the cold winter, and harvested in the summer.

Winter wheat   Kansas, Oklahoma, Texas and Colorado. The winters are not so severe. The wheat is planted in the autumn and lives through the winter so that it can be cut in the spring.

Most of the region has the rich chernozem soils (See p. 89) of natural grasslands, and consists of plains between 400 and 1,000 metres (1,500 and 3,000 ft) above sea level. The winters are severe, but the summers are hot with long hours of daylight, and there is enough rain to grow cereals or grass. Wheat is grown here as a commercial enterprise. Many Americans consider farming to be *agribusiness* rather than *agriculture*, and few even live on the land where the wheat is grown. The land is flat and extensive, which allows machines to work uninterrupted over many square kilometres. The land is relatively cheap but labour is expensive, so as large an area as possible is managed at one time. Average farm sizes vary from 160 to 280 hectares (400-700 acres), depending on the location, the prairie provinces having the largest farms.

The wheat lands, which also grow other crops like barley and sorghum, are dry, only receiving between 250 and 500 mm (10 and 20 in.) of rain a year. Drought-resistant varieties are used, and fertilizers, pesticides, fungicides and herbicides are supplied mechanically, often from the air. As little manpower as possible is used. In fact the farmers are often called 'weekend' or 'suitcase' farmers,

because they only visit their farms for a few days a month, and do regular jobs in town for the rest of the time.

Because of the scientific approach to plant breeding, fertilizing and crop protection, this system works, and these huge areas produce the greatest surplus of wheat in the world - about 40% of all the wheat that is traded.

There are still problems of wind erosion of the soil, and

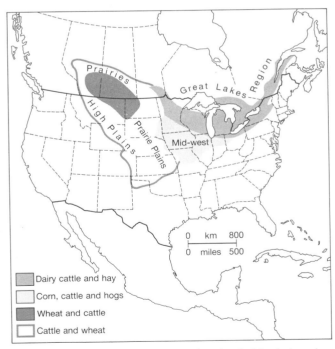

Fig. 13.3 *Wheat, corn, hay and dairy farming in North America. It should be noted that despite the common names 'Hay and Dairy Belt', 'Corn Belt' and 'Wheat Belt', in all the regions cattle are the first or second most valuable product.*

145

the 1950s saw dust clouds far greater than those that created the Dust Bowl of the 1930s. New techniques are now being used to prevent this. In the past the surface of the soil was crushed and powdered so as to retain the moisture below it. This encouraged wind erosion, so now the surface is ploughed into ridges and straw and trash are laid on the surface to keep in the moisture. In addition, irrigation has become much more common with major schemes in the prairie provinces around the South Saskatchewan River in South Saskatchewan and Alberta. Nevertheless, there is still a feeling in North America that land is cheap and too much time and money should not be spent on it. The land is planted in wheat and if there is a problem with erosion, it may be abandoned. If yields are low, barley or oats will be planted and fed to livestock, and cattle and pigs are not uncommon in the wheat belts. In some places, dry areas are sealed by being sprayed with asphalt, which is simply ploughed into the ground at planting time.

The Mid-West of the USA - corn, hogs and dairying

The plains and prairies have over 800,000 farms. The Mid-West has over 500,000, but here they are smaller, less than 80 ha (200 acres) instead of about 200 ha (500 acres). Here is a more intensive type of production, and a good income can be made from farms that are only two-fifths the size of those further west. This area, stretching from the Great Lakes to the Ohio River, is probably the world's most productive and richest agricultural region.

Traditionally the southern and slightly warmer part of the Mid-West, which has longer summers, has been known as the Corn Belt, because it specialized in growing corn and feeding it to pigs. Corn has the highest yield per hectare of protein and bulk of any feed grain. In the last 35 years soybean has also been grown, and the fodder has been fed to cattle as well as to pigs. Soybean oil has also been the basis of a margarine and cooking oil industry. Wheat and hay, and pasture crops like alfalfa and clover, are often rotated with the corn to revive the soil by adding nitrogen to it.

This approach to farming - growing crops to feed animals - has often been criticized as wasteful. If it was widely practised in food-deficient countries this might well be true, but the land in the Mid-West is so productive that both food crops and meat are produced in great surplus, and it is a problem finding somewhere to sell them. For a long time the US government actually paid farmers not to plant crops, and a farmer could get more money by buying land and not using it than by growing something on it. The world's famines and hunger are not caused by world food shortages, but by local poverty. It is the inability of nations to purchase available food that causes malnutrition and starvation.

The Mid-West is mainly an area of glacial deposition, including lake sediments. It is fairly flat or rolling country-side, and has been well drained by artificial means. Rainfall is over 750 mm (30 in.) a year, with about six months frost free, compared with three months in the prairie provinces. Farms are numerous, but get sparser towards the north. About one fifth of all US farm income comes from this region, and of this a large part is from the sale of livestock.

Further north, in Michigan and Wisconsin, dairying becomes important and is the main source of income. Summers are too short to get good results from corn, but hay and other fodder can be produced in abundance. Large amounts of butter and cheese are made, and as in all other areas there have been major improvements in milk production. In the last 30 years the average amount of milk per cow has doubled, and for beef the growing period has been halved to a mere 1.5 to 2 years before slaughter. Most of these cattle are fed concentrated feeds in large pens or feedlots, although they are often raised on ranches further west and then shipped in for fattening.

Throughout North America the farm population is still declining rapidly. In the Mid-West it was halved between 1950 and 1970, yet output increased.

1 Where is wheat grown for export besides North America?

2 What is wheat used for? Are all these things required in your country? Are there substitutes for some of them? How did Guyana try to reduce wheat flour imports?

3 What are the natural advantages of the American Plains for growing wheat?

4 Similar conditions exist in the Steppes of the USSR for growing wheat, yet the USSR imports millions of tonnes of wheat every year. Why do you think this is so?

14
Fishing and marine resources

A well-equipped long-line fishing boat from Florida unloads a large catch of swordfish for trans-shipment to New York. Christiansted, St Croix.

Although the Caribbean is one of the world's great groups of island nations, the sea and its resources have scarcely been exploited here. The Americans, Columbians and Japanese have frequently exploited the waters around the islands, and West Indian shops are full of salt cod and tins of tuna and sardines, but all are imported. The largest fishing fleets have been the foreign-owned shrimp fleets of Barbados, Trinidad and Guyana.

The settlers of most of the Caribbean countries, especially the Commonwealth ones, were farmers, aristocrats or slaves, and not fishermen. A notable exception were some of the Loyalist settlers of the northern Bahamas, who came from New England and settled on the small cays off the larger islands of Abaco and Eleuthera, depending on the sea for their livelihood. The Bahamas had no sugar economy but did have excellent fishing grounds. Today they have one of the most prosperous fishing industries in the region, and a large fishing boat can land a catch worth over US$100,000 after a ten-day trip. Only three countries - The Bahamas, Guyana and Suriname - are self-sufficient in fish.

It is best to think of the world's oceans as marine deserts with oases of life at certain points, mainly around the edge. Fish and other edible life require nutrients, and these are only found under certain conditions:

Where rivers and swamps enter the sea The Amazon and Orinoco Rivers provide the major input of nutrients in the West Indies, affecting the Guiana coastlands and Trinidad. About half of the world's fisheries are found near river estuaries and coastal wetlands. The Amazon River carries some 1 billion tonnes of nutrient-rich sediment into the sea every year, and the equatorial current (See p. 66) entering the Caribbean carries this along the continental shelf of the Guianas.

Where currents carry nutrients to the surface Eventually the nutrients that enter the sea sink too far below the surface to be used by fish, and are lost. In a few places shallow submarine currents of cool water rise to the surface, bringing the nutrients back up with them. Once in the sunlight photosynthesis creates abundant food and the result is some of the world's greatest fisheries, as off the coast of Peru, where the Peruvian current wells up. There is a similar situation on the Newfoundland Banks where the cold Labrador Current rises over the Banks and mixes with the warm Gulf Stream. There are no such conditions in the Caribbean region.

In shallow areas such as on banks and reefs Where the sunlight reaches the sea floor and creates vegetable life through photosynthesis. In this way beds of grass and coral reefs are formed, and certain areas of the Caribbean are well endowed in this way:

The Bahamas and Turks and Caicos Banks
The Cuban coastal banks
The Belizean coast
Several banks south of Jamaica, notably the Pedro Bank
Some other banks in the eastern Caribbean, e.g. Barbuda

We should not therefore expect the Caribbean to be abundant in fish. Its clear blue waters are clear because they are pure - and sterile. Less than 1% of the world's fish are caught away from coastal areas.

Fishing in the Caribbean is for several particular groups of species:

Pelagic fishing Pelagic fish are the fast, free-swimming types that keep near the surface of the sea. These include flying fish, dolphin, tuna, shark, bonito, mackerel. They are mainly the subject of *sport fishing*, which is related to the tourist industry, especially in The Bahamas, where Bimini is a world-renowned sport fishing centre. A few commercial fisheries also exploit these fish, the most prominent being in Barbados, where dolphin, flying fish, kingfish, shark and bonito dominate the annual catch. More recently, *long line fishing* has been introduced, particularly for the catching of swordfish.

In many ways this is a highly technological and capital-intensive method of fishing. The lines are anything from one to 100km (60 miles) long, and are equipped with chemical lights to attract the fish. Most fishing is done at night at a cost of about US$1,000, with an average catch of 650-700 kg (1,500 lb), per night. During the day marlin can be caught. A typical trip in a 20 metre (65 ft) boat can produce 10-20 tonnes of swordfish with some mackerel and other species. One such operation in the US Virgin Islands flies the catch from St Croix to New York in refrigerated containers, with a variety of fish left over for use in the tourist restaurants of Christiansted.

Reef and banks fishing Demersal (bottom dwelling) species are caught in this way. They include groupers, snappers, and smaller fish like grunts and croakers. Almost all the countries of the West Indies catch these fish in their shallow *inshore* coastal waters, although these areas are becoming rapidly fished out, notably around Jamaica.

During the last ten years the number of fishermen in Jamaica has approximately doubled, but the amount of fish caught has remained the same. Jamaica's economic crises have increased the demand for local fish, but at the same time limited investment in boats and engines. As a result the sheltered inshore waters have been the fishing grounds of an increasing number of fishermen who have of necessity been forced to take smaller and smaller fish. In many cases immature fish are now sold openly by 'higglers' on the roadside, and this will severely limit the reproduction and replacement of the most popular species. One restaurant owner in Ocho Rios reports that he has to drive right around the island to get enough fish to stock his restaurant each week. With the decline in bauxite earnings there has been a considerable increase in tourist activity, especially along the north coast. The pressure on the limited inshore area is such that even a three-month closed season for lobster fishing is unlikely to prevent a drastic decline in fish landings in the future.

Lobster fishing The spiny lobster (which has no claws) is prevalent throughout the region wherever there is a suitable *habitat* - holes and ledges for it to hide in. Both The Bahamas and Belize have a major export industry in lobster tails to the USA where the retail price is over US$10 a pound. The Antigua and Barbuda Bank, and the shallow waters around St Kitts-Nevis (which extend north to Saba and south to Redonda) are also important lobster grounds supplying the Leeward Islands' growing tourist industry, with occasional exports (Table 14.1).

Shrimp fishing This is a major activity along the South American coast from Venezuela to Brazil. It involves all the countries south of and including Barbados (as a base), and several foreign nations such as the USA, Cuba and Japan. This fishery has declined in recent years, despite the fact that the US market increased by 50% from 1982 to 1987. This is partly due to competition from shrimp farming in Ecuador, China and Taiwan, which have now surpassed Mexico as the main US supplier.

Mariculture Raising fish in salt water, and *aquaculture* (raising fish inland in lakes and rivers) are also practised in the Caribbean, and in the 1980s have shown signs of considerable increase as the technology has improved.

1 What are the basic requirements for good fishing grounds?

2 What parts of the Caribbean are most suitable for commercial fishing?

3 What marine products are imported into your country? Check some food stores and make a note of the country exporting the product.

4 For the countries you have listed (question 3), and with the aid of an atlas, suggest which fishing grounds your imports come from.

The Cuban fishing industry

Cuba has the largest fishing industry in the region, handling more than 200,000 tonnes per year in the 1980s. (A figure of 500-10,000 tonnes per year is typical of most West Indian countries.) Fishing was always important in this very large island, but after the Revolution it became much more adventurous. Thousands of Cubans were trained in Russian fleets and a major deep-sea fishing industry using fish-factory ships was started. Today about 65% of the total catch comes from Cuba's two long-range fleets, one in the Atlantic and the other in the Pacific. These two fleets alone include 26 fish-factory ships which process and can the fish on board. Another 300 ships roam the Caribbean and the Gulf of Mexico, sometimes moving illegally into the nearby Bahamian waters. The advent of 320km (200 mile) fishing zones around most countries has limited the activities of these boats, especially as many countries have equipped themselves with naval patrol vessels. Most of the catch is processed and exported to the Eastern bloc countries, and is valued at more than US$100 million per year.

Fishing in The Bahamas

The most important part of the Bahamian industry is the lobster fishery, which earns over US$20 million a year in exports to the USA. Large quantities are also consumed locally by the tourist industry and the local population.

Fig. 14.1 Fishing environments of the shallow-water banks. This profile is typical of the coastal fishing zones of most West Indian islands, and is the basis of fisheries on the banks of Belize, The Bahamas and the Leeward Islands. Compare with Fig. 14.3.

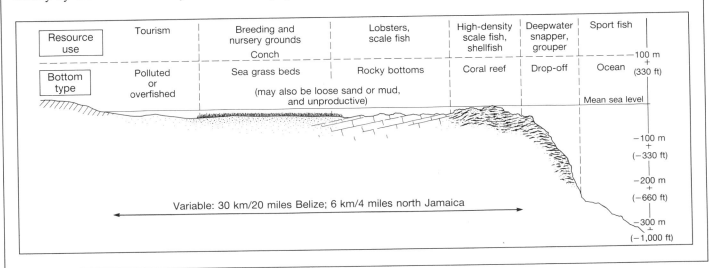

149

Laboriously hauling a pirogue (fishing boat) ashore at Mayaro, Trinidad. Note the small outboard motor.

The grouper and snapper catch has also increased considerably in recent years, owing to the discovery of large stocks of deepwater fish at 20-200 metres (60-600 ft) off the edges of the banks (Fig. 14.1). With the introduction of well-equipped vessels using electronic navigation aids, cold storage, and electric fishing reels, these areas have now begun to be exploited, and the export of surplus fish is being seriously considered. Potential markets are the net importers of fish in the region, such as Martinique, Guadeloupe, Jamaica and Barbados. However, at present there are cheaper supplies of fish available than from The Bahamas, and only about 10% of the catch is exported.

There is also a specialized local fishery for the giant mollusc, the *conch*. Probably over 1 million conches are consumed in Nassau alone every year, and the conch is a major element of the local diet. For this reason its export is banned so that stocks will not be depleted and the price pushed up.

Finally, the sport fishing industry in The Bahamas has a considerable value in its own right. The catch is sold on an *ad hoc* basis locally, but more important is the number of visitors it attracts, estimated at about 200,000 per year in the 1980s.

As there are large stocks, the possibility of increasing the catch to 10 000 tonnes a year, worth US$100 million, is excellent. However, there are also serious problems including poaching by Dominican Republicans, Cubans, and Cuban Americans (operating from South Florida); taking lobsters in the closed season; and bleaching the reefs.

The fishing industry of Belize

This has developed somewhat more recently than in The Bahamas, but is a very similar fishery (Table 14.1). Ninety per cent of the exports are lobsters going to the USA and Europe (Fig. 14.2), and most of the rest is conch, the export of which is allowed from Belize. Most of the other products are consumed locally.

The industry is based on five co-operatives set up by the

Table 14.1 Major Caribbean fish and shellfish production 1988. (1,000 tonnes)

Country	Scalefish	Shellfish	Total
Cuba	198	23	231*
Guyana	39	2.6	42
Dominican Rep.	18	1.4	19
Jamaica	9.9	0.1	10
Barbados	9.1	–	9.1
Guadeloupe	7.5	0.7	8.2
Bahamas	1.6	5.6	7.2
Trinidad & Tobago	2.8	0.4	3.2
Antigua & Barbuda	2.3	0.1	2.4
Belize	0.5	1.0	1.5

* Only 78, 000 tonnes is caught in the Caribbean (Source: F.A.O.)

FISHERIES REGULATIONS FOR CRAWFISH OR SPINY LOBSTER

— No person shall take in the waters of Belize or buy, sell or have in his possession crawfish:

a) if the tail weight is less than four (4) ounces;

b) between the 15th day of March and the 14th day of July, inclusive, in any year;

c) that has eggs or spawn;

d) that has had the eggs or spawn removed;

e) that has a soft shell.

FISHERIES REGULATIONS FOR CONCH (STROMBUS GIGAS)

— No person shall take in the waters of Belize or buy, sell or have in his possession, conch during the months of July, August and September in any year.

— No conch should be taken in the waters of Belize unless the overall shell length exceeds seven (7) inches or the 'market cleaned' weight of its meat exceeds three (3) ounces.

FISHERIES REGULATIONS FOR TURTLES

— No person shall take or have in his possession any turtle during the period from the 1st day of June to the 31st day of August inclusive in the year, or take any turtle at anytime when the same shall be found on the shores of Belize and adjacent cayes thereof.

— No person shall take or have his in possession any turtle eggs.

— No person shall set or attempt to set within one hundred yards of the shores of Belize or of the adjacent cayes thereof any net or seine or whatsoever for the purpose or with the intent of taking turtles.

— No person shall take, buy, sell or have in his possession any turtle of the following description:—

a) Green Turtle (Chelonia midas) less than 50 pounds in weight;

b) Hawksbill Turtle (Eretmochelys imbricata) less than 50 pounds in weight;

c) Loggerhead Turtle (Caretta caretta) less than 30 pounds in weight.

— No person shall export or attempt to export any turtle or any articles made from any part of a turtle otherwise than under a licence granted by the Minister.

Fig. 14.2 Belizean fishing regulations.

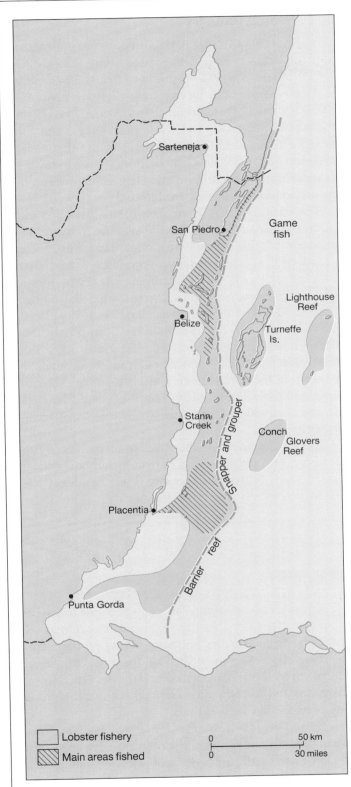

Fig. 14.3 Lobster fisheries off Belize. The environment of the shallow-water region between the barrier reef and the shore is shown in Fig. 14.1.

Cleaning sea eggs near the Crane, Barbados.

government in the 1960s, and the industry is fairly strictly regulated, with a quota for each centre so as to prevent over-fishing (See Fig. 14.3). Exports are now worth about US$7 million.

The industry depends largely on traditional small craft, such as skiffs, canoes and dinghies, with or without outboard motors. A few larger boats have been introduced, and some 1,700 fishermen are active. However, virtually all the fishing is done inside the barrier reef, and the high cost of providing boats to fish outside this zone makes it unlikely that new grounds will be exploited for some time. The co-operative approach has had the effect of industrializing fishing without the cost of fitting out large vessels, as there is never very far to go with the catch. Unlike The Bahamas, the straight coastline here means that most fishing grounds are within 15-40km (10-25 miles) of a co-operative port. The most successful centres are the two in Belize City (Table 14.2).

Table 14.2 Co-operative landings in Belize, 1984

	National (Belize City)	Northern (Belize City)	Caribena (San Pedro)	Placentia	Total
US$m	2.5	2.9	0.8	0.5	6.7
%	37%	43%	13%	7%	100%

The evolution of the Guyanese fishing industry

Guyana's offshore waters extend about 160km (100 miles) to the continental shelf, and in this area are varieties of fish that have supported two rather different kinds of fisheries. In addition, a quite distinct shrimp industry was superimposed on these (See text below and Table 14.3).

The older of the two main activities is the *snapper fishery* (including the grouper) which established itself as a commercial enterprise in the 1920s. The fleet (schooners using handlines) was owned by a single company which was also Guyana's ice-making company. This sort of enterprise was very unusual at the time, when virtually the whole of the West Indies fished from canoes and dinghies (*pirogues*). The continued emphasis on estate farming and imported fish prevented the expansion of the fleet until the Second World War (1939-45). At this point imports were restricted and the industry started to expand using the existing infrastructure. After the war the need to diversify continued the expansion slowly, and landings grew at about 5% a year into the 1960s. Unfortunately this expansion was in the number of boats, and not in technology, and the snapper fleet found itself fished-out in the traditional grounds, and unable to locate new ones. Even today the snapper industry could be expanded considerably if equipment and techniques were modernized.

The *silver fish* (mainly croaker, banga-mary and sea trout) industry developed as the snapper industry declined, and is one reason why the snapper industry was abandoned. The new fishery depended on new boats trawling for shoals of fish swimming just above the sea floor. Once the fishing grounds were identified, landings were high, and by 1958 silver fish landings had replaced the snapper fleet as the main industry. Surprisingly, this fishery never expanded any further, and most of the fleet on the continental shelf was non-Guyanese (53 out of 56 vessels). In those days there was no 200-mile (322-km) limit, and Barbados, for example, had a fleet of schooners on the shelf. 30-40% of Guyana's fish was still being imported.

The main reason for the collapse of the silver fish industry was the discovery of prawns (or jumbo shrimps) on the shelf. Nevertheless, enforced self-sufficiency has led to increasingly larger fish landings.

Table 14.3 Guyana - deep-sea fish production and imports, 1960-1988 (1,000 tonnes)

Year	Imports	Domestic catch	Shrimp landings	Size of shrimp fleet
1960	2.6	2.7	1.2	37
1965	2.7	7.2	3.8	103
1970	3.6	12.1	5.4	171
1975	(imports banned)	15.9	4.2	244
1980	0	27.6	3.2	169
1988	0	38.3	2.6	

The Caribbean shrimp fishery

The USA has been a major market for shrimps for a long time, and this demand was originally fed by catches in the Gulf of Mexico. By the mid-1950s large areas of the Gulf had been fished out and other grounds were being sought. A US research vessel surveyed the Guyanese continental shelf in 1958 and found abundant shrimps, and within a very short time a huge fleet of shrimp trawlers was fishing the shelf from Venezuela to Brazil. Most of these ships were US and Japanese owned, with bases in Georgetown, Bridgetown and Port of Spain, among others. The Barbados government had a shrimp fleet which operated until 1978. By then, 200-mile economic zones had been established by Guyana and Brazil (in 1977). Legally the continental shelf is now closed to foreign fishing, although inter-governmental agreements are possible.

Almost all of the shrimp catch was exported to the USA, with a small amount of processing, mainly the removal of the heads, being done in the Caribbean. At first most of the fleets working on the Guyanese shelf landed most of their catch there, but by the 1970s less than half did so. Bridgetown in Barbados, and Port of Spain in Trinidad, both became processing ports for Guyanese shrimp.

Guyana became a socialist country in 1970, and made several attempts to control the shrimp industry, and to profit by it. Only a small part of the profits made by the industry remained in the Caribbean, as there were only a few local fleets, and the processing was of little value. The Guyanese government banned fish imports in 1970, and in 1972 a Guyanese fleet was formed which had 22 vessels out of the 216 based in Guyana in 1973. It acquired 38 more when it nationalized the Booker group of companies. With the news that the government also wished to take over the processing and storage of shrimp, several companies moved their bases out of the country. In 1975 there was a major decline in yields due to overfishing, and the catch has continued to decline since then. Eventually, worried about the damage to its fishing grounds, Guyana closed them to foreign ships imposing the 200-mile exclusive economic zone.

During the shrimping bonanza little was done to expand the scale fish fisheries, although they grew slowly towards 20,000 tonnes a year. The total capacity of the shelf is estimated at 50,000-100,000 tonnes per year for demersal fish like the snapper, and about 70,000 tonnes per year for pelagic fish like shark and silver fish. An interesting but alarming feature of the shrimp industry was the enormous wastage of fish caught in the shrimp trawls. For every tonne of shrimp caught, over 5 tonnes of fish were brought on board, about 40% (over 80,000 tonnes a year) being edible species! However, as the shrimp was 15 to 40 times more valuable than the fish, most of the fish were thrown back. Given the fact that millions of dollars a year are spent importing fish into the region, and that over 40% of Caricom's population is deficient in protein, this was a terrible waste. In 1973 Guyana passed a law requiring each trawler to land one tonne of fish every trip (about every month). In 1978 the amount was raised to 2 tonnes. Only Guyana had this law, unfortunately, so once again there was a move away from having bases in that

country. In 1979, for instance, Cuba sent its 13 trawlers back home and closed its Guyana base.

In the 1980s the Guyana shrimping industry continued, mainly through licences to US multinational corporations who provided money and services in return for being allowed to fish within the 200-mile zone.

Until recently, 90% of the shrimp sold to the USA was caught in the sea, around Mexico and along the Brazil-Guyana continental shelf, but the huge demand from the USA has encouraged the development of very low-cost aquaculture production, especially in Asia. This has caused a 25% fall in the world price, and made the Caribbean fisheries much less profitable. By 1980 shrimp landings had fallen below 1,000 tonnes.

Despite this, since 1983 there has been a major revival in shrimping in this region, and Guyana, Suriname and French Guiana produced over 6,000 tonnes in 1988.

---

1 What are the main marine exports from the Caribbean?

2 Why is the fishing industry of Guyana so different from that of The Bahamas?

3 Describe the Caribbean shrimp industry and consider its probable future.

Mariculture, aquaculture and marine resources

Apart from the shrimp industry, climatic conditions in the Caribbean have encouraged the development of aquaculture. There is a great variety of these systems, many providing aquarium fish for export. A German-owned operation in Belize is worth US$16,000 a year and is expanding, and Abaco in The Bahamas opened a large (40 ha/100 acres) tropical fish hatchery in 1985, breeding clown fish for export. Trinidad also exports aquarium fish worth about US$250,000 a year. However, these are not raised artificially, but are collected from the larger swamps and include the pui pui, used as a scavenger in aquaria.

On a larger scale there are operations like turtle-rearing in the Cayman Islands, which was started in 1970 by an American company. After several setbacks, by 1978 it was worth US$3 million a year. US regulations on the importing of turtle meat and its products have now seriously affected this business, but it still operates as a tourist attraction.

In The Bahamas, the abandoned saltpans on Long Island

were taken over in 1984 by a US Virgin Islands company. They are being used to produce brine shrimp, and projected exports are valued at over US$10 million a year. However, such projects require considerable amounts of investment to sustain them, and the company had to spend over US$7 million to establish the venture. It will be some time before it can be considered successful, but the company, Maritek, already has a shrimp hatchery in St Croix, US Virgin Islands. There are also three fish farms raising tilapia, an African lake fish that is widely farmed around the world. To increase its attractiveness the fish is raised in salt water and called 'Bahama snapper'. The great advantage of aquaculture is that an increase in demand can be met much more cheaply than by investing in fishing boats and training fishermen. The danger is the threat of disease which can wipe out a whole farm.

Fishing is just one aspect of the exploitation of marine resources. For any territory there is a wide range of possibilities, as illustrated in Fig. 14.4.

A shrimp fleet from the Guyanese continental shelf at rest in the Careenage, Barbados.

1 What are the advantages of mariculture?

2 With reference to Fig. 14.4, what are the main areas in the Caribbean for: (a) grouper, (b) conch, (c) lobster, (d) sport fishing, (e) turtle, (f) sponges?

Fig. 14.4 Marine resources in the Caribbean. This diagram shows the diversity of resources in the Caribbean region. The list can be extended to include local and lesser-known fish, and items like aquaria and diving and other tourist attractions.

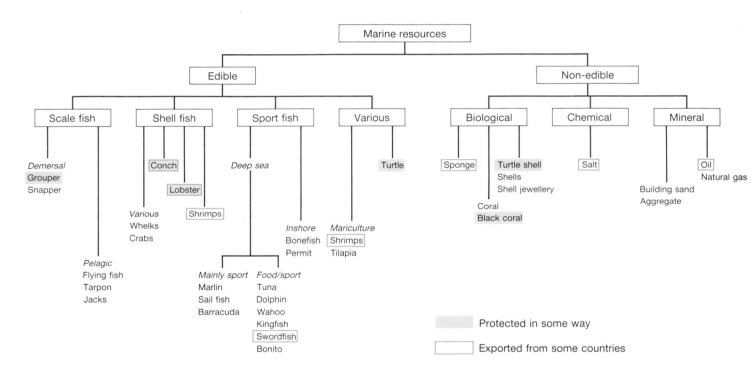

Fishing in British Columbia

Although the Caribbean produces a great variety of fish, it also imports a lot of processed fish. Much of this comes from the cold-water fisheries of North America, which produce different types of fish to those found in the Caribbean. Among the tinned fish is salmon, and the frozen fish include halibut fillets. Clams, oysters and crabs are also imported in the form of soups and pastes, and canned specialities are found in grocery stores and served in hotels. All of these are from the waters off the Pacific coast of North America, particularly off British Columbia.

As in the case of forestry (See p. 104), Canada is the world's largest exporter of fish products, but the value is

A typical salmon river with special facilities for sportsmen to catch the fish. What do you think is the function of the building to the left of the photograph?

much smaller (Canadian$2.8 billion in 1987). Production is also split between the west and the east, with the Pacific Ocean producing about 17% of the catch, but making up 26% of the value. Most of this is canned fresh salmon (Table 14.4), herring, cod and halibut, but as salmon accounts for two-thirds of the value of the Pacific catch, it completely dominates the fishery.

Only about 2% of the labour force of British Columbia (18,500 fishermen) are engaged in fishing, but they produce about 17% of Canadian fish from the relatively small stretch of water between the two main ports, Prince Rupert in the north, and Vancouver in the south (Fig. 14.5)

Commercial fishing began early in the twentieth century, and soon there were fish canneries all along the coast. Today most of these are closed and most of the processing is done on fish-factory ships that travel with the fishing fleet. The remaining fish is delivered to 49 fish-processing plants, most of them in Prince Rupert and Vancouver.

British Columbia has a highly indented coastline where the many rivers discharge into fjords (the glacially widened mouths of rivers). The numerous inlets and islands and the broad continental shelf provide shelter and food

Species	Atlantic	Pacific
Groundfish		
Cod	320	8
Flounder and sole	48	3
Haddock	34	0
Halibut	11	26
Pelagic		
Salmon	6	190
Herring	53	96
Shellfish		
Scallops	95	0
Lobster	283	0
Crab	78	6

Table 14.4 Most valuable Canadian fish, 1987 (Canadian $m)
The value of some of these species is often enhanced by processing.

Fig. 14.5 Fishing in British Columbia.

for both scale fish and shell fish. Canada has claimed a 320km (200-mile) exclusive fisheries zone since 1977, and this includes the entire continental shelf area, which is about 160km (100 miles) wide.

The most valuable fish is the salmon, which is worth more than all the other fish together. The salmon is what is known as an *anadromous fish*, which means that they return to the rivers where they were born in order to spawn. The young salmon (*fry*) stay in the rivers for a period of up to two years and then swim downstream to the sea. They stay

	Value 1984 (Canadian $)	1986
Sockeye (Red) salmon	86	143
Coho (Silver) salmon	60	39
Chum or Keta	33	38
Humpback (Pink) salmon	44	26
Spring salmon	47	20

Table 14.5 Value of different species of Canadian salmon

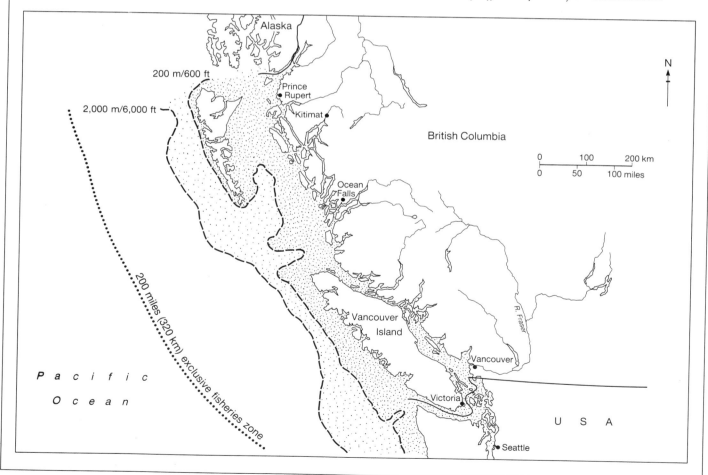

Type	Atlantic	Pacific	Total
Seafish, whole	180	277	457
Seafish, fillets	590	32	622
Seafish, frozen blocks	254	1	255
Canned fish	98	278	376
Salted (mainly cod)	124	0	124
Roe (mainly herring)	47	98	145
Shellfish, whole	282	17	299
Shellfish, shelled	320	13	333
Shellfish, canned	17	0	17
Total (including minor types)	2,065	763	2,828

Table 14.6 Value of Canadian fish landed 1986 (Canadian $m)
(Source: Canada Year Book, 1990).

in the sea for up to seven years, and then return to the river to spawn, after which they drift downstream and die. They are mainly caught when they gather together to find the entrances to the rivers, such as the River Fraser (Table 14.6), and while they are swimming upriver.

The flesh deteriorates rapidly, so little is sold fresh. Instead it is smoked, which gives it its well-known pink/red colour, or canned.

Because the rivers are large and powerful, HEP has been widely developed here, and the dams have interfered with the migrating fish. To counteract this, laws were passed requiring fishways, or fish 'ladders', to be built so that the mating salmon could still get upstream. This has worked, though not without some loss. Preserving the salmon fisheries has been a major conservation success, and production today is higher than it has ever been. There are also closed seasons for both salmon and halibut, and for the king crab.

As salmon return to the rivers to breed, they are particularly vulnerable to pollution from *acid rain*. Acid rain is produced when sulphur dioxide and nitrogen oxides, produced from burning fuels like coal and petroleum, are transformed into sulphuric and nitric acids in the atmosphere. Once in the atmosphere they can be transmitted great distances and then deposited via rain or snow on vegetation, soil, lakes and rivers.

Acid rain is the result of human pollution, and is particularly associated with electricity power plants. It is especially damaging to fish which can be killed by the acid, or store various toxic trace metals in their flesh. Fish taken from acid waters in Canada have shown high concentrations of mercury and other heavy metals. The control of industrial emissions (smoke and gases) is a major topic of debate between Canada and the USA at the present time.

15
Manufacturing: its nature and development

Building a fishing boat with hand tools at Marquis, on Grenada's windward coast.

Manufacturing is an activity by which wealth is created. A certain material is made into something else that is more valuable. The difference in value is the wealth that has been created.

Manufacturing fits into a three-part structure of economic activity:

1 *Primary*   The removal or cultivation of a natural resource, as in coal-mining, fishing or agriculture.

2 *Secondary* The processing or *manufacturing* of a primary product into something more valuable.

3 *Tertiary*   The provision of a service, such as transportation, banking and tourism.

In most cases manufacturing involves the processing of a *raw material* or, quite often, many raw materials. A raw material might be something quite crude such as iron ore, which, with coke and limestone, becomes steel, or it might be a basic product like steel or cement which is then used to produce a car or a house.

A manufacturing activity that produces a *finished product* is said to produce *consumer goods*; that is, something that can be bought and used as it is, like an umbrella or a book. Many factories produce goods for use in other factories, such as chemicals for drug firms, textiles for clothing factories, and glass for car and housing manufacturers. It is possible to identify several major groups of manufacturing industries. These are listed in Table 15.1.

Table 15.1 Classification and examples of manufacturing industries in the Caribbean

Market	Local raw material		Imported raw material	
Domestic	(1)	Rum, canned fruit, sauces, furniture, handicrafts, wooden boats	(3)	Rum, beer, soft drinks, clothing, plastic containers, paint
Export	(2)	Rum, alumina/aluminium, salt, petrochemicals	(4)	Rum, electronic products, petroleum, pharmaceuticals, sports equipment

Raw materials

The raw materials of an industry may be a natural resource, and if a country has suitable natural resources it is logical to expect it to develop industries that can use them. For instance, in the West Indies, clay might be the basis of a pottery industry, fruit might lead to a canning industry, or bauxite could be the basis for an aluminium industry. However, in practice development of these industries is not so common, for the following reasons:

1 The *cost* of building a factory may be very great.

2 Some types of manufacturing, for example the production of most metals, require large amounts of *energy*.

3 The skills, *technology* and scientific knowledge may not be available.

4 A trained *labour force* may not exist.

5 There may not be a local *market* for the product, and the cost of exporting it may be too high.

Usually, a West Indian manufacturer is either more expensive than a foreign one, or the local market is too small to support the factory. However, there are several types of manufacturing activity in the West Indies, and they use both *local* and *imported* raw materials.

Exporting

One answer to the problem of the small local market is to export - then (in theory) the market is as big as the world! However, this creates its own problems:

1 The product must be of a very high *quality*, especially in the developed countries of North America and Europe, which are the world's largest importers.

2 The *price* must be cheap enough, or other countries will capture the market.

3 *Output* must be large and reliable so that the importer can rely on a continuous supply.

4 A suitable means of *transport* must be arranged.

Under the right conditions, therefore, goods can be *exported as well as used domestically.*

Manufacturing in the Caribbean

There are several possibilities for manufacturing in the Caribbean region. Local raw materials can be used, or they can be imported, and the goods can be produced for the local market or for export. Table 15.1 shows examples of these four types.

It will be seen that rum can be placed in all four categories. Many industries overlap, their products can be used at home or exported, and they may have local raw materials mixed in with imported ones. In the case of rum, for example:

- Rum is produced in Barbados and drunk locally.
- Rum is produced in Jamaica and exported.
- Molasses is imported into St Lucia and the rum is sold locally.
- Molasses is imported into The Bahamas and the rum is exported.

In fact, in each of these four cases the rum is both consumed locally *and* exported, but the most important use is the one listed above.

Each of the four categories represents a major group of industries which have been most important in the development of the Caribbean's modern economy. These are described below, along with examples of each type of industry.

---

1 Is all manufacturing the same? Which of the following are Caribbean manufacturing activities?

(a) dredging sand for building, (b) solar salt, (c) mariculture, (d) boat building, (e) brown sugar.

2 Which of these are consumer products, and which are raw materials for another industry?

(a) Steel, (b) motor cars, (c) bauxite, (d) salt, (e) ammonia, (f) bread.

3 Make a list of activities in your country which have developed out of *necessity*. Which are manufacturing activities?

---

(1) Traditional industries - local raw materials, domestic markets

These are the oldest industries in the region. Some of them started in colonial days when imports were limited and the industrial revolution had not even begun. Two good examples are the making of rum as a by-product of sugar, and boat-building from local timber. The sugar industry is probably the oldest example of manufacturing in the Caribbean but in its early days it was mainly for export.

These manufactures were created from necessity. Food, drink and, for people who live on islands, boats, are all essential items. In the past there was a lot of simple processing of local agricultural produce, usually in an island's main town. Rum, however, was first produced in the countryside alongside the sugar factories. These are still in the country, but in most cases the rum distilleries have now moved into the towns, which are better for power supplies, labour, and distribution to shops and abroad. A waterfront location is common.

A similar type of activity is *fruit and vegetable processing*. Most countries have to face the problem that food is needed all the year round, but that each crop is harvested only once or twice a year. Some means of preserving the surplus is needed, such as bottling, canning, drying, spicing or freezing. The canning of fruit and fruit juice is traditional and widespread in the West Indies, especially in Jamaica and Trinidad. Similar means of processing are used to produce hot (pepper) sauce, tomato paste, and canned pigeon peas, for example.

Although traditional, these industries are not all extinct or dying, although many have gone. Often they have been encouraged or expanded, and new canneries have been opened. Populations are now larger and there is the possibility of exporting, especially within Caricom. Jamaica has set up canneries within several agricultural districts, such as in the vegetable-growing district in the southern part of St Elizabeth parish.

Although it would seem that this sort of industry is ideal for West Indian countries, they have not been very successful. In 1982 Jamaica had some 40 factories - agro-industries - in the agricultural processing field, but 60% of their capacity was not used owing to a shortage of agricultural raw materials. If factories are to work efficiently they need to be kept busy continuously, and therefore consume an enormous amount of produce. The traditional type of farming is not sufficient on its own to feed these modern, albeit small, plants. Consequently an agricultural revolution will be needed before agro-industries become major industries in the region. When this happens there will be considerable scope for increased production, such as in these four areas noted by the Jamaican Ministry of Agriculture:

1 Citrus processing to produce jellies, juices, jams, and cattle feed from the waste pulp.
2 Banana processing to make banana chips and baby food, animal feeds and industrial starch.

3 Pineapple processing. It is planned to produce juice, bakery products and animal feed.

4 The processing of non-edible beef products including leather, hair for brushes, bones for animal meal, and fertilizer from the various waste products.

Other examples of this kind of manufacturing are straw-work in Dominica, jams and jellies in Grenada, coconut cooking oil and margarine in St Lucia, and condensed milk in Barbados.

In the past many products were made out of wood, and many islands had significant boat-building and furniture industries. *Boat-building* ranged from the dugout canoe, still made and widely used in Jamaica and Hispaniola, to quite large schooners built in Nassau and Abaco in The Bahamas. Apart from the canoes, few boats are made today. Most of the wood has gone, and wooden boats are hard to maintain, liable to rotting and, above all, labour intensive to build. Compared with modern fibreglass boats they are simply too expensive to build commercially. As a result the industry has largely died out, but in a few countries, such as Barbados (See p. 166) it has survived by adopting modern technology.

The furniture industry has also suffered in part, as metals and plastics have replaced wood. However, Jamaica has had some success in promoting its own industry using local timber and other raw materials.

Overall, this class of manufacturing has changed radically. Easily available and cheap imports have replaced expensive local products. Most Caribbean countries do not have such low wage rates that they can compete with a mass-produced import. For example, 80% of the straw products sold to tourists in The Bahamas are foreign. In some cases tastes have changed and the market has disappeared. The straw industry originally provided necessities, such as hats, baskets, mats and floor coverings. Now these products are almost entirely aimed at the tourist market, and imported substitutes of paper, plastic and cloth have taken over the original role. In a few cases modern factories have been built to exploit under-used local resources. One of the few of any note is the cement industry, of which Barbados's new Arawak cement company is an excellent example.

The Barbados Arawak Cement Company

Until recently, Barbados acquired its cement from Trinidad. In the 1970s Trinidad's economy improved so much that it could not supply its own needs, and the supply to Barbados was cut off. For a while Barbados imported cement from a variety of countries, including Ireland, Venezuela, Columbia and Cuba (the last supplied most of the West Indies). By 1973 Barbados realized the need for its own plant, and building started in 1981, the plant being finished in 1984. Ownership is shared between Barbados (51%) and Trinidad and Tobago (49%), and the plant supplies Trinidad as well. The total cost of building the plant was about US$75 million.

The raw materials of the cement industry are limestone (75-80%), clay (20-25%) and gypsum (5%). The limestone is supplied from Checker Hall quarry, and the clay from the St Andrew's clay works. Gypsum comes from Jamaica. The maximum total output is planned at 300,000 tonnes a year, half to be exported to Trinidad and other Caribbean territories. In 1988 exports of about 165,000 tonnes were valued at US$5.5 million.

Cement plants are notorious polluters of the environment. The quarries and trucks create dust, the kilns produce smoke, and the buildings are usually large and ugly. The local environment of St Lucy has been taken into account and many anti-pollution measures are to be enforced:

- The site is well away from the main tourist and residential areas, and quite close to the raw materials. Nevertheless, the government-owned Heywoods Resort, opened in 1984, is only 3km (2 miles) to the south.
- The main areas of processing are acoustically sealed to reduce noise.
- Quarry blasting is limited to one blast per day, and dust will be reduced by water spraying.
- The works have a variety of filters and collectors, including a large electrostatic precipitator, which is the most effective method of controlling dust.
- The site is being kept as compact as possible, and is surfaced and landscaped as necessary.

---

1 Why are food processing, textile, and craft industries so common, even in less developed countries?

2 (a) What agricultural products in your country could be processed into a manufactured product?

(b) Which of the items listed in (a) are used in a local manufacturing industry? Which are not used, and why not?

3 Study the account of the Arawak Cement Company. If this was built in your country.

(a) Where would you locate it?

(b) What environmental problems would you consider?

This Bacardi factory takes advantage of the Bahamas' Commonwealth and EC status.

These are also 'traditional' industries in the sense that they started with the earliest plantations. As they served export markets they were usually established on a much larger scale, employed large amounts of cheap (originally slave) labour, and undertook only the minimum amount of processing necessary to make the product easily transportable. The *semi-finished product*, such as raw sugar, alumina, or cotton, was then exported to be finished abroad. A more recent example, and one that has been very successful in expanding the amount of processing done locally, has been the petroleum and petrochemical industry of Trinidad.

The *sugar industry* brought the first example of large-scale manufacturing to the West Indies, and illustrates many of the various factors that influence the location and economics of manufacturing in general. Originally there were numerous 'factories' - actually sugar mills and boiling houses - scattered over the countryside. There were few roads in the eighteenth century, and goods were carried by horse or by slaves. The cane could not be carried far, and as the main source of power was the wind, there was no need to, as windmills for crushing could be located almost anywhere. If the estate was too sheltered, animal-powered mills were used. For similar reasons there were many ports - ships were small and any of the many scattered anchorages around the coast could be used.

As time went on the extraction of juice and the production of sugar developed and factories became more expensive to run. It became cheaper to build one large factory rather than several smaller, old-fashioned ones. Roads and transport improved, allowing concentration on a few factories, and as the ships got larger only a few of the older ports remained suitable.

The result today is that there are only a few large and efficient sugar factories serving a sugar-producing area (See Fig. 15.2). Abandoned sugar mills far outnumber the working ones. Only the largest countries produce enough sugar to justify the cost of a large factory and a deepwater port. The smallest producer today is St Kitts, and islands like St Lucia have turned to other crops.

Coral blocks stacked and ready for use at a Barbadian quarry.

The comfith experiment

This was an experiment designed to study alternative uses of sugar cane. It was based on a self-contained *cane separator* which instead of crushing chopped sugar cane to extract the juice, carefully separated the rind (comfith) from the pith.

The process was invented by two Canadian scientists, and a pilot plant was built at Uplands in Barbados in the 1970s. The machinery carefully pared the rind off the cane so that only the pith, which contained most of the sugar, remained. The pith and rind could then be processed separately. The possible advantages of this were as follows:

1   The rind could be used as fibre for board manufacture. 20 tonnes per day of board could be produced from 320 tonnes of sugar cane stalks. A separate board manufacturing plant would have to be built, but the local construction industry could absorb it.

2   Wax and some sugar syrup would be removed from the rind and used commercially.

3   The pith could be used as a quality cattle food. This was the main purpose of the study, but it was found that to be economical a herd of 16,000 cattle would be needed to eat the product.

4   The pith could be processed into sugar in the normal way. Because it had been separated from the rind the sugar obtained came out much cleaner and whiter than from a crushing factory.

In general it was felt that at the time the possible benefits were not great enough to justify a full-scale cane separator and board manufacturing plant linked to a sugar factory. The new technology is nevertheless a possibility for the future.

An experimental mini sugar mill at Uplands, Barbados. The mill is designed to use the by-products of sugar - for example wax and pith - more efficiently.

There were also factories for most of the other plantation crops, such as for tobacco-curing and cigar-making, cotton cleaning ('ginning') and baling, and cocoa and coffee production.

After agricultural processing, the manufacture of alumina from bauxite is the next most important activity for the region (See chapter 11). As in the case of sugar, only the first stage of bauxite processing became widespread - that is, the making of alumina as opposed to the metal and its products. Alumina manufacture does not require excessive power and its reduced weight makes it more economical to export. It is always easier to ship bulk products like raw sugar and bauxite, or alumina, than finished products like refined sugar, aluminium ingots or consumer goods which need special packing.

The *petroleum industry* has already been discussed (See chapter 11), but unlike sugar and bauxite, there has been a considerable amount of processing in Trinidad. The petroleum industry can be considered to have several stages of production.

The first steps in the production of petrochemicals were taken about 30 years ago, to use the output of Trinidad's refineries more profitably. These refineries produced far more refined petroleum than the country needed, so it could be considered as a raw material, or it could just be exported. In fact less than 5% was used locally. One of the first products to be made was ordinary detergent, and then biodegradable detergent, mainly exported to Western Europe. At this time Trinidad and other Commonwealth countries had special duty-free access to Great Britain and the EFTA countries, and later on to the EC. The range of products was gradually increased to include many basic and intermediate chemicals, including those required to make nylon. Sulphur and lubricating oils were also made. In 1959 natural gas was used for the first time at Point Lisas, by Fedchem. This produced ammonia for nitrogenous fertilizers such as urea. The output of ammonia and its products has continued to increase steadily until the present time, and includes several plants that are partly owned by the government. In 1988 both oil and natural gas were being used as the feedstock to produce urea, ammonia and methanol for export. Trinidad and Tobago is now the world's second largest ammonia exporter, after the USSR.

Point Lisas industrial port

The idea of an industrial port was first thought of in the 1950s, but not launched until the 1970s when Trinidad had an oil boom, and it became apparent that major industrial development could be fuelled by the new finds of offshore natural gas. About 600 ha (1,500 acres) of land (Fig. 15.1), partly sugar cane and swamp land owned by Caroni, were purchased. Work began on the port in 1977 and is still in progress. The actual industrial estate covers about 80 hectares (200 acres)

Not all the industries planned are based on local raw

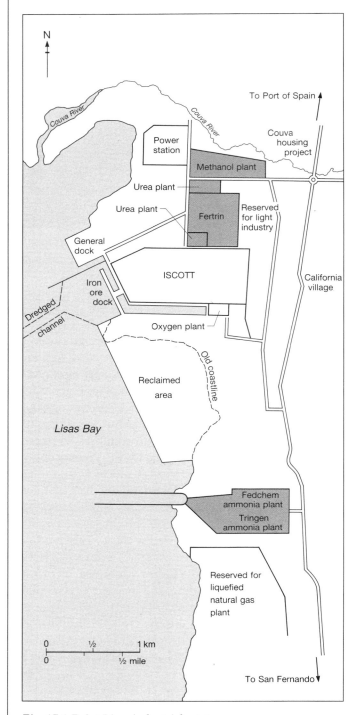

Fig. 15.1 Point Lisas industrial estate.

Use	1984	1986	(% of total)
Power generation	18	29	
Fertilizers - ammonia	29	27	
- urea	2	16	(new plant 1984)
Methanol	4	15	(new plant 1984)
Oil companies	45	11	(refineries at 25% capacity)
ISCOTT	2	2	

Table 15.2 Trinidad and Tobago - use of natural gas, 1984 and 1986

- It is centrally located, but separate from the congestion of Port of Spain.
- It has abundant flat land on the waterfront, which is ideal for major industrial development.
- The harbour is sheltered and suitable for developing into a deepwater port.
- It is near to the older natural gas pipelines and the Pointe-à-Pierre refinery.

It is common these days to gather major industries around a significant advantage, such as a deepwater port (See Freeport, p. 167) or a natural resource. In this way they share the cost of a very expensive infrastructure, such as the power supply, water supplies, and docks. Point Lisas has a large power station which is fuelled by natural gas, and several *heavy industries*, producing iron and steel (See ISCOTT, p. 169), methanol, ammonia and urea fertilizers (See Table 15.2). Heavy industries are those that process a raw material to make a primary product such as a metal or a petrochemical. These industries are often seen as Poles of Growth for other industries that will use their products. At Point Lisas, examples of *downstream* light industries that use steel are constructional steel firms and machine tool manufacturers, while those using petrochemicals include producers of plastics, and fertilizer companies.

---

1 What are the advantages and disadvantages of exporting raw materials or semi-finished products to developed countries? (This is a complicated problem, so it might help to give your answer under these headings: (a) economic, (b) political)

2 What is a 'growth pole'? Are any activities in your country of this type?

---

materials, but the presence of natural gas as both a fuel and a raw material (called a *feedstock*) was the most important factor. The Point Lisas area is particularly suitable for the following reasons:

Many of the industries in this category are small local enterprises. They are designed to produce consumer goods for the local market, and in many cases they first appeared after independence to replace imported goods.

Some have been around for a long time, such as baking and brewing, while others are quite big enterprises that hope to export as well. The Iron and Steel Company of Trinidad and Tobago (ISCOTT) is a fairly recent example. However, most are small and located on specially built industrial estates, such as Grazettes in Barbados. Quite often they have local or Caribbean Development Bank loans to help them get started. They are encouraged for several reasons:

- They reduce the amount of foreign exchange spent on imports, as importing the raw materials is cheaper than importing the finished goods.
- They provide employment.
- They provide a degree of independence from shortages and delays in shipments.
- They encourage the development of an industrial labour force.

Import-substitution industries also have some drawbacks, the most common being that the local product is often dearer than the imported one. This can be due to bad management, high labour costs, low labour productivity, or simply because the industry is too small to practise scale economies. Another problem is poor quality, often due to poor management, and shortages are common. These problems lead to demands for imports to be banned in order to *protect* local industry. Although some governments take this step, this usually causes prices to rise. An example from the 1960s was the *Pine Hill Dairy* in Barbados, which produced both fresh and condensed milk. The government, which owns 40% of the dairy, decided to ban the importation of Carnation and other brands, and was undoubtedly right in the long term. In the short term, cans of spoiled milk had to be returned to the dairy, and consumers had to adjust to the differences between the traditional and the new product. In the end the dairy became very successful and has not exploited the consumer. In 1988 it was producing 14,000 litres (3,000 gallons) of milk a day from 1,500 cows, which was 88% of consumption. By enlarging the herd to 1,800 cows, the dairy planned to make Barbados self-sufficient by 1990. Multinational companies are often richer than the countries that they export to, and could have driven the new dairy out of business so as to regain control of the local market. Nevertheless, protection for every industry would be most unwise.

Most of these import-substitution industries have a particular reason for being developed in the West Indies. However, only some industries are suitable for promotion in this way, and development depends on whether they fall into one of the following four categories:

1 The product *increases in weight* during manufacture, usually owing to the addition of water. Examples are beer, soft drinks and spirits; milk and ice cream; paints; and chemicals like bleach and detergents. These industries are common in the West Indies, either independently, like Barbados' Banks beer, or as a subsidiary, like Heineken in Trinidad and St Lucia. The cost of transporting empty cans and Coca Cola essence is much less than for carrying full cans.

2 The product *increases in size* (bulk) during manufacture. All bakery products are of this type, as are plastic bottles and containers, garbage pails and buckets. In The Bahamas one company produces nearly all the plastic containers needed for juices, water and milk. It is located on a government-owned industrial park housing twelve factories. Other examples in this category are mattresses, furniture, and many construction fittings such as windows. All of these are bulky and take up a lot of cargo space which has to be paid for by the cubic metre or cubic foot. The individual parts, such as glass and aluminium for windows, and wire, kapok and cloth for mattresses, can be brought in much more compactly and cheaply.

3 The product is *likely to perish* or go stale during transport, or has to be refrigerated. This means a very expensive method of shipment, such as air transport or refrigerated container. There are therefore many local bakeries and dairies, but it should be noted that some communities are quite willing to pay two to three times as much for an imported product, either because of a consumer preference, or for better quality or special variety. This is important, especially when related to the tourist market (See chapter 16).

4 There is a particular *local skill* available, such as needlework. The garment/clothing industry using imported cloth is probably the most important of all the industries in this category, but it also spreads across into the export category. In many countries this was often the first factory industry to be established (although like baking it was originally a *cottage* industry). The presence of the tourist market has been an additional incentive, and there is a demand, for example, for decorated T-shirts.

Unless an item is produced to take advantage of one of these four conditions, a local industry is unlikely to succeed. For example, a small valuable item like a watch or camera will gain nothing by being assembled locally, as its transport and labour costs are extremely small.

Both Trinidad and Tobago and Jamaica are sufficiently developed and have large enough markets to have several quite large industries (Tables 15.3, 15.4). Trinidad assembles gas cookers, refrigerators, radios, televisions and even cars and light trucks; Jamaica produces fertilizers, paints, detergents, toothpaste and car tyres. All of these are made up from imported parts or raw materials and result in a product that is considerably heavier and/or more bulky that the original imports. Additional advantages are that foreign currency is saved and employment is created.

Product	Output (units)
Gas cookers	19,300
Refrigerators	9,650
Radios	2,600
Televisions	20,600
Cars and trucks	15,700

Table 15.3 Trinidad and Tobago - import-substitution of assembly-type manufactured goods, 1984

Product	1984	1989	
Fertilizers	33,000	56,000	(tonnes)
Paint	6,800	10,700	(1,000 litres)
Detergent	7,400	8,200	(tonnes)
Toothpaste	900	950	(tonnes)
Tyres and tubes	2,700	5,100	(tonnes)

Table 15.4 Jamaica - import-substitution manufactures, 1984 and 1989

1 Make a list of import-substitution industries in your country. You might look at one or all of the following to help you:

(a) telephone directory,

(b) Chamber of Commerce list/directory,

(c) Industrial Development Corporation literature.

2 List some of the manufactured goods that are produced in your country. Match each to one of the four conditions given in Table 15.1.

Fibrepol

(Fibreglass boat-building in Barbados)

This company manufactures fishing boats that are a compromise between the traditional style of a wooden boat and modern hull design. The new design helped to remove problems of weak sterns (27 boats in Bridgetown harbour were destroyed during bad weather caused by Hurricane Allen in 1980) and wasted space. Most of the raw materials are imported, but these only account for about 10% of the cost. The plant is using temporary premises and is to be relocated on an industrial estate. Exports to the Eastern Caribbean and Trinidad are planned. One of the difficulties faced by the firm is that of finding professionally trained employees. Workers with good skills are available, but few have technical training in plastics and chemistry, for instance. As manufacturing progresses in the region, this is likely to be an even more severe handicap for continued development than financing.

Improving a traditional fishing boat. The Fibrepol company in Barbados makes fibreglass boats, but based on the traditional wooden design, with a large cold-storage hold.

166

ISCOTT
(the Iron and Steel Company of Trinidad and Tobago)

This is the region's most expensive and ambitious project. It cost more than US$1 billion to build, and has been running at a loss of over US$100 million a year. The reasons for this were partly a depression in export markets, but mainly the result of poor management which resulted in the plant only producing about a quarter of its planned output of 900,000 tonnes of iron a year. In 1988 it was sold to a West German company that had first taken over its management in 1984.

ISCOTT was originally government owned, and located at Point Lisas (See p. 163) where it uses natural gas as the main fuel. The plant is a small-scale version of the traditional integrated iron and steel mill, which has three functions:

1 The production of *iron*. There are two furnaces to do this. Iron ore is imported from Brazil, and the limestone is found locally.

2 The production of *steel*. There are two electric arc furnaces for this purpose using the iron from the plant and a certain amount of scrap. The steel is formed into long sections known as *billets*. In this form it can be exported or sent to the rolling mill.

3 The production of *milled steel*. There are two rolling mills which form the steel into constructional steel bars and wire rods. From these a variety of usable products can be made, including nails and screws, wire mesh, barbed wire, welding rods, upholstery springs and tyre wire. The manufacture of these items is typical of the *light industries* that can be encouraged downstream of a heavy industry (See above).

To a large extent the project was designed to supply the local building industry, which was extremely prosperous in the 1970s but had to import all of its steel products. It was made possible by the presence of natural gas, and it was always intended that it should become a major export industry. The first part of the plant opened in 1980 and it now employs over 1,000 people. Recently, contracts have been signed to supply Puerto Rico and the Dominican Republic with at least 200,000 tonnes of steel products a year.

(4) Offshore industries - imported raw materials, exported products

The previous three groups of industries were all linked to their location either by their source of supply or by the market. This group is unique in being located for quite different reasons:

1 The presence of a low-cost labour force - not necessarily 'cheap' but providing high productivity per dollar. This attracts *labour-intensive* industries, particularly of the *assembly* type.

2 The presence of *financial incentives*, such as tax holidays, tax avoidance, duty-free imports and exports. These can be applied independently to each industry in turn, or a complete set of facilities can be provided in a *freeport* - a port industrial area that is guaranteed free of taxes and duties. The *International Free Trade Zones* that are currently being established in some islands are variations on the freeport idea.

These factors usually attract major *capital-intensive* industries such as oil refineries, or smaller capital-intensive, *high-technology* operations which also have a significant need for labour.

Whether labour-intensive or capital-intensive, the industry is located 'offshore' in order to save money. High labour costs and strong unions might be the reason for a clothing company to locate part of its business in Jamaica, or cheap land with low taxes might attract an electronics industry to one of St Lucia's three industrial estates.

Assembly-type industries are quite varied. The clothing industry is typical, although not usually classified as such. The manufacture of automobiles is a much-quoted example because of its well-known assembly lines, but the assembly line in this case is merely the final stage of a multifactory industry which is largely of the non-assembly type. For instance, the assembly line will be supplied by glass companies, rubber companies, engine and radiator builders, and numerous other mechanical and electrical firms. Some of the earliest (1960s) industries of this type in the West Indies used the dressmaking skills of seamstresses. Not only did they smock imported shirts for re-export, and make lingerie and children's clothes, but they also assembled computer parts and electronic components. Some factories, as in Barbados, were located at an airport and the goods were shipped in and

167

out in a matter of days. In more recent times the industries have become larger and more complex. In the Commonwealth Caribbean there have been some considerable successes in attracting these 'footloose' firms, often the subsidiaries of multinational corporations. In Barbados, manufacturing now exceeds both sugar and tourism in export earnings; and in The Bahamas the development of Freeport, Grand Bahama has established a variety of large industries on what was once an almost uninhabited island. However, all of this is quite small when compared with Puerto Rico's massive manufacturing sector, whose output is greater than the whole of the rest of the Caribbean's manufacturing effort.

In 1984 Puerto Rico earned 59% of its GNP from manufacturing; this was worth US$6,669 million and employed 150,000 persons. By comparison, Trinidad and Tobago earned US$561 million from manufacturing, which represented 11% of its GDP in 1984.

Other countries of the Caribbean also have their attractions. For example, Haiti is quite close to the USA, and has low wage rates of about US$2 a day. Unfortunately its political climate, poor educational standards and lack of infrastructure have not encouraged development. The Dominican Republic and Jamaica have attracted more industries, but each has had political disturbances and economic setbacks which have stopped them developing further. Jamaica in particular has good infrastructure and educational facilities.

1 Give an account of the disadvantages and advantages of offshore industries.

2 In what ways might the disadvantages of offshore industries be reduced?

Industrial estates in Barbados

In 1966 Barbados had three industrial estates (parks), with another under construction (See Fig. 15.2 and Table 15.5). By 1982 it had 10 parks containing 161 factories, many of them import-export operations owned by foreign companies. Exports of manufacturers have grown rapidly. The greatest expansion was in the electronics high-technology field, with American companies the most prominent. An example was *Intel*, a major manufacturer of computer components. This company is based in California where microprocessor circuits are manufactured. These circuits were sent to Barbados for assembly, and also to two other plants in Penang, Malaysia, and Manila in the Philippines. The value added in Barbados was purely through the skill of the mainly female labour force. The labour force totalled about 900, of which 680 were production staff. Intel started operations at the Harbour Industrial Park in 1977, but then moved to its own property at Sargeants Village in Christ Church. Intel closed in 1986 (See p. 172). Barbados had 14 such industries in 1981, all but one receiving financial incentives under one of four Acts aimed at attracting industries.

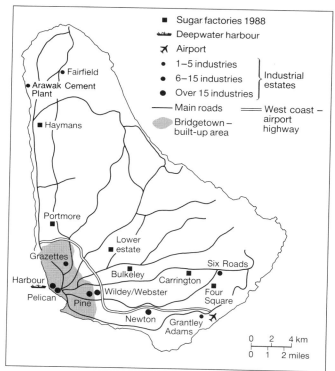

Fig. 15.2 Barbados industrial estates and sugar factories.

Commodity Group	US$ million		
	1980	1984	1987
Chemicals (mainly insecticides)	10.8	13.0	14.4
Electronic components	31.6	168.0	21.4
Clothing	24.6	32.4	15.2
Cement	–	–	4.7
Other manufacturers	32.4	33.8	20.0
Total of non-agricultural manufacturers	99.4	247.2	75.7

Table 15.5 Value of manufactured exports for Barbados, 1975-1988

Freeport, Grand Bahama

Freeport was established under the Hawksbill Creek Agreement in 1955. The agreement provided for a 99-year lease on 20,000 ha (50,000 acres) of land on which to develop a freeport and industrial complex (Fig. 15.3). Included in the agreement were the following terms which are similar for most such ports and trading zones:

(a) Freedom from all customs duties and taxes on imports, except for consumer goods.

(b) Freedom from real property taxes, rates, company taxes and personal taxes guaranteed until 1990 (extended to 2010 in 1990). The Bahamas does not have income tax at present.

(c) No excise (customs duties on exports) or other export taxes.

In return the leaseholders, mainly American and British businessmen, known as the Port Authority, had to construct a deepwater harbour and wharves, encourage local

Fig 15.3 Freeport-Lucaya, Grand Bahama. Only the most westerly part of the city has actually been built up, and most of the residential area is still vacant, although access roads have been laid out far to the east.

industry, and build schools and medical facilities. Later on tourist facilities were developed in an adjoining area known as Lucaya.

This venture turned out to be a major success, creating a town of 40,000 by 1990 and attracting a variety of major industries, including the following:

- a large oil refinery (partly closed down)
- a steel company (closed down)
- a cement factory (closed - now bags imported cement only)
- two major pharmaceutical companies
- several other chemical companies
- two distilling and blending companies
- two electric car research companies (closed)
- a variety of smaller factories.

Although some companies have now closed or left, several more have been attracted in recent years, and the 1980s saw a number of proposals for other countries to establish *industrial free zones*. This is the term now used to describe seaport or airport duty-free zones like Freeport. Barbados, Jamaica and Puerto Rico all have plans to develop zones of this type, but may lack the enormous amount of capital that is needed to build the necessary infrastructure.

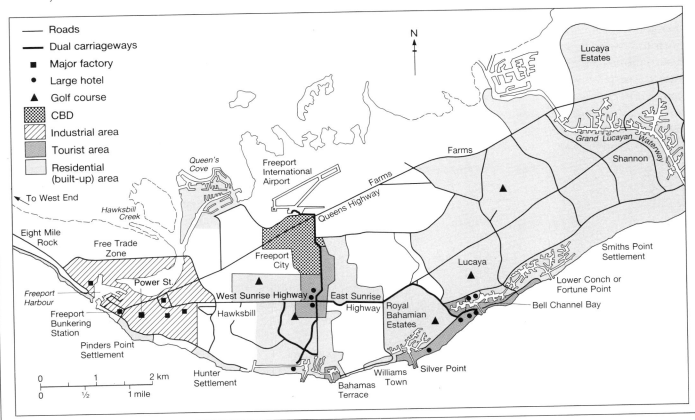

Puerto Rico - Operation Bootstrap and Fomento

There was nothing special about Puerto Rico's economy 50 years ago. In 1935 it had 65% unemployment and only the traditional industries of sugar, rum and tobacco. This was a time of worldwide recession, and the USA, which administered Puerto Rico, had started its recovery plan known as the *New Deal*. For Puerto Rico it was decided that industrialization was the answer to its problems, and the name *Operation Bootstrap* was given to the promotion of industry. At first there was little change, but the Second World War led to a much greater demand for manufactured products. It also provided a lucky break in the form of $160 million earned in duties on rum exported to the USA, which was refunded to Puerto Rico. This money was the main source of the capital used to lay down the necessary infrastructure.

Table 15.6 shows that there was significant growth from 1940 to 1950, when the Puerto Rican Industrial Development Company, known as Fomento ('promotion') was founded. The early success was based on the use of low-cost labour to produce things like furniture, clothing and tobacco goods, but as many other West Indian countries are finding out today, this rate of growth can only be continued for a limited time. The success of industrial development caused wages and living standards to rise so dramatically that low-cost labour became very scarce. It therefore became necessary to alter the promotion of industrial development to take this into account. For a period that continued into the 1970s, the emphasis was placed on attracting capital-intensive industries, particularly in the petroleum refining and petrochemical field. At one time it

Year	Income (US$million)	% GNP	Employment
1940	27	12	-
1950	89	15	-
1960	289	21	-
1970	958	26	136,700
1975	1,987	33	136,600
1980	4,809	52	154,600
1984	6,669	59	149,000

Table 15.6 Growth in the value of Puerto Rico's manufacturing and percentage of GNP, 1940-84

was thought that as many as 50,000 jobs could be created from the development of industries which used petrochemical products to make consumer goods. In 1984 this sector employed 16,000 persons, with the high-technology pharmaceutical sector being the most successful, but this was not as much as had been hoped for. The limits on growth were due to the lack of a cheap source of raw materials. Until 1974 Venezuelan oil, which cost about 30% less than US oil, could be used, but after the oil crisis this advantage disappeared. Puerto Rico had to find some other advantage with which to attract industry.

Ever since Operation Bootstrap the biggest advantage had been duty-free entry into the USA mainland, and exemption from US federal taxes. Also, Puerto Rico's own taxes are greatly reduced for the first 25 years. As neither low wages nor cheap labour were available, it was decided to pursue industries that would need neither, but would benefit from the use of skilled labour and financial incentives. The industries that responded turned out to be a group known as *high technology industries*, which include pharamaceuticals, mechanical and electrical machinery, computers and precision instruments. Intel (p. 168) was a typical example. However, there has been a development away from the routine assembly and return of components towards much more sophisticated processes of manufacturing, testing and quality control. The lower-wage jobs are now migrating to the less developed countries, and the higher-paid jobs are being attracted to Puerto Rico (Table 15.7). Nearly all managerial, scientific and professional positions (93%) are held by Puerto Ricans, and 30% of the national budget goes on education (Barbados spends 16%, Jamaica 18% and The Bahamas 23%), with 160,000 persons enrolled in higher education.

A typical Fomento estate at Juan Diaz, Puerto Rico.

It has often been said that the special relationship of Puerto Rico with the USA gives it an unfair advantage when competing with the rest of the Caribbean. Although it certainly benefits from this in many ways, the various other countries also have many special trading advantages, for example with the EC and the CBI (See p. 226). Businesses in Puerto Rico only survive by being internationally competitive. Although the majority of exports are to the USA, 15% (worth $1,395 million) go elsewhere, and this figure has increased every year since 1970.

Declining	Increasing
Food and associated products	Printing, publishing
	Chemicals[1] (+3%)
Tobacco	Rubber and plastic products
Textiles	Leather and leather products
Clothing	Machinery, except electrical[2]
Lumber and wood products	(+12%)
Furniture	Electrical and electronic
Petroleum refining and	goods (+5%)
products (−7%)	Transportation
Stone, clay, glass and	Instruments (+2%)
concrete products	Miscellaneous
Primary metals	
Fabricated metals	

Table 15.7 Declining and increasing industries in Puerto Rico, 1975-84

1 Pharmaceuticals +8%	All high tech industries +4.5%
2 Computers +16%	All manufacturing +0.5%

Part of the nature of manufacturing is the speed with which factories can be opened and closed. The closure of Intel in Barbados, and of the Lago oil refinery in Aruba in 1985, came with absolutely no warning, and 2,500 people lost their jobs. In the manufacturing sector there has to be a continuous recruitment of new firms to replace those that close down. This is well illustrated by studying a typical year in Puerto Rico: 1983 (See Table 15.8). A total of 84 factories closed causing the loss of more than 800 jobs. At one time these firms had employed over 4,000 people. Despite this, employment increased by 3,746, and in the long term represented a gain of 6,544 jobs. Much of this was due to the high-technology sector which included all of the fastest-growing industries. Now, 42% of all manufacturing employment is in high-technology industries, and 50% of the new jobs. In 1984, 42 high-technology projects with a potential employment of over 4,000 were awaiting approval.

New *clothing and food* industries, although in the less prosperous sector, are still opening, but their nature has changed and now involves a higher degree of processing. Clothing is now aimed at the high-fashion market.

Table 15.8 Number of firms opening and closing in Puerto Rico, 1983

	Number	Employment initial or closing	Maximum
Firms opened	173	4,570	10,554
Firms closed	84	824	4,010
Balance	+89	+3,746	+6,544
High-technology			
Opened	78	5,287	(50% of total)
Closed	26	1,875	
Balance	+52	+3,412	
Clothing and food			
Opened	44	2,672	
Closed	25	1,215	
Balance	+19	+1,457	

1 With the aid of an atlas map, and referring to Fig. 15.4, where in Puerto Rico would you locate:

  (a) a large petrochemical plant?

  (b) a factory making compact discs?

  (c) a clothing factory?

2 What advantages would you promote to encourage an investor in your country? Use these headings:

  (a) economic

  (b) social

  (c) political

The future of manufacturing in the Caribbean

Manufacturing is a particularly volatile area of employment. For example, in 1985 Intel, Barbados's largest manufacturer (See p. 168), announced plans for a major expansion, and then in 1986 announced its closure. This resulted in the loss of 900 jobs. Yet one of the great attractions of manufacturing is its almost 'instant' creation of jobs. Most West Indian countries have very high levels of unemployment (about 20-30%), and many more people are underemployed. Anything that can reduce this problem is most welcome, but unfortunately it is the very character of manufacturing that allows its rapid closure. In the Puerto Rico case study above it will be noted how firms opening were balanced against firms closing to give an overall picture of actual jobs gained. In Puerto Rico there are enough industries to cope with a certain amount of unemployment, but in a smaller island like Barbados, Curaçao or Aruba - all of which have had major closures - the whole economy can suffer. On each of these islands an oversupply of the item produced by the plant made it uneconomic to continue manufacturing on that island.

Offshore industries are most vulnerable to this kind of worldwide effect, and it is usually the overseas subsidiaries of multinational corporations that are the first to close. The Caribbean is usually an 'alternative location' for the world's major companies. If there is a sudden increase in demand for a product, then the Caribbean is a good place to locate a new plant. Because of its proximity to the USA, and a good infrastructure on the larger islands, new plants can be put into production quite quickly; when there is a slump, they can equally quickly be closed down. It is only realistic to see the Caribbean being used in this way in the future. As long as it is appreciated that offshore plants have these particular characteristics, then there is still much to be achieved. Perhaps this kind of development can be seen as a 'bonus'.

Offshore manufacturing is only one of several categories, and it is in these other areas that we can look for a more permanent and integrated type of development. The Second World War was probably the most significant event to throw the West Indies back on its own resources, both physical and human. Many of the ideas for import-substitution were sown in those years, and the opportunities of the post-war period led to the growth of new industries that are with us today - locally owned, and prosperous. We should not lose sight of the very real benefits of the many small-scale domestic enterprises that perhaps seem minute when compared with glamorous foreign operations. *Both* have a significant contribution to make, not only in employment and income, but in development.

Manufacturing, under control, is a fine asset. Various financial incentives are important to encourage new development (See Fig. 15.4) - but only up to a point. More important is a wholehearted commitment to manufacturing, above all:

Fig. 15.4 Rental and tax exemption zones for Puerto Rico. Both types of zone are designed to favour industries that locate in the mountainous interior or on offshore islands. Industries near San Juan are taxed sooner and pay significantly higher rents. Locations near large towns are also treated less favourably.

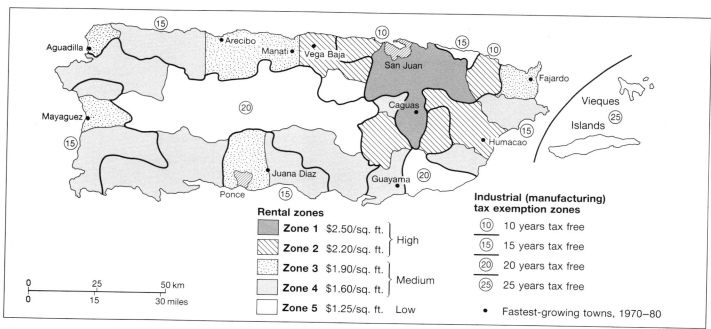

Rental zones

	Zone 1	$2.50/sq. ft.	} High
	Zone 2	$2.20/sq. ft.	
	Zone 3	$1.90/sq. ft.	} Medium
	Zone 4	$1.60/sq. ft.	
	Zone 5	$1.25/sq. ft.	Low

Industrial (manufacturing) tax exemption zones

- (10) 10 years tax free
- (15) 15 years tax free
- (20) 20 years tax free
- (25) 25 years tax free
- ● Fastest-growing towns, 1970–80

1   The systematic development of infrastructure - roads, seaports, airports, telecommunications, water, power, and the various public and professional services (See chapter 19);

2   an educated and trainable workforce that is cost-effective.

Without both of these, manufacturing will not develop to any great extent, and what does appear will be isolated from the community, probably physically, certainly psychologically and socially. Enclaves of manufacturing or tax-free estates will not provide the benefits of true industrialization. A population that is committed to modernization through the intelligent development and integration of manufacturing into its economy will find many benefits in the long term.

Some parts of the world do not suffer from the lack of resources nor the small market that is such a problem in the Caribbean. This is true of both developed and underdeveloped regions. The case studies that follow, describing the north-eastern states of the USA, and the Lower Ganges Valley, provide examples of industrial development based on a coalfield and access to major ports.

1   In what ways might other countries or associations help industry in your country (See also chapter 19)?

2   What infrastructure would you improve to help attract industry to your country?

3   How would your answer to question 2 also help (a) local people, (b) tourism?

4   (a) What incentives are there in your country to encourage manufacturing to locate in a particular area?

    (b) Is manufacturing discouraged in any areas?

The industrial heart of North America - a case study of the north-eastern industrial belt

The north-eastern part of the USA has the world's greatest concentration of manufacturing. It stretches 1,300km (800 miles) from the coast to the Mississippi in a belt 380km (240 miles) wide south of the Great Lakes (Fig. 15.5).

Historically, manufacturing developed early in the nineteenth century along the Atlantic coast, and spread inland to the coalfields and lake shores. Although still of immense importance, its manufacturing activity grew slowly after the 1950s, and since the 1970s there has been far more investment in other parts of the country, notably in the

Fig. 15.5 The north-east USA manufacturing belt.

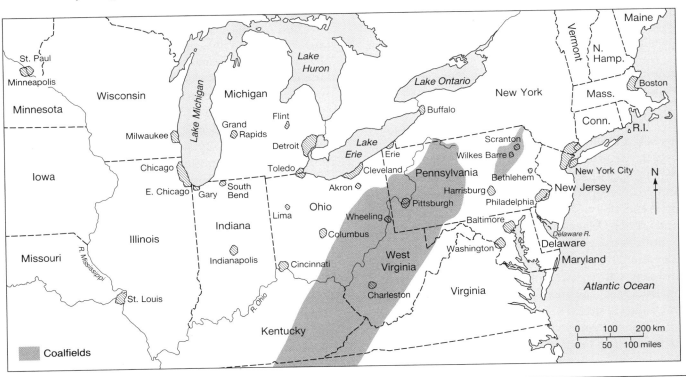

173

Charlotte, North Carolina is one of the newer towns in the South, competing successfully for the North's industries.

southern and Pacific states. The largest growth today is in the service industries, and some of the great industries of the past, including the iron and steel and car industries, have suffered many closures and redistribution to other parts of the country. Many parts of the region are now liabilities, with high unemployment, poor-quality housing and infrastructure. Severe inner-city decay and environmental pollution are common.

The manufacturing belt has a variety of assets. Of prime importance are the Atlantic ports of New York, Boston, Philadelphia and Baltimore, and the Great Lakes ports of Chicago, Milwaukee, Detroit, Toledo, Cleveland and Buffalo. These ports import raw materials for the manufacturing belt, and although the ports themselves have changed over the years they are still the most successful part of the region. The earliest port industries developed to handle and process exports from the interior. For example, Baltimore exported coal and wheat; Philadelphia and its sister ports on the Delaware processed foods (Campbell's) and built ships using Pennsylvanian steel; and the lake ports - Cleveland, Toledo, Erie, Gary and Chicago - produced iron and steel, with coal from the Appalachian states and iron ore from Michigan and Canada.

Coalfields stretch all the way along the Appalachians from eastern Pennsylvania to Kentucky. On the northern anthracite field (anthracite is the purest form of coal and pollutes the least), towns like Scranton were heavily in-

volved in mining (much coal was sent to the coast for domestic heating), metals and engineering (locomotives, wire rope), textiles and garments. This coalfield closed down in the 1970s and the region as a whole now suffers severely from unemployment.

Further south lies the much larger bituminous coalfield of West Virginia and southern Pennsylvania. This kind of coal is most suitable for making coke, the form of coal used by the iron and steel industry. It is exported to steel plants in Baltimore and Philadelphia (which receive iron ore from overseas); and to the lake ports which now get iron ore from Canada. Some is also used on the coalfield itself such as in Bethlehem and most notably in Pittsburg, America's most famous steel city. In the early days of the industry, iron ore was found with the coal, but now it comes from Canada. Many steel-making and steel-using industries are found in the Pittsburg area.

As well as being used as a fuel and for coke for the iron and steel industry, the coalfield supports a large range of other heavy industries such as glass-making, bricks, pottery, sawmills and pulp and paper factories. A chemical industry using coal as the raw material grew up in West Virginia, which is much less industrialized than Pennsylvania. Like most chemical industries around the world, the increasing availability of petroleum led to a changeover to petroleum feedstocks instead of coal as a raw material, and these old chemical plants have declined in importance.

Industrialisation brings its own problems, such as the ugly scars produced by the need to build roads and railways.

Pennsylvania was in fact the birthplace of the petroleum industry, when oil was discovered there in 1859. Today production is negligible and all the oil is imported to refineries along the coast or lake shores, or by oil and gas pipelines to inland centres. The main refinery and petrochemical industries are near Philadelphia on the Delaware River, East Chicago on Lake Michigan, and Lima (south of Toledo in Ohio), which is fed by a crude oil pipeline. Some

62 refineries, about 20% of the US total, are found in the manufacturing belt.

The industries described above were the basis of numerous other industries that produced finished products, most notably engineering products, and among these the chief was the automobile. The problem is today that the raw materials have either been exhausted or have been superseded, and competition has reduced demand. These are declining industries, and the growth industries like electronics, pharmaceuticals and high-technology electrical and mechanical engineering are not tied to a coalfield or port location. The new industries are increasingly located away from the dirt and dereliction of the north-east in California (e.g. Silicon Valley) or the southern states (Atlanta, Raleigh/Durham) - see Table 15.9 .

As a result, the relative importance of the north-east has declined, and its problems have increased. However, it is still the world's wealthiest market and many of those industries that benefit from being close to the market are still located here. This is explained partly in the study of New York (See p. 213).

The most difficult problems are faced by cities like Detroit which depended very much on one industry - automobile manufacturing. Detroit was hit by increasing competition from Japanese cars, by the 1974 oil crisis which forced companies to reduce the size of their cars, and rising labour costs. By the time the industry had reorganized itself, the American share of the market had shrunk, and what was left had spread to many new areas which had built modern plants. Detroit, and many other nearby cities that were dependent on the car industry (e.g. Akron, Flint, Grand Rapids, South Bend) have had to diversify into a much wider range of engineering.

The greatest growth in employment in the manufacturing belt is in the service industries. Those towns and cities that had the widest range of activities combined with good communications have continued to attract new industries and have prospered. The inland regions tied to the coalfield or to one basic industry have suffered most.

Table 15.9 Manufacturing value added by different states, 1982

Manufacturing belt states		Southern states	
State	Value (US$billion)	State	Value (US$billion)
1 New York	62.9	California	94.4
2 Ohio	49.6	Texas	53.3
3 Illinois	47.7	North Carolina	28.5
4 Pennsylvania	44.8	Georgia	19.2
5 Michigan	39.1	Florida	18.1
6 New Jersey	31.7	Tennessee	17.8
7 Indiana	25.7	South Carolina	12.2
Total North-East	301.5	Total South	243.5
Percent of US total	37%	Percent of US total	30%

The contribution of the top seven states in each region to manufacturing shows that although the North-East is indeed the most important region of the United States, the South is not to be ignored. California and Texas are the first and third most important manufacturing states respectively, and the South in general has more modern industries with higher growth rates.

1 What are the natural advantages of the north-east USA for industrial growth?

2 What is coal? Is all coal the same? Identify the characteristics of (a) anthracite, (b) coking coal, (c) steam coal. Is there any coal in the Caribbean?

The development of manufacturing in India: the Lower Ganges Valley industrial area

This large area includes two major industrial regions which are closely linked and very much dependent on each other. They are the Damodar Valley, a coalfield region in the State of Bihar, and Hooghlyside, the conurbation that includes Calcutta in West Bengal.

The Damodar River is not directly connected to the Ganges, but joins its delta below Calcutta. Calcutta itself is on a branch of the Ganges known as the Hooghly, and lies about 50 km (80 miles) from the sea. However, the Damodar Valley is a major routeway linking Calcutta to the Ganges Basin at Varanasi. It carries both the main railway (the Grand Chord) and the main road (the Grand Trunk Road) going to Delhi and the north-west. Calcutta is also linked to the Damodar Valley by a navigation canal that carries 2 million tonnes of coal a year, and by a coal-gas pipeline and electrical power lines.

Calcutta and Hooghlyside

Calcutta was a creation of the British Empire in India at the end of the seventeenth century. It is a good example of the advantages of location overcoming a bad site, for Calcutta has been called the 'City in a Swamp' (Murphy, 1964). It is situated on the banks of a distributary (the name for a branch of a river in a delta) in the Ganges delta. Deltas are wet and flat by nature (See p. 40), yet Calcutta has grown to cover some 50 km² of levée and backswamp, and has a population of more than 7 million. Along the banks of the Hooghly to the north are a string of individual towns which with Calcutta form the *conurbation* of Hooghlyside (Fig. 15.6). A conurbation is formed where the built-up areas of individual towns link-up with each other to form a continuously built-up area, in this case stretching for 50 km (30 miles) on both banks.

The reason for the growth here is that the lower Ganges region, which includes Bangladesh (once part of India), is an exceptionally fertile and productive region, and Calcutta is both its centre and its port. As masters of India's trade, the British built major ports all around India, notably Bombay and Madras, but Calcutta was the most important, and they made it the capital of India from 1773 until 1912. The main exports were textiles, and with the coming of steam power and railways, textile mills sprang up along the Hooghly, especially for jute. Jute is a coarse fibre, suitable for carpet-backing, that grows well in the delta swamps. The first railway was to the Damodar coalfield to bring coal to the new jute mills. Employment is still high in the jute and other textile industries, and in the clothing industry, despite a long decline that was due to the loss of Bangladesh, and to competition from artificial fibres. Metals and engineering are the other major employers, and Hooghlyside is noted for its production of consumer products like sewing machines, pumps and bicycles. Both the raw material and fuel for these industries come from the Damodar Valley, which has become the heart of India's industrial revolution.

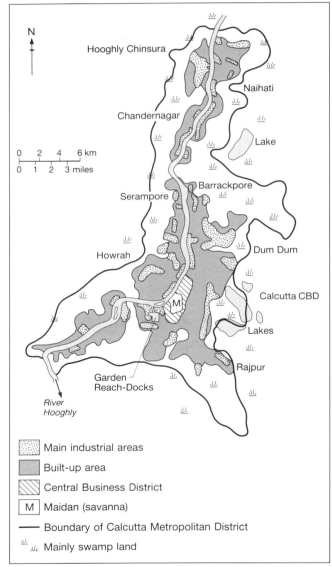

Fig. 15.6 The Calcutta-Hooghlyside conurbation. Based on B.L.C. Johnson (1979) India: Resources and Development, *Heinemann.*

The Damodar Valley

In the Damodar Valley is India's largest and most productive coalfield, and although there are other coalfields in India, only this one has coal that is suitable for making coke, an essential raw material for the iron and steel industry. There are many other mineral resources on this part of the Deccan Shield, notably mica (an electrical insulator), clay for china and for firebricks, bauxite, copper, lead and zinc, and huge deposits of iron ore. Like the Canadian Shield and the Guiana Shield, these old hard rock plateaus are often the most mineralized parts of a country and the basis for much of its industry.

The development of the Damodar Valley and its surrounding plateau began slowly in the nineteenth century but became rapid with the building of the railways after the Indian Mutiny. At this point the British took over the whole country, and the railways were especially important to them in maintaining control.

The oldest iron and steelworks were built early in the century at Jamshedpur and Burnpur (Fig. 15.7). The plant at Burnpur used iron ore found in the coalfield itself, but after it ran out, rich deposits near Jamshedpur were used for both plants. After Independence, three more integrated iron and steel works were constructed in the region, at Durgapur and Bokaro on the coalfield, and at Rourkela further south. There are many deposits of iron ore in this region, and large amounts are exported, especially to Japan.

The manufacture of steel was particularly important for the early railway industry, and locomotives and rolling-stock are still made at Chittaranjan and Jamshedpur. Today steel is used for numerous engineering products, such as shipbuilding, and is exported to many countries bordering the Indian Ocean.

Bauxite is the basis of an alumina industry at Purulia and Muri but the large amounts of electricity needed to refine aluminium has meant that this has to be sent to Hirakud or even further for the final stages. The product is much more expensive than current world prices, but India persists because it has little copper (all produced at Jamshedpur) and uses it as a substitute for copper in the electrical industry, which it has been developing since independence.

The heavy chemical industry is also well-established in the coalfield, especially at a huge government-owned fertilizer factory at Sindri. By-products of the coalfield are the main raw materials, but gypsum and salt, also major raw materials, have to be imported from the desert state of Rajasthan. Failures in supply and the cost of transport make this a high-cost industry, but heavy chemicals are an important export to the many light industries of Hooghlyside.

Together the Damodar Valley and Hooghlyside form the largest industrial region in India, and the only one that is based on coal. The Indian government has a policy of diversifying its industrial locations, however, and new steel plants, engineering works and chemical plants are being constructed throughout the country, with newly discovered mineral resources, scattered across the shield area of the Deccan Plateau, being developed to supply them.

---

1 What were the first industries to develop in north-east India?

2 Compare the natural resources of north-east India with those of north-east USA.

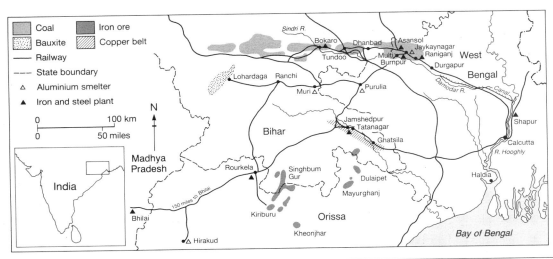

Fig. 15.7 The north-east industrial region of India.

16
Tourism

Tourism in the West Indies is a significant and widespread industry. It is important to large and small islands, to English, French, Dutch and Spanish speaking countries, and to democratic, socialist and communist states alike. It has proved to be capable of continuous growth, and is a relatively high employer of all classes of labour. In a few countries it generates income at a very high level and appears unaffected by economic recessions over a long period.

The very large tourist destinations are limited to The Bahamas, Puerto Rico and the US Virgin Islands, and these

The Lucayan resort area on Grand Bahama. Here there has been a heavy capital investment in canals, a golf course, shopping centre, marinas and roads.

three take about half of all tourists in the West Indies. The other half are distributed among 25 other territories. Only the three South American countries do not have a significant trade, and Belize and Cuba are relative newcomers with only a limited potential at present.

178

There are two main classes of tourist in the West Indies: the *stopover*, and the *cruise passenger*. The *stopover* tourist is particularly important because he or she stays at least one night in rented accommodation, e.g. a hotel, and brings income to the country visited. There are many features about tourists and their behaviour that need to be studied before their importance can be fully understood, and we examine these here.

Length of stay

This can vary, and may be from one day to six months, but a stay of four to ten days is the most common. The further a visitor has to travel, the longer he or she is likely to stay. A visit to Barbados averages 10 days compared with 6 days for one to the Bahamas. Europeans always stay longer than North Americans anywhere in the region, 10-12 days being common. Because there is a global trend towards higher incomes, more leisure time and more travelling, it can be concluded that tourists are taking longer vacations. On the other hand there are more flights to more destinations, and more accommodation is available. This means that tourists may stay longer on vacation, but may visit more destinations, so that average length of stay is a difficult statistic to analyse. For hotels a shorter stay is unprofitable, but for the airlines the extra travelling is beneficial. More information on the total movements of tourists in the Caribbean, as opposed to individual country statistics, would help us to understand this better.

Seasonality

This refers to the tendency of tourists to take their vacations at the same time of the year. For almost every destination there are two peaks and two troughs (See Fig. 16.1):

Antigua's summer carnival attracts tourists during the summer season.

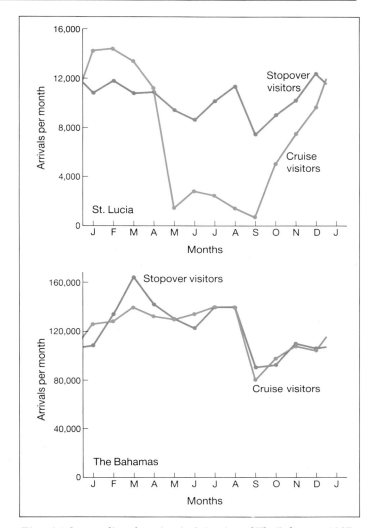

Fig. 16.1 Seasonality of tourism in St Lucia and The Bahamas, 1987.

(a) *The winter peak*, from Christmas to Easter, is the coldest time of the year in Europe and North America. This appeals to the more wealthy and to older people, and hotel rates are highest at this time. As children are at school, whole families are not so common for most of this season.

(b) *The summer peak* Younger people are out of school, college or university at this time, and whole families can travel together. July and August is a mini-peak.

(c) *The autumn trough* is the weakest period, with possibly only half the number in September that there were in the best month. Students return home, and the 'fall' is often an attractive season at home for many people, especially North Americans, who also celebrate their main public holiday, *Thanksgiving*, at the end of November.

(d) *The spring trough* is a popular time in the temperate countries, as the outdoors can be enjoyed again after the long winter. However, it is not nearly as severe a trough as the autumn one, and many people do travel at this time to take advantage of the off-season fall in prices.

Origin of visitors

It is important to know where tourists come from. Promotion, including advertising, has to be directed at the most appropriate markets, and the tourist facilities must suit the culture of the visitor. Tourists are likely to be those people with the time and money to be able to travel. Africa as a whole would not be a good continent to advertise in, but North America obviously is. Most Caribbean visitors come from North America, but other important areas include the following (See Fig. 16.2):

Western Europe, especially those countries with historical links to the West Indies, e.g. Britain with the Commonwealth Caribbean, France with Martinique and Guadeloupe, the Netherlands with the Dutch Antilles.

South America Most South Americans are as poor as their African counterparts, but there are rich communities in the cities of Columbia, Venezuela and Brazil who visit the West Indies and Miami, and take cruises.

West Indies West Indians often visit other islands, especially if they have friends or relatives there, and particularly during the summer.

The most relevant factor is *distance*. In general most tourists travel to the closest resorts, and this explains the popularity of Bermuda and The Bahamas in particular for US tourists. The further away a tourist is from home, the less important distance is - a European is just as likely to go to Barbados as to the Cayman Islands, and Canadians are also much more evenly spread than US tourists. West Indians favour other West Indian islands nearby, like Trinidad or Barbados for tourists from the Eastern Caribbean. The Bahamas, on the other hand, is not close enough or attractive to them.

The *purpose of travel* is also important, as many 'visitors' in the West Indies are actually visiting friends and relatives, who do not stay in hotels. The case of Puerto Rico is significant. In 1986/87, Puerto Rico recorded 1.9 million stopover visitors, but only one-third of these stayed in hotels. Many Puerto Ricans have migrated to the USA, especially to New York, and they return home frequently on visits. Although their expenditure is valuable, it is misleading to regard Puerto Rico as the largest tourist destination in the Caribbean. Based on expenditure it ranked second in 1987, on hotel nights it was just ahead of Barbados, and on length of stay its average of 3 days was the lowest of all Caribbean destinations.

Fig. 16.2 Origin of visitors to the Caribbean, 1987.

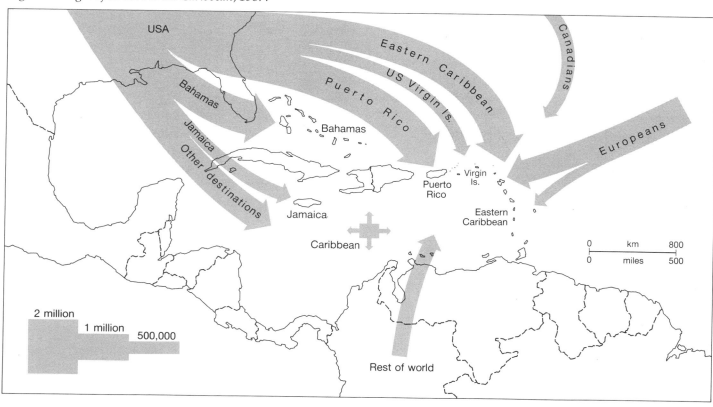

1 What sort of activities might a *day tripper* enjoy?

2 What tourist facilities might members of a business convention use?

3 Why do tourists not come to the Caribbean in the same numbers every month?

4 Why are there more North American than South American visitors to the Caribbean?

Hotel beds and airline seats

It is sometimes not realized that the number of stopover tourists is directly limited by these two factors. One 200-seater aircraft each week from New York can bring a maximum of about 10,000 tourists a year. Major destinations in the Caribbean in the 1980s have total arrivals by air of well over 100,000, which requires 10 average flights a week. Smaller destinations just do not have that amount of air traffic, and they would therefore have to persuade the airlines to establish more flights if they wished to increase the number of their visitors arriving by air.

Similarly every tourist needs a bed. It has been known for whole plane-loads of tourists to be sent straight back because the hotels were full. Roughly, 100,000 visitors a year staying for a week each will need 2,000 beds (100,000 ÷ 50 weeks). The average hotel room has two beds, and hotel sizes average about 100 rooms, so this figure would require 10 (2,000 ÷ (100 x 2)) hotels of this size.

In 1980 Barbados accommodated its 370,000 tourists in just over 13,360 beds, and The Bahamas 1,181,000 tourists in 23,000 beds. By using these figures for Barbados and The Bahamas, we can see what percentage of the hotel and other tourist accommodation was fully used; that is, the *occupancy rate* (Fig. 16.1).

In practice not all tourists stay in hotels, so the hotels were not as full as the calculated percentages suggest. The hotel occupancy rate was actually 69% in each case. The occupancy rate for hotel beds, and for aircraft seats, is a good indication of their profitability. In most cases they will need about 60% occupancy to be profitable, although the price paid by the tourist is also important. A winter tourist spends more than a summer package tourist, for instance. Often winter is the only profitable period.

Visitor expenditure

Income and employment are the two reasons for having a tourist industry. Every tourist spends a certain amount. The most important statistics are the total amount spent, the average per visitor, and what it is spent on.

Overall the figures are very high indeed. The West Indies received over US $3 billion in 1980, and US$6.7 billion in 1987, which worked out at about US $400-600 per tourist. However, different tourists spend different amounts, as shown in Table 16.2.

A stopover tourist is likely to spend over US$120 a day, while a cruise visitor spends US $50. In The Bahamas, 93% of the income is from stopover visitors, because the stopovers spend more per day and stay longer. The cruise visitor does not have to pay for accommodation, and usually has already paid for meals. On the other hand he or she requires very little infrastrucuture and spends a lot on shopping. Expenditure figures are similar for all tourists from the same origin. For instance, North Americans spend similar amounts whether in Jamaica or Barbados, and West Indians spend less wherever they go.

The amount of money spent that actually stays in the country is variable. Because food, transport and other facili-

Table 16.2 Visitor expenditure for The Bahamas, 1989

	US$	%
Total income	1,146 million	100
Average per tourist	372	
Total income from stopover tourists	1,064 million	93
Average income from stopover tourists	719	
Stopover expenditure per day	122	
Total income from cruise visitors	74 million	6.5
Average income from cruise visitors	52	
Cruise expenditure per day	52	
Day visitors total	8 million	0.5
Day visitors per day	50	

Table 16.1 Occupancy rates for Barbados and The Bahamas in 1980

	Total beds	Maximum possible no. of tourists (Staying 6 or 10 days)	Actual number of tourists	% occupancy (theoretical)
Barbados	13,360	487,640 (10 day stay)	370,000	76
The Bahamas	23,000	1,400,000 (10 day stay)	1,181,000	84

High-rise hotels from a bygone age in Havana, Cuba. The massive Habana Libre was once the Havana Hilton.

ties for tourists are often imported, and many of the hotels are foreign-owned, some of the money goes abroad. This is known as *leakage*, and can be quite high in some countries. For every dollar earned, as much as another dollar may be spent abroad on imports and services, and the net result might seem to be nothing! Fortunately this is not the case, for there is a bonus with every dollar spent, due to what is known as the *multiplier effect*. For instance, if a hotel earns a dollar, it may pay this to a maid. The maid may spend it in a shop on vegetables, and the shop may use it to pay the farmer. In this case the maid, the shopkeeper, and the farmer have all earned a dollar, and so the value has been 'multiplied'. Because of this there will always be some benefit to a country that is earning tourist dollars. In countries with a high foreign investment

and dependence, a dollar spent may be only 75 cents kept, but in a self-sufficient country it may actually be worth $1.25.

Finally we should note that a lot of tourist expenditure takes place outside the region. Tourists pay travel agents and airlines in their own country, and often pay for their accommodation there as well. It has been calculated that every American tourist spends $1.50 in the USA for every dollar that he or she spends abroad. In other words, tourists give more to their own country for their vacation than to the place being visited. This is not really a Caribbean problem, however - but it does explain why the USA encourages tourism.

1 How many different airlines regularly serve your country? What countries do they fly to?

2 What is a *charter airline*, or a *charter flight*? What is the importance of charter flights for tourism?

3 Referring to the examples on p.181, find out how many airline seats you would need to keep every hotel room full in your country.

4 Estimate what percentage of the money paid by a tourist for the following services is likely to benefit your country:

(a) a foreign airline's ticket

(b) your own airline's ticket (if your country has an airline)

(c) a stay in a large (over 100 rooms) hotel

(d) a stay in a small hotel

(e) an evening meal in a restaurant (not in an hotel)

(f) a shopping trip

Employment

In the present age of technological advancement, tourism is one of the few industries that has maintained a high demand for labour. The changes that technology has made in tourism have allowed it to expand and be more efficient, but not to employ fewer people. Computers have reduced delays in accommodation and flight bookings, and reduced errors in accounts. Rooms are more comfortable and may have satellite television and direct overseas telephone dialling. How-

The waterfront warehouse sector of Charlotte Amalie on St Thomas has been totally transformed into a dense network of tourist shopping plazas.

ever, an average hotel room in the Caribbean still needs one employee to run it, and the hotel generates further employment in the rest of the community. A survey of six major destinations in the Caribbean indicates that about three more jobs per room are created in areas such as shopping, casinos, taxi and tour guide services, water sports, airport services, and the provision of food supplies, utilities and government services.

A typical 100-room hotel might therefore create as many as 400 new jobs. Put another way, each 20 additional stopover visitors (or 350 cruise visitors) can generate a new job. (*Example*: 20 visitors staying one week each occupy a room for 10 weeks. At 80% occupancy, one room creates employment for four people, so 40 weeks of occupancy employ four people, or 10 weeks for one person.) This cannot be achieved without some cost, and a modern hotel room represents an investment of about US $100,000 in a destination such as Aruba or The Bahamas, or $25,000 per job. This can still be better than investment in some other areas. For instance, in 1980 a job was created by an investment of US $5,000-10,000 in hotel accommodation in Puerto Rico, compared with US $100,000 for a job in manufacturing.

In the region as a whole, about 100,000 people work in hotels and other accommodation, and the total employment dependent on tourism is between 300,000 and 400,000. *(Source: Caribbean Tourism Statistical Report, 1987, p. 52)*

Dependency on tourism

Some countries are very dependent on their tourist industry (Table 16.3). Countries like the Cayman Islands, the Virgin Islands and The Bahamas have no other comparable industry, and any decline in tourism will seriously disrupt their economies. A few countries have quite large tourist industries, but do not depend entirely on them, notably Puerto Rico and Trinidad. Most countries depend on their tourism even if it is not their most important activity, such as Barbados and Jamaica.

There is no doubt that Caribbean governments are concerned about their dependence on tourist dollars to run their countries. It is also frustrating for many of them to have recently become politically independent, but still to find themselves economically dependent on other countries. In order to understand both the advantages and disadvantages of large tourist sectors we need to look at several factors:

A modern beach resort with individual cottages linked to a central hotel. The golf course is nearby. Carambola Beach Resort, St Croix.

Country	Gross domestic product/capita (US$)	%GDP due to tourism (%)	% labour force in tourism employment*
Cayman Islands	12,910	44	35
Bermuda	12,900	56	63
Bahamas	9,460	52	48
US Virgin Is	8,930	62	23
Aruba	6,820	45	25
Barbados	5,290	28	13
Puerto Rico	4,080	6	2
Trinidad and Tobago	4,030	2	1
Martinique	3,640	18	3
Guadeloupe	2,990	17	5
St Lucia	1,390	40	10
Jamaica	1,040	25	5
Grenada	1,010	41	5
St Vincent	880	36	7

*Estimates based on size of labour force and employment in tourist accommodation

Table 16.3 Gross domestic product and tourism, 1986

1 Economic independence is virtually impossible for any country, and certainly not for one that wishes to become more developed. As examples, the USA's largest economic activity is agriculture, and its annual profitability depends very much on how much grain it can export to the USSR. Japan's new-found economic success depends very much on the whims and tastes of car, electronics and camera buyers in a host of foreign countries. In many ways, dependency on tourism is much better than dependency on a manufacturing product. Part of the problem for tourism is that the consumer is present in your own country, and his requirements have to be dealt with on a day-to-day basis. If we depended on grain or car sales, the dependency would be concealed from us most of the time. Only in a crisis would it become obvious (See p. 185).

2 Although dependency may be inevitable, it can be reduced by development in other sectors. Banking and finance is a very important second industry in The Bahamas and the Cayman Islands, and not insignificant in several others. It is an activity that is entirely the creation of human ingenuity. The Swiss watch and clock industry, and Dutch and Danish processed foods, are similar examples. The development of manufacturing in Barbados, and to a lesser extent in St Lucia, are equally praiseworthy in islands with strong tourist economies.

Redevelopment of downtown St Johns, Antigua, is aimed specifically at the tourist.

3 Tourism itself can be used to reduce dependence. The tourist is a consumer, and a considerable marketplace is created once tourism is established. This is particularly so for food and beverages, construction, transport, numerous services, furniture and fittings, and a range of manufactures. Many activities can develop and prosper with a tourist economy that could not do so without it. Not only does this reduce the imports - the 'leakage' of tourism earnings - but it also provides employment and goods and services for the local population. Unfortunately, this is not an area which has been successfully exploited so far. Starting and maintaining a business is a skilled and complex operation which needs careful planning and much assistance, especially on the financial side. Government and private institutions, such as the various Development Banks, have made a start in the Caribbean, but overall there is still much that can be done in all areas.

4 One of the problems that is often created by large-scale tourism is that of inflation of the cost of some goods and services. Handicrafts, originally locally-made products for the local market, and taxi rides are typical of items that were once available but which have frequently been priced out of the average consumer's reach. This naturally creates ill-feeling towards the tourist. It is another reason to pursue the development of local enterprises with the profits from tourism.

1 How can the tourist market be used to encourage other activities in: (a) agriculture, (b) manufacturing?

2 What effect is tourism likely to have on: (a) local shopping, (b) traffic on the roads, (c) litter, (d) water supplies?

People in the West Indies are sometimes misled as to the size of tourism in the region. The countries included in this book received 8 million stopover visitors in 1984, compared with 45 million going to Florida alone, or one million a month going to Great Britain. Clearly there are many other places for tourists to go, and tourism is not just a West Indian phenomenon, but a massive worldwide industry.

Most tourists come to the Caribbean for a combination of warmth and sunshine, beaches and the sea, and to experience something a bit foreign and perhaps exciting. Just which of the islands they choose to go to depends on the development of tourism there, and on the extent to which it is promoted.

Apart from investment in accommodation and tourist facilities, a destination has to be advertised in order to attract tourists. *Promotion*, as this is called, is expensive, and many countries have quite large budgets to do this. The Bahamas spent US$30 million in 1987, or $120 per inhabitant, compared with Barbados, which spent about US$30 per inhabitant. This reflects their differing degrees of dependency on tourism, as in terms of stopover tourists the expenditure works out fairly evenly at about US$20 and $16.50 per tourist, respectively.

Aruba - looking for growth

Aruba can be seen as a test case for the ability of investment to generate tourism, and for tourism to create wealth and employment. Until 1985 Aruba had a successful but stagnant tourist industry, showing little investment since 1979 and steady or declining arrivals (Fig. 16.3). In May 1985 the Lago oil refinery, which had supplied 17% of the country's gross domestic product, closed down, and it was decided to concentrate on tourism to replace the lost income. The budget was increased to $40 per inhabitant, and $17 per tourist (compare with Barbados and The Bahamas, above), and a major programme of promotion and building was started. By 1990 the number of hotel rooms had doubled to

5,000, with as many as 2,000 more projected for 1992. By 1990 tourist arrivals had increased by 61%, the highest growth in the Caribbean. Six casinos were operating in 1990, and eight more were planned. This compares with four casinos in The Bahamas.

Aruba will be well worth studying in future years to see if:

(a) The level of investment and new building can be maintained,

(b) tourist arrivals will continue to increase, and grow faster than in the Caribbean as a whole,

(c) tourism can replace the refinery as a revenue earner and employer.

Fig. 16.3 Tourism in Aruba, 1977-90.

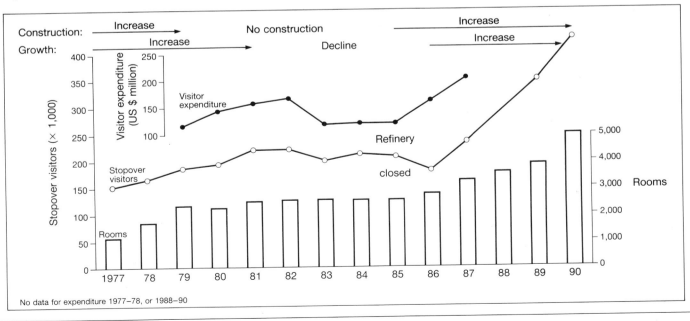

No data for expenditure 1977–78, or 1988–90

Tourist destinations in the Caribbean

The major destinations for the region include The Bahamas and Bermuda, which are strictly both in the Atlantic. However, they compete directly for the region's tourists (as does Florida), and are mainly visited for the same reasons. The major tourist centres are:

The Bahamas	Jamaica
Barbados	Puerto Rico
Bermuda	US Virgin Islands
The Dominican Republic	St Maarten

These have 72% of the total visitors. The remainder are shared by 20 other countries. The major destinations are the countries closest to the USA, with the significant exception of Barbados.

The reasons for the other countries having fewer tourists are basically all related to the amount of development that has taken place. The Windward Islands are mountainous with only a limited amount of level ground for airports and hotels, but so are the US Virgin Islands, which rank fourth in the region. It could be said that Trinidad is too industrial, but Puerto Rico, which ranks second, is far more urbanized, industrial and overcrowded. The marshy coastlands of the Guianas and Belize are not the real reason why tourism in these countries is limited, for south Florida is still mostly swampland, and most of the tourism is confined to a narrow strip of reclaimed offshore bars and lagoons. Even Florida's biggest resort of all, Disneyworld in Orlando, is an entirely artificial creation. With the proper development there is no territory in the West Indies that could not be a major tourist destination in the future.

1 What are the three largest tourist destinations in the world at present?

2 Referring to Table 16.3, several countries do not match the trend of high GDP and high employment in tourism. Can you explain this for (a) Puerto Rico, (b) Trinidad and Tobago?

3 Even though the Dominican Republic is not English-speaking, it is one of the largest tourist centres in the region. Why is this?

Cruise visitors

A common sight in the 1980s was the cruise liners crowded into Nassau harbour in The Bahamas.

Cruising has been an area of rapid development and new investment in the 1980s. It originally started using ocean liners that had lost their passengers to the airlines, and included ships like the *SS France*, now the cruise ship *Norway*. Since 1980 many ships have been custom-made for the cruise industry, and the number of cruise passengers has increased dramatically (Fig. 16.4).

Major cruise destinations in the Caribbean Region are The Bahamas, Puerto Rico and the US Virgin Islands, and these have 53% of all the total passenters (Table 16.4). Puerto Rico is also unique in having the only *originating* port, San Juan.

Table 16.4 Cruise arrivals, 1978 to 1989 (thousands)

Year	Bermuda	Bahamas	Jamaica	Barbados
1978	132	450	149	156
1981	105	597	140	136
1984	111	908	231	99
1989	131	1,645	444	337

The beautiful natural harbour of Charlotte Amalie in the US Virgin Islands has room for yachts, cruise liners, cargo ships and seaplanes.

Fig. 16.4 Caribbean cruising. This map shows a selection of routes from the various US ports that serve the Caribbean. For example, ships from New York serve a different area (the Eastern Caribbean) compared with those from the Gulf ports (Western Caribbean).

The main ports of embarkation are Miami (by far the most important), Fort Lauderdale, Tampa, and Port Canaveral, in Florida; and New York.

Cruising is much less important in terms of income and employment than the stopover tourist business, but it does have certain advantages that make it an important part of any economy:

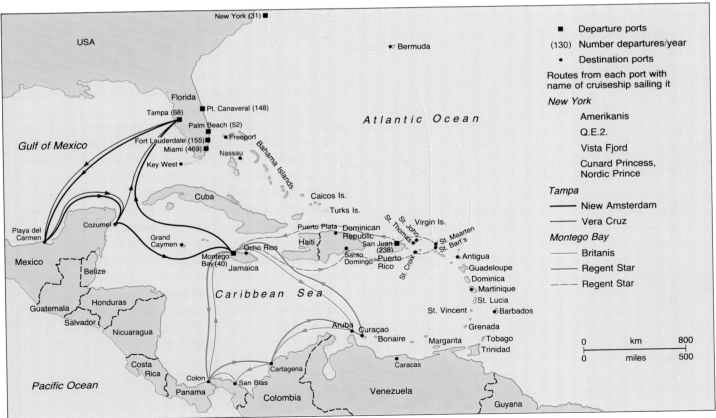

1   It requires little infrastructure, the most important need being for a deepwater harbour. In some cases such as the Windward Islands, ports built for another trade (bananas) can be used. Ocho Rios in Jamaica uses the bauxite harbour.

2   If no harbour is available, cruising is still possible. Large cruise liners have their own tenders and take the passengers into town or to a nearby beach, even on quite small islands.

3   Cruising benefits a certain sector of the economy that may not benefit much otherwise. Downtown shopping, often duty-free, and sightseeing tours, are particular attractions for cruise passengers.

4   The host country receives income from harbour dues, garbage collection, and perhaps water, fuel and food supplies.

5   Perhaps most important of all, many tourists use a cruise to see as much of the region as possible, and then choose one place for a long vacation. Cruise passengers are often 'window shopping'.

The cruise trade is, unfortunately, easily disrupted. As there is little investment needed by the shipping companies, they can move from island to island at will. Several labour disputes in Bermuda have caused a major slump in its trade, while The Bahamas with numerous potential harbours and anchorages has seen very rapid growth. Jamaica, too, after a bad spell up to 1981, has started to attract more ships, as has Barbados (Table 16.4). Caribbean tourism, dominated by hoteliers who see cruise ships as competition, has yet to respond to this growth. Major investment is needed in facilities specifically designed for short-stop cruise visitors.

1   What are the advantages and disadvantages of cruise tourists?

2   What could be done in your country to improve income from cruise visitors?

Barbados - an historic tourist centre

Possibly only Jamaica and the French Riviera have had such a romantic appeal as Barbados, where royalty and film stars took - and still take - their holidays. Every year until 1975 saw an increase in the number of tourists and the amount of income, and 1975 was only a minor setback resulting from the oil crisis of 1974. Right through until 1979, when stopover tourists reached 370,000, there was continued growth. Despite some recovery in 1983 and 1984, this total was not reached again until 1987. This decline is significant, for Barbados has a well-established industry and stable political and economic background.

Table 16.5 Percentage increase in tourist arrivals 1979-89

| | % change | |
	1979-84	1984-89
Barbados	- 0.9	+25
Bahamas	+11.7	+23
Aruba	+11.9	+64
Jamaica	+29.3	+19
Cayman Is	+32.3	+42
All Caribbean	+11.8	+38

Many other countries had problems in the early 1980s, but the important competitors have surged ahead, particularly The Bahamas, Jamaica and the Cayman Islands, and the region as a whole had a 12% growth (See Table 16.5). The Barbados government development plan for 1979-83 had assumed an annual growth rate of 8% for this period, and there was a 1% decline.

Only Puerto Rico has had a comparable decline, and although tourism is a large industry there, it only contributes about 5% to its GNP, so this was not so serious as it was in Barbados. In the 1960s in particular, but also in the 1970s, tourism kept the economy in Barbados healthy as sugar earnings fluctuated and declined. Tourism generated significant amounts of employment and foreign exchange. It encouraged infrastructural development, notably at the Grantley Adams international airport, one of the finest in the West Indies, and in Bridgetown harbour.

More recently (1984-89) Barbados has shown much improvement with a 25% increase in arrivals. However, at a growth rate of 5% a year this is well below the Caribbean average. 1990 saw no growth in stopover visitors at all, and only 1987 can be considered entirely successful.

Barbados has most of the geographical advantages associated with the Caribbean, but few of its extremes. It has a quite tolerable temperature, which is moderated by the trade winds, and there is no extreme rainfall in the coastal areas. Hurricanes are possible but relatively infrequent compared with areas further north.

The landscape is attractive without being mountainous, and the island is served by a well-maintained road system. Beaches offering both sheltered bathing and surfing are abundant and among the best in the region. The language is English and the government is often quoted as being one of the most stable and democratic in the world. As the island is well served by sea and air, all these advantages have made it extremely attractive to the prospective tourist, especially the knowledgeable one. The percentage of returning tourists is also high, being much higher than, say, for Jamaica.

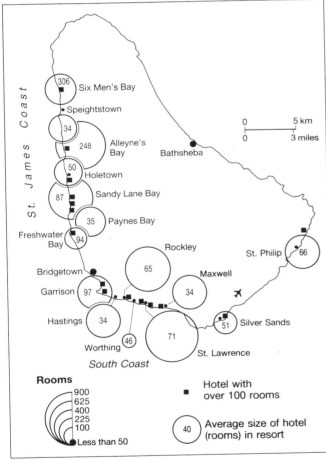

Fig. 16.5 Resort areas in Barbados, 1989. The tourist industry in Barbados is essentially located in two areas of overlapping resorts north and south of Bridgetown. Although the south coast area is more congested, there is no particular concentration of hotels in any one location. The even distribution of large hotels bears this out.

In recent years both wages and leisure time have increased. Many tourists have no real idea where Barbados, The Bahamas, or Bermuda are - and often confuse all three! - but they are most likely to go where there is an attractive package deal or their travel agent advises them. This is most likely to be a large hotel, and these have always had the best occupancy rates (Fig. 16.5). With a trend towards mass tourism in the Caribbean, proximity to North America has favoured the northern destinations. The special attractions of Barbados, which made up for its further distance from the USA, have not been so apparent to the tourist looking for an airline and hotel package holiday. The kind of accommodation offered in Barbados has been rather different from the rest of the West Indies: a much larger percentage of rooms - over half - is of the apartment type, which was very popular in the 1970s. The newest development here is a combination of hotels and apartments known as Heywoods Holiday Village, which has over 300 rooms in five hotels and two apartels. It is located on 12 ha (30 acres) of land well to the north of Bridgetown. It can also accommodate small conferences (up to 200 persons) and has a nine-hole golf course.

The causes of the recent decline in arrivals are very difficult to identify. It may be just a passing phase, or the result of random factors that have quite accidentally affected Barbados. However, there are some notable differences in the recent development of tourism in Barbados when compared with the more successful destinations.

1   Barbados has traditionally had small hotels, none having more than 200 rooms until recently. In 1989 it had 134 hotels and other accommodation, of which only 11 had over 100 rooms. Small hotels are very difficult to run profitably all the year round. Tour operators and travel agents prefer to book into large hotels where they can guarantee accommodation for charter parties, conventions and other large groups, and probably get instant confirmation via fax and/or computer. An American tour operator may only deal with three or four Barbadian hotels, and when these are full will simply switch to another island destination.

2   Sporting activities. Golf is a major American sport and often a requirement for American tourists. Hotels incorporating a top-class 18-hole golf course have now become a feature of many new resorts. Similarly, deep-sea fishing and scuba-diving are big attractions in some areas. (Cricket is largely unknown in North America!)

	1979	1981	1983	1985	1987	1989
Visitor Expenditure (US$Million)	187	262	252	309	379	500
Stopover visitors (x1,000)	371	353	328	359	422	465
Hotel and other beds (x1,000)	11.3	13.4	14.3	14.0	13.8	13.7

Table 16.6 Growth of Barbados Tourism 1979-1989

3   Those countries that have concentrated on North American tourists have suffered less from the strength of the US dollar compared with sterling or the European currencies. Barbados had a high percentage of UK/European and West Indian tourists, and it was these tourists particularly who stopped coming to Barbados. Equally, the weak US dollar in 1987 led to an increase in UK and European visitors (+54%), and not North American tourists (+6%).

4   Barbados is substantially further away from North America than many of its competitors, and North America accounts for 68% of the region's tourists, a proportion which has been slowly increasing.

5   The promotion of tourism is a crucial factor, and some countries have been much more successful at selling themselves than Barbados.

6   Barbados has far less room than many other islands. It may have to decide, for example, if it can continue to reserve marginal land for agriculture, or whether small hotels, guest houses and cottages should be allowed to use up the limited amount of valuable beach frontage.

1   Using the statistics in table 16.6, construct a graph for Barbados like Fig. 16.3 for Aruba.

2   Look at the diagram constructed from Table 16.6. Does there seem to be any link between the three items? Is Aruba like Barbados?

3   What is 'hotel occupancy rate'? Using the information in question 1 above, discuss the significance of occupancy in Barbados.

Tourism in Switzerland

Although the Caribbean is a popular destination for American tourists, with about 6 million visiting it each year, Europe is an even greater attraction for about 9 million American visitors. The main countries they visit are listed in Table 16.7.

Each of these countries has a large tourist industry, and in total any one of them receives far more tourists than the entire Caribbean. Switzerland, for instance, received about 19.5 million visitors in 1988 compared with 10 million for the Caribbean. Despite this, countries like Switzerland do not have as great a dependence on tourists as Caribbean countries, nor do their tourists visit them for the same reasons or at the same time. (See Table 16.8).

In 1987 Switzerland earned US $6 billion from tourism, which was about 10% of its export earnings (Table 16.10). The industry employed an average of 105,000 Swiss people, plus another 100,000 migrant workers, although this last figure varied quite a bit, being higher in summer and lower in winter owing to the seasonality of the visitors (Fig. 16.6). The peak season is the summer, and this is the time when most Americans visit Europe, but the winter period is valuable because tourists at this time stay longer and spend more money. A typical winter tourist is German or French and stays for five days at a ski resort. A typical summer visitor is also German, but could be British or American and only stay for two or three days, passing through on a coach tour or staying in low-priced accommodation such as a youth hostel or even on a campsite. In

Table 16.7 United States visitors to Europe - total nights spent in country, 1978

Country	Bed nights* (million)
Great Britain	22.5
France	10.3
Italy	4.9
Ireland	3.5
Spain	2.6
West Germany	2.4
Switzerland	2.2

*number of tourists x length of stay

Country	Nights (1,000)	%
West Germany*	14,970	43
Netherlands	2,875	8.5
Great Britain	2,590	7.5
France*	2,510	7
USA	2,270	6.5
Belgium	1,920	5.5
Italy*	1,530	4.5
Japan	680	2
Rest of world	5,380	15.5
Total foreign (46%)	34,626	100
Total domestic (54%)	40,050	
Total tourist nights	74,675	

*These border countries, along with Austria, account for 55% of all tourist nights. American tourists actually out-number all except the Germans, but as they stay for only a short period they account for relatively fewer nights.

Table 16.8 Total nights spent by tourists in Switzerland, 1988

the summer, hotels have about 45% occupancy compared with 37% in winter, but other types of accommodation, called *para-hotellerie* by the Swiss, are popular.

This variation in seasonality, accommodation and nationality reflects the varied attractions of Switzerland for tourists. The attractions include the following :

    Natural beauty, lakes, mountains
    Pure air
    Mineral/thermal springs
    Historic buildings, towns
    Distinctive culture (building style, clothes, food)
    Accessibility
    Climate (reliable snow in winter, sun in summer)

Table 16.9 Type of tourist accommodation in Switzerland, 1987

Type	Beds available (x 1,000)	Nights spent (million) Swiss	Foreign
Hotels	228	14.3	19.6
Apartments, cottages, etc.	360	14.1	10.1
Camp sites	273	4.9	2.1
Youth hostels	8	0.35	0.48
Motels	7	N/A	N/A
Sanatoria and convalescent homes	6	N/A	N/A
Other types*	235	5.0	2.0
Total beds	1,117	38.65	34.3

*Mainly group accommodation used by domestic tourists

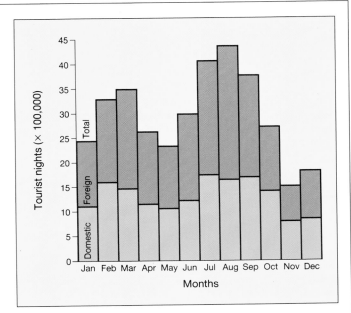

Fig. 16.6 Seasonality of tourists in Switzerland, 1988. Domestic tourism is the foundation of the Swiss tourist industry. In which months does it exceed foreign tourism?

Table 16.10 Switzerland: export earnings 1987

Industry	%
Metals and engineering	31
Chemicals/pharmaceuticals	15
Tourism	10
Textiles	4.5
Watches, clocks	4.5
Other	35

Most tourists come from the countries nearest to Switzerland, as this only requires a relatively short drive across the frontier. Germany has the best communications and by far the largest number of visitors - about one out of three - are German. The French and Italians have to cross the Alps, but are still the next most important, and in each case the Swiss speak the language of the country closest to them, so there is no language barrier.

1 Why do tourists go to Switzerland?

2 What are the main differences between accommodation in the Caribbean and in Switzerland?

The development of Swiss tourism

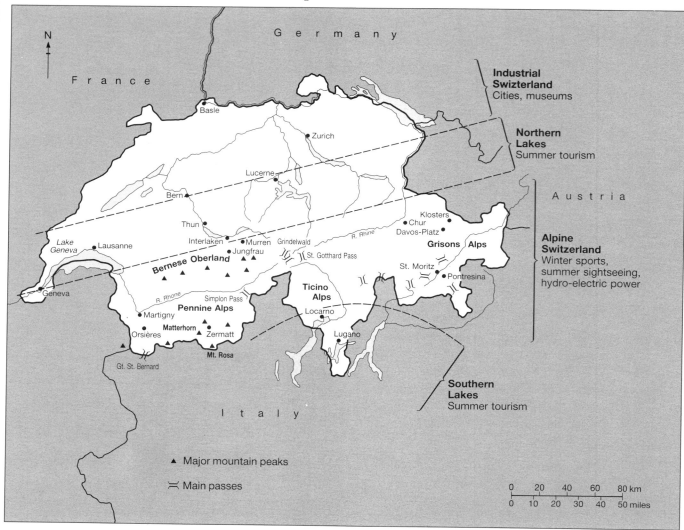

Fig. 16.7 Tourism in Switzerland.

The earliest visitors to Switzerland were English mountaineers, and it was an Englishman named Thomas Cook who introduced modern tourism to Switzerland. In 1863 he led an excursion to the Bernese Oberland, a mountainous region in the heart of the Swiss Alps which includes the famous Eiger mountain.

Thomas Cook is often considered the father of modern tourism, and he founded the world's largest travel agency. For a long time this was owned and operated by the British Government, and it is comparable to American Express, which was modelled on Cook's agency.

Cook's methods opened up Switzerland (and soon the rest of Europe) to tourists, and the Swiss in turn developed industry by investing heavily in transport and accommodation. Switzerland is a country of mountains, lakes and rivers, and severe winters. To make its scenery accessible

it had to develop its roads and railways in some of the most difficult circumstances in the world. Huge tunnels take the roads and railways through the Alps - several are more than 15km (10 miles) long. To provide the power to run the trains, ski-lifts, chair-lifts and cableways the Swiss developed hydro-electricity along the many rivers leaving the mountains. By 1961 total accessibility by electrified railway had been achieved, taking tourists quietly, cleanly and punctually to the highest peaks, whether they were winter skiers or summer sightseers.

Today the industry is concentrated in several areas (Fig. 16.7). The winter-sports industry is centred on three mountain regions:

1 The Bernese Oberland   Grindelwald
   (Jungfrau and Eiger Mountains) Kanderstaag
                                  Wengen
                                  Murren

2 Matterhorn and Monte Rosa   Zermatt
   Mountains   St Nicklaus

3 The Engadine Valley and   Davos-Platz
   Grisons Alps   Klosters
                                 St Moritz
                                 Pontresina

In summer the lake resorts are popular, although the winter resorts are also used:

1 Lake Geneva   Geneva
2 Lakes Thun and Brienz   Thun
                                 Interlaken
3 Lake Lucerne   Lucerne
4 Lake Zurich   Zurich
5 Lakes Maggiore and Lugano   Locarno
                                 Lugano

There are also many historic sites and towns with museums, castles, theatres and concert halls. Geneva, Basle, Bern, Lausanne, and Zurich are world-famous (Table 16.11). Equally famous are the health resorts and exclusive finishing schools scattered throughout the country. Sanatoria alone account for 6,000 beds, which is about the same amount of accommodation that is to be found in, say, Martinique or Aruba.

Table 16.11 The tourist regions of Switzerland - hotel accommodation and tourist nights, 1987

Mountains *Beds Nights+		Lakes Beds Nights		Cities Beds Nights		Other areas Beds Nights	
80.2	13.1	48.7	7.4	32.2	6.0	66.4	7.4
35%	38%	22%	22%	14%	18%	29%	22%

*(1,000)   +(1,000,000)

17
The Caribbean population

A Barbadian family in front of their home near Bridgetown.

The Caribbean region contains some 35 million people. The differences in population between countries are often very great, and vary from about 10 million in Cuba to a few thousand on many of the smaller islands. Ninety per cent of the total population live in just six countries, with the remaining 10% distributed among the other 21. However, this is not surprising, as the top six countries are by far the biggest islands. Only the four mainland countries (Belize, Guyana, Suriname and French Guiana) have similar areas, but these

Cuba	10.2	Spanish until 1898
Hispaniola:		
Dominican Republic	6.9	Spanish until 1844
Haiti	6.3	Spanish until 1697
Puerto Rico	3.6	Spanish until 1898
Jamaica	2.4	Spanish until 1655
Trinidad	1.2	Spanish until 1797
Total	30.6	

Table 17.1 Population of the larger West Indian islands, 1988 (millions)

have quite moderately sized populations. Without exception the largest populations have developed in those islands that were originally settled by the Spanish (Table 17.1). The Spanish had little interest in settling the smaller islands, and even in those where they did settle, development came later with the British, the French and from the United States.

Size

The size of the population is an important characteristic of any country. It determines the size of the labour force, the number of schools, colleges, houses, and the amount of food and water it is likely to need. These factors have a significant economic impact as well, so that the bigger countries have more say in what happens in the region and have the economic power to maintain that position. It is true also that when these larger countries have problems, they become everyone else's problems. Haiti may be of little account politically or economically, but because it has 6 million people its difficulties affect the entire northern Caribbean.

Smaller populations have the advantage - perhaps only in theory - that their problems are limited in size. Unfortunately the advantages that are possible with economies of scale are denied to them, as we have seen in the problem of developing industries for small local markets. Nevertheless, a country of 3 million people may have 1 million students and need 2,000 schools with 50,000 teachers, which is a major requirement by any standards. On the other hand, a large population can justify a university, museums, specialist hospitals, a national airline and many other things that smaller countries often have to do without. The absolute size of a population usually determines the size of everything else in the economic and social structure.

Density and distribution

Although size of population is what distinguishes one country from another, within countries it is usually the *density* that is the more obvious. Density means the number of persons per unit of land. A crude measure of density would be the number of persons per square kilometre, or for countries dependent on agriculture we could have the number of persons per cultivated hectare. Often much of the land cannot be used, so a useful measure is the number of persons per square kilometre of economically useful land. The actual distribution of population therefore depends very much on the natural landscapes, and the opportunities they provide for settlement (See chapter 1). The extent to which countries provide land that is both accessible and fertile is the main reason for the differences in density between them (Table 17.2).

These differences are not very great at all if the most densely populated country (Barbados) and the six least densely populated countries are excluded. The remaining 20 countries are all fairly close to the average of about 200 persons/

km² (500/sq. mile). However, the countries at the top and bottom of Table 17.2 cannot be ignored, and if they are examined more closely it will be seen that there is a reason for their extreme figures.

Barbados is unusual in being fertile over most of its land area. Its neighbours, like Grenada and St Vincent, are volcanic islands, with their populations restricted to the coastal areas. About half of these islands are uninhabitable, and if we take this into account it will be seen that their comparable densities for the habitable areas are quite similar, being 638 and 534 persons/km² respectively.

The very low figures for the bottom six countries tend to conceal the real situation, which is that here there are fairly high densities - typical for the West Indies - in the habitable areas. For instance, in The Bahamas the density for New Providence is virtually the same as for Barbados, but all the other large Bahamian islands have very low densities, owing to their lack of economic development at the present. In Guyana, Suriname, and French Guiana, only the coastal strip

Country	Persons/km²	Persons/sq. mile	Rank
Barbados	616	1,596	1
Puerto Rico	354	918	2
Aruba	345	893	3
US Virgin Is	322	833	4
Grenada	319	827	5
Curaçao	292	757	6
St Vincent	267	693	7
Antigua	261	676	8
Guadeloupe	259	670	9
Trinidad and Tobago	243	630	10
Jamaica	193	499	11
St Kitts/Nevis	191	494	12
St Lucia	186	482	13
Haiti	176	457	14
Martinique	128	332	15
Montserrat	120	310	16
Dominican Rep.	107	276	17
Dominica	97	252	18
Cuba	87	226	19
British Virgin Is	72	186	20
Cayman Is	56	145	21
Bahamas	20	53	22
Turks and Caicos Is	14	36	23
Belize	6	16	24
Guyana	3	9	25
Suriname	2	6	26
French Guiana	1	2	27

Table 17.2 Population density of West Indian countries in 1980

is settled densely; most of the rest is largely inaccessible. Belize also has large areas of swampland, and a limited number of areas suitable for settlement.

The distribution of population in individual countries is also influenced by landscape, but there are other factors that need to be considered. A study of Trinidad and Tobago shows that although the mountainous areas and swamps are the least settled, and the coastal plains and lowlands have the highest densities, there are certain areas where these 'rules' do not apply (Fig. 17.1). These *anomalies*, as they are called, can be explained once the history of settlement and the economic factors which influenced it have been understood. In the case of Trinidad and Tobago, we can note the following:

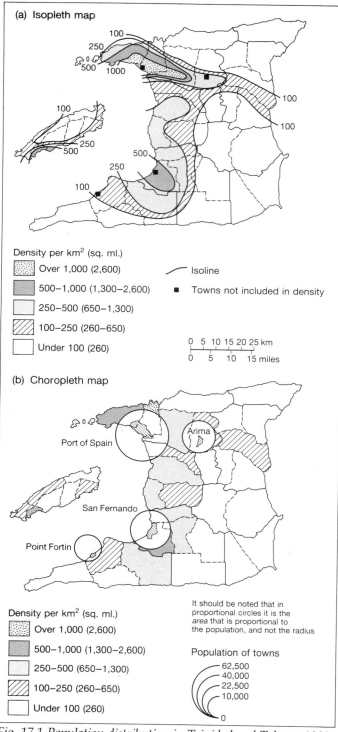

Fig. 17.1 Population distribution in Trinidad and Tobago, 1980. Both of these maps use data from the 1980 census for the wards and parishes of Trinidad and Tobago. The isopleth map uses isolines (lines joining points of equal density) which have been estimated from the ward densities and the map of settlement. The choropleth map only shows the ward densities. In both cases the population of the four boroughs has been excluded from the ward densities, but in the choropleth map they are shown by proportional circles.

(a) Mountainous areas may be inhabited owing to urban expansion (north of Port-of-Spain) or agriculture (coffee farming in St David).

(b) Coastal areas may be sparsely settled because of lack of access (Blanchisseuse, most of the south coast) or distance from Port of Spain (Mayaro).

(c) Inland areas may be densely settled owing to agricultural development and mineral deposits (rice growing and oil south of San Fernando).

Despite this, the settlement pattern is generally related to the natural landscape.

Population pressure, overpopulation and underpopulation

The size and density of a population are exact statistics, and other characteristics, like population growth and migration, can also be measured precisely. The *effect* of a population's size or density is much less exact, however, and brings us to the *concept* of whether a particular area is overcrowded or suffering in some way from the size and density of its population.

Overpopulation and *underpopulation* are the extremes of population pressure, and refer to the extent to which a country's resources can support its population. A country that is overpopulated is one that cannot provide the necessities for its population because at that time there are too many people. Haiti is the best-known example in the Caribbean. Two of the most densely populated islands in the world, Barbados (616 persons/km²) and New Providence (653 persons/km²) in The Bahamas, cannot be said to be overpopulated because in general their populations are well fed, housed and clothed. It should not be assumed that a high density means overpopulation.

Some overpopulated areas are in fact quite sparsely populated, such as many of the southern Family Islands of The Bahamas. This is largely a response to their lack of resources, and has been characterized by out-migration to Nassau. In fact most overpopulated places can be identified not by their density, but by their *out-migration*. Whenever a population shows itself willing to migrate on a regular basis it is a sure sign of strong population pressure. The continued emigration of Haitians throughout the twentieth century to the USA, The Bahamas, Cuba, the Dominican Republic and the French West Indies is a classic example.

Underpopulated describes a country that does not have the labour force to develop its resources. It is usually a magnet for migrants, and *in-migration* is common. Trinidad and Tobago is a country whose prosperity has attracted many migrants. (See Tables 17.3, 17.6).

Under or overpopulation are difficult ideas to apply to a country, and should be used with care. There is one viewpoint that neither of these conditions exists, but that overpopulation is really the underdevelopment of resources, and if we

Country	Population	% of total
Grenada	20,127	46
St Vincent	13,594	30
Barbados	3,918	
Guyana	2,766	
Others	4,445	
Total West Indians	45,850	4.2
Other foreign born	14,408	
Total foreign born	60,258	5.6

Table 17.3 Trinidad and Tobago - West Indian born population, 1980

use our abilities properly there should be enough for everyone. Probably the best examples of overpopulation are found in certain areas of a country, and only apply to certain conditions. For instance, Kingston in Jamaica is overpopulated, especially with respect to water resources, housing and jobs. The north coast of Jamaica can be said to be underdeveloped with respect to tourism, and could certainly support a much larger population. San Juan, the capital of Puerto Rico, has literally run out of space. It is overcrowded, housing is congested, and traffic jams are almost continuous during working hours.

1 What are the disadvantages of a small population? Do these apply to a country like Antigua?

2 What are the advantages of a large population? Do these apply to a country like Jamaica?

3 Is Barbados overpopulated?

4 Is Guyana underpopulated?

Migration deals with the movement of people. The most notable movement of this sort is into or away from a country:

immigration = in-migration

emigration = out-migration

There are other kinds of migration, however, such as *internal migration*. This includes the following:

(a) Movement from the countryside to the towns. This is also known as *urban drift* or simply *urbanization* (See p. 204).

(b) Movement away from the central urban areas into the suburbs.

(c) Movement from one part of the country to another as a result of development, as in the new tourist resort areas, or where a new mineral resource has been discovered.

Seasonal or *temporary migration* is also characteristic of West Indian societies. Most seasonal migration is in search of work during harvest time. For example, picking fruit in Florida has long been an attraction for Jamaicans and others in the Greater Antilles. Temporary migration includes two great labour migrations at the beginning of the twentieth century, during the building of the Panama Canal (1903-12), and the Florida railways. Thousands left islands throughout the Caribbean, and many never returned.

Similarly, there is migration within the Caribbean, and from the Caribbean to other parts of the world. These can best be studied by examining some recent migrations.

Queues for food in Havana are a common sight.

West Indian migration to Great Britain in the 1950s and 1960s

Starting in the 1950s and continuing through the 1960s, Great Britain and West Germany both had growing economies and a need for an increased labour force. By the 1970s West Germany had received over 2 million migrant workers, mainly from Turkey and Yugoslavia, and unemployment was at a record low of less than 1%.

Great Britain was neither so prosperous nor had such a low unemployment level, but as its economy developed it found it very difficult to recruit workers in low-paid or low-status jobs. These in particular included jobs in restaurants, hotels, hospitals, on buses and the underground trains, and in certain factories such as those for textiles and furniture. To meet this demand, workers from the West Indies were recruited, along with people from India, Pakistan and East Africa.

It is important to realize that the migration of West Indians to Britain was relatively well organized, and was aimed at filling the particular jobs vacant at the time. London Transport, for instance, maintained a recruiting office in Kingston, and Lyons Restaurants did the same in Barbados.

Whether they were recruited directly... or whether they moved through their own initiative, the bulk of West Indians were destined to fill vacancies for which there was either insufficient labour available, or which [existing] workers were insufficiently willing to fill

Ceri Peach, *West Indian Migration to Britain*, 1968, p. 94

The number of migrants, both men and women, varied according to the needs of the job market until about 1961, and ranged from about 15,000 to 45,000 a year. In 1962 the British government passed an Immigration Act requiring every migrant to have a work permit, and the number of these work permits was limited. This in turn restricted the numbers of West Indian migrants to about 15,000 a year, of whom most were the dependents of earlier migrants. By the late 1960s more migrants were returning to the West Indies than going to Britain, and the migration was over.

The effect of this migration on the West Indies was considerable for the islands that were involved. In 1970 there were 300,000 Jamaicans living in Britain, equivalent to about 15% of Jamaica's population, and they would have greatly affected the pressure on employment and social services had they stayed at home. Barbados, Antigua and St Kitts also sent large numbers, but none as high as Montserrat, which sent 4,000 out of its 12,000 population to Britain! The migration

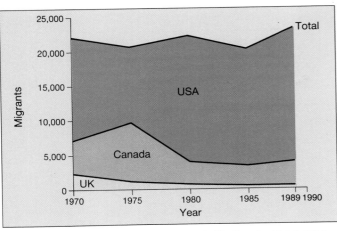

Fig. 17.2 Migration from Jamaica, 1970-89. See also Table 17.8.

was less attractive to people from Guyana, Trinidad and The Bahamas, but virtually every West Indian community did participate, and eventually there were about one million West Indians living in Great Britain.

Migration to Britain continues to this day, but is a fraction of what it used to be. Since the 1962 Act, more people have emigrated to the USA and Canada than to Britain. (Fig. 17.2 and Table 17.8).

Migration from Trinidad and Tobago in the late 1960s

The migration described above attracted mainly unskilled people seeking employment of any kind. Trinidadians also went to Britain in this migration, but not in great numbers, and in the years 1961-63 there were more Trinidadians returning than leaving. However, from 1964 to 1970, out-migration progressively increased until it reached over 17,000 a year. This was apparently due to an increasing degree of unemployment, but the effect was quite different from the earlier migration. The new Trinidad migration included skilled and professional people, mainly going to Canada and the USA. About 75% of the nurses trained in Trinidad went to North America in this period, and an increasing number of doctors also left. By 1968 some 38% of the university-trained labour force had migrated, along with 10% of the remaining labour. To some extent this also happened in Jamaica. This naturally caused great alarm in Trinidad, and considerable efforts were made to get these well-qualified people to return. Unfortunately both the USA and Canada accept migrants based on their training and skills, and so people with good qualifications find it relatively easy to leave home, especially if they already have contacts abroad to sponsor them (Table 17.4).

This trend - a 'brain drain' - has spread throughout the West Indies, with independence and better education in the 1970s and 1980s. It is encouraged by the large number of students who go to study higher education in North America, and then stay to work there. In time they may return, but their absence is partly responsible for the use of expatriate labour, especially in the professions.

The Haitian migration

The two migrations discussed above were prompted by *pull* factors - there was an attraction (jobs) in another country. Economic migration of this type is typical of many of the migrations that occur within the West Indies as well. There is another group of migrations, however, that are subject to *push* factors. In these cases conditions are so bad because of persecution, civil war, political oppression or poverty that people will leave to go anywhere. Such migrants are usually called *refugees*. The Vietnamese 'boat people' of the late 1970s were such an example, and Cubans fleeing to Miami from communism are another. The most persistent migrants of this type at the present time, however, are the Haitians, who have been called the Caribbean's boat people.

Haitians can only migrate illegally, by paying a boat captain to take them to 'Florida'. Florida is the apparent destination of all the Haitian boat people, but for various reasons they end up in the Turks and Caicos Islands, the Dominican Republic, and especially The Bahamas. Few of the boats are able to reach Florida at all, and in fact few of the boat 'captains' attempt to do so. They usually offload their cargo of 100-200 migrants at the first land they come to, which is sometimes uninhabited. Current statistics suggest that about 40,000 Haitians have reached Miami, and perhaps 25,000 are in The Bahamas. Most of those in Miami arrived in The Bahamas first where they worked as agricultural or building-site labourers, or as gardeners, jobs which few Bahamians apply for. More recently signifant numbers of Haitians have also been turning up in the French dependencies of Martinique, Guadeloupe and St Martin.

As is the way with many migrations, they create problems for the receiving country and in the end restrictions are placed on arrivals. In the case of the Haitians they are illegal to start with, and efforts have been aimed at stopping the migration and returning existing migrants. In 1980 there was an agreement between Haiti and the USA for the US Coast Guard to

Table 17.4 Trinidad and Tobago - natural increase and net migration, 1960-80

	Natural increase	Net migration	Population growth
1960-70	238,600	- 117,800	120,800
1970-80	195,000	- 70,400	124,600
1960-80	433,600	- 188,200	245,400

patrol off Haiti. This has been very successful in reducing the flow of illegal boats.

In 1985 Haiti and The Bahamas signed an agreement to repatriate most of the Haitians living there illegally. Nevertheless, boats still leave Haiti with hopeful refugees on an almost daily basis, despite the threat of the Coast Guard, repatriation, or the very real danger of drowning, starvation or even murder by unscrupulous boat 'captains'.

---

1 What foreign nationalities are there in your population, and why?

2 Where have natives of your country migrated to, and why?

Some other recent migrations

Cuba to Florida

This is undoubtedly the biggest movement taking place in recent times, and it involves hundreds of thousands of Cubans. The scale of this migration is encouraged by the USA's policy of classing Cubans as political refugees seeking asylum from communism. By 1980 there were over one million Cubans in America, and in 1980 a further 125,000 left Cuba in a massive flotilla of boats, subsequently known as the Mariel migration. Since then the flow of Cubans has been much smaller, but south Florida and Miami in particular are now dominated by Cubans. Current plans by the US government are to permit up to 20,000 Cuban migrants a year, mainly the dependents of those who are already in the USA.

West Indians to The Bahamas

The Bahamas (like the Cayman Islands and the Turks and Caicos Islands) have no income tax. They also have relatively high wage rates, partly due to the nearness of the USA, and a prosperous economy. Many West Indians have sought to work and live there, and the shortage of highly skilled and professional labour has encouraged this (Table 17.5). The Bahamas has a relatively small population for its land area, which is a little greater than Jamaica's.

In 1980 the total foreign-born population in The Bahamas was almost 12% of the total, although many of these were temporary residents with two-year work permits. They were mainly employed in teaching, accounting, banking, nursing, and the other professions.

Over-the-border migration

Six countries in the West Indies have land frontiers across which migration is common. These are Belize (with Guate-

Country	1970	1980
Haiti	*6,151	*8,832
Jamaica	3,526	2,571
Turks and Caicos	3,185	2,689
Trinidad & Tobago	388	257
Barbados	338	269
Guyana	263	151
Cuba	175	78
Others	459	302
Total Caribbean	14,485	15,149
% of population	9%	7%

*As most Haitians are illegal migrants, the census figures are believed to be less than half of the actual numbers.

Table 17.5 West Indian born population in The Bahamas in 1970 and 1980

mala and Mexico), Haiti and the Dominican Republic, Guyana (with Suriname and Venezuela), Suriname (with Guyana, Brazil and French Guiana), and French Guiana (with Suriname and Brazil).

The Belizean government estimated that there were 47,000 aliens in Belize in 1985, and a large unknown number who were illegal (Table 17.6). In 1988 the Belize government granted refugee status to 1,000 illegal migrants, 700 of them from El Salvador.

Since 1970 many Guyanese have gone to Suriname, and there are frequent reports of these people being sent back forcibly. When Suriname became independent, a large number migrated to the Netherlands, creating a shortage of labour in some areas. With the decline in the Guyanese economy in the 1970s, many Guyanese went to Suriname, but the government there has repeatedly taken steps to expel them. With the military takeover of the Suriname government in 1983, up to 5,000 Surinames fled to the Netherlands claiming to be political refugees. The Dutch government considers them illegal and wishes to repatriate them.

The Haitian situation is very similar to that in Guyana. Large numbers leave Haiti to cross the mountainous border to the Dominican Republic, but as their language is different,

Table 17.6 Population structure of Belize, 1985

Native born	112,000	71%
Guatemalan	10,900	
El Salvadoran	7,850	29%
Others	28,050	
Total	158,800	

being French-based, not Spanish, they are easily identified. More than half a million Haitians live in the Dominican Republic, where they work in the consturction industry and agriculture. Periodically the Dominican military and immi- gration officials round-up and deport thousands of Haitians. Both Suriname and the Dominican Republic still have large numbers of their neighbours within their borders, despite these efforts.

Population change

There are only two ways in which a population size can change. It may be added to by *natural increase*, or increased or decreased by *migration*. Most West Indian countries have lost population in the last 20 years as a result of out-migration, but all have had increases from natural increase. In nearly all cases the natural increase has been greater than the loss due to migration, and populations have grown. (See Table 17.7.)

Natural increase is the difference between the births and deaths in the population over a given period. Usually the birth rate, death rate, and natural increase are described in terms of numbers per thousand population (‰). Generally speaking the most backward and the most advanced countries have low growth rates. In the first case both the death rate and the birth rates are high, so that the large numbers of births are cancelled out by high rates of infant mortality and death from disease. None of the West Indian countries falls into this category today because medical and public health measures, often in the form of foreign aid, have reduced the death rate. Haiti has the highest death rate at 16/1,000, well below the figures of 30-40/1,000 for some African and South American countries. However, both Haiti and the Dominican Republic still have very high birth rates and this gives them a high rate of natural increase - over 25/1,000.

The rest of the region has passed through this phase of declining death rates and has reached a stable figure of about 6/1,000. Countries are now undergoing declining birth rates, but this is much less predictable than the decline in the death rate. Barbados is notable for its low birth rate - below 20/1,000. Cuba is the only other major country with such a low figure. Mostly the birth rates are between 20/1,000 and 30/1,000, but they have all declined from higher figures over the last 10-15 years, and so has the natural increase.

Obviously, if natural increase was the only factor, every country in the Caribbean would have had a sizeable increase in population in the ten years from 1970 - between 10% and 30%. In fact many had much less because of out-migration, and in St Kitts and Montserrat the population has actually declined because out-migration was so high.

In Jamaica there was a net out-migration for every year in the two decades 1970-90, apart from 1983. The average loss of population has been about 15,000 persons per year, or roughly one-third of the natural increase. This could be considered a fortunate reduction in population pressure, equivalent to a drop of about 9/1,000 in the birth rate, but it can also be considered unfortunate as about 20% of the workers migrating are professional or highly skilled people (Table 17.8).

Table 17.7 Vital statistics for selected countries, 1980, rate per thousand

Country	Birth rate	Death rate	Natural increase	
Haiti	41.8	15.6	26.2	High
Dominican Rep.	36.7	9.1	27.6	
Jamaica	27.5	6.7	20.7	Moderate
Bahamas	23.8	5.9	17.9	
Trinidad	27.6	6.9	20.7	
Cuba	19.7	6.3	13.4	Low
Barbados	18.9	8.8	11.1	

1 What are the disadvantages of a small population? Do these apply to a country like Antigua?

2 What are the advantages of a large population? Do these apply to a country like Jamaica?

3 Is Barbados overpopulated?

4 Is Guyana underpopulated?

Table 17.8 Migration from Jamaica to the USA, Canada and Great Britain, 1970-85

Destination	1970	%	1975	%	1980	%	1985	%
USA	15,000	68	11,100	54	19,000	83	18,900	86
Canada	4,700	21	8,200	40	3,200	14	2,900	13
Great Britain	2,400	11	1,400	6	600	3	300	1
Total	22,100		20,700		22,800		22,100	

18
Settlements, towns and cities

A small fishing community on the White River near Ocho Rios, Jamaica. Overfishing has seriously depleted the north coast's fish stocks.

What are they and how do they grow?

Any place where people live is a settlement. Many of the early settlements in the West Indies were small communities living around a source of employment provided by a landowner. Names often suggest this, for example Victoria Hill Settlement and Current Island Settlement. Frequently the word 'settlement' was dropped, so that only the owner's name was used, as in Dixon's or McKenzie's. In the sugar islands the word 'estate' would be used, e.g. Belle Vue Estate or Frankland's Estate; and similarly there would be Jackson's Pasture, Camden Park or Francois Farm. These often dropped their second name as well. All of these examples have been picked out because they represent a *primary* or original type

Havana is one of the largest cities in the Caribbean. It has large buildings and wide avenues.

of settlement. People earned their living from the land, and clustered around the centre of activity. Larger estates often had separate settlements nearby, particularly for their labourers, and these were usually called *villages*, e.g. Potter's Village, Murray Village. Sometimes the villages were colonies of freed slaves who practised farming on their own, but in all these cases we still have settlements associated with farming - these are *rural* settlements (See p. 234).

The other types of settlement common in the West Indies in the early years were the various ports and harbours. These had a quite different function, that of commerce, but in many cases they were administrative and government centres as well, e.g. Port of Spain, Port Royal, Port Antonio. These were *urban* centres, and supported the activities associated with *towns*, which is what many of them were called: Georgetown, Kingstown, Bridgetown. A few of these towns grew to quite a large size and became the capitals of their countries. As their importance grew it was customary for the town to be given the title of *city*, often as a result of it becoming the seat of a bishop and therefore possessing a cathedral. Bridgetown became a city in 1842 as a result of the creation of the Diocese of Barbados and the Leeward Islands in 1824. The Diocese of Nassau was formed in 1861, and Nassau was legally recognized as a city in 1882. The status of city gave the town certain rights in governing itself. In a larger country this would have given it some independence from central government, but in the West Indies the main advantage was to give the colony more self-government. Since independence the status of city has lost its significance, and the term is used much more loosely to indicate size and importance. Most West Indian towns and cities were not large, and few reached a population of 100,000 until recently, although Havana was this size in the nineteenth century, and its population exceeds one million today.

Every major town that became a capital in the West Indies was also that country's major port. Very often it was the only large town, or city, in the country. When a city becomes far and away the largest settlement, with the second town of no great significance, it is known as a *primate* city. For instance, Kingston is 12 times as large as Jamaica's second city, which is Montego Bay. San Juan is five times bigger than Ponce in Puerto Rico. In many cases there is only one large town, as in Barbados - Bridgetown. It is common for between 25% and 40% of the population to live in the main town or city. In a few cases the figure is much higher, and the capital is virtually the country itself in terms of population. For instance, Willemstad has about 70% of the population of Curaçao.

The nature of a settlement therefore depends on its purpose, or function, and size. The basic differences are between rural and urban, with urban settlements often being extremely large. It is possible for the majority of the population to be rural, and this is more common in the less-developed countries, such as in the Windward Islands, where the capitals are still quite small towns, and up to 70% of the people live in rural towns and villages.

Patterns of settlement

The arrangement of the different types of settlement gives us a *pattern*, of which several types are well known. The most common distinction is between a widely scattered population - *dispersed* - and one that concentrates in communities - *nucleated*.

In the West Indies a truly dispersed population is uncommon. It is only likely to occur when a population is able to farm independently over a large area, and as most of the fertile land was taken up by sugar estates, this was not possible. The best examples are in the hilly areas of the larger islands where freed slaves settled to make an independent living, as in Haiti and the Dominican Republic especially, but also in parts of Jamaica and Martinique. All the larger islands also have a nucleated pattern superimposed on this, especialy Jamaica which has a well-structured range of large and small towns dominated by Kingston. Barbados is rather different, for although it has its rural population clustered in villages (nucleated), there are no rural towns. In small islands the nearness to the one big town usually prevents the growth of a second town, so the pattern is that of one town and a large number of villages. Smaller towns and scattered farms (dispersed) are absent, but plantation homes are often numerous and form a special type of dispersed settlement.

---

1 Give examples of the following in your country:

   (a) a nucleated settlement

   (b) a city

   (c) a market town

   (d) a village.

2 How do you explain the distribution of population in your country? (Use a map.)

3 What is a dispersed population? Does it exist in your country?

Change and urbanization

The pattern of settlement has not remained fixed, although it is rare for the larger settlements to disappear or even stop growing. At the smaller scale, plantation homes, farms and the more isolated settlements have often been abandoned as agriculture has changed. Many of the central and southern islands of The Bahamas have lost population and their smaller settlements are no longer viable. Migration has caused a similar situation in Montserrat and St Kitts, and partly in Antigua. For instance, the Galways plantation in Montserrat operated from the 1660s until the 1900s, but was then totally abandoned until archaeological work rediscovered it in 1981.

The most important change, however, has been the rapid growth of the towns, and particularly the capital cities. This has been largely the result of a transfer of population from the rural areas to the towns. This type of internal migration is effectively the process of *urbanization*. It is not merely the growth of towns, as this can take place without urbanization. It involves an increase in the percentage of the population living in towns, with a consequent decline in the rural percentage. In the last 30 years urbanization has been very rapid in the West Indies.

Urbanization has been caused, like other migrations, by *push* and *pull* factors. The towns have certain attractions:

- They pay higher wages.
- They provide a concentration of employment.
- They provide a variety of services not available elsewhere, such as higher education.
- They have usually been the centres of any growth in manufacturing, and also often in tourism.
- They have a major psychological presence for most people, as most things 'happen' in the largest town, and it is therefore talked about continuously.

In the countryside, certain things have discouraged people from staying there:

- Lack of public services - electricity, piped water, health and school services.
- Lack of employment.
- Poor returns from agriculture, when compared with the growth of manufacturing and tourism.

In particular, young people today have enough education to seek a wider range of employment than that offered in farming. They are often exposed to an urban lifestyle because the senior schools and colleges are nearly always located in the larger towns. Like most migrations, urbanization particularly attracts the young single adult.

In the larger countries urbanization usually occurs in stages, with migrants moving to the nearest town, and then moving to a bigger town a bit later. This has the effect of focusing urbanization on the largest towns - the capital cities.

Unlike migration to foreign countries, return migration is rare - once settled in a town the migrant usually stays an urban dweller for the rest of his life.

Problems of urbanization

In many cases urbanization is a healthy response to economic development. During the first hundred years of the Industrial Revolution in Great Britain the population changed from 80% rural to 80% urban. The availability of labour in the towns led to the rapid growth of numerous industries, and the presence of a large population in the limited space of a town encouraged the development of consumer industries and services. Mass production and mass consumption are mainly associated with urban and industrialized populations. Unfortunately, in the less developed countries, including the West Indies, many people moved to the towns in the *hope* of getting a job, which is rather different from a move directly into employment.

Urbanization has always created considerable social problems, especially for housing, health services and schools. In time a prosperous economy can afford to pay for these, but if the new population is arriving regardless of the need for labour, they do not create any wealth. The services are still needed, but now they cannot be paid for. This kind of urbanization creates slums, shanty towns and poverty. Parts of West Kingston suffer from this as well as the outskirts of Port au Prince, San Juan and Santo Domingo. It is even present in patches on gullied land around Port of Spain. Nowhere, except in Haiti, are the extremes of poverty found that exist in the Far East, Africa or South America, but the problems are still large and serious for the people involved.

The answers to the problems created by urbanization are limited. Even if low-cost housing has been provided it cannot be afforded or maintained by unemployed people. Basic services such as drinking water, electricity and waste disposal need to be provided, but they have to be subsidized by the rest of the community. The ideal is to provide employment and this is undoubtedly the main objective of every government in the region. The fact remains that there is scarcely anywhere which has less than 20% unemployment, and creating jobs is a very difficult business. Just keeping major industries profitable is often a problem; one example is the bauxite industry, where many previously 'secure' jobs are now being lost.

Dealing with the problem of unemployment and poverty in the towns is often impossible. In some countries serious attempts are made to create work in the countryside, and to improve conditions so that people will not feel the need to leave. This can be done in many ways, or example:

- Reviving existing agriculture, such as replanting coffee and coconut trees, re-stocking banana plantations and replacing obsolete infrastructure.
- Developing new agriculture, often with the aid of irrigation.
- Providing land for lease or sale. Many farmers have no land to farm, particularly in the larger islands. Jamaica, for instance, has bought up vacant land in its 'land-lease' scheme and prepared it for small farmers.
- Taking the basic utilities and services to the rural areas. This includes health clinics, rural electricity, piped water and secondary schools. This was particularly promoted in the 1980s with aid from Caricom and the EC.
- Establishing manufacturing industries in rural areas. Puerto Rico has a system where its tax exemptions are lowest around San Juan, and higher for the rest of the country. This has in fact been very successful in getting industry to locate away from the capital (See Fig 15.4).
- Building new towns. Often this is an extreme measure, but Belmopan in Belize and Freeport in The Bahamas are good examples, being totally independent towns with great potential for growth. There is a larger number of smaller new towns, such as Portmore to the west of Kingston, Jamaica, that are mainly housing estates linked to the nearby city. They start off by providing good-quality housing and social services which allow people in the city to move out of the slums, which can then be redeveloped. Eventually industry grows up in and around these suburbs and allows for a more orderly expansion.

We must remember that towns and cities grow in the same way as the country as a whole - by natural increase and migration. Generally the natural increase in urban areas is not much different from the rural areas, so that without migration both areas would grow at the same rate. The towns would get bigger, but this would not be urbanization. It is the transfer of population to the towns that is the key factor. This does not mean that the population in rural areas declines, although it may do so. Often it is the surplus population produced by natural increase that migrates, as is the case in Puerto Rico (Table 18.1).

Large populations on the larger islands have led to overcrowding in the towns. Cap Haitien, Haiti.

Urbanization in Puerto Rico

Puerto Rico has undergone considerable urbanization since 1970, with two out of three people now living in the towns. The national rate of growth was 15%, but towns grew more than twice as fast as this, and the rural population actually declined. An interesting feature of this growth was the capital city itself, San Juan, which actually lost population (See Table 18.1).

This is explained by the extraordinary growth of the five municipal districts immediately outside San Juan which increased their population by over 50% (Fig. 18.2). The original San Juan is now completely built up and increas-ingly commercial. The population has to settle on the outskirts, which in 1980 had 100,000 more people than the

Puerto Rico	1970	1980	% change
Urban areas	1.6m (58%)	2.1m (67%)	+36%
Rural areas	1.14m (42%)	1.06m (33%)	-7%
Total	2.7m	3.2m	+15%

Table 18.1 Population growth in Puerto Rico, 1970 to 1980

Fig. 18.1 The Greater San Juan area.

Toa Baja

US navy base

Navy

US army base

San Juan

Bayamon

Carolina

Guaynabo

Trujillo Alto

■ San Juan

▨ Built-up area – outer San Juan

— Divided highways

0   8 km
0   5 miles

District	1970	1980	% change
San Juan	452,749	433,901	– 4
Adjacent districts:			
Toa Baja	35,874	73,141	+104
Bayamon	147,552	189,753	+ 29
Guaynabo	55,310	76,378	+ 38
Trujillo Alto	18,477	47,844	+159
Carolina	96,990	159,055	+ 64
Total	354,203	546,171	+ 54
Greater San Juan	806,952	980,072	+ 21

Table 18.2 Population in San Juan and adjacent districts, 1970 to 1980

Town	1980 population	% change
Humacao	26,300	+112%
Vego Baja	30,800	+ 80%
Aquadilla	48,600	+ 70%
Caguas	105,200	+ 63%
Manati	21,700	+ 61%
Juana Diaz	20,800	+ 58%
Arecibo	52,500	+ 48%
Fujardo	26,900	+ 48%

Mostly it is the smaller towns that had a population of 5-15,000 in 1970 that have had the greatest increases.

Table 18.3 Fastest growing towns in Puerto Rico, 1970-80

city itself. In 1970 they had 100,000 less - they added 200,000 to their population in just 10 years!

These districts are now really part of San Juan, and we could refer to the whole area as:

Inner San Juan   433,901
Outer San Juan   546,171
Greater San Juan 980,072

Greater San Juan has increased its population by 21% since 1970. As this is less than the national rate of +36% for urban areas, it indicates that other parts of Puerto Rico have had even greater urbanization (Table 18.3).

1 What is urbanization? As it causes so many problems, why does it take place?

2 What can be done to reduce excessive urbanization?

3 What examples of urbanization are there in your country? Can you calculate the percentage in population living in town(s) for 1950, 1960, 1970 and 1980?

4 What are (a) slums, (b) shanty towns, (c) bustees, (d) suburbs, (e) dormitory towns?

The nature of towns and cities

Most accounts of West Indian towns and cities are historical. An historical description tells us why a town is where it is, what people did there in the past, and how it grew. The best accounts *explain* why many of a town's special features are there, and this is very useful in understanding how a town works. Towns and cities are among man's most complex creations. They are very difficult to manage and plan for, and virtually every major town in the world has its own serious problem, such as slums, traffic congestion, crime, and in some cases, bankruptcy and total decay.

To understand these things we have to do a bit more than simply sketch the historical development of a city, which is a bit like writing the biography of a person. We also have to examine the internal structure and see how these parts relate to the other parts. This is more like an anatomy lesson, and the study is more one of biology than biography.

The fruit and vegetable market is an important part of the CBD in Bridgetown, Barbados.

Most studies of large towns and cities reveal that there are certain parts of a town that specialize in certain activities, or have certain uses. These are described on the following pages.

Central Business District (CBD)

The CBD is an American term for the town centre. Even in very large towns it is usually not too big, and in smaller towns it is often just the two sides of the main street. It usually has several of the following features:

- The main government buildings.
- The head offices of banks, insurance companies, and various professional services like accountants and lawyers.
- Large shops, department stores and others specializing in clothing, luxury goods, jewellery and so on. Food stores are not common, but there may be produce markets for vegetables, fish and meat, like Stabroek Market in Georgetown, Guyana.
- Entertainment, restaurants, bars, clubs, etc.
- A bus station, taxi stands, possibly a ferry, boat and ship docks, and travel agents.

Many West Indian towns are quite similar in their central area. The commercial banks are represented, for instance. In the Commonwealth Caribbean, the Royal Bank of Canada and a few other Canadian banks, and Barclay's Bank, often dominate the main street. Their buildings are usually the largest and most modern in town, and they contrast strongly with the other buildings beside them. This is because they are based on designs used in the developed countries, and the materials (usually concrete) and style (usually an undecorated or blank face) are quite different from the local architecture. Places as far apart as Bridgetown, Belize City, and Georgetown in Grand Cayman all show this impersonal business character in their main streets. Nearby are the only department stores in the country, and in between, especially in the larger tourist centres, are jewellers, hi-fi shops, camera shops, chemists, perfume stores, fashion boutiques and restaurants, often including some of the American 'fast food' type. More recently a government central bank may have been built, as in Bridgetown and Nassau, while many professional offices are located within the larger bank and insurance buildings.

The list can be extended, but most of the buildings are there to provide essential services, usually involving large amounts of money. The CBD is the natural focus of a city and therefore it is the most valued location (Fig. 18.2). Only services with a very high income can afford to buy or rent the land, and so it becomes economically restricted to just a few activities.

As time passes the CBD becomes too crowded for everything to fit in, so some services move out to other areas, and secondary shopping centres start up. This is encouraged by

Fig. 18.2 Land use in central Bridgetown, Barbados. Bridgetown's central business district is clearly defined by a southern boundary of warehouses and related land use, and a ring of government and public buildings, more wholesaling, and housing. It has expanded along avenues of commercialization both northwards and eastwards.

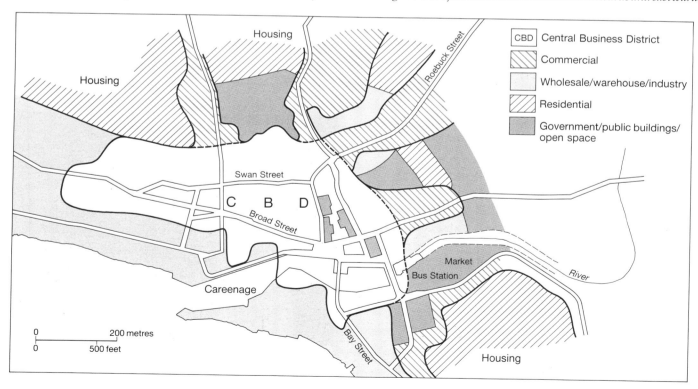

traffic jams and lack of parking space. The land in the central area is usually too expensive to allow street widening or space for car-parking lots. This spread to the suburbs is aided by the growth of a commuter zone which includes a high proportion of the wealthier population. A supermarket and a small bank are typical of these local shopping centres.

---

1 Do all the features of CBDs that are listed on p. 208 exist in your largest town?

2 What nationality are the main banks in your country?

3 How do CBDs grow? What happens to the activities they replace?

Modern bank and office buildings can destroy the character of West Indian towns if they are not carefully designed. Georgetown, Grand Cayman Island.

Warehouse and transition zone

This zone is very distinctive in its activities, but much less predictable in its location. Originally, before the use of modern road transport, it was much more compact and formed a ring around the CBD, but today it is found in other areas as well, such as along major roads leading out of town. Nowadays locations can be quite scattered depending on the availability of suitable land and nearness to good roads.

The warehouse zone naturally deals mainly in bulk goods and wholesale or manufactured products. Storage and distribution are the main activities, and they need fairly large amounts of land close to their main markets. Roebuck Street in Bridgetown, Barbados is a dying example of this type of land use, and many of the firms once located there have had to move further away in order to find the room they need for expansion. One company moved about a kilometre further out to Eagle Hall, onto what can be called Bridgetown's inner ring road (Fig. 18.2), and has built a bottling plant 14km (9 miles) away on a plantation site in Christchurch. This is typical of the changing land use in a growing city, and Roebuck Street is being swallowed up by the expanding city centre. The main concentration of warehousing has traditionally been to the south of the city centre on either side of the Careenage, but an increasing amount is now being found near the deepwater harbour to the north. The Careenage will eventually be closed to shipping.

In the past this zone comprised most of the town centre. The towns began life as ports, and the handling of merchandise was their main purpose. The modern CBD came much later, and in the less developed countries the chief town still has this 'pioneer' image. In Castries (St Lucia) and Belize City this zone dominates the central area, and the CBD is scarcely more than a department store, a bank and the post office.

Even in Bridgetown the CBD and warehouse zone near the Careenage overlap considerably, and the same is true of Nassau along East Bay Street on its eastern side. Only in the larger cities like Kingston, Havana and Port of Spain have the two become quite separate areas.

---

1 Many West Indian countries have a deepwater harbour and an original small-boat harbour. How many examples can you give?

2 What are the conditions necessary for locating a new deepwater harbour?

3 *Either* (a) Why was your country's deepwater harbour located where it is, and what was necessary to make the site suitable?

or (b) Where should a deepwater harbour be located in your country, and what changes will be necessary? (Consider both the onshore and offshore environments.)

Inner housing area

Towns have their businesses near the centre and their housing around the edge. As towns get bigger, housing is added further and further away from the centre, and the CBD expands. This means that there is always an older area of housing between the first two zones and the most recent housing. Some of this is being taken over by the expanding central area, and some of it remains.

The older houses are abandoned by the original owners as

Low-cost housing developed by the Barbados government at Warners.

the inner area becomes less pleasant to live in. The houses are old but the land is valuable, so in order to keep rents low for lower-income families, the larger houses are split into apartments. Under the worst conditions *slums* develop, but the inner zone of housing can also be well maintained. What is most unlikely is that it will be replaced by more housing. When it is finally pulled down, the occupants move further out of town, and the land is used for commercial premises. Often the replacement of slum areas is part of a government policy. In Kingston, Jamaica, for example, a large new town has been built west of the city at Portmore. When this fills up, building will be extended into the Hellshire Hills (See below). In Nassau, large low-cost housing estates have been built in the suburbs at Yellow Elder and Elizabeth Estates. (See Figs. 18.3, 18.4, 18.5, 18.6).

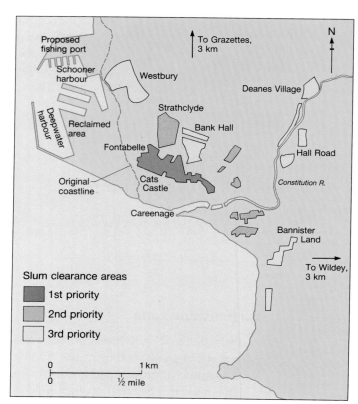

Figs. 18.3 Slum clearance proposals for Bridgetown. These areas are identified in the 1970 Physical Development Plan for Barbados, and much development has taken place since then. The provision of low-cost housing is a necessary part of the proposals, and between 100 and 400 units have been built each year in areas such as Grazettes to the north and Wildey to the east.

Fig. 18.4 Kingston, Jamaica.

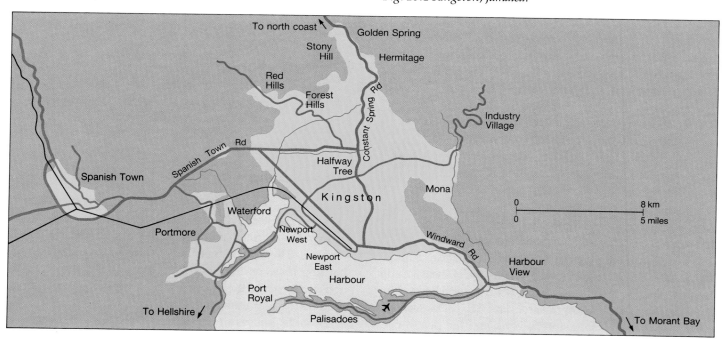

Jamaica's Hellshire Hills development

The Hellshire Hills project was approved in 1975 (Fig. 18.5). Essentially it is an overspill scheme designed to house some of the 1.2 million people expected to be living in the Kingston region by the year 2000. This population would be distributed as follows:

Kingston city	– present	600,000
	– additional	200,000
Spanish Town	– present	50,000
	– additional	50,000
Portmore		80,000
Braeton		45,000
Hellshire		175,000
		1,200,000

Ultimately Hellshire would have a capacity of 400,000, and with Portmore would be something of a 'twin city' with Kingston proper.

It is now clear that progress will in fact be much slower than these figures suggest, mainly owing to the sluggishness of the Jamaican economy, damage caused by Hurricane Gilbert in 1988, and the present expansion of Portmore, which is closer to Kingston. Growth would be faster if more employment could be created in Hellshire itself. Initially a tourist-based economy was planned here, and several national parks and nature reserves have already been established. In fact the urban area will only be 30% of the total area.

In practice, employment has come from two natural resources: the local limestone which is used as commercial marble and for making tiles for the construction industry; and fish farming in the Great Salt Pond.

Hellshire Bay is being developed first, and had about 3,000 inhabitants in 1990.

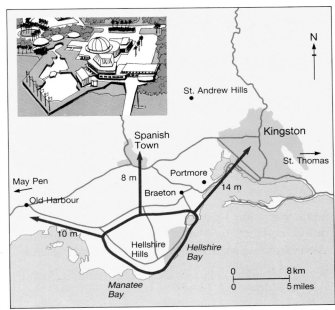

Fig. 18.5 Hellshire New Town, Jamaica. Hellshire Bay is the first of a group of planned settlements in the Hellshire Hills, each of which will eventually have a population of about 50,000. Construction started in 1975. Manatee Bay will be the second settlement.

The large Portmore new town, outside Kingston. The Hellshire Hills are in the background. By 1990 most of the land in Portmore had been built on.

In Trinidad, major housing projects of two quite different styles have been built in areas where industrial development is planned. Couva is quite traditional, in the form of a British new town residential area, with curving access roads, cul-de-sacs and low-density single-storey detached cottages. This National Housing Authority project is situated just to the north of Point Lisas industrial area. The Maloney project near Arima is dominated by medium-density four-storey apartment blocks, which is rather unusual in the Caribbean and more typical of inner-city redevelopment in Europe. Single family dwellings are also included in the project, which would benefit from landscaping (Fig 18.7).

Outer housing area - suburbs

This is the main residential area, and although it is concentrated into neighbourhoods, districts, subdivisions and so on, it is always on the outer edge of the continuously built-up area, with clusters along the main roads. As well as housing, this zone contains many of the following features:

(a) Shops, especially food and other *consumer non-durables* - that is, products that will perish eventually, or have a short life, like cigarettes, flowers, alcohol or gasoline.

(b) Various services like laundries, garages, dentists, doctors and the trades.

(c) Schools, clinics, and some other government and charitable services.

(d) Entertainment, like tennis courts, parks and cinemas.

Often a district is laid out according to a plan and has a particular style. As the houses are similar they attract people in the same income group, who have the same spending habits, and a range of shops and services will be provided to suit them. So in this zone we can recognize neighbourhoods for low-, middle- and high-income families, and businesses in them will have goods and prices to suit each group of people. This is why each residential area has its own particular character and is usualy classified in some way by those who live in and around it - for example a 'nice' area, a 'rough' area, and so on (Fig. 18.6).

Commuter zone

Commuting is still a novelty in many parts of the West Indies, and did not exist on a large scale anywhere in the world until automobiles became widely available. Even in Europe commuting did not develop until the 1950s, and in the West Indies it came much later. Kingston provides one of the best examples, with quite large communities of people living as far away as Stony Hill and Golden Spring to the north, and in the

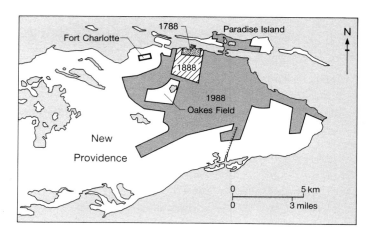

Fig. 18.6 Growth of built-up area in Nassau, 1788-1988, the town grew slowly to 1788 and 1888, and remained compact. The spread to the east and south has been rapid since the introduction of the motor car and bus services. The southern margin is likely to disappear rapidly as the few remaining vacant areas are filled in and the built-up area becomes continuous as far as the coast.

new town of Portmore to the west (See Fig. 18.4). Smaller communities dot the surrounding hillsides in a complete semicircle from Red Hills in the west to the coast as far as Yallahs in the east. Port of Spain has also seen a similar flight to the hills (especially on the slopes of the Maraval, St Ann's and Cascade valleys) and along the coast to the north-west as far as Chaguaramas, and including the Diego Martin Valley (Fig. 18.7). The major commuting zone is in fact along the Eastern Main Road as far as Arima, and compares with Kingston's northern A3.

The actual location of commuter settlements depends very much on the presence of a main road linking them to the CBD, so that a string of settlements like those along the Stony Hill A3 road, or Trinidad's Eastern Main Road, is a typical development.

Fig. 18.7 Port of Spain commuter zone.

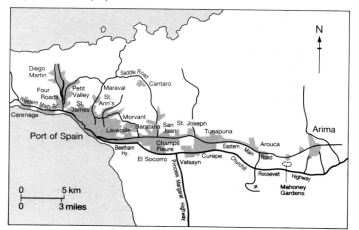

Usually these communities were originally villages where the first commuters bought houses. As their numbers increased the character of the village changed, and many of the suburban services already described started to appear to take care of the domestic needs of the newcomers. Despite this the commuter belt is distinct, as it remains detached from the continuously built-up area and lacks many of the city's other amenities. Most of the population is absent during the weekday, and often the settlements within it are known as 'dormitories', or even 'dormitory towns', as they mainly provide night-time and weekend accommodation only.

1 Why do some governments feel it necessary to construct low-cost housing?

2 What services do housing areas need? Give examples of these in the suburban districts of a town near you.

3 What are the problems of unplanned housing development?

4 Compare the site and situation of Kingston and Port of Spain.

Social groupings in towns

It has already been mentioned that different income groups are likely to be concentrated in different parts of a town. This is a *socio-economic grouping* where class-consciousness and wealth have combined to bring people together. Cultural origins such as race, colour and language also have this effect, and this sort of social grouping is often found in the very mixed societies of the West Indies, especially among the newer immigrants and the poorer people. Mostly this is a natural clustering of people who have similar needs. Newcomers tend to go where their language is understood, for example the Indians (in nineteenth-century Trinidad and Guyana), the Chinese (about 100 years ago in Jamaica), and the Haitians (in The Bahamas today). After a while these groups become acclimatized and spread out among the population as a whole, a process known as *assimilation*. If immigration ceases, the clustering may eventually disappear, as it has done with the Chinese in the West Indies to a very large extent. Racial segregation is not as common as it once was, but under colonial conditions the towns were much more socially 'stratified' than they are today. With the exception of recent migrants, social groupings are becoming much less common, and income groupings, mainly due to the expansion of 'middle'-income families, or the building of low-cost housing, are much more likely to be the critical factors.

A study of social and ethnic segregation in Port of Spain up to 1970 found that employment, income and education were becoming increasingly significant in the residential location of the population, and that ethnic differences were becoming less important (Stephanie Goodenough, *Race, Status and Ecology in Port of Spain, Trinidad*, 1978). The poorest people still inhabited the poorest areas, which included steep slopes such as in the Laventille Hills and along Maraval Valley, and swampy coastal areas. High-income neighbourhoods, such as around the Savannah, still existed, but these had also spread out of town to Maraval, the St Ann's Valley and the Cascade Valley - basically following roads along the valleys to the north. The largest development was in middle-income housing as this grew rapidly and spread west and east of the city, especially along the Diego Martin Valley and along the Eastern Main Road (See Fig. 18.7).

New York City

New York and its surrounding region have a population of about 15 million. As a settlement it can only be compared with other great metropolitan centres such as London, Paris or Tokyo, and as a city there is no direct comparison with any settlement in the Caribbean.

The city is best known through its commercial, financial and cultural activities which are concentrated on Manhattan Island, but this is only a small part of New York proper (Fig. 18.8). The built-up area extends about 30 kilometres (90 miles) in all directions, and includes Queens and Brooklyn (on Long Island), Bronx (in New York State to the north), Staten Island, and Newark and Jersey City in New Jersey. Because of the various islands, and the Hudson River, East River and Harlem River, many bridges and several tunnels are used to link up the various communities. Like Calcutta (See p. 176), it is a *conurbation*.

New York's success is due to its excellent accessibility from all parts of the continent and, via its harbour, from the Atlantic and Europe. At one time Manhattan Island was the main port area, but today its numerous docks are derelict or have been reclaimed for other uses. Only the passenger ship terminal on the Hudson River is still in use, and this is the centre for the cruise liners, many of which serve the Caribbean. For the last 30 years most of New York's cargo has been handled in Newark Bay where a huge container terminal is located, and in Brooklyn, which also has a container port. New York is by far the largest port in the country, and handles about 15% of the country's imports, and 3% of the exports.

Freight is distributed in several directions:

- North and east into southern New England, until the trade area overlaps with Boston.
- North along the Hudson Valley, and then along the Mohawk westwards as far as Buffalo on Lake Erie. This is the most important routeway of all and is heavily industrialized.

Fig. 18.8 New York City.

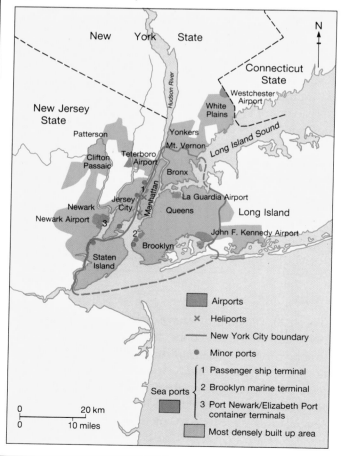

- South west to Philadelphia, Baltimore and Washington.

New York is therefore an important industrial centre for petroleum refining, chemicals (including soap and paint), non-ferrous metals and food processing. These are mainly found near the docks in New Jersey. Other industries are scattered throughout the built-up area and are much more dependent on the size and wealth of the market than on access to raw materials. Many are directly related to service activities, like transport, publishing and retailing. They include vehicle assembly from kits, furniture and furnishings, clothing (including furs), jewellery, cosmetics and printing. About 18% of the workforce work in manufacturing, mostly in small factories (See Table 18.4).

New York is also most successful in its various service industries, including tourism. Its historic attractions, museums, entertainment, shopping and lifestyle attract millions every year. Together with its financial services based on Wall Street, it is essentially a city where people meet people to do business, unlike, say, Detroit (See p. 175). It has three of the country's largest airports, at Kennedy (27 million passengers 1980), Newark (9 million) and La Guardia (17 million). Railways handled 45 million passengers, and buses another 75 million, although each on successively shorter journeys. Public transport is much more important in New York than in any other American city, with about 30% of the commuters using trains, subway and buses, which have special lanes allocated to them on the freeways - in other large cities the figure is 15% or less. Transportation accounts for about a quarter of the land used by the city and is undoubtedly its single biggest problem, as it is in London and Tokyo.

Table 18.4 New York City employment categories, 1982

Category	Number (thousands)	Percentage labour force
Manufacturing	600	18
Retail	434	13
Finance	521	16
Other services	1,064	32
All other employment	663	21
Total	3,282	100

These figures refer to New York City only. The total employed in manufacturing in the greater built-up area, which extends into New Jersey and Connecticut, is 1.23 million, a decline from 1.64 million in 1967.

19
Routes, trade and economic associations

Buses (tap-taps) *are the main form of public transport on most islands, especially in Haiti, where few can afford cars.*

Routes develop between *destinations*, and *transport* is used to carry goods or passengers along them. Destinations with special facilities for receiving goods or passengers are *ports* - seaports or airports. Routes are so numerous, and so variable, that we must distinguish between the various types (Fig. 19.1).

As most West Indians live on islands, they are very conscious of the main shipping and airline routes. However, the majority of movement is along a great variety of internal routes, mainly roads, but including many other types.

The routes are used by domestic travellers, for freight, exports and imports, and by tourists. Although some of these overlap, especially passengers and tourists travelling by air, the vehicles used on each route are usually designed to serve one market. If we look briefly at the main categories and at some examples, we can see how specialized some routes are.

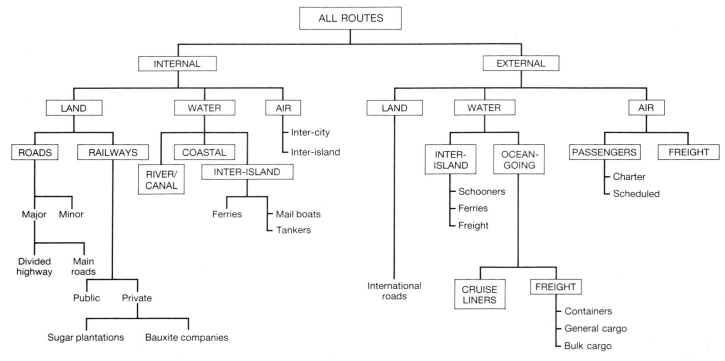

Fig. 19.1 Types of routes.

Internal routes and transport

Major roads

In the Caribbean these are mainly designed to link the interior and/or coastal regions to the main port. Most of them were laid down in the days when plantation agriculture was the only significant economic activity. The road maps for the sugar islands of Barbados (Fig. 15.2) and St Kitts (Fig. 12.1) show this well. Very few major roads have been built along new routes since those days, although naturally the old roads have been greatly improved. The following are some examples of new routes:

Town or city throughways and bypasses An example is the urban motorways in and around San Juan, Puerto Rico. Every West Indian town with a population over 100,000 suffers from serious traffic congestion, but very few new roads have been constructed. This will be one of the main areas for new building in the next 20 years. Jamaica already has a programme of bypass construction for towns such as May Pen, Mandeville and Bog Walk. Barbados's Industrial Access Highway links the airport to the St James coast and is in effect a Bridgetown bypass for most of its 30km (19 miles). It was completed in 1989.

The completion of coastal roads Contact along the coast, as opposed to between the coast and the interior, was not a

priority in colonial times. With the need for better access and administration, and the use of the coastal areas for tourism, coastal routes have been developed or completed, like the Barbados East Coast Road built in the 1960s, and its extension southwards into St John in the 1980s.

The construction of mountain roads These are the most important new routes and represent major advances for islands like St Lucia, Dominica and Montserrat, which have exceptionally difficult terrain for roads. St Lucia's new road from Castries to Dennery, and on to Vieux Fort, and a similar development in Puerto Rico, from San Juan to Caguas and Ponce, have so improved communications along these routes that they have become ribbons of development for industry and settlement along them. Dominica's road system was completely rebuilt largely in response to the damage done by Hurricane David. There is now an excellent system of modern coastal and mountain roads, completed 1985-87, which has encouraged development in many new areas.

New roads from the growing airports and harbours Most countries have constructed international airports in recent years, and new roads have had to be built to serve them. In addition, the new deepwater ports have generated a lot of heavy dock traffic, including the sealed container. This has made it neces-

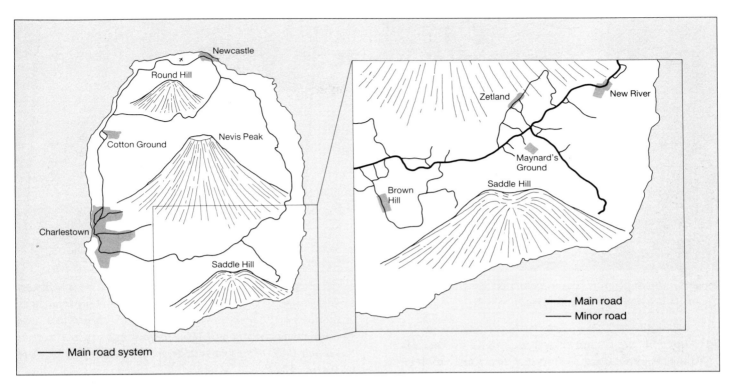

Fig. 19.2 Road system, Nevis. This map should be compared with that of Barbados (See Fig.15.2), which has a radial system of roads to feed an unobstructed interior from a harbour, and that of Cuba (Fig. 19.3), which has a linear trunk route with minor branches to serve a similar but lengthy interior. Volcanic islands like Nevis have circular systems with minor access roads.

sary to build new or improved roads, such as the multilane highways serving the Kingston dock area and its extension to Newport West; and the Spring Garden Highway from the deepwater harbour in Bridgetown to Highway 1.

Minor roads

These are largely *access* roads. They connect housing areas to major roads; farms and villages to towns; and provide access to the more remote areas - this last group including many dead-end roads. In the more wealthy countries these roads are well paved and graded, but elsewhere they are more likely to be tracks and footpaths, and this is how most of them began. Barbados is exceptional for its high degree of accessibility, while Haiti is virtually a land of footpaths.

Transport

The types of vehicles on roads needs little explanation. The main consideration should be given to bus and truck movement, as these are the most economical forms of transport, and the roads that suit these normally suit cars as well. In the

1980s containers became increasingly important as a means of transport, and many roads, and especially their junctions and bends, are too narrow to accommodate them. Road widening has therefore become necessary in most towns.

Containers

These have transformed the transport industry world-wide. Their use has been widespread since the 1960s, and Kingston, San Juan and Port of Spain have had large container terminals for some time. Almost every West Indian community has had to make certain provisions for them. The main features of containers are these:

(a) A uniform size, 6 or 12 metres (20 or 40 ft) long. This means that warehouses, ships, loading ramps, etc. can all be built to the same sizes.

(b) The standardized size has meant that many existing facilities are not suitable for containers. The 12-metre container is much larger than the average truck.

(c) The containers are weatherproof and may be refrigerated. They do not need to be covered and can simply be stacked out of doors until needed. The main requirement is a very large container park, which on the smaller islands has not always been easy to provide.

(d) Containers are locked and sealed, which reduces damage, theft and loss of small items. This in turn reduces insurance and assists customs inspection.

217

Mountains are difficult and expensive to cross. A highway across the Chaine de Belance, near Gonaives, Haiti.

(e) Above all the container system speeds up cargo-handling. A general cargo ship that previously took eight days to discharge can now unload in two days. The labour force is also much reduced, which is not always an advantage as unemployment among unskilled labourers is high. In total, this makes cargo-handling cheaper.

(f) Containers are best suited to general cargo (not bulk, such as sugar or oil) and have had the biggest impact on international sea transport and road haulage.

Railways

Railways are rare in the West Indies. The Kingston-Montego Bay line is subsidized by the Jamaican government, and has run at a loss in most recent years. Despite this the line is well used with over 1.25 million passengers in 1987, and additional services for commuters and tourists have been provided. There are no other passenger lines operating except in Cuba, which has a fairly comprehensive network (Fig. 19.3). Railways are limited in usefulness because:
* they only serve their stations
* they have a high capital and maintenance cost
* they are labour-intensive
* they only operate at fixed times
* goods require extra handling on and off the trains

These disadvantages can be minimized if:
* the lines run directly to the final destinations, such as into a mine or a port
* the line can be used continuously
* handling is largely automated, such as by using conveyor belts for bulk cargoes.

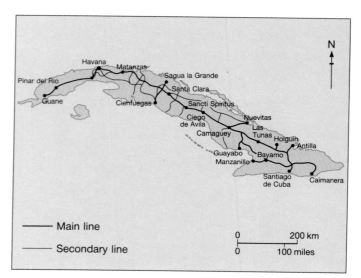

Fig. 19.3 Cuban railway system. Railways in Cuba are used almost exclusively for the sugar industry. Cane, sugar and sugar products accounted for 90% of the cargo carried in 1975. There is also some passenger traffic, amounting to 11 million passengers a year. However, this is only 0.5% of the total of 2,260 million passengers, 99.5% of whom travel by bus.

Under these circumstances they are still efficient. Originally they were more widely used in the Caribbean in just this way, as they are in Cuba today, for the sugar industry in such places as Antigua, St Lucia, St Kitts, Jamaica and Trinidad. These narrow-gauge railways have all been closed down. The bauxite companies use railways to carry their products to the ports in Guyana and Jamaica, and this function accounts for 85% of the revenue earned in Jamaica.

Gregory Park railway station on Jamaica's only railway line.

1 What are the advantages of (a) air travel over sea travel, (b) sea transport over air transport?

2 What are the advantages of road over rail transport?

3 What are the advantages of using containers for cargo transport?

4 What are the problems of constructing a road along

   (a) Trinidad's north coast?

   (b) Belize's coast?

5 What types of mechanization are common in transport today?
      Consider (a) airports (b) docks (c) warehouses.

Much Caribbean cargo now travels in containers on ships like this one.

Domestic water routes and transport

The degree to which water transport is used depends almost entirely on the local geography. Generally it is a declining means of transport, but will certainly not die out. There are three main systems.

Rivers and canals

These are the least important. There are few canals and they are little used. Some Guyanese canals, which were originally built to drain the coastal areas, are used to carry sugar cane and rice in small boats or barges. In earlier times rivers had the advantage that they provided access to the interior without having to be built. They were used by the logging industry in Guyana and Belize. They still have some value, but to be used on the same scale as the North American rivers they would have to be much bigger and more reliable. All the West Indian rivers have major interruptions like waterfalls, rapids and sandbanks, and are liable to flooding or drying up. Ironically, rivers are more of an obstacle than an asset to good communications, and ferries to get across them are more common than river boats to go along them.

Domestic coastal shipping

For a long time coastal shipping by schooner was the only means of communication between many coastal settlements, even well into the twentieth century. This was particularly true of the smaller fishing villages, such as in St Lucia between Castries and Soufrière. These were not accessible by road until quite recent times. However, once roads were completed the shipping services disappeared.

In the larger countries a more regular trade for heavy goods has been maintained, despite the dangers of a sea journey for small boats. Coastal services run on a regular basis in both Guyana (Georgetown to Berbice and Essequibo provinces) and Belize (Belize City to Stan Creek and Punta Gorda).

Domestic inter-island shipping

At first sight it might seem that this would be quite small, but in fact nearly all the countries of the West Indies have dependent islands and all of these have to be served. The main links are listed below, but there are several others:

1 Belize to her offshore cays such as Ambergris Cay.

2 The Bahamas - at present about 60 ports are served by about 20 government-licensed mailboats sailing to 26 Family Islands. There are also private services, such as those provided by the oil companies.

Nassau's fine natural harbour is the base for the mailboat fleet that serves the many islands of The Bahamas. Potters Cay (under the bridge) is the main dock.

3   Antigua to Barbuda.

4   Grenada to the Grenadines.

5   St Vincent to the Grenadines, especially to Bequia.

6   Grand Cayman to Cayman Brac and Little Cayman.

7   Trinidad to Tobago.

8   Guadeloupe to Marie Galante.

9   To and among the US and British Virgin Islands.

10 Puerto Rico to its offshore islands, notably Vieques.

Despite the distances and rough seas that may be encountered, the small populations of the dependent islands and the shallow harbours available mean that the boats are small. They are used to carry both cargo and passengers, and may take from three hours to several days to complete their journeys. The longest routes are in The Bahamas, and sailings here are often restricted to only one a week. Virtually all the food and general goods, cooking gas, building materials, machinery and so on go by the mailboat. Fuel is often taken separately by a small oil tanker owned by one of the large oil companies. Passengers usually travel by air these days, but most boats have regular passenger accommodation.

---

1   What is RO-RO, and what are its advantages?

2   Which countries in the Caribbean have ferries, and what is their function?

3   What types of innovation are there for high-speed boat travel? Are there any of these in the Caribbean?

Air transport

Despite its higher cost, the airplane is rapidly becoming the main mode of long-distance travel within the West Indies. Its usefulness is obvious in the larger territories, such as the mainland countries and the Greater Antilles, but there are air links between dependent islands of even quite small countries. The savings in time are enormous, and modern aircraft ensure moderate fares for as few as five persons, and as many as fifty. The Bahamas government operates 27 separate services to 19 Family Island airports, and there are a variety of other charter and private lines also serving the islands. Internal flights in Jamaica, Trinidad and Tobago, Guyana and Belize are commonplace, and some smaller countries, including St Lucia, Antigua and the US Virgin Islands, also operate internal services.

A nine-seater plane is all that is needed for the smallest communities. Tourists, local people and the district nurse visit Codrington, Barbuda, after a 20-minute flight by LIAT from Antigua.

Apart from speed, the airplane is immensely flexible in its routeing, as there is virtually nowhere it cannot fly over. This gives it a considerable advantage over shipping, which must quite often make large detours around the coast. Its great disadvantage is the need for an airport and the cost of equipment, fuel and maintenance. For passengers, most of whom travel by air only occasionally, the cost is acceptable, but the opposite is true for cargo. Very few commodities are light enough and valuable enough to justify air transport. Mail and spare parts for machinery are the most common items carried by air other than personal baggage. The transport of food and livestock is sometimes economical by air, but generally the cost is too high. For example, the two Jamaican airports handled 26,000 tonnes of freight in 1987, compared with 11.7 million tonnes by shipping.

Many of the existing air services are in fact subsidized by governments because they provide particular advantages:

1   *Accessibility* for purposes of development, tourism and research.

2   *Internal security* Police or the military can maintain order and surveillance.

3   *Social services* Visits by doctors, nurses, teachers, politicians, etc. can be made, and the outlying population can also have access to services that are only found in large towns, such as hospitals, international travel, higher education, shopping, and so on.

Much of what has been said above about internal routes is equally valid for external routes. However, there are some major differences, and these are described below.

International land routes

These are negligible in the Caribbean. Probably the only one of any significance is the road from Belize through Mexico to Texas and the USA. Although it is a long route (2,000km/1,200 miles), it is being increasingly used. It was one factor involved in the recent purchase of 280,000 ha (700,000 acres) of land for citrus production by several US companies, including Coca Cola Foods. This land is right on the Mexican border.

International sea routes

These are of two quite different types.

Cargo routes

For the most part the cargo routes are quite specific, such as the Geest Line, which brings general cargoes out and takes bananas back to Britain. Sugar outwards, oil inwards, cars from Japan, and general cargo in containers, are also carried by the major shipping companies. However, these large shipping lines only serve a few Caribbean ports, mainly San Juan, Kingston and Port of Spain. A second level of ports includes Havana, Santo Domingo and Bridgetown. These are all trans-shipment ports to varying degrees, and the other much smaller ports are served by a much more numerous fleet of small ships sailing between the various islands (Fig. 19.4). For instance, Bridgetown serves as the main port of entry for many of the Windward Islands, and San Juan for the Virgin Islands. There is also a regional trade in West Indian produce and manufactures, such as cement, foodstuffs, beverages and some fuels and machinery. Quite often a deepwater harbour serves the larger ocean-going ships, and near to it is the small boat or 'schooner' harbour. Bridgetown and Nassau both have this kind of development (Fig. 19.5).

Cruise liners

These have already been referred to in chapter 16. Their routes are still the product of supply and demand as for all other types of transport, but nothing is actually traded. Cruise liners may use ports like Nassau or San Juan, but often the

Fig. 19.4 Major ports in the West Indies.

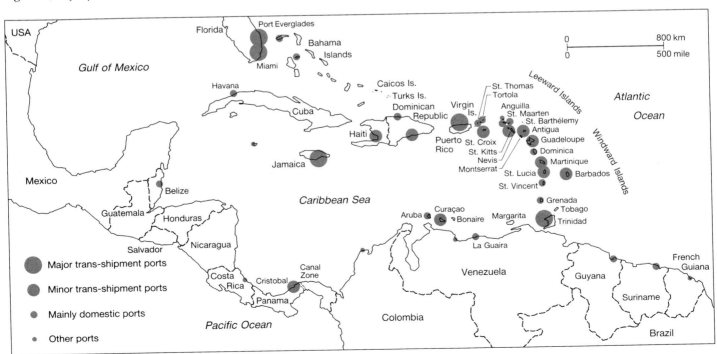

221

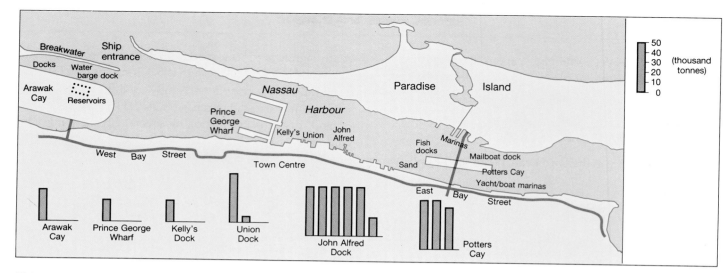

Fig. 19.5 Cargo handled in Nassau harbour and docks, 1987. The Potters Cay dock is exclusively for the internal mailboat service. Prince George Wharf is mainly for cruise liners. Arawak Cay has become an overflow for additional container traffic, and bulk materials for construction. Oil, cement and other bulk cargoes are handled at an outport at the western end of the island.

capital cities are by-passed and calls are made at secondary ports which have more suitable tourist attractions. Table 19.1 shows that although Kingston is by far the largest port in Jamaica, it receives the fewest liners.

Some cruise ships make a point of going to uninhabited islands, and ferry their passengers to the beaches. The larger liners may simply anchor offshore and use the ship's launches to take passengers ashore - for example the *Norway* and *QEII* in the eastern Caribbean.

International air travel

Air travel is also a two-tiered operation, with the major international airlines feeding the various regional carriers. Most larger countries have international airports capable of taking the largest jet aircraft caryying anything from 150 to 400 passengers. Most of the other islands have airstrips that can take 30- to 50-seater aircraft. As a result there is a system of long-range routes focusing on the main airports, and a denser network of short-range routes serving the surrounding territories. For instance, long-range jets bring West Indians and tourists to St John's, Antigua, from the UK, Europe and North America (BWIA, British Airways, American Airways, Pan Am, Air Canada, and various charter companies). From St John's, LIAT (Leeward Islands Air Transportation) serves the nearby islands of Montserrat, St Kitts/Nevis, Anguilla, St Maarten, Dominica, and the British Virgin Islands. A similar system serves Grenada, St Vincent and St Lucia from Barbados.

The development and expansion of international airports and their access roads is a continual process as air traffic increases every year. Some countries have already built airports for the future, notably Martinique, Guadeloupe and Barbados. The terminals at Nassau, and Trinidad's Piarco airport, are to be replaced. Grenada had her Cuban-built airport completed with US assistance in 1985. Only a few islands cannot receive large jet aircraft - these include Dominica, St Vincent, Montserrat, Nevis, Anguilla and the British Virgin Islands.

Table 19.1 Number of cruise liners calling at Jamaican ports in 1978 and 1987

Port	Number of calls	
	1978	1987
Ochos Rios	121	195
Montego Bay	95	104
Port Antonio	81	1
Kingston	33	1

1 What is bulk cargo, and what types of bulk cargo are there in the Caribbean?

2 What is a STOL aircraft, and what is its importance in the Caribbean?

3 What is the flying time from your country to (a) Miami, (b) New York, (c) London?

4 For question 3 what time differences are there between these cities and your country, and why?

Trading is the importing and exporting of goods and services. Most West Indian countries export one or more of:

- agricultural products
- certain mineral products
- minor manufactured goods

and in turn they import nearly all their requirements of:
- processed food
- fuels
- manufactured goods.

Table 19.2 shows how this works for three different countries and provides a 'balance of trade'.

West Indian countries have very limited resources and small international markets. This means that they cannot command world markets with their exports, nor substitute for imports. Many other countries in the world find themselves in a similar situation, and have reacted in a variety of ways to protect themselves. Some of the typical measures used individually by countries are described here.

Table 19.2 Balance of visible trade by standard international trade classification

1 With reference to Table 19.2, which country (a) has the most trade, (b) has a positive trade balance, (c) depends heavily on agricultural exports?

2 With reference to Table 19.2, what is the link between items 3 and 5 for Trinidad?

3 How do you account for the very high values for item 3 for The Bahamas in Table 19.2? (Help? Turn to p. 119)

Customs duties

Virtually all countries charge customs duties, which serve two purposes:

1 They are a form of taxation to raise money.

2 They provide 'protection' against low-cost imported goods, and helps to stop them destroying the business of local producers.

The second purpose has the most relevance to trading. By raising or varying customs duties it is possible to control the imports of a particular product. Generally, consumers do not

Commodity		St Kitts and Nevis, 1984			Trinidad and Tobago, 1985			The Bahamas, 1986		
		Imports	Exports	Trade balance	Imports	Exports	Trade balance	Imports	Exports	Trade balance
0	Food and live animals	10.3	12.7	+2.4	212.0	24.6	−187.4	163.9	21.5	−141.4
1	Beverages and tobacco	1.4	1.0	−0.4	9.3	9.3	−2.7	30.5	11.6	−18.9
2	Crude materials inedible except fuel	1.1	0.1	−1.0	42.7	4.9	−37.8	16.9	15.2	−1.7
3	Mineral fuels, lubricants, etc.	5.7	0.0	−5.7	34.5	1,161.0	+1,126.5	663.0	545.3	−117.7
4	Animal and vegetable oils and fats	0.9	0.0	−0.9	13.9	0.0	−13.9	1.6	0.0	−1.6
5	Chemicals	4.3	0.1	−4.2	98.6	178.0	+79.4	130.5	266.4	+135.9
6	Manufactured goods	9.8	0.1	−9.7	211.0	30.5	−180.5	160.1	8.5	−151.6
7	Machinery and transport equipment	10.3	2.1	−8.2	315.0	42.9	−272.1	200.5	12.3	−188.2
8	Miscellaneous manufactured goods	8.1	3.4	−4.7	97.6	5.8	−91.8	158.9	2.5	−156.4
9	Commodities not elsewhere stated	0.1	0.0	−0.1	3.8	3.2	0.6	0.0	0.6	+0.6
	Total	52.0	19.5	−32.5	1,039	1,458	+421	1,526	884	−642

like customs duties as they make goods more expensive than they should be. Foreign countries resent them as they limit the amount they can export. On the other hand, local manufacturers and farmers frequently request protection from imports so that there is less competition for their own goods.

The decision on whether to have customs duties, and if so how much to charge, is a very complex matter. Rates of duty often vary with the season, or are changed quite often.

Basically there are two trends:

1 *Free trade* This involves the removal of customs duties between trading countries. Ideally there would be no duties, and free trade between all nations, leading to international co-operation of the Caricom type. The EC (below) is to remove all customs duties between its 12 members in 1992.

2 *Protectionism* This is practised by countries with good resources that wish to build up or maintain their industries in the face of competition. The USA and Japan are in many ways protectionist. India allows very few consumer items to be imported, and encourages multinational corporations to set up local factories, which should eventually help Indian manufacturers to develop similar products. (The Coca Cola company was expelled from India for failing to do this.)

Quotas and bans

Sometimes an absolute limit on the amount that can be imported is applied, or the product is banned altogether. US quotas for West Indian sugar and the US ban on Jamaican shirts in the 1970s are examples.

Free trade associations

Small countries, because they have small markets, are often interested in free trade with other countries so that they can sell their goods to more people. There might simply be a customs agreement (*a customs union*) between two or three countries. The countries of Western Europe have long provided examples of this type of co-operation; the *Benelux* countries - Belgium, the Netherlands and Luxembourg each produced things the others wanted - mainly coal, steel and machinery. A similar agreement involving the Benelux countries, France and West Germany was known as the *European Coal and Steel Community* (ECSC). These two organizations later became the foundation for the much more elaborate EC (See below).

EFTA, the European Free Trade Association, was mainly a customs-free agreement between Great Britain and the non-EC countries until Britain joined the EC. Carifta was a similar agreement which led on to Caricom (See below). EFTA still exists, and includes Austria, Iceland, Norway, Switzerland and Sweden. As well as requiring free trade between members, it now also has almost complete free trade in industrial goods with the EC countries.

Economic associations

It is often felt that nations should co-operate to a much greater extent. For instance, they could share in major research and development projects (like the EC's Euratom) or in the operation of a university (like Caricom's UWI). Co-operation can be carried to the extent of having a separate government, laws, and even currency, and agreement would only stop short of replacing a nation's own *sovereignty* - that is, the country's right to govern its own affairs. There are associations that replace governments in many internal areas, and these are known as *federations*. Countries such as India, Australia and the USA are federations of states or provinces, and these states have the right to elect governors and charge taxes independently.

Despite the attractions of free trade and economic associations, many have failed, and none has succeeded in the majority of its aims. See Table 19.3. Two of the longest surviving examples are the EC and Caricom.

The European Community (EC or Common Market)

Apart from the internal advantages of a free trade association, further agreement can bring great advantages for external trade. The USA is by far the world's greatest economic power, and the countries of Europe felt that they must unite if they were to compete with it. In many ways the European Community has been successful in this. It has developed European agriculture so rapidly that surpluses (as in the USA) are more of a problem than are shortages. Collaboration on aircraft construction has created the only major airliners to compete with, and be sold in, the USA (European Airbus A300, Concorde). Europeans are free to travel, live and work in any of the member countries. Despite this there is much disagreement among the members, mainly on payments to the common fund, and on what the money is spent. Trade between the 12 members of the EC and the Caribbean is governed by the Lomé Convention (See below).

The Caribbean Community (Caricom)

The EC includes over 300 million people, Caricom just 5 million. There is really no comparison between the two groups apart from their ideals. The population of Caricom is so small and so spread out that it makes virtually no difference to a large producer whether or not he or she can sell their product duty-free to another member. Most West Indian countries produce the same basic products, and mainly im-

EEC	Caricom 1973-74	OAS	OECS 1981	British Commonwealth	ACP states 1975	CBI 1983	Caribcan 1986
1958 Belgium Netherlands Luxembourg France West Germany Italy 1973 United Kingdom Ireland Denmark 1981 Greece 1986 Spain Portugal	Antigua & Barbuda Bahamas (not Common Market) Barbados Belize Dominica Grenada Guyana Jamaica Montserrat St Kitts-Nevis St Lucia St Vincent & the Grenadines Trinidad & Tobago	All Caribbean countries except Belize, Guyana	Dominica Grenada Montserrat St Kitts-Nevis St Lucia St Vincent & the Grenadines	All British colonies on becoming independent	All Caricom and also: Suriname Aruba Netherlands Antilles (Bonaire, Curaçao, St Maarten, Saba, St Eustatius) British West Indies (Anguilla, Br. Virgin Is, Cayman Is, Montserrat, Turks & Caicos Islands)	All Caricom countries except Guyana, and also: Aruba Dominican Republic Haiti Netherlands Antilles Costa Rica El Salvador, Guatemala Honduras Panama Also eligible: Anguilla Cayman Is Guyana Nicaragua Suriname Turks & Caicos Is	All British Commonwealth countries and dependencies

Table 19.3 Membership of economic associations

port things from outside the region, not from each other. Cars, most processed foods, fuels and machinery are typical examples.

The main advantage of Caricom is that it can act as a single voice with a single policy when making agreements with other countries or trade blocs. This has been advantageous since Britain joined the EC, and the sugar trade came under EC control. Trade relations between the EC and the Caribbean states are governed by a convention (like a treaty) which was named after the place where it first met, *Lomé*.

Many of the other activities of Caricom are social, and often include arrangements that existed before 1973, or would have developed anyway, such as for health, meteorology and shipping.

Its greatest achievements have been in the economic and social development of individual countries through the Caribbean Development Bank. For the purpose of providing aid, Caricom is divided into the More Developed Countries (MDCs - Trinidad, Jamaica, Guyana and Barbados) and the Less Developed Countries (LDCs - all the others). As in the EC, funds paid to the Bank are spent on development projects in the region, with the emphasis being placed on raising the economies of the poorer members (LDCs) to the level of the others. Unfortunately none of the Caricom members is very large or very rich, and they all have severe economic problems of their own. This makes it politically difficult for funds to be diverted to, say, a Windward Island, when the largest member, Jamaica, is itself heavily in debt. However, the system does work, and foreign aid is much more easily obtained for Caricom purposes, through the Development Bank, than it would be independently.

Within Caricom the LDCs have found it necessary to help themselves, and in 1981 founded their own community, the *Organization of Eastern Caribbean States* (OECS) It was originally proposed in 1975. It includes all the Caricom members of the Eastern Caribbean - seven states in all - and five of these states have become independent since the formation of Caricom in 1973. These countries felt that they could benefit more from their Caricom status as LDCs if they organized themselves. The objectives of the OECS are basically to promote economic integration and to form an Eastern Caribbean *common market* (another term for a free trade area). More general aims are to promote co-operation, and provide a united front in matters of foreign trade and policy. As a small unit of just over half a million people, the OECS can be seen as a co-ordinating body working within the Caricom framework to ensure that its member's interests are not neglected. Its most recent achievements have been in the securing of grants and loans for the development of infrastructure, including more planes for LIAT, a secretariat in Antigua, road improvement, port construction and telecommunications facilities. There have also been moves towards closer ties among OECS members, and Dominica, Grenada, St Lucia and St Vincent are proposing a political union independently of the other three members.

---

1 What is *protectionism*? Does your country have restrictions on imports, and if so why?

2 What is the importance of the EC to the Caribbean?

3 What was the West Indies Federation? What are the main differences between it and Caricom? (Help? Look in a history book.)

4 What are the Lomé Conventions? Do they affect any exports from your country?

Other organizations

The Organization of American States (OAS), and the British Commonwealth

Unlike the previous economically oriented groups, these two have a much broader scope and represent spheres of political and historical interest. They do have an influence on trade, however. The *OAS* is restricted to most of the countries of the western hemisphere, which all have an equal say in its policies. Its main activities are to provide a meeting place for discussion about the region, and to promote research and development by providing technical assistance and finance. Its activities in the Caribbean region have not been very great until recently, but areas such as tourism have received attention, and the Caribbean Tourist Research and Development Centre based in Barbados is one of its creations.

The *British Commonwealth* consists of the great majority of the independent countries that once belonged to the British Empire. It has no constitution, but aims for mutual co-operation and assistance. Economic concessions are available and include access for exports to the UK, and therefore the EC, which is often denied or heavily penalized for non-Commonwealth members. The Commonwealth Caribbean has benefited greatly from this, as many US companies have set up in them so as to be able to export to the EC countries. The American Texaco company in Trinidad, and the Bacardi company in The Bahamas, are both examples of companies with significant exports to EC and EFTA countries. There is also a 10% reduction in tariffs for Commonwealth goods entering Britain.

However, both of these organizations have been overshadowed by two other bodies of much more recent origin, which were established to deal more directly with the economic needs of the Caribbean. These are the *Lomé Conventions* and the *Caribbean Basin Initiative*.

The African, Caribbean and Pacific (ACP) states, the EC and the Lomé Conventions

When Britain joined what was then called the European Economic Community (EEC) in 1973, the status of the colonies and ex-colonies of the European countries became a vital issue. Until then, each country had had special arrangements for trade with its own colonies or commonwealth members. It was realized that the other EEC members could hardly be expected to observe the British agreements, and so it was decided to set up a completely new set of rules to govern trade between these countries. The 10 EEC states recognized 64 independent countries and about 26 dependent ones that needed special assistance. About half of them were members of the British Commonwealth or were British colonies, and most of the rest had associations with France or the Netherlands. Because of their location in three distinct areas, they were called the *African, Caribbean and Pacific (ACP) states*. All the Caribbean countries except Cuba, Haiti, the Dominican Republic, Puerto Rico and the US Virgin Islands were included.

In 1975 a five-year agreement was reached in Lomé, and this became known as the *Lomé Convention*. In 1980 and 1985 it was revised, the revisions known respectively as *Lomé II* and *Lomé III*. Lomé IV started in 1990.

The main provisions of Lomé IV are in these areas:

- Agricultural co-operation and food security
- Development of fisheries
- Development of mining and energy potential
- Transport and communications
- Development of trade and services
- Regional co-operation
- Industrial development
- Cultural and social co-operation
- Environment

Special provisions for sugar, rum and bananas were also included. In addition, precise quantities and prices were set for 48 agricultural products that could be exported to the EEC. This scheme is known as STABEX, and is intended to provide stable export earnings for countries dependent on agricultural exports for much of their income. Similar arrangements have been made for mining products and manufactured goods. The following are some recent examples of projects funded in the Caribbean:

Major projects over US $10million

Guyana Rehabilitation of sea defences, quarries, transport and water supplies. 1988: $18million.

Guyana Rehabilitation of the bauxite industry. 1988: $38million.

Jamaica Reconstruction following Hurricane Gilbert, especially galvanized roofing and fertilizers. 1988: $22million.

Other projects US $1million - 10 million

Bahamas Family Island electrification. 1987: $3million.

Barbados Construction of jetty and marketplace for Speightstown fishing port. 1985: $4 million.

Grenada Repairs to Eastern Main Road. 1984: $2million.

Dominica Roadbuilding and resurfacing. 1983: $3million.

St Lucia Rural drainage improvement. 1984: $2million.

Suriname Rice production at Coronie. 1985: $9million.

In total, Lomé III committed the EC to spend about US$8.5 billion on the ACP countries in five years. It is by far the most important long-term trade and aid arrangement that the Caribbean countries are involved in.

---

1 Why does the EC undertake expensive projects in the Caribbean?

2 What is the difference between emergency aid, short-term aid, and long-term aid?

3 What is the difference between a grant, a 'soft' loan, and a regular loan? What is 'hard' currency?

The Caribbean Basin Initiative (CBI)

This is rather different from the other schemes in that it involves only one donor, the USA, and it appears to operate as a series of *bilateral* agreements; that is, separate agreements are made between the USA and individual countries. These include the non-communist Central American countries as well as the West Indies.

The Initiative originated in 1983 and coincided with the invasion of Grenada. Clearly there are political reasons for an increased US involvement in the West Indies, as it wishes to counterbalance Cuban acitivity. In economic terms it seems that the Initiative is planned in a much longer-term fashion than other US aid schemes, of which there have been several since the 1930s. As more information becomes available, and projects are set up, it is likely to develop into a Lomé-type agreement, which can only be good for the region.

The following are important features of the CBI:

1 It does not provide aid. It allows items produced in the Caribbean under certain conditions to be imported into the USA duty-free. To qualify for CBI acceptance, a manufactured product has to be substantially different from the raw materials that are used to make it, and 35% of its value must have been added in the Caribbean. It also allows for the import of agricultural produce such as citrus.

2 Certain non-economic conditions may be imposed on the receiving country, such as access to private bank accounts, before trade agreements are reached. For instance, conventions held in Jamaica are tax-deductible for American companies, but this is not allowed in The Bahamas, which has refused to exchange tax information with the USA.

3 There are bans or quotas on certain major commodities which are therefore excluded from CBI. These include sugar, bananas, textiles, footwear, petroleum products and leather goods, all of which could have been important exports for the West Indian countries.

4 Manufactured goods, once accepted by the CBI, are guaranteed 12 years of duty-free access to the USA. This is a major incentive and should encourage the development and modernization of industry, and especially of market research into what the US public is prepared to buy.

Between 1983 and 1988 the value of all goods exported to the USA actually fell by US$700 million. However, most of this was due to a decline in the export of the main traditional goods, namely petroleum, bauxite and sugar. Trade in non-traditional goods actually increased by about US$700million, and it is clear that the USA does not wish to support industries that it sees as competitive with its own production. Instead it is attempting to diversify the industrial and agricultural structure into more profitable areas such as those found in Puerto Rico. Jamaica has probably benefited the most in this respect, with some 70 factories assembling goods originally manufactured in the USA, particularly clothing. By 1988 this type of development had created 20,000 jobs in Jamaica.

Caribcan

This is a version of the CBI introduced by Canada for the benefit of the Commonwealth Caribbean in 1986. Like the CBI it requires that manufactured goods have a certain percentage of value added in the Caribbean country, in this case 60%. Certain manufactures that compete with Canadian produce will still be taxed, notably textiles, clothing, leather goods, lubricating oil and methanol. Unlike the CBI, virtually all of the traditional exports presently sent to Canada will be allowed in duty-free.

Caribcan is intended to encourage the development of manufacturing and production of goods that are not presently exported from the Commonwealth Caribbean.

The future for trade in the West Indies

The Caribbean cannot hope to have a positive trade balance in the near future. This does not mean that it will become economically bankrupt, however, as it has many 'invisible' resources to sell. These include its climate, location, and labour. The USA currently has the world's largest trade-gap, but also has an extremely healthy economy, as shown by the value of the US dollar. A simple negative balance of trade does not mean that a country cannot survive or develop. There is no reason why the Caribbean region's assets cannot continue to be developed and traded. Experience has shown that the major economic groupings provide the most stable conditions for trade, and that individual alignments (such as Cuba's with the USSR) and protectionism, which has been widely practised in the Caribbean, prevent it.

---

1 Why does the USA want to help Caribbean countries?

2 What other American countries have aided the Caribbean states besides the USA and Canada?

3 Why was it necessary to divide Caricom into LDCs and MDCs?

4 Why is The Bahamas not part of the free trade agreement in Caricom, but is otherwise a full member?

Part Four
Practical Skills

20
Mapwork

Aerial photos are often just as good as maps. Can you identify this important town in Jamaica?

Maps are used mainly to show *location*. They are the results of *surveys* in which a surveyor records information about the location of particular features. As this information can either be about the land or the sea, we have to distinguish between *maps* (land) and *charts* (sea). (See Fig. 20.1).

Basic features of the landscape are usually the first things to be surveyed. On land we call this *topographic* information, and this gives us *topographic maps*, which are the types of map used in schools or colleges to show the area in which you live. The same kind of information about the sea produces a *hydrographic chart*. Over the centuries most countries have developed similar styles of maps and of charts, and once you have learnt to use one country's maps or charts, you can use those of any other country.

Other maps can be derived from these, and this is usually done in two ways. *Thematic* maps show one particular feature, for example settlement; or add data from another source, such as a census, to produce a *population* map, for example. Other features are removed so that only population or settlement is shown. Other examples are *relief* maps and *road* maps. (See Fig. 20.2).

Another way in which the basic information can be shown is at different sizes, or *scales*. A map that has a scale larger than 1:5,000 is usually called a *plan*. These larger-scale maps are used for construction work, such as new roads, pipelines or airports. Details about these can be added later to existing maps.

Smaller-scale maps are often called *atlas* maps, although this includes any map showing a large area on a single sheet, such as a wall map. The scale may be as large as 1:150,000 for a map of Barbados in a Caribbean atlas, or as small as 1:100,000,000 (1:100 million) for a world map. Most countries are shown at between 1:1 million and 1:10 million. Atlas maps concentrate on showing relief and drainage, and settlement and communication.

Fig. 20.1 Maps and charts

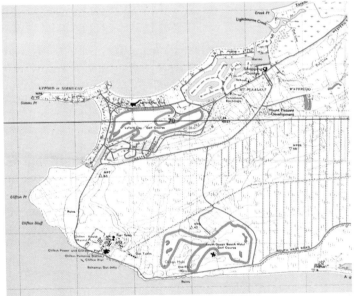
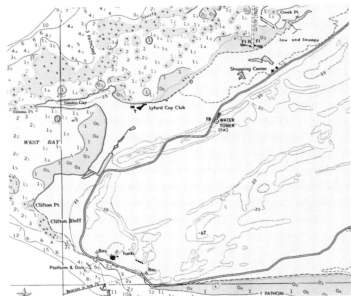

Map information

The information shown on most maps and charts falls under a limited number of headings, and once each of these headings (or classifications) is understood separately, it is much easier to understand the map itself, which of course shows everything together.

1   *Height or elevation*   This shows the height above sea level of the land surface by contours or spot heights. *Relief*, which is the shape of the land surface, can be interpreted from this to a certain extent, and may be further illustrated by contour shading, hachures, and by symbols for rocky and cliff outcrops, and depressions.

2   *Land use*   This is of several types.

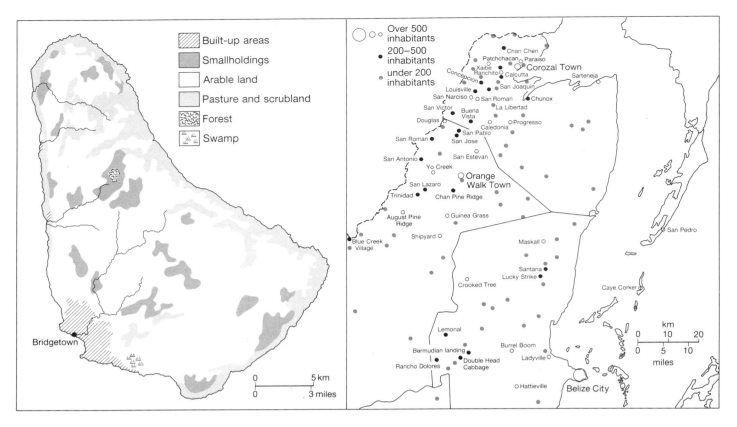

Fig. 20.2 Two examples of thematic maps. The map of Barbados (a) shows land use by means of tonal shading, and is known as a choropleth map. The map of Belize shows the distribution of population by means of symbols. It is called a point distribution map.

(a) Natural vegetation, the most common being forest and swamp.

(b) Cultivated land, sometimes with the crop named.

(c) Settlement, with a variety of common buildings identified by symbols or letters.

(d) Bare ground, usually rock, sand or mud.

3 *Drainage* This is nearly always shown in blue and includes everything to do with water such as lakes, rivers, waterfalls, wells, reservoirs and canals.

4 *Boundaries* Maps are often used to show property and ownership, and therefore have a variety of administrative and legal boundaries which are shown by different lines. Single red lines, which are often broken, are common. Walls, fences and hedges are also included.

5 *Communications* These are always highly visible lines on topographic maps, often enhanced in width or colour to show their importance. They include roads, paths, railways and canals. Related to these are power transmission lines and pipelines. All are carefully described in the key to a map.

6 *Survey marks* These are mainly of value to the surveyor and include trigonometrical stations and bench marks, both of which often have a precise height next to them.

7 *Names* These are numerous and widespread, but as with the other features the particular colour, size, style or typeface has a specific meaning. Often this is *not* in the key, but can be determined from a careful inspection of the map. For instance, on the Dominica 1:50,000 topographic map (See Fig. 20.4)

(a) *Sloping capitals: SOUFRIÈRE RIDGE* always refers to a district.

(b) *Blue lettering* refers to a marine feature, e.g. *Grand Bay*.

(c) **Bold lettering** refers to settlements: lower case for villages, e.g. **Tète Morne**; capitals for small towns BEREKUA; large capitals for large towns ROSEAU (only one).

These seven classifications are each quite simple, but when combined on a map the result is complex. The easiest way to understand the map is to seek out each set of features separately.

232

Map exercises

The following exercises are for the 1:50,000 Dominica map and the 1:25,000 Montserrat map, but can easily be adapted to any other country's topographic maps. Whenever possible the full sheets should be used, but where these are not available, Figures 20.4 and 20.5 can be used. The outlines and the grids of these maps should be traced for use as *base maps* (i.e. maps on which further information is to be added). Reference should be made to the section on *Interpretation* (See p. 238) for assistance with the techniques for doing these exercises.

Exercise 1 - Height

(a) With reference to the Dominica 1:50,000 extract (Fig. 20.4), construct a key showing the intervals at which the colouring between contours changes.

(b) With the aid of the grid on the Montserrat map, locate all the spot heights given for mountain tops (only). What do the symbols next to these heights mean?

Exercise 2 - Natural land use

(a) Using the Dominica extract, draw on your own base map the area covered by forest.

(b) Using the Montserrat extract, draw the areas of beach (sand or mud) on your base map with a red felt pen.

Exercise 3 - Human land use

(a) Locate all the churches on the Dominica extract and transfer them to your base map. Name the village or town to which each one belongs.

(b) On your Montserrat base map, draw the approximate boundaries around these settlements: Davy Hill, Rendezvous, Gerald's, Old Norwood, St John's, Judy Piece, Dick Hill and Mango Hill.

Fig. 20.3 (a) Two atlas maps showing Trinidad. At these scales maps can only show a few of the things that are shown on topographic maps.

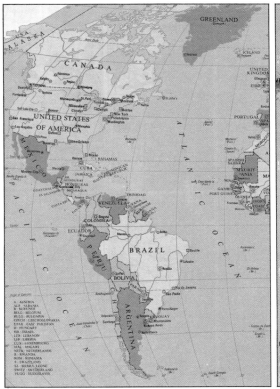

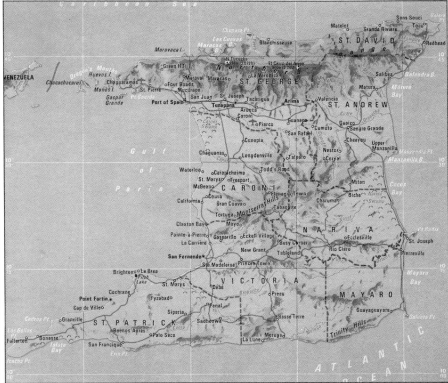

Height or elevation

.1250   Heights in feet given to ground level

         Contours, vertical interval 250 ft

         Embankment

Land use   Natural features

Forest and woodland

Swamp

Sand or mud

Cliff, rocks

Human features

Named building

R   # Rem   Other building/Ruin/Remains

■ Ch   ■ C   ■ Sch   Church/Clinic/School

■ PS   ■ H   ■ PO   Police Station/Hotel/Post Office

■ WM   ■ T   ■ CtH   Windmill/Toilet/Court House

■ Hosp   Cem   Hospital/Cemetary

● Tk   ● Tk   Oil tank/Water tank

● Twr   ○ Chy   Tower/Chimney

Drainage

● (T)   ● (PT)   ● (U)   Springs – trapped partly, trapped, untrapped

Watercourse – intermittent , dam, waterfall

Watercourse – permanent, waterfall

● Hope   Reservoir (named)

Boundaries

Parish boundary

Forest reserve and National Park boundaries

Fence, hedge, wall

Communications

Bridge   Surfaced road with bridge

Culvert   Unsurfaced road with culvert

Track and four-wheel-drive trail

Footpath

Pipe   Pipeline

Survey marks

Cut line

△   ▽   Trigonometrical station – primary, secondary

Names

ST ANN'S BAY   Large Town

RETREAT   Town

CARRON HALL   Minor Town

Chester   Village

Fig. 20.3(b) Some of the symbols that are commonly used on larger-scale maps

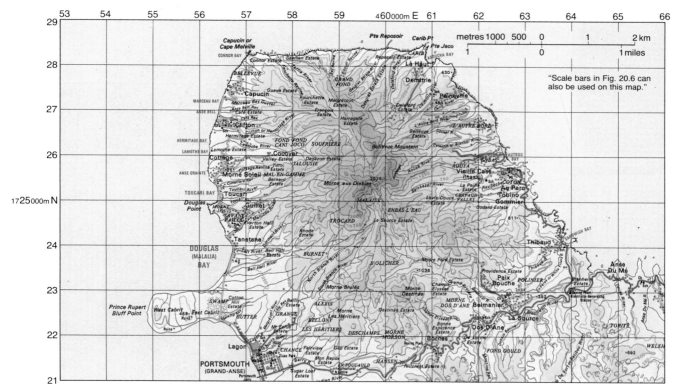

Fig. 20.4 Northern part of Dominica, 1:50,000 (not to scale)

Exercise 4 - Drainage

(a) On your Dominica base map, draw in the following rivers with their tributaries:

Indian R.	Lamothe R.
Blenheim R.	Taffia R.
North R.	Demitrie R.
Bell Hall R.	Balthazar R.
Manicou R.	Thibaud R.

(b) On your Montserrat base map, using a round blue symbol, locate and name all the reservoirs.

Exercise 5 - Boundaries

(a) Draw and name the Forestry Reserve boundary on your Dominica base map.

(b) Name four places or features on the Montserrat map that mark the parish boundary between St Peter and St George (See inset).

Exercise 6 - Communications

(a) On your Dominica base map draw in (using the same symbols) all the surfaced roads.

(b) On your Montserrat base map mark in the following :

- The footpath from St John's to Katy Hill
- The unsurfaced road around Potato Hill
- All the bridges that are shown by a symbol on main roads (these are the large bridges)

Exercise 7 - Names

(a) On the Dominica extract, what kinds of features are shown by:

- Blue lettering?
- Upright lower-case lettering?
- Sloping lower-case lettering?
- Sloping capitals?
- Bold upright lower-case lettering?

How many other types of lettering are there?

(b) What are the four main kinds of feature named in blue on the Montserrat map? (Some of them are subdivided into minor types - what are they?)

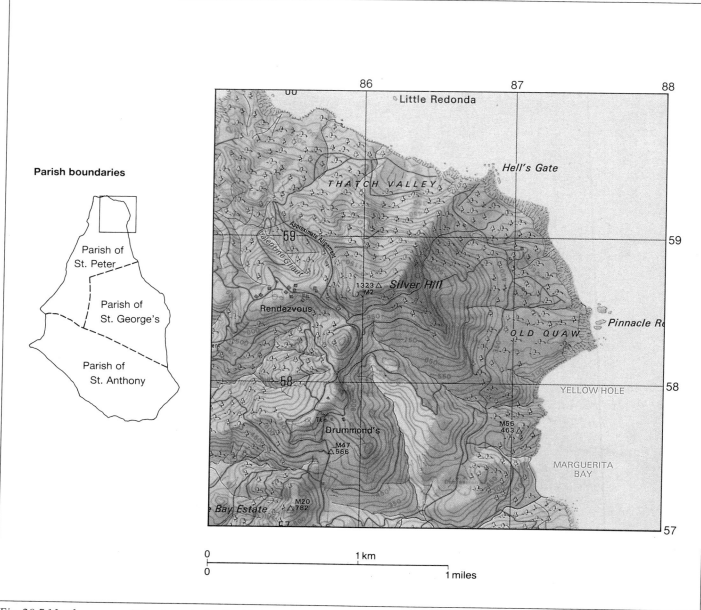

Fig. 20.5 Northern area of Montserrat plus Parish Boundaries, 1:25,000 (not to scale)

More map information

Scale

It will be clear by now that scale tells us the size of a map and that it is the most common way of describing one. The notation 1:100,000 means that 1 cm on the map equals 100,000 cm on the land, and as 100 cm equals 1 metre, and 1,000 metres equals 1 kilometre, then:

$$1 \text{ cm} = \frac{100,000}{100 \times 1,000} \text{ kilometres, or}$$

1 cm represents 1km on the ground. The advantage of the scale ratio is that it has *no units* and has the same meaning in any country in the world.

On the maps for your country, the scale ratio will be given together with *scale bars* showing distances on the map in the units most common in your country (usually inches/miles and centimetres/kilometres). The most common scales are the following:

236

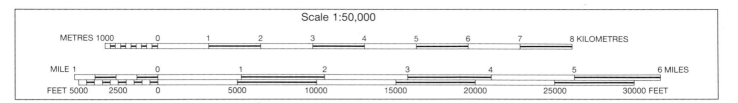

Fig. 20.6 Scale bars from the 1:50,000 (not to scale) map of St Kitts and Nevis. The scale bar is intended for use with a pair of dividers. The two simplest ways to measure distance are as follows:

1) *Set 1 unit (mile or kilometre) on the dividers, and 'walk' the dividers carefully along the route, counting each step. At the end section, close the dividers to the remaining distance, and measure the distance in tenths on the scale to the left of zero.*

2) *Spread the dividers along the distance to be measured, or along part of it, for example along a straight stretch of road. Measure the gap between the points of the dividers in whole units (to the right of zero) and tenths (to the left of zero) against the scale bar. Repeat this until the total distance has been measured, and add up the separate measurements to find the total.*

1:10,000 1cm = 0.1km or 100 metres	6 inches = 1 mile (approx.)
1:25,000 1cm = 0.25km;	2.5 in = 1 mile (approx.)
1:50,000 1cm = 0.5km;	1 inch = 0.75 mile (approx.)
2cm = 1km;	1 inch = 1.5 miles (approx)
1:1,000,000 1cm = 10km;	1 inch = 15 miles (approx.)

Gradient

This is a mathematical relationship to show the slope of the land. It can only be estimated from a map. Like scale, it is usually shown as a ratio such as 1:10, which is spoken as 'one in ten' and means that the land rises (or falls) one unit for every ten units horizontally. Like scale it has no units and is universally understood.

On a map it is used in conjunction with the contours. It can only be estimated between places for which the height is given on the map. If the distance between the coast (0 metres) and the 500-metre contour is 5 kilometres, then the gradient is 500 metres in 5 kilometres, or:

$$500 \text{ metres} \quad : \quad 5 \text{ kilometres}$$
$$= \quad 500 \text{ metres} \quad : \quad 5,000 \text{ metres}$$
$$1 \text{ metre} \quad : \quad \frac{5,000}{500} = 10 \text{ metres}$$
$$1:10 \text{ or 'one in ten'}$$

You can use a set-square to compare the gradient of Morne aux Diables with the theoretical gradients in the lower part of Fig. 20.7. By calculation it is as follows:

Height: Distance

$$2,828 \text{ ft} \quad : \quad 11,088 \text{ ft (2.1 miles} \times 5,280 \text{ ft)}$$
$$\text{or} \quad 1 \quad : \quad \frac{11,088}{2,828}$$
$$= \quad 1 \quad : \quad 3.9$$

or nearly 1 in 4, as is indicated graphically.

---

1 Construct your own gradient graph and draw the slope of Silver Hill on the Montserrat map (Fig. 20.5), from the summit to Hell's Gate on the north-east coast. What is the gradient:

(a) graphically

(b) by calculation?

Fig. 20.7 Average gradient from Morne Aux Diables to the East Coast (Dominica 1:50,000 map)

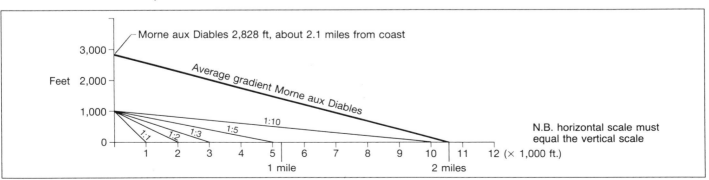

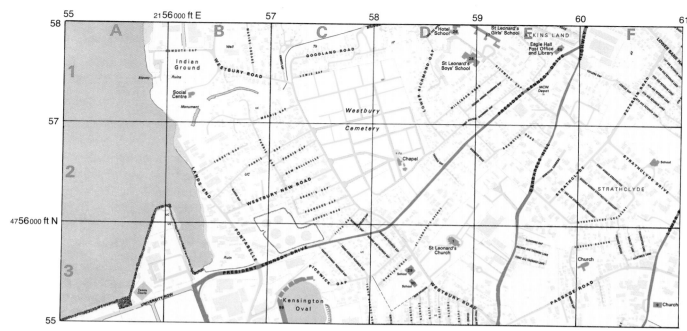

Fig. 20.8 Grid system used on 1:5,000 Bridgetown plan. A simple letter/number grid has been superimposed on the British West Indies Grid, which can also be used.

The grid

Most maps have a grid of squares superimposed on them. The lines of the squares are usually 1, 2 or 4 kilometres apart, depending on the scale, and so are excellent for estimating distance and areas on topographic maps. (The Dominica 1:50,000 map does not show the grid, but the margin of the map has the divisions for it so that it can be drawn in.)

The grid is actually a network of lines that the cartographer uses to construct the map from the survey. The nature of the grid depends on the projection used to convert the spherical Earth onto a flat piece of paper. Small-scale atlas maps use different projections and their 'grid' is the network of lines of latitude and longitude. Larger-scale maps avoid the problems of these variable lines (lines of latitude vary in length,

lines of longitude appear curved) by using a rectangular grid, although the map will also have lines of latitude and longitude on it.

The grid is widely used for identifying a location on a map. Using the Montserrat extract (Fig. 20.5), the approximate area of Silver Hill is given in *four figures*, namely 8658. The 86 refers to the vertical line (called the 'easting') labelled with the bold figures 86, and 58 refers to the horizontal line (the 'northing'). The feature you are looking for (Silver Hill) is in that box. If the squares of the grid are divided up into tenths, accurately or by estimation, a *six-figure grid* can be given and the location found more precisely. For 861 587, move 0.1 (one-tenth) of the way from the 86 easting to the 87 easting, and follow that line down to 0.7 (seven-tenths) of the way from the 58 northing towards the 59 northing. This will locate the spot height of 1,323 feet on Silver Hill.

Simple grids using a letter/number combination, such as on the Bridgetown 1:5,000 plan, are often found on maps that are likely to be used by the general public or by tourists.

Map interpretation

So far we have *described* maps so that we can extract information from them accurately and easily. This in itself is a valuable skill. Map interpretation uses the map information *in combination with* geographical knowledge to provide a greater understanding of the natural and human features shown on the map.

To assist in interpretation there are three main techniques which can be used to extract the necessary information: cross sections, transects, and topic ('sketch') maps.

Cross-sections

These are a means of showing the relief along a line on the map. In the accurate version the height of each contour is plotted against a vertical scale. If the horizontal scale is the same as that of the map (that is, it is 'true') but the vertical scale is not, the cross-section will have a vertical exaggeration. Wherever possible both scales should be the same.

For instance, if the horizontal scale is 1:25,000, or 1 cm to 250

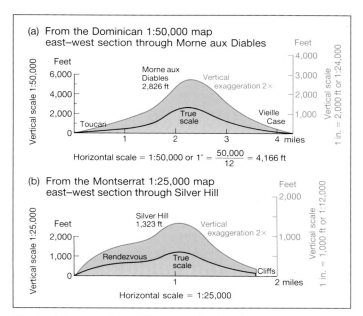

(a) From the Dominican 1:50,000 map east–west section through Morne aux Diables

Morne aux Diables 2,826 ft

Vertical exaggeration 2×

True scale

Toucari

Vieille Case

Horizontal scale = 1:50,000 or $1'' = \dfrac{50,000}{12} = 4,166$ ft

(b) From the Montserrat 1:25,000 map east–west section through Silver Hill

Silver Hill 1,323 ft

Vertical exaggeration 2×

Rendezvous

True scale

Cliffs

Horizontal scale = 1:25,000

Fig. 20.9 True scale and distorted sketch sections. (a) 4,000 ft on the vertical scale on the left should actually be 4,166 ft. For a sketch section this is close enough and there will be no vertical exaggeration. At 1in.=2,000ft on the right, the vertical scale is 1:12in.x 2,000ft.=24,000 and there is a vertical exaggeration of $\dfrac{50,000}{24,000}$ or about 2x.

(b) The comments above about the vertical scale also apply to this section. Note too that the true-to-scale sections of each hill give the impression that Morne Aux Diables is very much like Silver Hill. It is of course more than twice as high. Only if the horizontal scales were also the same could we compare the altitude visually.

metres, but the vertical scale is 1 cm to 500 metres, there is a *vertical exaggeration* of 2 x, and the relief is distorted so that all slopes appear to be steeper than they actually are. On a 1:50,000 map using the same vertical scale, the exaggeration is 4 x.

A *sketch* section is usually a quite acceptable way of illustrating the relief. In this case the same scales are used, but the profile is drawn freehand instead of by measurement. This is much quicker and with practice little 'accuracy' is actually lost.

Cross-sections are used to get a visual impression of the relief in an area. They are particularly useful when combined with some other feature, such as a road or vegetation.

In the case of a road the section can be taken along the route of the road to illustrate its relief. The vegetation could be added to the section to see if there is a relationship between the two.

Transects

This is a powerful technique that also has applications in field enquiries (See p. 245). The axis of the transect usually follows a straight line or a road. It is similar to a cross-section but it goes further by including as many categories of map information as necessary. This is taken from the area immediately adjacent to the transect line, perhaps 0.25km either side on 1:25,000 map, or 0.5km either side on a 1:50,000 map (Fig 20.10).

Fig. 20.10 Transect from Charles Fort to St George's Ghut Mouth on the St Christopher and Nevis 1:50,000 map.

This transect has five components:

- *relief is shown with an annotated sketch section, and includes all prominent features within one kilometre of the transect line, notably the edge of Brimstone Hill and Mt. Liamuiga*
- *drainage is shown diagrammatically*
- *vegetation in blocks*
- *roads and paths using the map symbols*
- *settlement in the style of the map symbol, but to approximate scale only.*

In all cases care is taken to align each feature horizontally so that its relationship with the other features is clear.

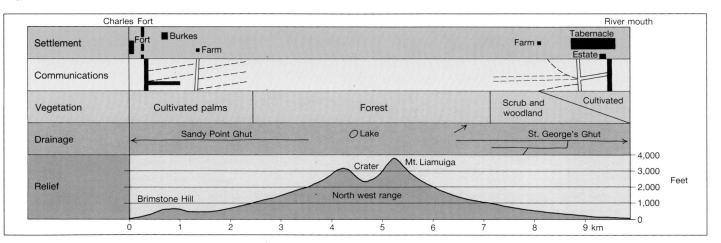

Topic maps ('sketch' maps)

These are often referred to simply as 'sketch' maps, but this term is misleading. A *sketched* topic map requires certain information to be extracted from a map and recorded separately, by eye, on a base map. For instance, we could show towns from the St Lucia 1:50,000 map (Fig. 20.11). The coast is drawn in by eye, and the settlements located, again by eye.

An *accurate* version is sometimes required, but this takes much longer. For this it is necessary to draw a grid (or use the map grid if this is suitable) on the map, and an identical grid at a smaller (or larger) scale on the paper for the topical map (Fig. 20.12). It usually helps to label the grid A,B,C, etc. vertically, and 1, 2, 3, etc. horizontally if there is a lot to copy. The coast is then drawn on the topic map by following its path carefully across each square in turn. Then the position of each settlement in its square on the map is noted, and the settlement symbol is located and named in the same part of the square on the new map.

This technique has an important advantage over the other two in that it can cover the whole map, and not just part of it.

Its simplest use is to compare two topics, such as relief and settlement, relief and communications, relief and drainage, or

Fig. 20.12 Reducing and enlarging accurately with the aid of a grid. The coast line and the main road have been drawn in each case.

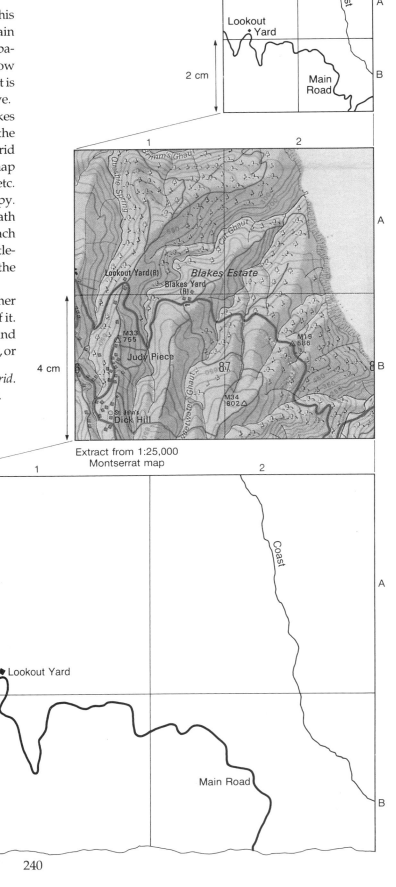

240

Fig. 20.11 Sketch map of settlement from the 1:50,000 St Lucia map. Settlement is shown at three levels based on the style of lettering used on the 1:50,000 map. Only those settlements shown in capitals have been chosen.

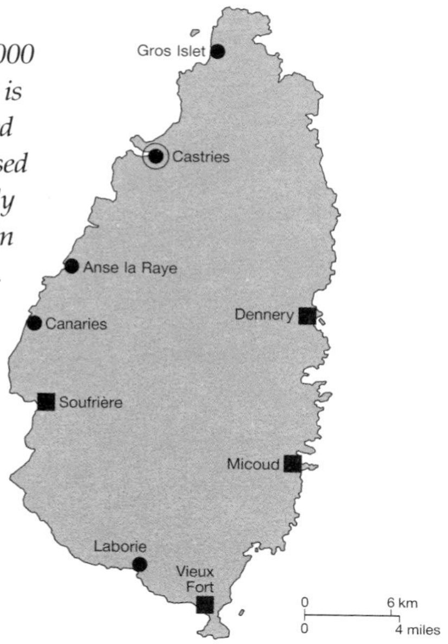

relief and vegetation. These can be combined to a certain extent, for example relief, drainage and vegetation, or relief, settlement and communications. More complex comparisons gain little by using topic maps - it is just as easy to use the existing map. The great advantage of the topic map is that unwanted information is removed from the mass of data on the full map. Once three or four topics have been put on a new map it is likely to be just as 'confused' as the original, and a lot less accurate.

1 With reference to Fig. 20.1, make a list of all the things that are:

(a) shown on both the map and the chart,

(b) only shown on the chart.

2 With reference to any Caribbean atlas, find a map of Trinidad and a world map:

(a) How much bigger is Trinidad on the Trinidad map than on the world map?

(b) What features does the world map leave out?

3 Using the extract from the 1:50,000 Dominica map:

(a) Draw a sketch map to show the relief and drainage. Describe the drainage pattern.

(b) Draw a sketch map to show the relief and the roads. Account for the road system.

4 Using the extract from the 1:25,000 Montserrat map:

(a) Draw a sketch map to show the settlements. Describe the settlement pattern.

(b) Draw a sketch map to show land use and height. Discuss the relationship between vegetation and height.

Interpretation methods

The three techniques described above are means of *describing* graphically features on a map. In themselves they are not an interpretation, but are the first step towards it.

Interpretation should be systematic: it should follow a sequence of procedures and reach a conclusion. A typical sequence might be:

1 *Observation* - visual examination of the feature(s) on the map.

2 *Display* - graphical portrayal of the features by a standard technique.

3 *Comparison* - a descriptive account of the relationship of two or more topics.

4 *Interpretation* - an explanation of the relationships observed.

5 *Conclusion* - a summary of the reality and its explanation.

It should be noted that the first three steps are descriptive and only use - and isolate - information on the map. No attempt to bring in outside knowledge should be made until this is complete.

For instance, if we are studying relief and communications, we should not start by saying, 'The roads follow the valleys'. We should describe what the roads do, which might be: 'Eight roads penetrate the mountains. Five of these follow the valley floors, two follow the crests of the interfluves, and one crosses three valleys and ridges with a series of hairpin bends.'

Almost every interpretation will eventually have to account for:

• the majority of cases
• a minority of cases
• exceptions

and therefore three explanations will be needed. It is at this stage that further geographical knowledge about the principles of settlement or communications, as discussed earlier in this book, should be used.

21
Fieldwork

Geography is one of the 'field sciences', and like geology, botany, zoology, oceanography, climatology and some others it depends on first-hand information from which to draw its conclusions. Work in the field generally falls into one of two categories: either *observation*, or *investigation*.

Upper-school students collecting data on a small farm in Eleuthera, The Bahamas.

Field observation

This includes any field visit to obtain visual information about a geographical topic, either in the physical or human field. Examples would include, for instance, observing features of erosion and deposition along the coast, or a visit to a sugar factory. To be effective, such visits should be planned in advance by the students and teacher together. Tasks are then set for each group of observers to complete.

The simplest way to do this is to decide what the purpose of the visit is, and what is to be learnt from it. A checklist, which can be in the form of a personal questionnaire for each student, is prepared in advance. During the visit the student answers the questions on the list as the field visit proceeds.

This may involve examining certain objects and asking questions. The notes made on the questionnaire ensure that nothing is missed on the trip. The knowledge gained can be integrated into subsequent follow-up work as it is needed.

Typical check lists/questionnaires for two visits are given below. Every student should answer each point by *making the observation*. Direct questions should only be asked when an observation cannot provide the answer (these are marked with an asterisk). The information to be obtained can usually be divided up among students, so that all are not searching for the same answers at the same time.

Visit to a Factory

Note: Refer to chapter 15. Manufacturing requires raw materials, processing, transportation, market and a site, and has an impact on the environment. The check list should take account of this, and of the country.

1   What are the raw materials?

2   Where do they come from?

3   How do they get to the factory?

4   What type of energy is needed to run the factory?

5   When did the factory open?

6   How big is the site?

7   Why is the factory located here?
   (a) Economic reasons*
   (b) Environmental reasons*
   (c) Social factors*
   (d) Other factors*

8   What exactly are the processes involved?

9   What are the products?

10 What are the markets for each product?*

11 How big is the labour force?*

12 What is the nature of the labour force?
   (e) Nationality*
   (f) Male/Female ratio
   (g) Special training/skills required
   (h) Seasonal requirement*

13 Does the company benefit from any national or international taxation or trade agreements?*

14 What does the factory do with its waste products?
   (a) Gases
   (b) Liquids
   (c) Solids

15 Is there any recycling or by-products?

16 Is there a visual impact or excessive noise?

17 Is the factory stable, expanding, declining? Why not?

*A direct question rather than an observation is probably required. For some other items observation may have to be supplemented with a question later.

Visit to the Coast

Note: Refer to chapter 5. The nature of the coast depends on the geology, on wave and current action, biological activity, the climate, and human impact. The checklist should take account of this and the nature of the coast to be visited. Samples should be collected.

A In an area with cliffs

1 What is the height of the cliffs? Give estimates for different sections.

2 What is the rock type(s)? (*Collect sample(s)*)

3 What structures can be seen? (*Sketch required*)

4 What signs of erosion can be seen?

5 What is the size of the rocks or boulders, if any?

6 What is the slope of the cliff face?

7 What is at the foot of the cliff?

    (a) Beach

    (b) Rocky platform

    (c) Sea

8 Where is the high tide mark/low tide mark? (*Sketch required*)

9 Is there any vegetation visible?

10 What are the waves like?

11 Describe any artificial features.

B In an area with a beach

1 What is the texture of the beach material? (*Sieves*)

2 What is the beach material made of? (*Collect samples*)

3 How wide is the beach?

4 Where is the high tide mark/low tide mark? (*Sketch required*)

5 What slopes does the beach have? (*Sketch required*)

6 Are any rocky surfaces visible?

7 Describe the nature of any rocky outcrops.

8 Is any vegetation present?

9 Describe the location and type of any vegetation *on* the beach.

10 Describe the waves.

11 Describe any artificial features.

Field enquiry

In this type of fieldwork students go into the field *to collect data*. Field enquiries are at the heart of all geographical research and the student field enquiry is simply a scaled-down version of what is required for a research project.

In its complete form the formal field enquiry consists of the following:

1 Choice of a *topic* - identifying a problem or a question.

2 Choice of *technique* and *preparation* for fieldwork.

3 *Collecting and recording* data in the field - the *field notebook*.

4 *Analysis and interpretation* of the data, and presentation of the results.

5 *Conclusion*.

Choice of a topic

The range of geographical topics is almost infinite, but for a limited field enquiry by school students the choice is much more restricted.

The choice of the topic must take into account:

- the time available?
- the distance to be travelled? and
- the quantity of data needed to complete the enquiry?

In combination these rather obvious restrictions limit the enquiry considerably. It cannot be emphasized too strongly that it is at this stage that *the exact answers to these three questions above must be known. If there is not enough time, transport is not available, or data not collected, the enquiry will be a failure.*

The choice of topics, although limited, is still large. To ensure that the enquiry is completed, the following guidelines should be noted. In particular, the choice of a suitable simple technique (next page) will greatly assist this.

(a) Decide on the time first. Three hours in the field can easily yield enough data for several inquiries if the technique is suitable. If time is a limitation, a class can break up into groups, each with a different area to work in. This multiplies the data without adding to the time.

(b) It is always preferable to work within walking distance of the school. The shorter the distance to the field area, the more time is available for the enquiry.

(c) You must know exactly what data is needed and be sure that your technique allows it to be collected in the time available. In particular, *questionnaire surveys should not be used*. Apart from requiring a lot of experience to design and interpret them, there is no control over the quantity and quality of information received. They are rarely of any value on their own.

The technique and its planning

The technique is the method you will use to collect the data. The following are a selection of the most common techniques suitable for school-based field enquiries.

The Transect

As in mapwork, this is a powerful technique by which a lot of comparative data can be collected quickly, and which is capable of being used in many aspects of physical and human geography. The two examples here illustrate the preparation needed and the style of notebook entry.

Natural vegetation survey

The objective is to see if there is a relationship between the vegetation and the rest of the landscape. We should record information about *vegetation type, soil, rock, slope* and *water table*.

As in all fieldwork, the data for each category has to be subject to *identification, measurement* and *recording*. The planning is done in the classroom, and it has to be decided what will be recorded and how it will be identified.

Vegetation   The areas to be visited should include a succession of types of vegetation, and this has to be simplified so that plants can be recognized easily. This is done by having a few species for each typical association:

Coast	Sea grape
	Sea oats
	Spider lily
	Railroad vine
Swamp	Saw grass
	Buttonwood
	Red mangrove
Pine forest	Caribbean pine
Rain forest	Mora
	Cocoplum
	Fig
	Silk cotton
	Air plants
Mixed hardwood forest (in limestone or drier areas)	
	Poison wood
	Gum elemi
	Pigeon plum
Scrub	Cactus
	Cinnecord
Grassland	Grasses

Different islands have different plants, so the list will be different for each country. A sheet should be duplicated for each student showing the identifying characteristics of each plant. The more unusual plants should also be identified in the field before the survey begins. Note that this is not a

Fig 21.1 Preparing the field notebook for a transect style survey

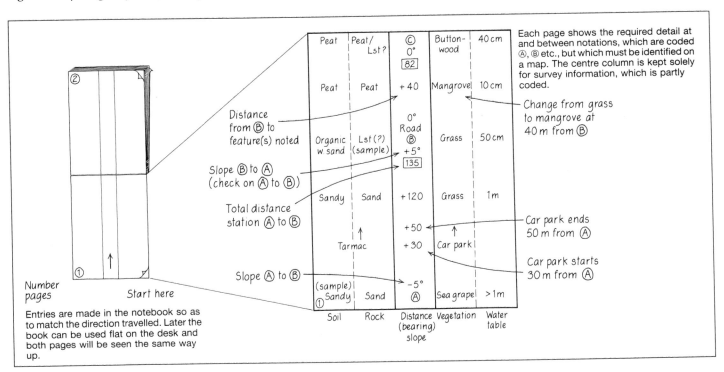

245

Harvesting potatoes on North Andros, the Bahamas.

botanical survey, but one to show the relationship of the vegetation with other things. Where the vegetation changes is more important than a list of species.

Soil Samples of the top horizon can be taken. Usually it is sufficient to record the *colour, texture* and *depth*, which can be measured with a thin steel rod down to about 1 metre (3 feet). Local soils should have been studied in advance (Ch. 9)

Rock Samples can be taken. The known geology of the area should be discussed in class, and typical rocks identified.

Slope Each separate slope section should be measured forwards and backwards, using a simple clinometer.

Fig. 21.2 Sketch map of urban area to be surveyed. The Urban area has been split up into four zones which can be surveyed by four teams of two students. Note that the boundaries do not split the streets, both sides of which are surveyed by the same team. A clear sketch map, not necessarily drawn to scale, must be made for each survey and given to each team, to ensure that no street is left unsurveyed.

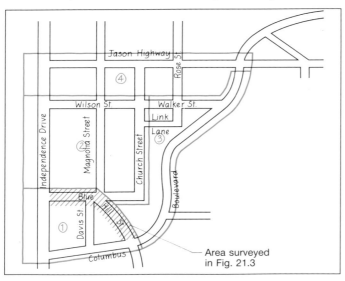

Water table If this is not visible in depressions it may be found using the probe. Only depths less than one metre are recorded.

The *preparation* is most important. *Recognition* (soil, plants) is important, so this needs to be studied carefully in advance. *Sampling* and *surveying* can also be used, so sample bags, hammers and trowels, and marker pens should be supplied to students. Use of a simple clinometer can be practised in the school grounds.

The *purpose* of the fieldwork is *to collect data*, not to learn plant or rock types. This is therefore made as simple as possible by doing everything possible in the classroom first.

In the field, work can be divided between groups, and usually the *change of slope* is the basis for a subdivision of the

Fig. 21.3 Using the field notebook for a street survey. This survey records the land use on either side of Blue Hill Street. The position on Blue Hill Street is indicated by the location of other named streets. The buildings are coded as suggested on p247

No attempt is made to position the spacing between buildings to scale. The amount of page used up is determined by the frequency of entries on the right-hand side. for example, the distance from Columbus Blvd. to Magnolia Street might in fact be greater than from Magnolia Street to Independence Drive.

A sketch-map (Fig 21.3) should coordinate the survey area.

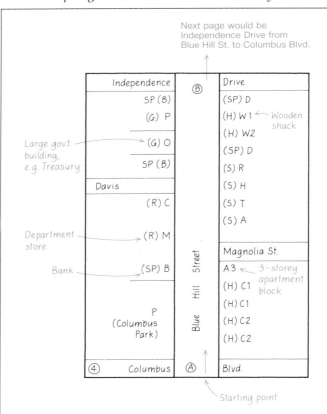

transect into recording sections. Groups can be changed at suitable intervals.

On a minor road or path, 15 students could probably survey 2 kilometres (just over a mile). In uncleared vegetation, progress would be much slower, so it is best to keep to established paths.

Housing and services survey

Once the transect technique is mastered it is easily adapted to urban surveys. In the example given here, streets are surveyed to record numbers and types of housing and services. The preparation requires *a map of the area* (Fig 21.2) and a list of *housing characteristics* and *service types* to be recorded, as well as a *coding system* to use in the field notebook.

The following is a guide to what may be used. A large number of variations are possible but it is best to limit the choice to the most essential.

Housing (H)			Services - Retail (R)	
Wooden	W		Food	F
Concrete	C		Clothing	C
Number of storeys 1, 2, 3+			Hardware	H
Apartment	A		Pharmacy	P
			Multiple	M
			Electrical	E
			Florist	F
Services - Professional (SP)			Services - Personal (S)	
Doctor	D		Launderette	L
Dentist	T		Garage	G
Optician	O		Hairdresser	H
Lawyer	L		Dry cleaner	D
Bank	B		Restaurant	R
Insurance	I		Take-away food	T
Travel agent	A			
Government services (G)			Miscellaneous	
School - primary	SP		Other use	Q
- secondary	SS		e.g. (R) Q = other retail use	
Post office	P		Vacant lot	V
Offices	O		Derelict building	X
Police station	L		Park	P

As Fig. 21.3 shows, the centre line of the transect is the street, and either side of the centre is used for the two sides of the street. Location is identified by drawing in the junctions with other streets.

The area to be surveyed is divided up among the students with two or three in each group. A large amount of information can be collected in 2 hours.

Many variations are possible. In a residential area, housing can be described more thoroughly to include roofing material, number of windows on front wall, state of repair, presence of TV/satellite aerial, presence of car, and so on. In a downtown area a separate category can be devised for tourism and/or recreation. Downtown areas might need a greater subdivision of the types of shops and services, and allowance for multiple use of different floors can be considered.

Movement study

This is another very flexible technique which yields a large amount of accurate data in a short time. It has the additional advantage that comparisons in time can be made, such as between morning and afternoon, or between different days, or different seasons.

The two most obvious subjects of study are vehicles and pedestrians. Each of these could be limited if necessary; for example, vehicles - goods or passengers; pedestrians - locals or tourists.

The operation of the survey divides itself into two concerns:

(a) What to record?

(b) Where to record it?

Some examples are given below.

Vehicular flow

A suitable survey point is at a major intersection which will provide 8 recording stations (Fig. 21.4), enough work for 16

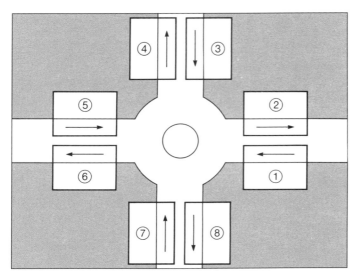

Fig. 21.4 Plan for traffic survey. Any major intersection can be used. Eight teams are split up as shown (1-8). Vehicles are recorded according to an agreed system on a prepared sheet. One student observes, and one or more record, depending on the density of traffic. As everything entering the intersection must leave it, the sum of every category at stations 1,3,5 and 7 must equal those at stations 2,4,6 and 8 - a valuable check on the fieldwork. The check should be included as part of the field enquiry.

students. Each pair records the traffic leaving or entering the intersection and classifies it according to a prepared code:

Car	C	No. of passengers: 1, 2, 3, 4
Motor cycle	M	(including driver, for car, motor
Truck	T	cycle and taxi only)
Taxi	X	
Bus	B	
Tanker	K	No. of axles: 3, 4, 5
Container	N	if more than two (gives idea of
Public utilities	U	size) for truck, bus, tanker, etc
Van	V	

Several variations are possible. Passengers only can be surveyed, or the number of school children counted during school rush hours. Goods and utility vehicles can be subdivided further. Whatever is chosen should be stated in the form of a hypothesis or a question:

Hypothesis Between 10 and 12 in the morning there are more female drivers than male.

Question Do most cars only have one occupant?

The scope for expansion and development of this sort of survey is considerable:

- One intersection can be compared with another.
- Traffic at the same intersection can be compared for different times of the day, days of the week, and times during the year. Even one year's study can be compared with that of a previous year.
- Comparison can be made between four or five roads away from major intersections. Road use rather than direction will then be suggested.
- Traffic densities in different areas can be compared.
- All the above can be done by category, for example private passengers, public passengers, goods, services, etc.

Pedestrian flow

A suitable busy area is needed such as downtown or at a shopping centre. Care must be taken to choose a location where there is a definite flow, and not a lot of stationary people, as in a car park. A busy street between intersections is suitable, away from major stores or pedestrian crossings. Pedestrians can be classified as follows:

Male/Female	M/F
Child (estimate up to 18 years old)	C
Infant (being carried in any way)	I
Tourist	T
Business (wearing traditional clothing, e.g. suit)	B
Carrying shopping	SH
Carrying briefcase	B/C
Carrying camera	CAM

A hypothesis or question is formed as before, and a variety of other classifications and time or place comparisons are possible.

Material study

This technique is suitable for studying small objects such as beach material, river sediments, flotsam and jetsam (marine litter), litter, agricultural produce and a few similar materials. The items are collected over a specific area and can be compared with similar areas and over a given period of time.

Beach debris survey

Several sections of beach of equal length are chosen with teams of about 10-12 students for each one. Densely used or maintained beaches are not suitable, as the object is to find all the debris that has collected on the beach. (Litter can also be collected along roads, in open spaces such as parks and car parks, etc., but in these cases the health risk must also be

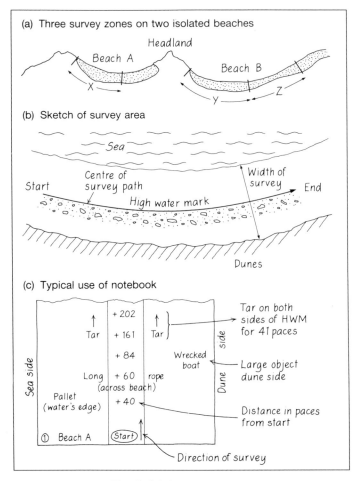

(a) Three survey zones on two isolated beaches

(b) Sketch of survey area

(c) Typical use of notebook

Fig. 21.5 Survey of beach debris

Fig. 21.6 Use of field notebook for general observations

considered. Beach debris is usually cleaner than land debris, but protective gloves should be available and students should be warned about tar deposits. Tar remover should be taken into the field.)

Items	Additional description	Code
Wooden objects		
Metal objects	Old/Recent	O/R
Glass objects	Seaborne	S
Plastic/polystyrene	Can float	F
Paper/cardboard	Marine origin (boat parts,	M
Organic, incl. food	fishing line, nets, buoys,	
Cloth/leather/rubber	ropes, etc.)	
Large objects		

The beach debris should be classified in advance and collected in sturdy garbage sacks. Large objects should be noted, but left behind. A typical classification might be as follows:

As the objects are separated and placed in previously labelled sacks, the actual recording and analysis can be done back at the school. Only the large objects have to be recorded in the field, but the notebook should be used to indicate density and location on the beach. As the party moves along the beach together, the distance from the start is measured (paced, or staked out in advance) and the point at which every 20 (or 10 or 100 depending on the state of the beach) objects (say) are picked up is noted. Also noted would be the general location such as high water mark, or dunes, or the water's edge.

As in the movement study, comparisons can be made between places and times, although the time interval should

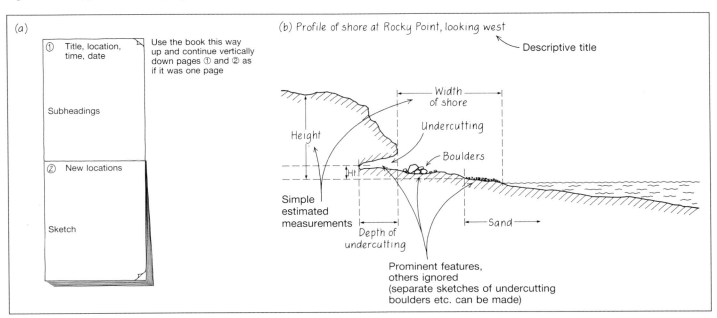

249

be at least a week. In addition a series of weekly or monthly surveys will provide *rates* of accumulation.

If this is done, a summary of the *wind direction* for the period should be included.

The field notebook

By the time the field is reached, the nature of the entries will have been decided and pages in the notebook may already have been prepared.

Apart from the specific entries which depend on the nature of the enquiry, the *principle* of a field notebook should be borne in mind:

> *A field notebook should be kept in such a way that any other trained observer should be able to use the notebook to replicate the observations without any other assistance.*

This is important, because field surveys are always expensive. Businesses or agencies cannot afford to repeat surveys if something should happen to the original observer. Historically this has been of great significance. David Livingstone, the African explorer, kept meticulous field notebooks, so that even today his footsteps across Africa can be retraced. Henry Morton Stanley, who discovered Livingstone and later followed the Congo River to its main source, kept such poor records that the course of the Congo remained unknown for many years after his death.

The following points should be noted when completing a field notebook.

1   It must be written clearly in pencil or a non-soluble ink so that the writing cannot be spoiled by water. The pencil should be soft enough to erase, and dark enough to read easily in poor light.

2   The notebook should have a hard cover, and be usable when the note-taker is standing up holding the notebook in one hand. The pages should be thick enough to write on both sides and have a secure binding so that leaves do not become detached.

3   The name of the observer should be on the outside, with an address for its return if lost. Inside, the pages must be numbered and every piece of work must have the date, time and location. The initial location must be clear enough for another person to find the exact starting point easily. All movements from then on must be recorded.

4   Annotated sketches save many words. They should always show directions and distances and the place at which they were made. Simple line drawings with clear labels are better than artistic impressions.

5   The field notebook should only include observations in the form of descriptions or data. It is not the place for

Fig 21.7 Typical display diagrams. This is a very simple and accurate way of displaying a lot of information. Many variations and additions are possible - some of these are shown here.

In this display the exact figures are easily found and the totals can also be included and compared. It would take several histograms or other diagrams to display all of this information, and some of it would be concealed.

A graph is best used to show a trend, in this case the change in vehicles per hour during 1988. The same graph can be used to show previous years, or a breakdown between cars and other vehicles. A similar graph can be used to show change over a period of years.

(a) Histogram (Beach survey)

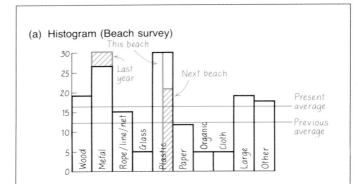

(b) Table/chart (Housing survey)

Type \ Zone	1	2	3	4	Total
Wood 1	82	12	0	84	178
Wood 2	31	16	0	72	119
Wood 3	3	0	0	8	11
Concrete 1	28	58	3	5	94
Concrete 2	4	23	0	0	27
Concrete 3	0	0	0	0	0
Apartments	0	1	2	4	7
Total	148	110	5	173	436 / 436

Check on arithmetic

(c) Graph (Vehicles/hour at 9–10 a.m. at observation point)

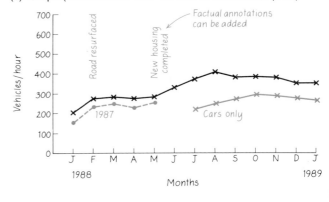

250

opinions or notes from other sources. It should only contain entries made in the field.

6 If the route followed depends on the use of a *sketch map* then this map should be attached to the field notebook. If it depends on a published map, the sheet number and title should be included. If a *coding system* for entries is used, the code should be included or attached. Only *standard abbreviations* should be used, e.g. m for metres, N for north.

7 Once in the field, all the available data should be recorded. Numbers should not be reduced or rounded up or down, averages should not be made. Once the observer has left the field, the notebook is the only record of the observations. These can be reduced, averaged or analysed later. *Entries can always be discarded; they can never be added without another visit to the field.*

Analysis, synthesis and presentation

Once the data has been collected, all the statistical and geographical methods of interpretation can be applied as necessary. These are numerous, but some of the particularly quick and clear techniques for presentation and comparison are suggested below:

• Annotated sketch map - to show relationships, e.g. land use.
• Distribution and location - use a base map and enter the data on it, e.g. traffic survey.
• Histogram or vertical bar graph - excellent for showing and comparing quantities (Fig. 21.7 (a)).
• Table - some data is best left in numerical form, especially if there are a lot of items and some are very small, e.g. survey of housing and/or services (Fig. 21.7 (b)).
• Transect charts with a sketch or accurate cross-section, e.g. vegetation survey with topography.
• Simple line graph - to show the change in directly related data over time, e.g. sequence of surveys of traffic at same site and hour, but over a period of time.

In addition to the *method* of display, the type of *analysis* is variable:

• Comparison by total, by ratio, by percentage.
• Comparison of an individual site survey with the average of a large number.
• Comparisons in time - hour, day, week, season or year.
• Trends - nature of change: increase, decrease, stable, variable.
• Rate of change - rate of increase or decrease for a succession of measurements.

In each case the diagram should have a specific purpose related to the original question or hypothesis, and should be clearly and accurately drawn. No unnecessary diagrams should be drawn. Direct reference to the analysis should be made in the conclusion.

The conclusion

This should be the natural outcome of the field enquiry. Whether the hypothesis was proved or disproved, and why you think so, must be stated clearly and with reference to the data collected and its analysis.

It is also necessary to be honest, and this is done by being complete in the examination of the data. You should therefore also state the following:

• Any known errors in the work, and why they were made.
• Any anomalies, and how they can be explained.
• Any factors that might affect the validity of the results, such as a survey falling on a holiday, or exceptional weather conditions.
• Reasons why a definite conclusion could not be reached, together with an explanation and suggestions for further study.

Although the conclusion is related to the field enquiry, it is sometimes acceptable to make a reference to other similar studies. This should be done briefly, and full references given.

Bibliography and guide to further study

There are many well-known texts on the Caribbean and its various countries, and there is no need to list them here. The reader studying geography is cautioned, however, that many of these books are now dated, and it is in an attempt to correct this situation that the following sources are listed. In general they will provide up-to-date statistics and commentary on West Indian affairs, or deal with the fundamental nature of the physical environment.

Official publications

These include - for each nation - the following:

(a) *Population censuses*, often with an invaluable summary at the beginning.

(b) Annual summaries of *meteorological observations*, and the annual *Monthly Weather Summary* for the whole region published by the Caribbean Meteorological Institute, Barbados.

(c) *Annual reports on tourism, agriculture and fishing*, and some other topics, depending on the country, e.g. forestry, sugar, bauxite, petroleum, etc.

(d) Social and/or economic reports. Unlike statistical digests, these contain commentaries on each economic or social sector. Jamaica's *Economic and Social Survey* is an excellent example.

Topographic maps, and atlases

(a) General-purpose maps, ranging from scales of 1:10,000 to 1:100,000, exist for virtually every island. A collection of these is invaluable for all geographical purposes. The larger scales are suitable for fieldwork.

(b) Good atlases exist for most countries, for example *Atlas de Cuba, Atlas of the Commonwealth of the Bahamas, Atlas of Belize*. All are suitable for educational use and include maps showing social, economic and physical distributions.

(c) *Atlas for Caribbean Examinations*, edited by M. Morrissey, Longman, 1991. The first 50 pages of this comprehensive atlas deal specifically with the countries and the issues discussed in this book.

Handbooks and yearbooks

(a) A variety of regional handbooks is available, but most are of little value and are really directories mainly devoted to advertising. One exception is *The Caribbean Handbook*, published by FT Caribbean, PO Box 1037, St John's, Antigua. This gives a balanced treatment to *all* the countries of the Caribbean, not just the English-speaking ones. The British *Statesman's Yearbook* (Macmillan) is also excellent, and covers all the countries of the world.

(b) Several countries publish yearbooks or annuals. Many of these are simply tourist guides, but a few provide valuable articles and information about their countries, notably *The Settlers Handbook for the US Virgin Islands*, available from PO Box 894, Christiansted, St Croix, US Virgin Islands, *The Cayman Islands Yearbook*, from PO Box 1365, Grand Cayman and *Bahamas Handbook* from PO Box N7513, Nassau, Bahamas.

Lesser-known textbooks (especially those dealing with the physical background).

These include the following:

(a) *Minerals and Rocks of Jamaica* by A.R.D. Porter, T.A. Jackson and E. Robinson. Jamaica Publishing House, 1982.

(b) *Natural Resources of Trinidad and Tobago*, edited by St G.C. Cooper and P.R. Bacon. Edward Arnold 1981.

(c) *Flora & Fauna of the Caribbean* by P.R. Bacon. Key Caribbean Publications, Trinidad, 1978.

(d) *Bahamian Landscapes* by Neil Sealey. Collins Caribbean (now Longman), 1986.

(e) *Mineral Industries of Latin America*, Bureau of Mines, US Department of the Interior, 1988.

Institutional and international publications

on specific topics, for example:

(a) *Caribbean Countries - Economic Situation, Regional Issues and Capital Flows*. World Bank, 1988.

(b) *Caribbean Tourism Statistical Report* (annual publication). Caribbean Tourism Research and Development Centre, Barbados.

(c) *The Haitian Problem* by Dawn Marshall. Institute of Social and Economic Research, UWI, 1979.

(d) *Caricom Statistics Yearbook*, Caribbean Community Secretariat, Guyana.

Regional journals and newsletters

(a) *Social and Economic Studies*, quarterly. Institute of Social and Economic Research, UWI. The Institute also publishes original research in book form, and *Occasional Papers*.

(b) *Caribbean Geography*, twice annually. Dept. of Geography, U.W.I., Jamaica.

(c) *Caribbean Insight*, every month. West India Committee, 18 Northumberland House, London, WC2 5RA. This is a newsletter covering events, especially economic and political affairs, throughout the region. Many of the recent statistics in this book were obtained from this source.

(d) *Courier*, every 2 months, free. General Secretariat of the ACP Group of States. Avenue Georges Henri 451, 1200 Brussels, Belgium. A 100+ page journal of development in the African, Caribbean and Pacific countries, with one or two in-depth country studies, and topical studies, in each issue.

(e) *Jamaican Geographer*, the newsletter of the Jamaican Geographical Society. Twice annually, Dept. of Geography, U.W.I., Jamaica.

International journals

There are literally hundreds of these, but occasionally they publish articles of considerable importance to the region. Whenever possible the major geological, geographical and tourism journals should be searched for relevant articles.

Index

Published by the Press Syndicate of the University of Cambridge
The Pitt Building, Trumpington Street, Cambridge CB2 1RP
40 West 20th Street, New York, NY 10011 – 4211, USA
10 Stamford Road, Oakleigh, Victoria 3166, Australia

© Cambridge University Press 1992

First published 1992

Printed in Great Britain at the University Press, Cambridge

A catalogue record for this book is available from the British Library.

Library of Congress Cataloguing in Publication applied for.

ISBN 0 521 37764 1

The author and publishers would like to acknowledge the assistance of the Lands and Survey Departments of Montserrat, The Bahamas, Dominica and Barbados for use of map extracts in this book, and the US Defense Mapping Agency for permission to reproduce a
section of their chart 26309.

Cover photograph of Tortola by Anne Bolt
Cover design by Chris McLeod